RAYMOND IRWIN ON THE ENGLISH LIBRARY

Volume 2

THE ENGLISH LIBRARY

THE ENGLISH LIBRARY
Sources and History

RAYMOND IRWIN

Routledge
Taylor & Francis Group
LONDON AND NEW YORK

First published in 1966 by George Allen & Unwin Ltd.

This edition first published in 2022
by Routledge
2 Park Square, Milton Park, Abingdon, Oxon OX14 4RN

and by Routledge
605 Third Avenue, New York, NY 10158

Routledge is an imprint of the Taylor & Francis Group, an informa business

© 1966 George Allen & Unwin Ltd

All rights reserved. No part of this book may be reprinted or reproduced or utilised in any form or by any electronic, mechanical, or other means, now known or hereafter invented, including photocopying and recording, or in any information storage or retrieval system, without permission in writing from the publishers.

Trademark notice: Product or corporate names may be trademarks or registered trademarks, and are used only for identification and explanation without intent to infringe.

British Library Cataloguing in Publication Data
A catalogue record for this book is available from the British Library

ISBN: 978-1-03-216165-5 (Set)
ISBN: 978-1-00-324758-6 (Set) (ebk)
ISBN: 978-1-03-216173-0 (Volume 2) (hbk)
ISBN: 978-1-03-216211-9 (Volume 2) (pbk)
ISBN: 978-1-00-324752-4 (Volume 2) (ebk)

DOI: 10.4324/9781003247524

Publisher's Note
The publisher has gone to great lengths to ensure the quality of this reprint but points out that some imperfections in the original copies may be apparent.

Disclaimer
The publisher has made every effort to trace copyright holders and would welcome correspondence from those they have been unable to trace.

The English Library

SOURCES AND HISTORY

RAYMOND IRWIN
M.A., F.L.A.

Professor of Library Studies in the University of London
Director of the School of Librarianship and Archives
University College London

London
GEORGE ALLEN & UNWIN LTD
RUSKIN HOUSE MUSEUM STREET

FIRST PUBLISHED IN 1966

This book is copyright under the Berne Convention. Apart from any fair dealing for the purposes of private study, research, criticism, or review, as permitted under the Copyright Act, 1956, no portion may be reproduced by any process without written permission. Enquiries should be addressed to the publisher.

© *George Allen & Unwin Ltd. 1966*

Parts of this work were published under the title *The Origins of the English Library* in 1958

Revised and enlarged under the title *The English Library*, this book first published in 1966

PRINTED IN GREAT BRITAIN
in 12 on 13 point Bembo type
BY C. TINLING AND CO. LTD.
LIVERPOOL, LONDON AND PRESCOT

This book is dedicated with respect and affection to the memory of J. L. Stocks, Fellow of St John's College, Oxford, and Professor of Philosophy in the University of Manchester. Forty-five years ago he and Lady Stocks gave far more encouragement and friendly help to a young undergraduate at St John's than they probably realized at the time.

ACKNOWLEDGEMENTS

I am indebted to the Council of the Library Association for allowing me to reprint material that has appeared in various articles in *The Library Association Record*, and to the Editor of *The Library Review* for his permission to base part of my introductory chapter on an article that was published in his journal.

The poem by the late Arundell Esdaile on p. 28 is reprinted by kind permission of his family.

I gratefully acknowledge the help and advice of many good friends, including Professor Eric Turner and Professor James Sutherland of this College, Dr Paul Kaufman, Sir James D. Anderson, K.C.I.E., Dr J. N. L. Myres, the library staff at University College London and my colleagues at the School of Librarianship and Archives. Miss Mary Piggott has kindly undertaken responsibility for the index.

CONTENTS

PART ONE

I.	Introduction	13
II.	Callimachus and the Alexandrian Library	24
III.	The Byzantine Age	42
IV.	Seneca	64
V.	In Roman Britain	80
VI.	In Saxon England	97
VII.	Colonnade and Cloister	113
VIII.	The Dispersal	124
IX.	Physical Handicaps	143
X.	Gabriel Naudé and the Problems of Mass Production	160

PART TWO: The English Domestic Library

XI.	The Beginnings	173
XII.	From Sir Thomas More to Samuel Pepys	188
XIII.	From Samuel Pepys to Dr Johnson	209
XIV.	The Infectious Habit	227
	§1: The epidemic begins	227
	§2: Scanty Intellectual Viands	238
	§3: In Humbler Quarters	253
XV.	The Nineteenth Century	258
	§1: The Scholars and the Essayists	258
	§2: The New Population	276
	§3: Childhood Reminiscences	287
LIST OF SOURCES		294
INDEX		301

Part One

CHAPTER I

Introduction

WHEN eight years ago *The Origins of the English Library* was published, some objection was taken to its title, as not being properly descriptive of the contents. For this present edition a new title has been adopted, not because the old one was inappropriate, but because the earlier edition has been so changed and expanded as to constitute what is virtually a new work, more worthy, it may be hoped, of its companion volume, *The Heritage of the English Library*; and for a new work of this kind a distinctive title is surely justified. In point of fact all three titles, *Origins, Heritage* and the present one, seem equally appropriate to a series of studies depicting the conditions and circumstances under which English libraries of today have come to birth. They have their roots in the past, and it is these many-branched roots that we are here investigating and exploring, in the confident belief that they are as important to contemporary developments as the hidden roots of a plant are to its visible blossoms. Our aim is to dispel the illusion that the libraries we see around us today have nothing to do with Athens, Alexandria and Rome, with Constantinople and Islam, with Monte Cassino and Monk Wearmouth, with S. Columban, and S. Francis, with Alfred the Great and Henry VIII, and with many other seemingly remote people and places. If they appear remote, this is only because our eyes are turned in a different direction. A man climbing a ladder commonly looks upwards, but if he is wise he will remain conscious of the rungs beneath him which are his only link with solid earth.

A few doubtless see little sense in history of any kind. Rather more would question the value of history as applied to a subject so narrowly specialized as libraries. Both these views are misguided, but both are in a measure understandable, and need an honest answer. I suppose that the basic motive inspiring all historical enquiry is curiosity: a natural and fundamental instinct in all normal human beings and in many animals, and an instinct moreover that is primarily responsible for most intellectual and scientific progress. Disciplined curiosity is one of man's most valuable assets. Undisciplined, it may be fatal to men as well as to cats: and we must recognize that, like all instincts, it can be abused if given a free rein. There are examples of its abuse around us in many fields of knowledge; in history itself, in biography and literary criticism, in science. In all these fields the acquisitive and inquisitive instincts can tempt us to a vain hoarding of unfruitful and unproductive facts; and in biography they can turn us into Peeping Toms, prying into things that concern neither us nor anybody else. But a disciplined and discriminating curiosity is one of the chief blessings of intelligent man.

Some will defend the careful investigation of the past by its practical value today, dwelling on the so-called lessons of history and the repetition of cause and effect.[1] There is danger here, for such lessons as history can teach are inconclusive, uncertain and double-faced. It has been said that you can prove anything from the Bible; so also any policy, any cause can be supported by history, and the fact that history could be made to condemn it with equal ease will be ignored by the single-minded. If history were a game of chess, with bishops, knights and castles moving on fixed and undeviating paths, then we could indeed follow its lessons with some confidence. But in the real world bishops, knights and castles, let alone queens and kings and the humble pawn, have no set paths; they can never be trusted to react to similar situations in similar ways; their movements are erratic and unpredictable, and the wisest forecasts of their actions are little more than guesswork. If we seek immediate value in the study of history, we should do well to regard it as a source of inspiration rather than practical guidance. This is what Plato and Seneca meant in urging children to make friends with the great men of past ages, choosing thereby some model for the conduct of their own lives.[2] This no doubt is what Montrose found in Sir Walter Ralegh, John Buchan in Montrose, Sir Winston Churchill in Marlborough, and (rather

---

[1] As for example General Sir John Glubb, in *The Course of Empire*, 1965, in which he propounds his thesis of the social and political cycle followed by all the empires of history. Arnold Toynbee and H. A. L. Fisher could also be cited in this connection.

[2] Plato, *Protag.* 326; Seneca, *De otio*, 1 1.

INTRODUCTION

differently) both Thomas and Oliver Cromwell in Machiavelli, and Lenin in Marx and Engels. This indeed has always been the stock justification for the art of reading, that you could learn from books of the nobility and greatness and virtues of those who had gone before you.

But history is more than hero-worship; more than the search for a guiding star; more than the praise of famous men and our fathers that begat us. The special gift of Clio is the power to see the temporal universe as a whole: the recorded past, the momentary present and, so far as we can penetrate it, the misty future, as a single span of human thought and activity, much as a traveller views the whole landscape from a mountain top. If we close our eyes to the breadth of the landscape, we have only a myopic view of the passing moments, discontinuous and unrelated to past and future. A sailor, navigating his ship over the lonely sea, can only plot his course for home if he knows his present position and the course he has so far been following. So the historian takes his bearings on the future by reference to the past, and history becomes the science of navigation through time. The idea of history as a voyage of discovery is useful, because it underlines the continuity of the course we are travelling from one year to the next, linking the centuries and the generations of mankind. The historian's view is thus a faint and inevitably distorted reflection of the divine view ('before Abraham was, I am') in which the present moment loses its illusion of overwhelming significance, and you see the landscape of time as a whole, holding 'infinity in the palm of your hand, and eternity in an hour'. Like Browning's Grammarian, we might cry 'What's Time? Leave Now for dogs and apes! Man has Forever.'

This may well be admitted, but the sceptic may still doubt the value of extending historical studies to narrower and narrower fields. 'Leave history to the historians', he may say, 'and let us concentrate on our current technology.' And here the professional historian may support him, for no professionally trained student welcomes the interference of amateurs. The scientist holds (with some justice) that only the man trained in science can profitably study the history of science. On the other hand, history being a subject in its own right, only the trained historian should attempt the history of science or any other subject. But 'double firsts' are rare birds, and specialization is no guarantee of scholarship. The scholarly amateur will sometimes obtain a truer view of a subject from the outside than the specialist can from the inside. Nobody surely can doubt the need for specialized histories, to set a limited field in its right historical perspective. Scholarship demands this insistently, even if technology finds it a waste of time. A man can become a successful farmer without any knowledge of the history of agriculture; a skilled carpenter or engineer or sailor without any knowledge of the history of navigation or engineering or woodwork. A man can even, though with some difficulty, become a skilful artist or musician, without knowledge of the history of music or art. But can we doubt that he would be a better artist or musician, if aesthetics or musicology were not a closed book to him? He would certainly find far greater happiness and satisfaction in his work. This is probably true in a measure of most of the skills to which men devote themselves. If a man merely wants to make farming pay, he need give little thought to agricultural problems in times earlier than the present. If, on the other hand, he dedicates himself to farming as a way of life for its own sake, curiosity will surely drive him to learn something about Jethro Tull and Turnip Townshend and William Cobbett; and the presence of a combine harvester on his farm will not blind him to an interest in sickle, flail and threshing floor, and perhaps even the skill to use these ancient tools. Turn from farming to an even more all-pervading and fundamental interest. Reading and writing and the making of books have always been the distinctive accomplishments of civilized man. How can the lover of books fail to be absorbed in the story of these accomplishments, how they began and how they changed and grew through the centuries, spreading over the whole civilized world? We are all lovers of books, and all therefore amateur librarians to a greater or lesser degree; and the tale is thus of universal interest. And the professional librarian neglects this study at his peril. In this field as in most others, the line between amateur and professional grows sharper year by year, but in becoming a professional a man need not cease to be an amateur in the true sense. His professionalism lies in the art of handling books in their thousands to good effect, and if this drives out the love of individual books for their own sake, he is no librarian, merely a technician. As such he can doubtless earn a good living; as a librarian, on the other hand, he can look forward to a happy and rewarding life. The two ideals are not conflicting.

The sceptic, agreeing to all this in theory, may object that the force of the argument loses much of its significance in the changing conditions of today. Our whole attitude to the past is, he would suggest, undergoing a radical change. There has in recent years been a technical and cultural revolution that has turned our way of life upside down; and many people, impressed by the apparent completeness of this upheaval, tend to minimize our dependence on tradition and history. In part the revolution is due to developments in electronics and automation; in part to the applications of nuclear power; in part to the devastation of two world wars, with the possibility of a third ever present to the imagination; in part to the spread of materialism and agnosticism, with its doubts of the validity of traditional religious doctrine and its consequent preoccupation with human life and welfare on earth, which is the only reality it acknowledges. There is indeed hardly any phase of our thinking or our living that has not, in the minds of many, been violently reversed; and on a short-sighted view it seems almost that history is starting afresh with a blank sheet. The relevance of the past has been obscured, and it seems hardly worth while to waste time in examining it. History (so it is thought) is harmless as a field for romantic or nostalgic fiction, or for the inquisitive curiosity that inspires the current interest in archaeology, popular because it combines the elements of hard physical work, skilful detection and the chance of a lucky discovery; for practical purposes however it can in this technological age be disregarded.

This attitude is surely mistaken, but it is widespread and perhaps not unnatural. Never has so much seemed so out of date as it does today. On a much smaller scale the same feeling was abroad in Tudor times when the invention of printing and the so-called 'new learning' made the manuscript learning of the medieval period seem out of date. Here again the change combined with new industrial and scientific advances (including the new art of navigation which made possible the discovery of America) to divide the old order more sharply from the new. Today once again we are faced with a new world in which everything seems completely different, in our social and ethical life, in politics, in science, in travel and in communications. The welfare state, nuclear warfare, television, automation—everything that matters in our lives seems brand new. Only the wickedness of man remains, and even this is a new wickedness, with new powers for evil. How can a young man profit today from learning of the struggles of his forebears in a totally different and alien world? Ambitious young readers in Victoria's reign may have drawn inspiration of this kind from Samuel Smiles, but how many read Samuel Smiles today? To the young scientist of our own time, or the young engineer, or the enthusiast for space travel, this kind of advice rings hollow. Their concern is for the revolutionary hypotheses that are current today, and the exciting researches and discoveries that are promised for tomorrow, rather than with the gropings and errors of yesterday. Robert Boyle and Sir Kenelm Digby, Joseph Priestley and the Brunels, father and son, are interesting names perhaps, but they have little apparent relevance to the complications of science and engineering in the late twentieth century.

These are, as we have said, short-sighted views, however natural they may appear. The real changes are considerably less than we imagine, and the world of today is not as new as it might seem. There is no impassable gulf between yesterday and today; enthusiasts for the excitement of space-travel would do well to recall that the history of modern astronomy starts with the astrology of the Chaldeans, just as modern chemistry has its source in medieval alchemy. There is still 'no new thing under the sun'. Since man first emerged on this earth, he has not passed through more than a thousand generations—a very brief period in the terms of evolution —and what we have called the 'golden chain'[1] is still unbroken; indeed it is stronger today than it ever was.

Nevertheless the upheavals of the last twenty or thirty years are startling enough, and they rightly give us pause to think; pause also to make fast the cables that bind us to the past. The upheaval is as noticeable in the care of books as in any other walk of life. The technology of librarianship (by which we mean the art of handling books and information on a large scale) has developed in recent years in a way that would make it unrecognizable to librarians of an earlier generation. The storage and retrieval of information has become a problem demanding all the complex devices of mechanization and electronic computation for its

[1] *Heritage*, p. 26.

INTRODUCTION

solution. Analytical bibliography is also using these aids to establish (not always very convincingly) conclusions regarding questions of authorship and book-production which would be impossibly laborious to reach by manual labour. The development of text-reproduction by photography and micro-photography is solving many practical problems for the librarian and making more material available in more places for the reader. Mechanical devices for recording loans of books are becoming commonplace.

The young librarian using, or learning to use, mechanical aids of this kind, may be forgiven if he doubts whether the study of famous librarians of past ages, Leibniz perhaps, or Naudé or Panizzi, can profit him anything in this new sort of librarianship. They worked under entirely different circumstances for apparently different purposes, and he may suppose that they can teach him nothing that he cannot absorb far more effectively from X or Y or Z at whose feet he is sitting and from whom he is learning the new techniques. And he feels instinctively that he can learn more of practical value from these than from people who lived in the strange and unfamiliar days of the past. Hero worship after all is just one other thing that is out of fashion. We are not so ready as we once were to give our hearts away, especially to those shadowy gods that reigned in the primitive world of yesterday. What can the soldier of today learn from Caesar or Montrose or Cromwell? By the same token, what can the young librarian learn from Sir Thomas Bodley or Richard Bentley or Humfrey Wanley?

He can in fact learn much. These questions are natural enough, but the answer is equally natural and completely overwhelming. If all that interests the young librarian is a bread and butter wage as a technician, then there is little in history that he need bother about. But if he is not content with mere mechanical competence: if what he seeks is not a job, but a vocation, a way of life; if he hungers, not for so many pounds a year, but for that inner satisfaction and joy which is the reward of a devoted life; if the faith and fire within him kindle a burning zeal that drives him to give all of himself in return for the only things that matter—then inevitably he will be impelled far beyond the confines of his technical skill, into that supreme happiness which is the mark of every true ideal, every land of heart's desire that man has pictured.

THE ENGLISH LIBRARY

Where beauty has no ebb, decay no flood,
But joy is wisdom, Time an endless song.

This is neither exaggeration nor romantic fancy. Those who have tasted this happiness will know what I mean. It is within the grasp of every true librarian if he has the will to seek it; but he must be prepared for a life of self-dedication and devotion.[1] The gulf between a bare professional existence on the one hand, and a rich life on the other, is a formidable barrier, but it is one you can surmount if you give your heart to it. We are lucky in our profession. Few others give such generous opportunities to exchange poverty for true wealth and penury for riches; and if anyone imagines I am discussing salary scales, the light is not in him.

The wealth that you will find takes many forms, both intellectual and spiritual. It has perhaps three characteristic features. One is the ability to stand back and view your work and your purpose honestly as a whole. Only those who have achieved this kind of detachment are qualified to talk about the philosophy of librarianship. These alone have a clear view both of the wood and of the trees that go to make it; these alone rise above the distracting worries that turn the daily round into slavery. Another of its features is a sense of proportion: a realization that our individual lives are but tiny fragments of the universe, and that today is an infinitesimal fraction of eternity. It is a contemporary habit to worship the present moment as though it were the one critical point in our history, and as though all the future depends on what we do now: the past is dead, tomorrow is ours to fashion and all that matters is today, the here and now. There is neither wisdom, nor logic, nor piety in this view. Those who cling to it forget that every today was once a tomorrow, and that in every age the present has appeared as the turning point of history. If history itself teaches us anything, it is that life is a constant succession of turning points, each in some sort a legacy of the past, and none of them much more decisive in reality than any of the others. And a third characteristic feature is a boundless sympathy, not so much an emotional as an intellectual sympathy, and not merely with the men and women around us today, but with those of yesterday and

---

[1] The devotion need not be directed to history itself; it may be given to other aspects of our work, e.g. classification or bibliography. But the historical element is present in all these.

INTRODUCTION

tomorrow as well. This sympathy is partly an infinite curiosity; partly a genuine love for human beings who share this world with us; but more especially a freedom from those preoccupations and prejudices which are so apt to bind us hand and foot. It is this kind of sympathy which enables us to enter selflessly into the intellectual problems and interests of others, to sift and weigh and judge their difficulties and their enthusiasms, and to give the sort of guidance and companionship that is genuinely worthy both of the people of every kind who seek our help, and of the books of every age that are in our keeping. These are surely the marks of a true and happy vocation to librarianship.

What is more natural than that many librarians, seeking this richer understanding of their mission in life, should be led to explore the history of their profession? How indeed can they help it? They want to build up in their minds a picture of their work as a whole; and if they leave out its historical roots, a great part of the picture will be missing and the rest will be distorted and false. The urge to explore is all the more impelling because these roots of ours are inextricably embedded in the history of scholarship and civilization. To learn about one is to learn about the other, and in this common ground we meet with the origins of every science, every art and every philosophy that man has developed. All these fall into perspective as we trace our story up to the present day, and little that we meet with in our daily work is then entirely unfamiliar; we recognize at least its relations and place in the scheme of things. This is nothing so silly as a claim to omniscience, but it does claim a right perspective and breadth in our view of human achievement, and a knowledge of the geography, so to speak, of the intellectual world. Take two simple illustrations. Our own history involves a knowledge of the history of the Royal Society from its beginnings in the seventeenth century. This knowledge may be comparatively superficial; less detailed probably than a good scientist would need. But if our knowledge is at all genuine, what better qualification could we have to enable us to talk on level terms with the scientist who uses our library; to understand his language, his prejudices and interests and purposes? Or again: our library is used by students, many of whom have worked, or will need to work, in the British Museum. Moreover, our own daily work may well bring us into contact with the

Museum, so that any ignorance of its activities and its aims would be unpardonable. But how can we claim any familiarity with the British Museum Library, unless we know something of its foundation collections, and their wealth and origins; unless, that is, we know something of the history of English libraries at least since the sixteenth century? This surely and beyond all doubt is part of the necessary equipment of the good librarian.

Many similar illustrations could be added, but I cannot think there is need. Having said so much, however, let me add one thing. The history of our libraries is reasonably well documented, and a good deal of it is more easily accessible to the ordinary reader than it was a few years ago. But a vast amount of research still remains to be done, and the librarian with a historical bent will find it a fascinating and rewarding study, and one in which his professional knowledge will be of special use. Some of our library histories, admirable as they may be, suffer because they were not written by a professional librarian; the layman may so easily give a wrong emphasis to some detail, or miss the significance of some point that would not escape a trained librarian. There is in particular a need for detailed regional surveys that will trace the growth of every type of library in a particular district from monastic times onward; very few such historical surveys exist, and they would add much to our knowledge of the libraries of our own country. I commend this to the historian-librarian, wherever he may be, who is in love with his work and is prepared to give his whole heart and soul to a task that will be laborious, but engrossing and infinitely satisfying.

I would, however, add one note of caution. A history of libraries, whether regional or national, can acquire vitality only if it is intimately related to the literature that the libraries contain, and the social circumstances of the people who use them. Such a history must be treated as one aspect of both social studies and literary history, and it will not come to life unless this is recognized.

When I was a small boy, an uncle presented me with a fragment of carved stone which he had brought back from his travels in Asia Minor. This came, he said, from the city of Smyrna, and had once been part of its library. Much later, when I chanced to read Strabo's description of 'this beautiful city with its harbour and Metröum and gymnasium, its streets in straight lines, paved with stone, its great two-storied porticoes, and its shrine of Homer, to whom the inhabitants lay special claim,' I found that he added, as an afterthought, ἔστι δὲ καὶ βιβλιοθήκη 'there is also a library'; and the memory of this fragment came back to me, bringing to life the building of which it had once formed a tiny part.

There must have been something prophetic in this gift; or perhaps it started a train of thought which bore fruit in later days. My interest in the history of our libraries grew, and a kind fortune allowed me to spend much time in reading all I could find about them. But that casual note of Strabo's kept recurring to me: 'there was also a library'. Without my treasured fragment of carving, it would doubtless have been overlooked or forgotten at once. So much of the history of early libraries is of this nature: bare statements that once upon a time a library existed here, an otherwise almost unknown person was the librarian there, certain not very interesting works are known to have once been in this library, and in that was kept a certain manuscript now visible in a glass case in a famous museum. Such statements are apt to appear sterile and unsatisfying; their significance is hard to seek. Yet ever since Lipsius produced his *De Bibliothecis Syntagma* in 1602, histories of libraries have been largely composed of such statements. Lipsius himself is indeed more interesting than most of his imitators, for he did clothe the bare bones of his subject with a little flesh, while his successors for the most part contented themselves with summarizing his facts. And it must be admitted that the recorded facts are often meagre and unilluminating. But the subject lies so near to the heart of all that we value in our civilization that a little digging beneath the surface will often uncover unexpected treasure; and if the disciplined imagination of the historian can be brought to bear on the relics unearthed, they will acquire a new and satisfying life.

I have tried, therefore, in this present work, as also in its sister volume, *The Heritage of the English Library*, to provide, not indeed a new history of our libraries, but studies of certain aspects of their history which will give vitality and interest to the often meagre facts and set them in perspective against the development of our civilization.

CHAPTER II

Callimachus and the Alexandrian Library

THE story of the libraries of Athens has been sketched in *The Heritage of the English Library* (ch. IV).[1] If the facts were known, the tale would probably start in Homeric times; perhaps even in Mycenaean times. We reach firm ground when we come to the classical period of the fifth century BC; and even firmer ground in the fourth century, when three of the four great schools of philosophy established their libraries: Plato's Academy about 385 BC, Aristotle's Lyceum about 336 BC, and the school of Epicurus in 306 BC. Alexander the Great, who had been Aristotle's pupil, died in 323 BC and Aristotle retired from his school to Chalcis, where he died the following year. This was a turning point in literary as well as political history. Within a year or two the end of the classical age was sealed by the passing of two of its greatest figures, Demosthenes and Aristotle. The new age was heralded by the coming of the New Comedy; Menander produced the first of over one hundred plays in 321. In 318 Demetrius of Phalerum began his ten years' rule as governor of Athens: a period of prosperity for the schools, and of elegant decadence in morals and manners. He made an abrupt exit from the city however in 307, and withdrew to Boeotia to write the story of his years of office. Ten years later he was in Alexandria, his head full of ideas as to how a philosopher-king could organize the scholarship and learning of his kingdom, and repeat on a grander scale the achievements of Aristotle's Lyceum. It seems probable that the plan for a great museum and library at Alexandria must be credited to Demetrius. He was himself a Peripatetic; he knew the work of the Lyceum at Athens intimately, and had seen the advantages of security and permanence which the state could lend to such an institution. He planned a similar foundation for the new royal city of Alexandria, in a conscious attempt to adorn

[1] Cited as *Heritage* in references in the present work.

the government and culture of the country with all the trappings of oriental magnificence.

Alexander had conquered the whole world from Greece and Egypt to India. On his death this great empire was broken into three pieces: Macedonia, Syria and Egypt. In a measure he had been the first imperialist to dream not merely of world domination, but of a world commonwealth, a great international union of peoples embracing the known world, something indeed approaching what we now term the brotherhood of man. The dream of course was unrealized, but we see a reflection of it in the international university which the Ptolemies built up in Alexandria. When Alexander died of fever in Babylon, only thirty-three years old, he had already achieved imperial divinity. His body was brought to the new city of Alexandria for burial, but though antiquarians are still searching for his tomb, there is little chance of its discovery today. It remained for long however an object of veneration and a temptation to plunder. The golden sarcophagus in which he lay, embalmed with spices and perfumes, was stolen by Ptolemy IX, who is said to have substituted a coffin of glass. Cleopatra stole other treasures from the tomb. Octavian examined the remains in 30 BC, clumsily breaking the nose. Later Caligula removed Alexander's cuirass, and later still Septimius Severus filled the grave with books plundered from local shrines; while his son Caracalla, deeming himself a second Alexander, laid his tunic, rings and belt on the coffin to signify the reincarnation in himself of his divine predecessor.

Alexander's ablest general, Ptolemy Soter, on the emperor's death seized Egypt for himself. He became satrap in 323 BC, proclaimed himself king in 304 BC and extended his kingdom by annexing Palestine, Cyprus and other possessions in Asia Minor and the Aegean. His son, Ptolemy Philadelphus, became joint ruler with him in 285 BC, and assumed full power two or three years later. The Museum and Library of Alexandria was established early in that century, possibly by the first Ptolemy, though it did not come fully into operation till the time of his son, Ptolemy Philadelphus.

During its first and probably its greatest years the Museum was the focus for the researches of a band of scholars, writers and editors of outstanding ability, whose work is of profound importance in the tradition of Greek learning and letters. Their teaching and writing and editorial work was indeed the channel into which the body of Greek classical literature was organized and through which it passed in due time to Constantinople and eventually to the Western World. Many of these scholars were connected officially with the Library, and none of them has secured a firmer niche in literary history than Callimachus.

It is perhaps surprising how few of those who in earlier times held office as librarians are remembered today; the ordinary man would be hard put to it to recall more than two or three: Leland and William of Malmesbury in our own country; in Germany perhaps Leibniz; and in the ancient world Callimachus, though unless he were a classical scholar, Callimachus would perhaps be little more than a name to him. And yet in a sense this is not surprising. The librarian as such is neither a maker of history, nor a maker of literature. He is an intermediary, whose only memorial lies in the books he preserves and the scholars who read them; his fate is to serve as the anonymous channel of recorded tradition. It is noteworthy that the librarians of former ages, if they are remembered at all, are always remembered for something other than their librarianship. Leland is the antiquary; William of Malmesbury is the historian; Leibniz is the philosopher and mathematician, so also Callimachus is the poet or the school teacher. If, indeed, there is one lesson that the history of libraries teaches us, it is that something over and above technical knowledge is needed to make the great librarian: a library cannot live on librarianship alone.

The classical scholar has, of course his own reasons for his interest in Callimachus. The interest of the librarian is due to the fact that Callimachus occupied a central position in the history of the Alexandrian libraries, through whose agency the literary heritage of Greece was handed down to us. On both sides he is a figure of supreme importance.

It would be out of place here to estimate his literary achievements. That he was a great poet is agreed on all sides. J. U. Powell observes that at his best he had the lesser poetical gifts in a pre-eminent degree: wit, invention, and an extraordinary dexterity in handling his medium; his greatest power lay in telling a story with artistic ease and charm, and this is seen at its best in his elegiac poem, *The Bath of Pallas*.[1] He had an immense reputation in the ancient world, and his influence on the Augustan poets in Rome, and through them on our own literature, is remarkable. Though he produced, according to *Suidas*, over 800 works, comparatively little has actually survived, and much of this is fragmentary. There is, however, the excitement of knowing that further discoveries of his pieces are likely. To many he is perhaps best known by the epigram which the lovely lines of Cory's translation have made familiar: 'They told me, Heraclitus, they told me you were dead.'

Callimachus was born *c.* 310 BC, a few years before the establishment of the Alexandrian Museum; he died about 240 BC. With his friend, the poet Aratus, he was educated at the Peripatetic School in Athens under Praxiphanes, who himself had been one of Theophrastus' pupils. After his student days Aratus went to the Macedonian court, but Callimachus set up as a school teacher at Eleusis, a suburb of Alexandria. Later he secured a court appointment at the Alexandrian library as a junior assistant. The order and dates of the Alexandrian librarians are uncertain; the three authorities for our list (the Byzantine lexicon *Suidas*, the twelfth-century scholar Tzetzes, and the papyrus fragment known as *POxy.* 1241) disagree.

But assuming that Zenodotus was the first head of the library, three of his successors (Apollonius Rhodius, Eratosthenes and Aristophanes of Byzantium) are said to have been pupils of Callimachus, who never himself attained the headship. We know sufficient of his life and work to build up a fairly true picture of the man: he was a highly skilled poet, elegant, graceful, polished, blasé, not a little precious, blessed with a certain dry humour, very much a modernist, something even of a revolutionary in temperament and technique and hence inclined to be contemptuous of old-fashioned ways of thought and composition. He had nevertheless a profound knowledge of his country's literature and in particular of all the curious byways of mythology, and he never lost an opportunity of airing this knowledge in his writing, overloading his verse with recondite allusions for no obvious purpose other than to display his learning. He must have been a thoroughly able teacher;

---

[1] J. U. Powell and E. A. Barber. *New Chapters in Greek Literature*, 1st series, 1921, p. 100. The best general study of the work of Callimachus is Dr Friedrich Schmidt's *Die Pinakes des Kallimachos*, Berlin, 1922.

such men, indeed, often teach extremely well. But we have the picture of a man who, for all his erudition and artistic skill, is morose, with an acid tongue and bitter temper, soured perhaps by his humble origin and early struggles. Some of his epigrams reveal his bitterness vividly. 'I hate (he cries) the old familiar songs that everybody sings; I hate the vulgarity of the common herd; I hate the paths that everybody takes, the delights that everybody raves about.' He set himself very much apart from other men, or rather above other men, for there was a good deal of the literary snob in him. It was of this aspect of his character that Arundell Esdaile was thinking when he wrote his epigram *Callimachus in London*:

> Be sure it's willy-nilly if I'm seen in Piccadilly,
>   From the British Public's haunts I hie me far;
> It simply makes me quail to read the *Daily Mail*
>   Or Captain Coe's predictions in the *Star*.
> I hate the picture-papers with their bathing-beauties' capers,
>   And I never do my drinking at a bar;
> For I'm the kind of person who has to call a curse on
>   Whatever things are really popular.[1]

We can well believe that it would be dangerously easy to pick a quarrel with such a man, and this fate befell the unfortunate Apollonius Rhodius. We do not know the exact history of this quarrel, but the works of both are full of evidences of it, and we can guess at its basic cause. Professional jealousy may partly explain it, for the honour of the directorship of the library, never bestowed on Callimachus, was given to his three famous pupils. The real dispute was, however, on a major point of literary criticism. Callimachus the modernist believed that the Homeric epic was dead; that the future of poetry lay not in the long narrative poem, but in neatly turned pieces of shorter length. Apollonius betrayed his master's teaching by writing an epic himself, the *Argonautica*; and he did this, it is said, while he was still a young student of 18 or 19, presumably working under Callimachus' tuition. On its first publication the *Argonautica* is alleged to have been a failure, though it later acquired a great reputation, and if this is so, the hostility of Callimachus may have been responsible. Athenaeus tells us that it was a dictum of Callimachus that a big book is a big evil. This

---
[1] From *Moments: epigrams and verses*, 1932. See *Anth. Pal.* XII, 43.

does not refer to the difficulties of storing outsize volumes, though it might well do so. It is simply Callimachus' dislike of the long epic. He replied to the *Argonautica* by producing the *Aetia*, an equally long poem dealing with obscure mythological legends, but episodic rather than epic in character. There followed a battle of mud-slinging on both sides (some of it can be found in the *Anthology*), culminating in the lost work of Callimachus called the *Ibis*, which Ovid may have used in part as a model for his poem of the same name. Ovid's poem has been described as a comprehensive curse on somebody who had been persecuting his wife. Callimachus' work is believed, on the authority of *Suidas*, to have been an equally comprehensive curse on Apollonius, and in it he is generally supposed to have reached the limit of obscurity and abuse. Strabo describes the ibis as a bird swarming at every street corner in Alexandria, a foul and omniverous scavenger, battening on the offal from the fishmongers' and butchers' shops, and this presumably is how Callimachus regarded his enemy. At this Apollonius retired defeated to the comparative peace of Rhodes, where they welcomed him and made much of him. There he revised his *Argonautica*, adding a few new lines to punish once more the unkindness of his old teacher.

The Alexandrian library was closely attached to the Museum. This was not so much a university as a research foundation under royal patronage. Its Director was a president-priest appointed by the king (or in Roman times by Caesar), and under him there was a Board of Regius Professors and of research fellows with royal endowments. There were two libraries closely attached to the college: the main library in the Brucheium, founded by Ptolemy Philadelphus, c. 285 BC, and the daughter library in the temple of Serapis, founded about fifty years later by Ptolemy III. The college (and probably the library also) was divided into faculties or subject departments. The intention was to build up a great international research library, incorporating not only all Greek literature, but translations into Greek from the other languages of the Mediterranean, the Middle East and India.[1] One of the great

[1] The close contact between India, Syria and Egypt, at least from the time of Antiochus I and Ptolemy Philadelphus, is well described in G. T. Garratt, *The Legacy of India*, 1937, pp. 11 ff. There was a settlement of Buddhists in Alexandria, according to Clement of Alexandria, and a prosperous trade was carried on between Pataliputra and Syria, and between Alexandria and the coast of Malabar.

achievements of the library was indeed the translation of the Septuagint.

The *Letter of Aristeas*, which is the authority for the account of the origin of the Septuagint, suggests that it was in the first place intended for the use of Greek-speaking Jews in Alexandria who knew neither Hebrew nor Aramaic. The writer of this letter was a Greek at the court of Philadelphus, and the letter is addressed to his brother. Demetrius of Phalerum, here given the title of librarian, is said to have obtained Philadelphus' consent to a proposal for an official translation of the Pentateuch for the library, and an embassy was sent to the High Priest Eleazar inviting him to despatch six elders from each of the twelve tribes to carry it out. These duly arrived, bringing with them a copy of the Law written in gold on a parchment roll. They were given a building on the island of Pharos for their work, which they finished in seventy-two days. Demetrius then read the translation to the king, who ordered it to be preserved with great care. This story is repeated with less credible additions by Aristobulus and Philo (both Alexandrian writers) and by Josephus. The legendary character of the story is recognized by most modern writers, but it probably had some foundation in fact.[1]

During its first century or two, however, the library must have been mainly Greek in spirit and fact, and all its known officials were preoccupied with the arrangement of the obviously vast stock of Greek writings in their own special subjects. There are traditions that the original stock of the library came from the collection at the Lyceum at Athens, and there may well be some ground for this story. Many of the volumes must, however, have been specially produced in Alexandria at the library's own scriptorium. Book production in the third century BC was, of course, in a primitive state, and there had been no previous experience of the physical problems of a really large library. There are varying estimates of the number of volumes in the Alexandrian library, but it is certain that the total soon reached several hundred thousand. The late Byzantine scholar Tzetzes tells us that four-fifths of the stock was composite, or mixed, the remainder being

---

[1] The *Letter of Aristeas* is printed in Swete's *Introduction to the Old Testament in Greek*, 1900, and there is a valuable study of it in the first chapter of this work. See also H. G. Meecham, *The Oldest Version of the Bible*, 1932, and the same author's *Letter of Aristeas*, 1935; also S. R. K.Glanville, *Legacy of Egypt*, 1942, p. 237.

'unmixed'. The reference comes from a Plautine scholium, based on a commentary by Tzetzes on Aristophanes, and surviving in both a Greek and a Latin version. The composite volumes were perhaps (like many medieval books) collections of miscellaneous and unrelated pieces. The 'unmixed' rolls were probably those that had been edited, re-copied and rearranged. The phrase used in the Latin scholium (*simplicium autem et digestorum milia nonaginta*) implies this clearly; earlier in the same passage, the departmental heads of the library are described as editing and collating the Greek poets in just this way (*in unum collegerunt et in ordinem redegerunt*).[1]

The library authorities, faced with the organization of a new national collection of unprecedented size, saw as clearly as we should see today that two preliminary steps were essential: (1) a comprehensive bibliography of Greek literature must be compiled; and (2) the existing texts, most of which were probably in a confused state, must be edited and reproduced in a standard form of roll suitable for easy reference and for storage on a large scale. These indeed formed the first great tasks undertaken by the library, and they proceeded simultaneously.

The editorial work was carried out by the various subject specialists. It included not merely a revision of the texts, but their arrangement into 'books' of suitable length for whatever standard form of roll was found convenient for storage. Thus Zenodotus, who produced the first scientific recension of Homer, arranged the *Iliad* and the *Odyssey* into the 24 books that we are familiar with today; a roll of average size might hold two or three books of the *Iliad*. Similarly, Aristophanes of Byzantium edited Pindar, arranging his works in 17 books, and produced standard editions of the plays of Euripides and Aristophanes, and the fifteen Platonic dialogues, the latter being arranged in trilogies.

The elaborate editorial programme of the library during its first century or so included the establishment of the Alexandrian canon of Greek poets, the publication of many select bibliographies of Greek literature, and the gradual introduction of systems of punctuation and accentuation.[2]

The second task was the compilation of a national bibliography,

[1] Professor H. J. de Vleeschauwer discusses possible meanings of συμμιγεῖς and ἀμιγεῖς at some length in *Mousaion* 71 (History of the Library in Antiquity, Pt. 6, Pretoria 1963). His interpretation of these terms seems much the same as ours.
[2] *Heritage*, p. 94.

and this was entrusted to Callimachus. This great reference work is no longer extant, though a few probable extracts from it can be identified in Athenaeus and in certain scholia, and it was available to scholars in the Byzantine period; a similar, but less important, bibliography was produced at Pergamum. In the select bibliography of Callimachus given in *Suidas*, the penultimate item is a work called *The Museum*, of which nothing is known; it may in fact be the title of the concluding entry which is *Tables of eminent writers with bibliographies*, in 120 volumes. The first table is sub-titled *Table and register of dramatic poets, chronologically arranged from the earliest times.* The subsequent tables deal with epic and non-dramatic poetry, laws, philosophy, history, oratory, and miscellaneous topics. The entries seem to have included bibliographical and biographical details for each author, with the incipit for each book and the stichometric record. The latter was based on an artificial unit (originally a hexameter) used for checking the completeness of the copyist's work and assessing his pay; it suggests plainly that in this case the editing, re-copying and cataloguing of the stock was a combined operation at Alexandria. The use of the word 'Pinakes' (Lat. *tabulae*) might also indicate that it was based on a shelf-list engraved on tablets. The system of storing the rolls at Alexandria is not known, but certain architectural remains at Pergamum and elsewhere indicate that racks of pigeon-holes were sometimes used for this purpose, and this method is possible at Alexandria. It is certain that there was some ready means of identifying and producing a particular roll. S. H. Steinberg states in a recent work[1] that the incipit of the book was used for this purpose. This, however, is most unlikely. Title pages did not, of course, exist, and both in the classical and the medieval period the opening words often served as a title; e.g., Lucretius' *De rerum natura* might be called *Aeneadum genetrix*. But descriptive titles were in common use for many classical texts, and though the title might be concealed like a colophon at the end of a text, nevertheless rolls in the Augustan period were identified by labels or tickets, and a similar practice may well have been followed at Alexandria. Judging from the entries quoted by Athenaeus, it would appear

---

[1] *Five Hundred Years of Printing*, 1955, p. 105. Steinberg here suggests that the incipit corresponds to the modern press-mark. In reality however, it was merely a substitute for the title. See *Heritage*, p. 103.

that the main heading was the author's name, with the incipit and other details following. A chronological arrangement was used, either for the authors or for the material under each author, or for both. An alphabetical arrangement of authors is, however, possible, as the Greeks were quite familiar with this method of arranging names.

The entertaining anecdote told by Vitruvius in the preface to Book VII of the *De architectura* makes it clear that a given roll could be produced at short notice. The story (too long to repeat here) describes Aristophanes of Byzantium as a librarian who daily read every book in his library with zeal and diligence; this means, of course, that he knew his stock from A to Z, as a good librarian should.[1] The tale tells how Aristophanes, relying on his memory of Greek poetry, was able to check the authorship of certain passages by producing at once the original texts from the bookcases where they were stored. This sleight of hand so impressed the king that he immediately promoted Aristophanes to be chief librarian. There is another story that later Aristophanes received an invitation from Pergamum to take charge of the library there. Before he had a chance to reply, Ptolemy settled the matter by throwing him into prison. Modern library authorities may occasionally discourage their librarians from accepting more profitable posts, but I do not recall that they have ever adopted so effective a method as this.

The problem of the arrangement and identification of rolls in ancient libraries is raised also by Ezra VI, where the prophet describes how Darius the king ordered his archivist to have a search made in the national record office in Babylon, for a copy of the decree made by his predecessor Cyrus authorizing the rebuilding of the temple at Jerusalem; the decree was duly produced.[2] The dates of Darius were 521–486 BC; the decree was made in the first year of Cyrus' reign, i.e. 559 BC. In such a case a chronological arrangement would of course be natural. But there is no need to assume that either the Persian archivist or Aristophanes of Byzan-

---

[1] Other librarians are said to have had this uncanny knack, notably Henry Bradshaw of Cambridge and Thomas Watts of the British Museum; once a book had passed through their hands, it was ever afterwards engraved in their memory, and they could go straight to it in the dark, like a homing pigeon. The librarian today, searching vainly for a volume which he knows is somewhere in his collection, may console himself with the thought that very few of his colleagues have achieved such a standard of infallibility.

[2] See R. Ghirshman, *Iran*, 1954.

tium had any elaborate system of what in current technical jargon is known as 'information retrieval'. A search of the actual rolls, guided perhaps by the memories of the staff, would normally supply what was needed.

The rolls at the Persian record office were on parchment. This is confirmed by Diodorus Siculus 2.32, where Ctesias of Cnidus is said to have employed the time of his captivity under Artaxerxes II in writing his history of Persia, based on his researches among the royal parchments. Herodotus 5.58 also confirms that parchment was the normal material for writing amongst the barbarians (i.e. the Persians) in his day.

There is one important piece of information which we might have expected to find in the catalogue entries of Callimachus, but which is missing in the few extracts which have survived: this is the number of rolls occupied by the work in question. Bibliographically, this information seems essential; and that it was sometimes included in book lists is shown by an inscription from Rhodes dated not later than 100 BC, giving a list of works (possibly part of a subject catalogue of a library) in which each title is succeeded by a figure giving the number of rolls; e.g., a work of Theodectes which was in three 'books' is marked 'four', i.e., in four volumes.[1] Athenaeus included the stichometric measurement in his extracts, and one supposes he would have included this also if it had been present.

Callimachus, if we interpret the Tzetzes scholium aright, completed the cataloguing and description of about one-fifth of the stock of the library (90,000 volumes), and the task was continued by Aristophanes of Byzantium, who revised and supplemented the entries, and no doubt by later librarians. The technical routine of compiling the bibliography was probably carried out by slaves, but the credit belongs to Callimachus himself. Knowing a little of his temperament and character, we may perhaps wonder whether he was fitted for so laborious a task. He has been likened to Ben Jonson in temperament; some of his verse may make us think of Browning or Swinburne or even Gerard Manley Hopkins, and it is difficult to imagine any of these devoting their impatient vitality to the meticulous labours of this vast compilation. We should

[1] J. U. Powell and E. A. Barber, *New Chapters in Greek Literature*, 2nd series, 1929, pp. 83–7. See *Heritage*, pp. 62–3.

remember, however, that Callimachus was something more than a poet. He was a professor of literature and an erudite literary historian, with an altogether abnormal knowledge of all the minutiae of mythology which formed the background of both Greek religion and literature; and from this point of view, no happier choice could have been made for the compiler of a bibliography of Greek writings. In one of his extant fragments, Callimachus writes: 'I sing nothing unattested, nothing that is not checked and authenticated'; a wholly admirable motto for a good bibliographer. If he carried this spirit, so evident in his poetry, into the field of descriptive cataloguing, then his work must have been a good deal more trustworthy than most of the classical attempts at bibliography which have come down to us. Our complaint against Callimachus may be, not that he had too poetical a mind for the labours of bibliography, but that he had too bibliographical a mind for the passions of poetry.

The bibliographical work of Callimachus was continued by at least two of his successors at the library. The first was Aristophanes of Byzantium, who was a pupil not only of Callimachus himself, but of two of the directors of the library, Zenodotus and Erastosthenes (could any man receive more distinguished tuition in his profession?). In addition to much textual and editorial work, he revised and expanded the bibliographical work that Callimachus had started. The second was Aristarchus of Samothrace, in whose work textual and literary criticism at Alexandria reached its high-water mark. He was himself a pupil of Aristophanes and his successor at the library; and he founded a school whose influence lasted till Imperial Roman times. These two librarians flourished during the early years of the library at Pergamum, and there is plenty of evidence of contact and indeed rivalry between the two libraries. Aristophanes and Aristarchus were responsible for propounding the grammatical theory of analogy, against which the Stoics at Pergamum under Crates of Mallos (the first head of its library) put forward their theory of anomaly. This rather artificial argument at least suggests that the two libraries exchanged their publications.

The true Alexandrian period lasted through the reigns of the first four Ptolemies. Many autocrats have sought to enhance their fame by the endowment of scholarship, but there has rarely been a hereditary succession of four monarchs prepared to devote their revenues as lavishly as the Ptolemies to the cause of literary research. The Museum and Libraries survived for some centuries into the Roman period. The firing of the dockyard in 47 BC by Caesar is said to have damaged the library, but the story is uncertain and if any damage occurred, it was slight.[1] Doubt also surrounds Plutarch's rumour of a gift by Antony of 200,000 volumes from Pergamum to Cleopatra for her library; indeed, Plutarch himself was suspicious of it.

Julius Caesar, defending the city on behalf of Cleopatra against Ptolemy XIII, was forced to set fire to the seventy-two warships in the harbour and dockyard. This seems to have been a strategic necessity; he had no intention of damaging the Museum, and it is doubtful whether any serious damage was actually done. Caesar himself does not record it.[1] Plutarch, Dio Cassius, Ammianus Marcellinus, Aulus Gellius and Orosius imply that the library was destroyed, though the word Dio Cassius uses (ἀποθήκη) might refer to a storehouse rather than a library. Seneca suggests that 40,000 books were burnt. Orosius, the Spanish priest and pupil of S. Augustine, writing five centuries later, turns the figure into 400,000, but he knew little Greek and is not a trustworthy authority.[2] Some writers have held that Caesar was storing the books in the dockyard to await shipment to Rome for Varro's projected library;[3] an interesting and ingenious theory, but there is no warrant for it. Strabo, who worked in the library twenty years later and tells us most of the little we know about its organization, does not refer to it. Nor does Cicero, who a little later was asking Cleopatra during her visit to Rome to procure him some books from Alexandria. The Museum and Library were in the northern sector of the city, not far from the harbour where Caesar had his quarters. There was no general burning of this part of the city, for Caesar continued to occupy the position after the fire; moreover the palace buildings were of stone, not wood. The silence of Caesar and Strabo is significant, if not conclusive, and in these circumstances we can only guess that if any damage occurred to the library or its books, it was not as serious as Plutarch suggests. The

---

[1] Caesar, *De bello civili*, 3. 111.
[2] Plutarch, *Caesar* 49; Dio Cas. 42, 38; Amm. Marc. 22. 16. 12: Gellius 6. 17; Orosius 6. 15; 3. Cicero *Ad Att.*, 14. 8; 15. 15.
[3] *Heritage*, p. 76.

loss of some of the library's possessions might account for the extraordinary editorial activity of Didymus, who was a pupil of Aristarchus and worked at the library late in the first century BC. He is said to have produced four thousand works, commentaries, biographies, literary histories and lexicons, including reconstitutions of lost recensions of Homer by Aristarchus. So voluminous an output earned him the nickname βιβλιολάθας; forgetful of what he had written in earlier volumes, he kept falling into self-contradictions. This fever of editorial work might reasonably suggest some serious disorganization in the library, but only guesswork can connect it with the fire.[1]

Some time before the battle of Actium in 31 BC, in which Antony was defeated by Octavian, there occurred the alleged transfer of 200,000 books from Pergamum to Alexandria as a gift from Antony to Cleopatra. Our only authority is Plutarch. White, accepting Plutarch's statement, quotes the suggestion in Pauly-Wissowa that the existing remains of the eastern chamber in the Pergamum library indicate that it may have been re-constructed for other purposes after the removal of the books.[2] The story is, however, improbable. First, the remains of only four small rooms of the Pergamum library have survived. The eastern room is the largest, measuring 42 by 49 feet, and it has been estimated that this could not accommodate more than 17,000 rolls.[3] Secondly it is scarcely credible that so large a consignment of books from one library to another or such a dramatic crisis in history could have gone unrecorded by other writers. Plutarch's reference is as follows. Prior to the battle of Actium, deserters from Antony's cause who had been ill-used by Cleopatra came over to Caesar with a report of Antony's will, which had been deposited with the vestal virgins. Caesar seized it and read it to the Senate. Antony had directed that his body, even if he died in Rome, should be sent to Cleopatra. Amongst various charges levelled against Antony was one that he had given Cleopatra the library of Pergamum, containing 200,000 separate volumes. But (Plutarch adds) these stories were regarded as invented for the occasion. We have all been misled by similar inventions in the wars of our own

---
[1] The best discussion of the problem is in J. W. White, *The Scholia on the Aves of Aristophanes*, Boston, 1914 (Introduction).
[2] Plutarch, *Antonius* 58; J. W. White, op. cit., p. XXX; *Real-Encyclopidie*, 3. 414.
[3] E. V. Hansen, *The Attalids of Pergamum*, 1947.

century, and without further evidence it can be discounted. A gift of books to Cleopatra is of course likely enough, but not a gift on this scale.

From this time onwards a gradual decline of the Museum and Library set in, but it continued to attract scholars for at least four more centuries. Domitian (AD 81–96) sent scholars there from Rome to make transcriptions for the replacement of books in the Octavian library damaged in the fire of AD 80.[1] Hadrian, visiting Egypt AD 130, met the professors of the Museum, and propounded many problems to them; the Emperor himself however announced the solutions to his problems, the embarrassed professors being perhaps reluctant to commit themselves.[2] Many writers who worked in Alexandria must have been familiar with the resources of the Museum: Strabo himself of course; Appian the historian (AD 95–165); Claudius Ptolemaeus the astronomer and geographer in the mid-second century; Athenaeus (*c.* AD 200) whose *Philosophers at the Dinner Table* includes much gossip about libraries; Christian and neo-Platonist scholars such as Clement of Alexandria, head of the Catachetical School (*c.* 200), Origen, Ammonius Saccas, Plotinus and Longinus; and lastly Theon the mathematician with his famous daughter Hypatia who took part in the revival of neo-Platonism in the fourth century. Hypatia, who held a chair of philosophy at the Museum, was murdered by a Christian mob, AD 415. The Museum seems gradually to have taken on the typical form of a Greek university, devoted more to teaching rather than research. Bishop Synesius, Hypatia's devoted student, refers to its professors as *scholastici*,[3] a not entirely complimentary term with an implication of pedantry which may have been deserved. Some of Hypatia's disciples migrated to Athens, where neo-Platonism took root at the Academy, losing itself eventually in a fog of mysticism and magic under the doubtful guidance of Proclus. Bishop Synesius wrote with scorn of the University of Athens in his day; the students (he said) boast of their acquaintance with the Academy, the Lyceum and the Stoa, but they know less about Aristotle and Plato than we do in Alexandria.[4] When Justinian closed the University AD 529, the last head of the

---
[1] Suet. Dom. 20.
[2] Spartianus, *Hadrian*, 20. 2.
[3] *Ep.* 105.
[4] *Ep.* 54, 136.

Academy, Damascius, with six of his professors travelled first to Persia and then back in despair to Alexandria, finding no welcome anywhere.

There can indeed have been little left at Alexandria of any academic institutions or libraries. The palace and Museum, including presumably its library, were destroyed in the civil war under Aurelian, AD 272, and were never rebuilt. The political centre of the city seems to have been transferred to the temple of Serapis, where Apthonius a century later describes the magnificence of the acropolis, built on rising ground above the Serapeum, with its temple, colonnades and library, and the great staircase with a hundred steps, with a propylon fitted with bronze grilles leading from the temple to the acropolis above.[1] For a time during the third and fourth centuries there seems to have been some co-operation between Christians, Jews and pagans at the Museum. Eusebius records that Anatolius, Bishop of Laodiceia, was head of the school of philosophy there, and there were Alexandrian commentators on Aristotle with names such as David and Elias. But in 391 the Serapeum was destroyed by Theophilus, patriarch of Alexandria, and a church and monastery took its place. It is curious that Bishop Synesius has no reference to the end of the Serapeum in his letters; he was proud of his association with the Museum, and was a correspondent of Theophilus, who had indeed consecrated him bishop. Though teaching no doubt continued, the library may no longer have been a living institution in 391. Orosius writes that, about 418, he saw only empty presses in the temples of Alexandria. Two centuries later in 641 the Museum, or what little remained of it, came to its final end with the Muslim conquest of Egypt. Nobody believes the story of the destruction of the library by the invaders and the use of the books as fuel for the baths of the city, for which purpose the supply is said to have lasted six months.[2] This tale comes from the pen of Abulpharagius, whose *Dynasties* was not written till six centuries after the event. Earlier historians such as the Patriarch Eutychius make no mention of an event so astonishing that they could scarcely have overlooked it. Nor indeed would such an act accord with the principles of Muslim teaching, which forbade the destruction of Christian and

---

[1] Apthonius, *Progymnasmata*, 12.
[2] On this story see also p. 73 *infra*.

Jewish works and permitted the use of foreign works of philosophy and science by the faithful. It is possible that the University in some degree survived the conquest, for Hellenic studies continued there at least till 718 when the University was transferred to Antioch.

To return to Roman Egypt. So far as we know, there were no other great libraries at Alexandria other than the two at the Museum. There was probably a library at the Catachetical School made famous by Clement and Origen, but details are lacking; Origen's own library was mainly collected at Caesarea. There were doubtless archive collections in the temples, and there was the record office housing the Land Register, introduced by the Romans as a repository of title deeds to real property.[1] Private and business archives are illustrated by the Zenon papers. Apollonius was the Egyptian finance minister in the mid-third century BC. He held a large agricultural estate in Philadelphia, with property also in Alexandria, and a merchant fleet with trading connections throughout the Middle East. Zenon was his business manager, and the surviving archives throw much light on the economic history of the time. Amongst these papers are a partial list of books which Zenon sent to his brother, and an inventory of furniture, including κίσται (book chests?), compiled by a certain Dionysius who is described as βιβλιοφύλαξ, i.e., library keeper—presumably in Apollonius' household.[2]

We can assume the existence of school libraries, and various fragments from the Oxyrhynchus papyri contain lists of books which might refer to school, or perhaps booksellers' catalogues. Palladas of Alexandria (c. AD 400), who has over 150 sardonic epigrams in the Anthology, was an impoverished dominie. In one of his epigrams he cries out that he is abandoning his schoolmaster's job and selling the tools of the Muses, the books that brought him nothing but tears and misery.[3]

Of private collections the best instance is that of Synesius, who became Bishop of Ptolemais (AD 370–403), the friend of Theon and Theophilus, and perhaps also of Palladas. From a literary point of view, he was one of the most attractive of Greek Christian

[1] S. R. K. Glanville, *The Legacy of Egypt*, 1942, p. 215.
[2] M. Rostovtzeff, *A Large Estate in Egypt*, 1922; *Social and Economic History of the Hellenistic world*, 1941; and C. C. Edgar, *Zenon papyri in the University of Michigan collection*, 1931; also *The Legacy of Egypt*, pp. 266, 272, 276.
[3] *Anth.Pal.* IX. 171

writers. He tells us in his letters that he had inherited his father's library, and that he had greatly enlarged it during his own lifetime. We hear of him exchanging books with his brother, and in his treatise on dreams he says that his whole life had been devoted either to his library or to the chase. In one of his letters to Hypatia he sends her two of his unpublished works, and complains that his library had been criticized because it contained unrevised copies of his books.[1] There is a portrait of Synesius in Kingsley's *Hypatia*.

[1] *Ep.* 65. 154.

CHAPTER III

The Byzantine Age

THE library traditions established at Alexandria passed in the fourth century of our era to Constantinople, which for over a thousand years was the fountain and source of scholarship in the Eastern Empire. It is well at this point to bear in mind the differing political and racial conditions under which the traditions of scholarship and libraries were handed down in the East and the West. In the East, there was throughout this period a single great city, the capital of an Empire, with a single language which in its literary form did not differ radically from the classical Attic model; while the spoken form of Greek, the κοινή, which had its birth perhaps in the conquests of Alexander the Great and is enshrined for us in the language of the New Testament, developed gradually the characteristics of modern Greek. The existence of these two forms of the Greek language, the classical and the colloquial, served to fix the classical language in a comparatively pure form, and its teaching in the schools of grammar and rhetoric, and its use by the Church for liturgical purposes, helped to stabilize it.

In the West, conditions were very different. There was no single city to act as the focus for literary tradition; Rome never achieved the position that Constantinople held in this respect. There was no single succession of dynasties to lend enlightened patronage to letters, such as Alexandria enjoyed from the Ptolemies, or such as Constantinople had through all its long history. There was no commonly acknowledged tradition of culture to compare with that of Constantinople, or even that of Islam. There was indeed no single spoken language after the sixth century. No families of pure Roman descent were left, and Latin was being learnt largely by ear by the differing races in Italy, Spain, Portugal and France. Latin was of course a younger language than Greek. It lacked refinements such as the articles and the distinction between the aorist and the perfect tense, and these refinements, necessary for easy conversation, were supplied in different ways in each different country. Being acquired by ear, it mingled the more readily with local non-Latin dialects, and a series of languages was evolved, differing from each other to a far greater extent than the various dialects of the Greek κοινή. Such scholarship as remained was thus diffused among many widely separated centres. The one stable element in this variety was the Church, which through the teaching in its own schools succeeded in fixing a universal language of its own in the shape of ecclesiastical Latin; and a few at least of these schools preserved in addition some knowledge of classical Latin in their teaching of grammar and literature. But the proportion of laymen who could both read and write or had any familiarity with Latin literature diminished almost to vanishing point; and it was a very fragile thread that linked the Western medieval world with classical Rome. The tenuous thread survived, however, and in due time was strengthened and restored by Greek thought percolating westwards from Byzantine and Arabic sources.

The Byzantine Age extends from the founding of Constantinople, AD 330, to its capture by the Turks in 1453; and the significance of the continuous Greek tradition of scholarship and libraries at a time when the West was all but submerged in darkness and illiteracy, is evident. From first to last in the East there was an unbroken succession of commentators, editors, encyclopaedists, theologians, historians, biographers and lexicographers, whose work, whether good or indifferent or bad by modern standards, was far in advance of contemporary Western achievements. To their labours we owe in great part the preservation of the texts of classical Greek. Moreover the work of a great many of these Byzantine scholars, especially perhaps of the encyclopaedists, the lexicographers and the historians, inevitably smacks of the library bookshelf; so much so that we can be reasonably certain that generous library resources of some type were available in Constantinople in every part of this period. There was no city in the West, not even Rome itself, of which the same could be said in the period under review.

Constantinople itself, whose magnificence and natural advantages are well described by Gibbon, and even better perhaps by

Robert Byron,[1] may well have been an even larger and more splendid city than Rome. Throughout it had to a remarkable degree not merely a literate but an educated population, and the standard of culture seems to have varied little in the whole thousand years of its history. 'All sensible people admit that education is the first of the goods we possess' was the confident assertion of S. Gregory Nazianzen, and as J. B. Bury affirmed,[2] 'every boy and girl whose parents could afford to pay was educated'. This was at the time when darkness lay heavily over the West, and literacy scarcely existed at all amongst laymen. In Constantinople on the other hand, the educated life was the ideal of almost every citizen, and illiteracy was not merely a misfortune but almost a crime.[3] The general plan of education followed the earlier Greek pattern fairly closely, but a sharp distinction was maintained between secular teaching and the theological schools. The boy began work at the age of six at an elementary school, where he learnt his 'orthography', that is, reading and writing the classical form of the language. At ten or twelve he was promoted to grammar, which included not merely syntax but a close study of classical texts, and especially of Homer, with detailed commentaries and much memorizing; it seems to have been common for the young student to have the whole of Homer by heart. Synesius in the fifth century speaks of his nephew learning 50 lines of Homer a day, and in the eleventh century Psellus claimed to have had the *Iliad* by heart at fourteen. The sharp distinction made between Christian and pagan culture made it possible for the Byzantines to regard Homer very much as we regard our fairy tales, and the stories of classical and Scandinavian mythology simply as part of our literary and cultural background, and unrelated to the orthodox doctrine which the Byzantine child probably imbibed from his parents before he ever started school.[4]

At fourteen the pupil embarked on the various subjects which made up his academic career: Rhetoric, which included the study

---

[1] Gibbon, ch. XVII; R. Byron, *Byzantine achievement*, 1929. For the period in general, see N. H. Baynes and H. St. L. B. Moss, *ed. Byzantium*, 1948; Steven Runciman, *Byzantine civilization*, 1933; J. M. Hussey, *Church and learning in the Byzantine Empire, 867–1185*, 1937; *The Byzantine world*, 1957; and Cambridge Medieval History, vol IV, 1965

[2] Quoted by Georgina Buckler in Baynes and Moss, *op. cit.*, p. 200.

[3] Runciman, *op. cit.*, p. 223.

[4] Baynes and Moss, *op. cit.*, pp. 202–3.

of Demosthenes and Greek prose writers in general; Philosophy; and the four arts of Arithmetic, Geometry, Music and Astronomy; and for the specialist, Law, Medicine or Physics could be added. Although its history is obscure, there seems to have been a secular university in Constantinople for practically the whole period; it was re-organized or refounded on more than one occasion, but if any actual interruptions occurred, they cannot have lasted long. Outside Constantinople there were other universities, especially in the earlier period: Antioch, where Libanius taught; Alexandria, where Hypatia taught and St Gregory Nazianzen studied; Gaza, with its schools of Rhetoric; Athens, where, although Justinian closed its university in 529, some academic studies must have continued, for Theodore of Tarsus received his education there in the early seventh century; Berytus with its Law School, destroyed in the earthquake of 551; and the Nestorian schools of Edessa (closed by the Emperor Zeno in 487), Nisibis in Persia and Gandisapora, where scholars were translating the Greek texts into Syriac and instructing the Arabs in philosophy and medicine.

The Empire was administered in its capital city by a vast and highly efficient civil service, and one of the main purposes of the secular teaching at the Imperial University was that it served as a training ground for civil servants; its evident value in this respect was no doubt responsible for its almost continuous history through so long a period. One is reminded of the part played by professional civil servants in the government of China over the last 2000 years; a university with a system of written examinations was founded for their training in the first century BC, and the system has worked with remarkable efficiency. Literacy was high in all classes.[1] The civil service in Pharaonic and Ptolemaic Egypt, staffed by the royal scribes, and administering the complex fiscal and legal system of a totalitarian state, may also be regarded as comparable, though little is known of how it actually worked.[2]

It is noteworthy that most of the senior posts in the Byzantine civil service were held by eunuchs. This was indeed the source of its strength, for it prevented the concentration of feudal power in a hereditary nobility, and provided a governing class that could be

[1] R. Dawson, *The Legacy of China*, 1964, p. 322.
[2] A. H. M. Jones, *Egypt and Rome*, in S. R. K. Glanville, *The Legacy of Egypt*, 1942, pp. 218–48.

trusted by the Emperors. No disgrace was felt at castration, and the ambitious were apparently ready to accept mutilation as the key to advancement.[1]

Side by side with the Imperial University at Constantinople there was a Patriarchal School about which little is known for certain. It was in the main a theological school, but preliminary grammar schools at various churches in the city were associated with it. Schools were also attached to the monasteries, but these were normally intended only for oblates. Though St Basil had been prepared to admit children of lay families in the neighbourhood to monastic schools, this practice was forbidden by the Council of Chalcedon, and the schools were restricted to children dedicated to the religious life. Teaching at monastic schools was narrowly confined to religious subjects, and it is probable that their libraries reflected this; theological and patristic works, histories, chronicles, *Vitae* and the works of the mystics would have been included, but few classical texts. Many of the monasteries were actively engaged in welfare work, providing hospitals, hostels, orphanages and refuges both for the poor and disabled and for aristocratic families temporarily out of favour at court; and these charitable occupations may possibly of course, have extended their libraries into more secular fields. There were no monastic orders as in the West, no detailed monastic constitutions governing practice, and no patriarchal control comparable to that exercised by Rome. In consequence, monastic standards were probably lower than in the West, except where they were maintained by an exceptional figure such as Theodore of Studium in the early ninth century, who prescribed very strict rules for his scriptorium and for monastic studies. The four outstanding houses were Studios (or Studium) in Constantinople. Mt Olympus in Bythinia, the monastic republic of Mt Athos, and the monastery of St John the Evangelist on Patmos, founded by Christodoulos in the eleventh century. An inventory of the Patmos library in 1201 reveals that it possessed 330 manuscripts, of which only 17 were of a secular nature, including Josephus and an unspecified volume of Aristotle. Most of the manuscripts were on parchment, but 63 were on bombycine, i.e. paper made from silk or cotton.[2]

[1] Runciman, *op. cit.*, p. 203.
[2] J. M. Hussey, *op. cit.*, p. 192.

Most, if not all, of these various institutions, whether academic, patriarchal or monastic, were evidently equipped with libraries, though detailed evidence is scanty and often circumstantial. It is equally certain that there were many private libraries, often very rich collections, especially in the prosperous time of Justinian and in the later period from the time of Photius in the ninth century onwards.

The Byzantine age (which, as has been said, extends from the founding of Constantinople by Constantine the Great, AD 330, to its capture by the Turks in 1453) is conveniently divided into three periods: first from 330 to the death of Heraclius in 641; second, the dark age from 641 to 867, which includes the period of the iconoclasts; third, the final period, with its literary revival under Photius from 867 onwards.

Both the Imperial Library and the Patriarchal Library had their beginnings under Constantine the Great, and both probably existed side by side throughout. It is probable that the Imperial Library was to begin with mainly Latin, though Latin must soon have given way to Greek; its last surviving stronghold would have been the Law School at Berytus, which remained a Latin island till the destruction of the city in 551. The Patriarchal library would have been mainly Greek in language and theological in content from the start; one of its earliest acquisitions was the set of fifty copies of the scriptures on vellum made to Constantine's order probably at Caesarea. It has been suggested that the Codex Sinaiticus and the Codex Vaticanus were rejected copies of this order.[1]

The Imperial Library seems to have grown rapidly during its first century. Julian the Apostate provided a building for it, and may have transferred to it the books he had appropriated from the library of George of Cappadocia, the Arian Patriarch of Alexandra. Two of Julian's letters[2] refer to this transaction: one to Ecdicius, the Prefect of Egypt, asking him to seize George's library, which contained many works of philosophy and rhetoric as well as works of the 'impious Galileans'. The latter were to be destroyed. George's secretary was to be told to carry out this task

---

[1] Eusebius, *Vita Constant.* 3; T. C. Skeat, "The Use of Dictation in Ancient Book Production, *Proc. Br. Acad.*, vol. LXII, 1956; C. H. Roberts, "The Codex," *Proc. Br. Acad.*, vol. XL, 1954.

[2] Julian, *Ep.*, 9, 38 (Wright).

with a promise of freedom as a reward, or torture if he failed; and Julian significantly added that he was familiar with the books, for George had lent him some when he (Julian) was in Cappadocia (that is, when George was at Caesarea and Julian under detention there by Constantius). A second letter repeats the demand as the matter was urgent; this is addressed to Porphyrius, who may have been George's secretary. Elsewhere[1] Julian records the Empress Eusebia's gift of a collection of the historians, philosophers, orators and poets to accompany him on his campaign in Gaul 'in such quantity that even my longing for them was quenched, though in reading I am quite insatiable'. Whether his books found a home in the Imperial library is not known; the foundation of a secular library by Julian in the royal palace is, however, recorded.[2]

In 372 the Emperor Valens attached a staff of four Greek and three Latin copyists to the library, their salaries to be paid from Imperial funds. The University was reorganized by Theodosius II in the early fifth century as a counterpoise to the fast decaying University of Athens. Thirty-one professors were appointed, paid by the State: ten professors of Greek literature and ten of Latin, five Greek sophists and three Latin, two jurists and one philosopher.[3] The library was burnt in the rebellion of Basiliscus in 476, and it is said then to have contained 120,000 volumes, but it must soon have been restored.

The period of Justinian in the middle of the sixth century was a time of high achievement and prosperity and of considerable literary activity. The great church of Santa Sophia took shape under the guidance of a band of famous architects, painters and sculptors. The Emperor began to rebuild Constantine's church in 532, and it was completed in 537: 'one of the mightiest creations in all architecture', it has been called, and 'a marvel of stability, daring, fearless logic and science', so that Justinian had reason for his exclamation 'Glory be to God who hath deemed me worthy to complete so great a work. I have outdone thee, O Solomon'.[4] There was nothing to compare with it in the West, either at this time or for many centuries afterwards. In literature this was the time of Procopius, the historian of Belisarius and Justinian; of

[1] Julian, Or., 3.
[2] Zosimus, 3. 11. 3.
[3] Runciman, op. cit., p. 224.
[4] Baynes and Moss, op. cit., pp. 166-9.

Agathias, the historian and poet, who published an enlarged and re-arranged edition of Meleager's *Anthology*, containing much of his own work, including the lovely piece known as the *Swallows*;[1] of Paul the Silentiary, probably the greatest of the Byzantine poets, whose three long poems on Santa Sophia and on the Pythian Baths in Bithynia were commissioned by Justinian and Theodora; and of Musaeus, who made the story of Hero and Leander immortal.

Fine manuscripts such as the magnificent codices written and illuminated on purple vellum with gold and silver ink, belong to this period: works such as the Vienna Genesis, the Rossano Gospel and the Vatican Joshua Roll are examples[2]. By Justinian's time the Imperial Library is said to have amassed 600,000 books, and the great houses of the city were filled with works of art and stores of books. One mansion included the Aphrodite of Praxiteles, the Hera of Lysippus and the Zeus of Phidias, together with a library of 120,000 volumes.[3]

This was also the great age of legal codification. The issue of Justinian's *Pandectae* in Latin and *Novellae* in Greek superseded the old law of the twelve tables, and reduced to one great system the whole range of Roman law; and it was during this time that the law schools of Berytus and Constantinople reached the height of their reputation. Western Europe inherited its Roman law directly from Justinian through the University of Bologna; and in England, Bracton's *De legibus et consuetudinibus Angliae* was based on the work of the celebrated lawyer Azo of Bologna, which was probably available then at Oxford. Each of the three law schools recognized by Justinian (Berytus, Rome and Constantinople) must have been equipped with its law library. At Berytus, the school was under an 'oecumenical master' or rector, and the normal course of study lasted four years, with an optional fifth year; students were drawn from all parts of the Empire. Teaching was in Greek, but copies of the Latin texts were studied.[4]

Justinian's reign was notable for the rescript in 529 closing the

---

[1] *Anth. Pal:* V. 236.
[2] Baynes and Moss, *op. cit.*, p. 176; Runciman, *op. cit.*, p. 268. The Rossano Codex, written in silver uncials on purple vellum, came to light in 1879 at the Greek monastery in Rossano in Southern Italy. See Thompson, *Med. libs.*, 1957, p. 336.
[3] F. A. Wright, *History of Later Greek Literature*, 1932, p. 383.
[4] Baynes and Moss, *op. cit.*, p. 214.

University of Athens. It had indeed all but disappeared before that date in the shadowy mists of Neo-Platonism. Readers of Gibbon will remember how unfortunate were the later developments of Neo-Platonism at Athens under Proclus when it became debased by the practices of magic and witchcraft. As a philosophy, it had its fruitful beginnings at Alexandria in the third century with Ammonius Saccas, among whose pupils were the two Origens (one, the Christian theologian who moved to Caesarea, the other a Neo-Platonist) and Plotinus, who became a teacher of philosophy in Rome. Plotinus is of great importance as the link between Plato and Christian mystical theology. The philosophic tradition which led from Plato and Plotinus to S. Augustine and eventually to medieval scholasticism is described with admirable clarity by Professor David Knowles in his *Evolution of Medieval Thought*, 1962.

The dark age of Byzantine history covers the period of the iconoclastic Emperors. There is no certain information about the progress of the University and the libraries at this time, but there cannot have been any serious interruption either to secular or theological studies. The story that Leo III closed the Oecumenical College, expelled its rector and twelve professors, set fire to the library and threw the professors into the flames, is now regarded as a myth, possibly invented by later writers to blacken the character of the iconoclasts. Two events of this period are significant from our point of view. The schools of Syria and Persia were active in translating the Greek texts into Syriac and instructing the Arabs in philosophy and medicine; Arab scholarship was indeed largely borrowed from Greek, Persian and Indian sources,[1] but it produced two of the three cultural centres of the early medieval world at Bagdad and Cordova. At Bagdad the Caliph Al-Ma'mun (813-33) established his great school and library of translations; the greatest of the translators at this school was Hunayn Ibn Ishaq (809-77) who translated the whole corpus of Galen's works, including 100 Syriac and 39 Arabic versions.[2]

[1] Arabic scholarship was in fact largely the work of Persian scholars using the Arabic language. Most of the great translators were either Persian or Jewish. Persia in the sixth-ninth centuries was a fertile meeting-place for Greek, Jewish, Christian, Hindu and Chinese influences, but detailed information about the intermingling of these various cultures is lacking. See G. T. Garratt, *The Legacy of India*, 1937, p. 336, and A. J. Arberry, *The Legacy of Persia*, 1953, pp. 292 ff.

[2] Arnold and Guillaume. *The Legacy of Islam*, 1931, pp. 316, 331.

The third centre of culture was of course Constantinople, 'the city guarded by God', 'the glory of Greece' and the most highly civilized city of the medieval world. Bagdad, which sprang to life in 762 'as by an enchanter's wand' was a close second to Constantinople, and the Court of the Abbasids has been described as a 'real garden of learning, science and the arts'. Cordova in Spain arose in the tenth century as the most brilliant city in Western Europe, 'the wonder and admiration of the world', with its 70 libraries and 900 public baths.[1] It was destroyed by the Berbers early in the eleventh century, after which Toledo took its place as the centre of learning in Spain. Toledo was conquered by the Christians in 1085, and became one of the main channels by which Arabic translations filtered through to the West.

It is perhaps of interest to note that it was in this period of the ninth century, when the iconoclasts reigned at Constantinople and Arabian culture was spreading from Bagdad through North Africa to Cordova, and when in England Alfred the Great was trying to overcome the illiteracy of his subjects, that the printed book first began to appear in China. The earliest extant printed book, the Diamond Sutra Scroll, AD 868, is now in the British Museum.

Printing apparently first reached the West in the form of paper money printed in Pekin, and also at Tabriz after 1294. Some block printing was done in Egypt on Chinese models at the time of the Crusades.

Gibbon tells the story of the spread of Arabian civilization in his own picturesque way.[2] From Samarkand and Bagdad westwards to Cordova and Toledo the pursuit of learning was decked out with the luxury and extravagance appropriate to the country of the Arabian Nights. Softened by wealth, the Moslems found that the study of the Quran no longer satisfied their needs, and they reached out into the fields of medicine and science. In Syria, Armenia and Constantinople their agents sought out manuscripts of Aristotle, Euclid, Ptolemy, Hippocrates and Galen, and these were translated either from the original or from Syriac versions by Syrian, Persian and Jewish interpreters, but mainly by Jewish

[1] Baynes and Moss, *op. cit.*, pp. 315–16.
[2] *Decline and Fall*, ch. LII.

scholars.[1] They poured out their treasure in the endowment of schools and libraries. 'In every city the productions of Arabic literature were copied and collected by the curiosity of the studious and the vanity of the rich. A private doctor refused the invitation of the Sultan of Bokhara because the carriage of his books would have required four hundred camels. The royal library of the Fatimites consisted of 100,000 manuscripts, elegantly transcribed and splendidly bound, which were lent without jealousy or avarice to the students of Cairo... the Ommiades in Spain had formed a library of 600,000 volumes, 44 of which were employed in the mere catalogue.' The age of Arabian learning, which lasted 500 years till the great eruption of the Mughals, is illustrated by the story of the philosopher and physician Avicenna, who was born in Bokhara, AD 980. At the age of 16 he took up medicine, which is not (he tells us) one of the difficult sciences. Then he devoted a year and a half to an intensive study of philosophy, during which he read Aristotle's *Metaphysics* forty times. Called to attend the ailing Amir of Bokhara, he made thereby his début as a physician. The Amir allowed him to use his valuable library, and he tells of his delight in this privilege, reading books nobody had ever heard of. In all the 'prince of physicians' wrote over 100 treatises, including the Qanum which in a million words systematized all ancient and contemporary medical knowledge.

In Egypt, the Museum had come to an end in 641 with the Moslem conquest of Alexandria. Its School of Philosophy lapsed towards the end of the sixth century, but the medical school continued for a further 50 years. A gap of three centuries then ensued before any academic teaching was resumed in Egypt. In 972 the Al-Azhar mosque in Cairo was founded by the Fâtimid Caliphs, and this developed into the official university of the Islamic world; it claims indeed to be the oldest of all surviving universities, serving as the recognized repository and guardian of orthodox Islamic theology and still drawing students from all over the Moslem world, though today it is to some extent overshadowed by the modern Egyptian university.[2]

[1] There is an admirable survey of the very substantial Jewish contribution to this work, both in the East and in Spain, in E. R. Bevan and C. Singer, *The Legacy of Israel*, 1927, esp. pp. 173–282.
[2] S. R. K. Glanville, *The Legacy of Egypt*, 1942, p. 351. On Muslim libraries in Persia, Egypt and Spain, see S. K. Padover's chapter in J. W. Thompson, *Medieval Libraries*, 1957.

Further East, Moslem libraries established in India belong to the period of the Mughals, and were royal or aristocratic rather than academic. They had a considerable influence however on Indian culture. Although in its early period (thirteenth century) Moslem rule resulted in the dissolution of Sanskrit academies and the persecution of scholars, many of the later rulers and nobles gathered rich collections of books as well as other treasures: notably Humāyūn (d.1556), who met his death in the library he had built, which still stands in Delhi; Akbar, his son (1556–1605), who founded a university at his mosque in Fatehpur, near Agra; Shāhjahān, the grandson of Akbar (1628–58), the creator of the Tāj Mahal at Agra; and his son Dārā Shikoh, a brilliant scholar and the collector of a large library. Calligraphy and illumination flourished during this period. The later Emperor Aurangzib (d. 1707) is said to have reimbursed himself for his personal expenses by selling copies of the Quran made by his own hand.[1]

In Constantinople, the end of iconoclasm in the middle of the ninth century was signalized by a literary revival under the Patriarch Photius, who had a tremendous reputation as grammarian, logician and philosopher. Disciples flocked to his house to hear his lectures on Aristotelian logic, and his interests and scholarship are reflected in his two best known works: his *Lexicon*, a glossary based on the work of earlier lexicographers, and his *Myriobiblion* or *Bibliotheca*, which was a reading list of classical prose, compiled for his brother Tarasius, who had asked for details of the books discussed at Photius' house during his absence. It is a bibliographical guide in 280 chapters annotating and criticizing a similar number of prose works with a wide range from Herodotus to Synesius.[2]

One of Photius' pupils was Arethas, Bishop of Caesarea, whose success as a book collector is testified by several extant manuscripts. His copy of Plato was acquired by the monastery at Patmos, where in due time it was rescued from a heap of manuscripts on the floor of the library by Edward Daniel Clark in 1801, and brought back to the Bodleian Library. This copy bears a statement that it was written by John the calligraphist for Arethas, November 895. The Arethas manuscripts provide some of the earliest dated

---

[1] G. T. Garratt, *The Legacy of India*, 1937, pp. 249, 298, 304.
[2] On Photius' library, see J. W. Thompson, *The Medieval Library*, 1957, pp. 317–19.

examples of the Greek minuscule hand of the middle ages. A facsimile of a portion of his Clemens Alexandrinus is reproduced by Sandys.[1] The rising value of good editions is illustrated by a note on his copy of Euclid that it was purchased for four nomismata —perhaps £12 in modern money.[2]

Another of Photius' pupils was Leo the Wise who was himself a writer; his son, Constantine Porphyrogenitus was a very voluminous writer indeed. He is perhaps chiefly remembered for his encouragement of the unfortunate Byzantine tendency towards the compilation of abridgements and epitomes and excerpts of classical works. This tendency, which was also a feature of the later medieval period in the West, can be regarded as evidence that the libraries were suffering from overcrowding and confusion, and were in need of reorganization. In both cases the attempt to restore their value to students by such means resulted in the loss of original texts.

To this period (the tenth century) belongs the compilation of the work we know now as the Suidas lexicon (this is the title, not the author). This is an immense reference work, arranged alphabetically, and of special value for the biographical and bibliographical information which it summarizes. It is based on a wide range of earlier lexicons, histories, biographies and scholia, and is obviously the product of extensive research among the libraries of Constantinople. Some original texts are used, such as Homer, Sophocles and Aristophanes, but unfortunately many of the sources were themselves abridgements. In spite of its deficiencies, it is a most important authority for the lives and work of classical writers. The bibliographical lists would not of course satisfy modern standards of accuracy and completeness, and many are cut short with κ.τ.λ.

It was probably the work of many hands; its many contradictions suggest this.

Though details are lacking it seems probable that both the secular and ecclesiastical schools and libraries continued to function during the iconoclastic period and in the centuries that followed. After the restoration of the icons in the late ninth century the secular university was reorganized in the Magnaura Palace, possibly in an attempt to rival the new University at Bagdad.

[1] *Hist. Class. Schol.* I. p. 395.
[2] Runciman, *op. cit.*, p. 228.

Though its secular nature was preserved, some of its most distinguished teachers, such as Leo the Mathematician and Photius, were ecclesiastics. Under Constantine Porphyrogenitus, four professorial chairs are recorded, of philosophy, geometry, astronomy and rhetoric, with teaching also in arithmetic, music, grammar, law and medicine.[1] There seems to have been a decline in standards in the early eleventh century, and there may even have been a break in the academic tradition, though some teaching certainly continued. A fresh literary revival set in about the middle of the eleventh century, and in 1045 the University was either reopened or reconstituted in two faculties of Law and Philosophy; no fees were charged, and it was evidently intended mainly as a training ground for the civil service.[2] The academic leaders at this time were the philosopher Michael Psellus, with his friends Xiphilinus, the head both of the Law School and the Law Library, which were in the newly founded monastery of S. George, John Mauropous, who drew up the constitution of the Law School, and the Latin philosopher John Italus, who succeeded Psellus as head of the university. Psellus was a Platonist, a writer of encyclopaedic range, and evidently a great teacher. In one of his works he laments the decay of learning, which flourished in his time neither in Athens, nor Nicomedeia, nor Alexandria, nor Phoenicia, nor in Old Rome, nor in New Rome;[3] and the production of a further series of lexicons and epitomes confirms the difficulties which academic study had to meet.

Two other features of the post-iconoclastic period can be noted. One was the development of mysticism, especially under the influence of Symeon the Young in the eleventh century. This is one of the only two fields in which Byzantine civilization developed any marked creative impulse, the other of course being in art and architecture. Symeon the Young began his religious life as a monk at Studios, though probably owing to jealousy he was banished from that monastery. For twenty years he lived at the neighbouring house of S. Mamas, and afterwards founded a house of his own at Chrysopolis, across the water.[4] Although his sermons

---

[1] Baynes and Moss, *op. cit.*, pp. 216–17.
[2] J. M. Hussey, *op. cit.*, pp. 51–72.
[3] Sandys, *op. cit.*, I. p. 401.
[4] J. M. Hussey, *op. cit.*, pp. 193–225.

reveal the fact that reading was part of the daily monastic routine, especially in summer, nevertheless the dangers and sterility of humanist studies are emphasized. 'Possess God, and you will need no book,' he declared; S. Francis of Assisi might have used those very words. Yet Symeon himself seems to have been an educated man of considerable intellectual ability, demanding clear logical thought from his hearers.[1] In the Western medieval world, the writings of the mystics had their part in establishing a climate of literacy in which reading habits could be formed. In the East, where secular education and literacy were already firmly established, they must also have had a part in stimulating both religious and secular life with a measure of clear thought and disciplined study.

The other notable feature of this period was the spread of monastic houses and libraries. The chief architect of the monastic revival of the ninth century was Theodore of Studios, who began his religious life at Saccudio under Abbot Plato, his uncle and mentor, succeeding Plato as Abbot in 794. In 799 he moved to Constantinople and became Abbot of Studios (or Studium), a house that already had a long tradition of monastic discipline behind it. Here Theodore established the strict code of rules which he had developed at Saccudio, and which were later borrowed or copied by other communities. In a sense he parallels the work of S. Benedict in the West, though owing to the absence of definite monastic orders and the independence of eastern communities, his influence was restricted to a smaller scale than that of S. Benedict and was less enduring. In Theodore's *Constitutions*, the library and scriptorium occupy a prominent part. The hierarchy of officials included a custodian of the library, and the leisure time of the monks (i.e. the time not devoted to manual labour) was spent in study or in the copying of books. Both Theodore and his uncle Plato were expert calligraphists, and severe penalties were imposed on careless or slovenly copying. There is no information about the contents of the library at Studios, but the citations in Theodore's own works are mostly from patristic theology; and this, no doubt with some grammar, must have formed the bulk of the library. In his funeral oration on Plato, Theodore speaks of his uncle's zeal in collecting books for Studios and its various daughter houses, and the beautiful hand which he wrote, and there is little doubt that

[1] J. M. Hussey, *op. cit.*

Theodore's influence led to the general adoption of the new Greek minuscule hand, in place of the earlier uncial; this had its origins in the Imperial Treasury, where Plato, and possibly Theodore also, acquired their calligraphy.[1] The traditions established by Theodore were followed closely at other Greek monasteries, including Mt Athos, during the succeeding two centuries, and many specimens of this beautiful hand still survive.[2] It appears that the uncial hand continued in use at Studios for service books, the minuscule hand being used mainly for literary works intended for the library.

Theodore's life coincided with the period of iconoclasm, and his disputes with the Emperors involved him in exile on three occasions and the closure of his monastery for a period. But the tradition established by Theodore lived on. The Studite rule, which was the only definite supplement to S. Basil's rule which the Byzantine houses produced, was the basis of the rule adopted by Athanasius in the tenth century for the foundation on Mt Athos.[3] Indeed it became normal practice in Byzantine monasteries, including the only other foundation about which much information has survived, namely, the monastery of S. John the Evangelist on Patmos which was founded by the monk Christodoulos in the eleventh century. This house flourished especially in the twelfth century, when it had as many as 150 monks; the inventory in 1201, revealing the contents of its library has already been noted; and Christodoulos evidently had the same care for accurate work in the scriptorium that Theodore had at Studios. Similarly in Russia the Studite rule was adapted for one of the earliest foundations, the Monastery of the Caves at Kiev, 1051.[4] Theodore's influence probably extended also to the Greek monasteries in Southern Italy, of which about 13 were founded before the Norman Conquest. Nilus of Rossana is known to have read Theodore's works with his monks.[5]

In the later centuries a further literary revival took place, and in Constantinople itself intellectual life remained at a high level till

[1] Alice Gardner, *Theodore of Studium*, 1905, pp. 77, 230–4.
[2] According to Maunde Thompson, about 139 examples from the ninth and tenth centuries (codices vetustissimi) survive, and about 400 from the eleventh and twelfth centuries.
[3] J. M. Hussey, op. cit., p. 167; R. Curzon, *Visits to the Monasteries of the Levant*, 1849.
[4] Baynes and Moss, op. cit., p. 378.
[5] Isabella Stone, *Libraries of the Greek Monasteries in Southern Italy*, in Thompson, *Medieval Libraries*, 1957, pp. 330–8.

the end. There is little information about the progress of the Imperial and Patriarchal libraries. When the city fell to the Franks in 1204, the university moved to Nicaea; it was restored to Constantinople after its recapture in 1261, when a Patriarchal school was also reopened at S. Paul's Church. In the early fifteenth century, Pope Pius II was still able to describe Constantinople as the 'home of letters and citadel of high philosophy'.[1] In the absence of direct accounts of the libraries, it is noteworthy that in these last centuries, perhaps the most important literary productions were in the field of history, in which the resources of good libraries would seem to be essential. The princess Anna Comnena with her *Alexiad* in the twelfth century, and Nicetas Acominatus with his account of the capture of the city in 1204, were historians of no mean calibre; and the final period was covered by four historians of considerable merit.[2] The standard of historiography in the later Byzantine period was markedly higher than any of the Western histories and chronicles of the same period.

We can note in passing, however, that in China at roughly the same time historiography reached an even higher level, and was far more systematic. A commission set up in the seventh century AD to fill certain gaps in the existing histories developed into a permanent Historical Bureau which survived till the end of the empire. Its function was to collect and preserve official documents, and to edit and publish them at the end of each reign or dynasty in the form of chronicles or 'Veritable Records', which thus became an official national history. In later centuries the preservation of documents and the compilation of histories by teams of officials was elaborately organized.[3]

The twelfth century is marked by the name of John Tzetzes, the author of two prodigious didactic poems: one, a commentary on Homer; the other, a long review of Greek literature and scholarship, with citations from over 400 authors, and displaying an immense range of learning. He was not a wealthy man, and he complains that on one occasion he was compelled to sell his own library (which must have been extensive), retaining only his copy of

---

[1] Baynes and Moss, *op. cit.*, p. 218.
[2] Laonicus Chalcocondyles of Athens, Ducas, George Phrantzes and Critobulus of Imbro; the latter wrote a history of Mahomet II in the style of Thucydides. Baynes and Moss, *op. cit.*, pp. 233–4.
[3] Raymond Dawson, *The Legacy of China*, 1964, pp. 154–6.

Plutarch, in which exception he surely showed good sense. His works are full of inaccuracies which charity might ascribe to the fact that he had to part with his books. He is remembered by librarians for his scholia on Aristophanes, which give valuable information on the Alexandrian library in its early period.[1] In the same century the satirist Theodore Prodromus was complaining bitterly of the penury to which scholars were subject, and of his inability to buy the books he needed.[2]

This is the period also of another great scholar, Eustathius, Archbishop of Thessalonica (*ob.* 1198), the author of commentaries on Pindar and Homer, and a historical work on Thessalonica. The commentaries were written in Constantinople before he received his archbishopric, when his house was the literary centre of the city, rivalling (it was said) in brilliance the Academy, or the Lyceum in Athens. While he was in Thessalonica there occurred the invasion of the Normans from Sicily, when the second city of the Empire was sacked. Eustathius stuck to his post, earning thus the commendation of Gibbon, who found little to commend in this period.[3] Monastic standards had evidently fallen sadly at this time, especially at houses at a distance from the capital. Men entered the religious life for unworthy reasons, as it assured them of a livelihood unearned by work; their only purpose was to add to the property of the house, and greater wealth brought greater worldliness. The monks were coarse and illiterate; study was neglected, and valuable books in the libraries were sold for cash. Eustathius bitterly and vainly upbraided them for these abuses, begging them not to part with their books, but to preserve them for future generations that might set a higher value on learning than they did themselves.[4] Eustathius' friend and pupil, Michael Acominatus, became Archbishop of Athens at about this time. He also paints a sorry picture of his times. He saw desolation and desecration all around him in the once noble city. Sheep were feeding in the Painted Porch. When he preached in the Parthenon, that had now become his cathedral, on the glorious heritage of the city, his congregation could not understand his words; their speech was the 'barbarous' local dialect, and Michael complained

[1] See p. 27, 30 *supra*.
[2] J. M. Hussey, *op. cit.*, p. 112, Baynes & Moss, *op. cit.*, p. 213.
[3] Gibbon, ch. LVI.
[4] Eustathius, *De emendanda vita monastica*, 128; Sandys, *op. cit.*, I, pp. 420-2.

that residence in Athens made even him a barbarian.[1] There were no libraries in Athens, and Michael was forced to bring his own library from Constantinople, storing it in two chests near the altar in the Parthenon; it contained works of Homer, Aristotle, Thucydides, Euclid and Galen.[2] When Eustathius died, Michael preached a funeral oration over his friend, hailing him as the last survivor of the golden age. With the coming of the Franks, Athens became a Latin see, and Michael ended his life as an exile on an island in the Aegean.

Only in Constantinople did any degree of literacy and learning survive. The city fell to the Franks in 1204, and a series of disastrous fires caused the destruction of many books and works of art. Here it was the Franks, not the Greeks, who were illiterate. Michael's brother Nicetas Acominatus, the historian, describes them as unlettered and uneducated barbarians (ἀγραμμάτοις βαρβάροις καὶ τέλεον ἀναλφαβήτοις) who scoffed at the city of clerks and bookworms, carrying through the streets in procession a pen, an inkhorn and paper as emblems of their derision. The city was recovered in 1261.

The significance of the Byzantine period for our purposes lies in the careful conservation by its libraries of so great a proportion of the texts of Greek literature. Long before the coming of the Turks, Greek manuscripts were filtering into Western Europe through Venice, and Arabic works, often translated from Greek or Syriac, were arriving in Sicily and Spain. At the end of the eleventh century the Norman occupation of Sicily and the re-conquest of New Castile brought many Arabic-speaking subjects under Christian rule, and both Sicily and Toledo became centres for the translation of Arabic works into Latin. The first English scholar to take part in this task was Adelard of Bath early in the twelfth century; the best known of his contributions was a version of Euclid's *Elements*. From then on, a succession of scholars joined in the work of translation, of whom Michael Scot the mathematician who figures as the magician in the *Lay of the Last Minstrel*, Alfred the Englishman who was papal legate in England in the time of Henry III, and Hermann the German are notable examples.[3]

---

[1] Baynes & Moss, *op. cit.*, pp. 265-6.
[2] Sandys, *op. cit.*, I, p. 422.
[3] See E. R. Bevan and C. Singer, *The Legacy of Israel*, 1927, esp. pp. 204-38.

According to Archbishop Eustathius, the Franks during their invasion of Thessalonica sold the books they had plundered for a song to Italian merchants, and Michael Acominatus reported that Italian vessels were sailing from Constantinople laden with books even before its capture in 1204. Both Venice and Pisa had commercial quarters in Constantinople as well as in the other ports of the Eastern Mediterranean. Greeks themselves moreover were travelling westwards; Matthew Paris described the arrival at King John's court of Greek philosophers from Athens, c. 1202.

Constantinople suffered twice: first in 1204 at the hands of the Franks and Venetians; finally in 1453 when it was taken by Mahomet II and his Turks. On both occasions the damage to books and libraries, as well as to the other treasures of the great city, was enormous. Probably the greatest losses were suffered in 1204, when the destruction seems to have been more indiscriminate. By 1453 the market value of books was to some extent realized. Moreover, Mahomet II, barbarous as he may have been in some respects, was something of a scholar and a linguist (he knew Greek and Latin), and he was not ill-disposed to genuine scholars. He could do little of course, to curb the excesses of his army during the three days' pillage of the city, but books were then recognized objects of merchandise, and many must have been salvaged, or sold contemptuously for a trifle. There were, of course, fewer books in the city in 1453 than in 1204.[1]

There is reason to believe that most of the Byzantine texts which have disappeared were in fact lost long before 1453. For example, the bibliography compiled by Photius in the ninth century comprised 280 authors. Two thirds of the items mentioned are now completely lost, and no writer quotes any of these lost works after the date of 1204.

Gibbon's assertion that 'more books and more knowledge were included within the walls of Constantinople than could be found dispersed over the extensive countries of the West' is almost certainly true; but it became considerably less true after 1204; though even in these last two centuries Byzantine scholarship (and especially, as already noted, historiography) was in advance of Western scholarship. We in the West owe our recovery of the Greek classical tradition in no small measure to the dispersal of

[1] On this event see Steven Runciman, *The Fall of Constantinople, 1453*, 1965.

Greek scholars, as well as of Greek texts, in the final period; and in this respect, Constantinople's loss was our gain. After 1453, Greek scholarship disappeared almost completely from Constantinople, and Greek scholars went into exile. The Orthodox Church, so far as it survived under Turkish rule, survived as an almost uneducated and illiterate body. The victory of Islam over Christianity had the result that the Russians in Moscow deemed themselves to have inherited the cultural traditions of Constantinople and the championship of the Orthodox faith.[1]

Greek culture survived for a further eight years in the more or less independent empire of Trebizond, on the South Coast of the Black Sea, which surrendered to Mahomet II in 1461. The palace is known to have contained a fine library, and the cultural traditions of the city stretched back for many centuries, at least to the time of Tychicus of Trebizond in the early seventh century. The Armenian, Ananias of Shirak, Tychicus' friend and pupil, said that he lived for eight years with Tychicus and read with him many works not so far translated into Armenian, for he possessed an enormous library, both secret books and open, ecclesiastical works and profane, scientific and historical, medical and chronological.[2] Tychicus settled in Trebizond after reading philosophy at Athens (which implies that academic teaching was still to be had in Athens, in spite of the closure of the university—Tychicus may well have been at Athens at the same time as Theodore of Tarsus); and his fame as a teacher attracted many young men from Constantinople, at a time when academic studies at Constantinople were apparently at a low ebb.[3]

Hard things have been said about the literary shortcomings of the Byzantine period, the absence of creative work in letters however strongly it was evident in art and perhaps mystical theology, the inaccuracy, the pedantry and indeed the dullness of a great proportion of the editorial and critical work that was carried out. From our point of view, the importance of the period rests less on these things, than on the *preservation* of the ancient texts in their keeping. It is precisely this for which the Byzantine age can justly claim credit. This, after all, is the first duty of the librarian—

---

[1] Baynes and Moss, *op. cit.*, pp. 325, 369 ff.
[2] Ananias of Shirak, trans. Conybeare, in *Byzantinische Zeitschrift*, VI, p. 572.
[3] Runciman, *op. cit.*, p. 225.

the curator, the keeper, of books. It is a duty which can only be satisfactorily and securely carried out by librarians working in stable and organized libraries; and we can assume that the principal part in this task was undertaken by the great libraries in Constantinople, the Imperial, University and Patriarchal libraries, however shadowy and uncertain their activities appear from a historical point of view.

Doubtless still more ancient texts would have been preserved, had not literary research slackened its efforts in the dark period of the eighth and ninth centuries. After the ninth century, Byzantine scholars possessed little more than we do today of pre-Alexandrian Greek texts, though they were better supplied with the works of later historians and commentators.[1] Known losses can be ascribed partly to the inactivity of the dark age in these two centuries, and partly to the compilation of excerpts and epitomes in the centuries immediately succeeding. On the whole, the libraries of Constantinople carried out their task of preserving the literature of ancient Greece with remarkable success and fidelity.

[1] Sandys, *op. cit.*, I, pp. 426–7.

CHAPTER IV

Seneca

THE villa libraries which form so striking a feature of Roman civilization can be traced back to the middle of the second century BC, when an interest in Greek literature was first awakening. At that time, many Greek scholars were visiting Rome; not the least famous was Crates of Mallos, the head of the school and library of Pergamum, whose stay was prolonged by a curious and distressing accident. He fell into the Cloaca Maxima, breaking his leg, and his convalescence gave him the opportunity to lecture. Suetonius explains, however, that the new interest was at first hampered by the shortage of books, and study circles were limited to their own compositions and to public readings[1]. About the same time, after the victory of Pydna, the Roman general Aemilius Paulus allowed his sons to plunder the Macedonian royal library and to bring it back to Rome. A thousand Achaean hostages were also brought from Pydna, and these, by a fortunate chance, included Polybius, who occupies a very high place indeed among Greek historians. Polybius became tutor to the general's sons, the younger of whom was Scipio Africanus Minor; and his account of his friendship with the young Scipio makes delightful reading. He describes how the boy's interest in Greek culture was caught through the books Polybius was able to lend him. Nevertheless Scipio, good Greek scholar though he became, remained a true Roman at heart, claiming that he owed more to experience and to his home life than he did to books. There resulted in due course the famous Scipionic Circle—a band of enthusiasts devoting themselves to the study of philosophy and letters, and thereby exercising a considerable influence on Hellenic studies in Rome. There was, of course, opposition to the infiltration of Greek thought in some quarters, but even that staunch old conservative Cato himself was constrained to learn the new language. A century later we find Cicero complaining that 'we Romans have

[1] Suet. *De Grammaticis*, 1-2.

gone to school in Greece; we read their poets and learn them by heart, and then we call ourselves scholars'.[1]

The villa libraries reached their highest pinnacle in the hundred years or so that separates Cicero from the elder Pliny. Early in the first century BC there was obviously a considerable importation of Greek books into Rome. There is, for example, the story of the Peripatetic books which Sulla seized in Athens and brought to Rome about 86 BC. Sulla's librarian, Tyrannion (who was the teacher of Strabo, the authority for this story) put the books in order and arranged for them to be edited and indexed by Andronicus of Rhodes, and an authorized edition, the basis of all our present texts, was published.[2] Lucullus brought another great collection back from the East in 63 BC, to form the basis of the famous library at his villa at Tusculum. There is a glimpse of this library in Cicero *De Finibus*, 3.2.7.

Our most intimate pictures of the villa libraries come from the letters of Cicero and the younger Pliny. Cicero seems to have had three collections, one in Rome and the others at Antium and Tusculum; and his correspondence (especially with the collector and connoisseur Atticus, who acted as his agent in Athens, and as his publisher) gives us intriguing pictures of the life of a Roman scholar in his study.[3]

From Cicero's time onwards, the possession of a private library was becoming a necessity to every scholar, teacher, writer and man of affairs in Rome. The bilingual character of Roman culture made this need all the more imperative; the educated man required his Greek library as well as his Latin books, just as the Roman temple libraries had their separate Greek and Latin departments. All the Augustan poets had their private collections, and their dependence on these is often evident. Ovid, for example, leant heavily on his books to stimulate his pen and provide him with material. During his years of banishment at Tomis, he was crippled by the enforced separation from his library. The effect of this is

---

[1] Cicero, *Tusc*. 2. 27.

[2] The full story is given in Colin Roberts, *Buried Books in Antiquity*, 1963, pp. 7–10. See also *Heritage*, pp. 66–9.

[3] 'The passage which I recollect with the greatest pleasure in Cicero, is where he says that books delight us at home, *and are no impediment abroad;* travel with us, ruralise with us. His period is rounded off to some purpose: "*Delectant domi, non impediunt foris; perigrinantur, rusticantur*".'—Leigh Hunt, *My Books*.

apparent in the poems of his exile, although despair and loneliness no doubt had their part in this as well. So also with Catullus at Verona, mourning his brother's death and protesting that grief has silenced his music. But he adds another reason for his silence; his home was at Rome, and all his library was there; 'when I come to Verona, I bring with me only one little box out of the many I have' (*una ex multis capsula*), and this means, he says, that he is without resources for composition.[1]

Horace, on the other hand, was glad to escape from the excitements of Rome to his Sabine farm, but he took with him his library; and in *Satires*, II. 3. we learn that this included the early Greek poet, Archilochus, as well as examples of the Old, Middle and New Comedy. His Latin volumes would, of course, have included the work of Gaius Lucilius, the member of the Scipionic Circle whom Horace regarded as his master and indeed as the founder of literary satire. In *Satires*, II. 6. we hear again what his country cottage meant to him; how with the books of old writers and sleep and idleness he could banish his cares. And in *Epistles*, I. 18. 107 Horace gives us his own personal prayer:

> ... *et mihi vivam*
> *quod superest aevi, si quid superesse volunt di;*
> *sit bona librorum et provisae frugis in annum*
> *copia* ...

that he may have the remaining years of his life to himself, with abundance of books and food enough for his needs. Abraham Cowley had a similar dream in the seventeenth century:

> *May I a small house and large garden have;*
> *And a few friends, and many books, both true,*
> *Both wise, and both delightful, too.*

Nahum Tate echoed the sentiment a little later when he petitioned Heaven for a rural seat, rather contemptible than great, in which very wisely

> *Some books I'd have, and some acquaintance too;*
> *But very good, and very few.*

---

[1] Ovid, *Tristia* III. 14. 17; Catullus LXVIII. 33. See also L. P. Wilkinson *Ovid Recalled*, 1955; and on the background of the Augustan poets, Gilbert Highet's delightful study, *Poets in a Landscape*, 1957.

Charles Lamb, in *The Superannuated Man*, quotes an English version of these very lines from Horace, and thousands condemned to town life dream the same dream today. The good Thomas Fuller was of much the same mind: 'It is a vanity', he wrote in *The Holy State*, 'to persuade the world one hath much learning by getting a great library ... few books well selected are best.'

The joy of the simple country life was a common theme in Augustan Rome. Tibullus is full of it. His dream was to live for himself alone on his own little farm; in his poems only Sulpicia, longing to be in Rome for her birthday, found no pleasure *rure molesto*, in the hateful country. But though Tibullus glories in the peace of his cottage fireside, he nowhere mentions the books which must have been at his elbow; his debt to his Greek models is as real, though not as obvious, as that of Catullus and Propertius. As for the scholar poets Lucretius and Virgil, their dependence on their predecessors is on a far greater scale, and though we know little of their life histories, neither is likely to have written within reach of any libraries but their own.

All through the first century AD similar conditions obtain. The 'villa poems' of Statius reveal clearly the literary atmosphere in which the Roman country gentleman lived. Persius, whose work owes much to both Horace and Lucilius, is credited by his biographer Probus with a library of 700 volumes. Even the indigent Martial had a bookshelf or two in his third-storey tenement. And the dependence of prose writers such as Quintilian, Suetonius and Tacitus on their libraries needs no explanation. The elder Pliny explains that in writing his *Historia naturalis* he had to consult 2,000 volumes, collecting 20,000 facts from 100 authors, and most of this research must have been done in his own library. The younger Pliny describes in detail the library at his Laurentine villa, with the 'built in' bookcase in his study where he kept the volumes which he delighted in reading over and over again.[1] Knowing Pliny, we may guess that copies of his own books lived here; and perhaps it was in this room, too, that his fond wife, Calpurnia, through her affection for him, developed a passion for

---

[1] Pariete eius in bibliothecae speciem armarium insertum est, quod non legendos libros, sed lectitandos capit. (Pliny *Ep.* 2. 17). The obvious way of providing cupboard accommodation in a stone-built house is by leaving holes for storage: just such a hole in the wall, in fact, as Jimsy Duthie in *A Window in Thrums* used to keep his little store of books, including the *Paradise Lost* on which he drew in writing his great epic, *The Millenium*.

reading, and especially (as he naïvely tells us) for reading her husband's works. And all Pliny's friends and correspondents quite evidently had similar libraries in their own homes. Books, reading and writing were definitely in fashion; and the architect Vitruvius warns his readers that their villa should face east to catch the morning light and forestall damage to the papyrus from damp. The elder Pliny is described as reading and being read to at every conceivable opportunity; even while he was at the baths, a stenographer was at his side to jot down the ideas that occurred to him.[1] Horace, describing the current craze for scribbling, notes that both young and old, while dining, dictate verses to a waiting scribe;[2] we all scribble poetry today, he says, both learned, and ignorant alike. And he rightly points out that this has its value, for poetry exerts an educative and refining influence on the ordinary man.

But there was a dark side to the picture of Roman life in the first century of our era. The families of pure Roman descent, whose traditions had made Rome what she was, were dying out. They were being replaced by a class of freedmen, mostly foreigners from Greece and Asia Minor: newly-rich profiteers making large fortunes in trade and commerce, and flaunting their wealth in extravagantly furnished villas. The old standards of education were disappearing. Tacitus, writing about AD 80, complains of this in his *Dialogus*; ignorant slaves, he says, were employed as teachers; the old Roman tradition of home education was gone, and with it all that was best in Roman character. The disreputable ruffians described by Petronius in his picaresque novel, the *Satyricon* (probably written in Nero's time), are good examples of what was happening. In this the story of Trimalchio's Banquet centres round a freedman who had more money than he knew what to do with, and no education to guide him in spending it. At the banquet he carries on a bantering conversation with an ill-educated teacher of rhetoric, and in the course of this he cries out, 'Don't think me an ignoramus, I have two libraries of my own; one Greek and one Latin.' And then he tries to prove his learning with some shaky mythological allusions, adding airily, 'Of course, I used to read this stuff in Homer as a kid.' The interest of this trivial

[1] Pliny, *Ep.* III. 8. Others doubtless have had the same luxurious habit. Margaret, Duchess of Newcastle, had a servant always handy at night to take down her sudden inspirations; she would summon him by calling out, 'John, I conceive . . .'.
[2] Horace, *Ep.* II. 1. 109.

incident is that it is the first evidence of a Roman library intended solely for display—a piece of furniture one acquires as a way of spending money, and as a mark of one's opulence. This is the result not merely of the rise of a new moneyed class, but of the existence of an active book market in which books are gaining artificial values.

There had been bookshops in Athens for long enough, but in the Empire they were everywhere; more of them probably than in England before the eighteenth century. Rome had its Charing Cross Road, or S. Paul's Churchyard, in the Argiletum. Pliny heard with delight that his own books were on sale in Lyons, and bookshops are mentioned by Aulus Gellius at Brindisi and by Martial at Vienne. Cicero, however, warns his brother Quintus, who was collecting a Greek and Latin library, that really good books are hard to come by in the Roman shops, and that it pays to employ an agent who is 'in the know'; Cicero himself employed various agents, including Atticus.[1]

The fashion of collecting libraries for show called forth, as one might guess, the prophet who could thunder against its depravity, and in first-century Rome that prophet was Seneca. Lucius Annaeus Seneca was the second son of the elder Seneca; Spanish by birth, and an expert rhetorician. Against his father's wish, the son, though trained in rhetoric, leant rather to Stoic philosophy. He became entangled in the more scandalous side of Imperial politics, suffered banishment at Messalina's hands to Corsica on an improbable charge of adultery, endured his exile with un-Stoic discontent, returned to Rome as a result of Agrippina's intervention, became Nero's tutor and later his minister, was concerned first in Agrippina's murder and then in the Pisonian conspiracy, and in AD 65 met his final self-inflicted punishment with a courage that had been lacking in his early life.

Seneca's character presents curious problems. Some of his moral writings, taken at their face value, reveal him as one of the wisest of the Romans; it might be supposed that he had reached the dignified pinnacle of Stoic philosophy—the highest peak of an admirable creed. Some of his actions stamp him as a despicable

---

[1] Aulus Gellius, IX. 4. 1; Martial, VII. 88, Cicero, Q. Fr. III. 4. 5. Commercially produced books had a bad reputation, and copies made in one's own scriptorium were in general more trustworthy. See Colin Roberts, *op. cit.*, p. 11.

hypocrite and an unscrupulous profiteer. His medical history ascribes both sides of his character to a psychopathic disorder. As a tragedian and a philosopher he was the idol of the Middle Ages; indeed he was regarded as all but a Christian. His tragedies, written for reading rather than acting, imply that his public had their private libraries; although they were one of the influences that moulded Elizabethan drama, they are today unread and unacted. And few now read his essays and dialogues.

The famous passage on the evils of book-collecting is contained in the dialogue *De Tranquillitate Animi*. In this he leaves Livy to praise the glory of the Alexandrian libraries, reserving for his own pen a bitter condemnation of the vainglory of them—the extravagant, senseless multiplication of books by books to make a magnificent display, not for scholarship, but for show. Then he turns his arrows on the upstart, the make-believe scholar, who wants books not for study but to adorn his dining room. Better to waste your money on books, you say, than on old masters or Ming vases? No, for all excess is wicked. How can you excuse the man who buys bookcases of expensive woods, and piling into them the works of unknown, worthless authors, goes yawning amongst his thousands of volumes? He knows their titles, their bindings, but nothing else. It is in the homes of the idlest men that you find the biggest libraries—range upon range of books, ceiling high. For nowadays a library is one of the essential fittings of a home, like a bathroom. You could forgive this if it were all due to a zeal for learning. But these libraries of the works of piety and genius are collected for mere show, to ornament the walls of the house.

The collection of libraries for show rather than for study became fashionable again in the eighteenth century, when it drew forth some rather pale imitations of Seneca's vigorous attack. Professor R. M. Wiles quotes some examples.[1] The *Lay-Monk* (No. 8, December 2, 1713) describes an 'Upholsterer in Learning', Sir Gregory Bookworm, a country gentleman of wealth who orders books by the yard to fill his shelves. A letter in the *Universal Spectator* (No. 254, August 18, 1733) requests a shipment of books to stock up the library of Sir Tinsel Wormius. Sir Tinsel's chaplain writes, 'I'm to order you to send down with Expedition, five yards of Folios, Theologists, Philosophers, Schoolmen or Romances; but

---

[1] *Serial publication in England before 1750*, 1957, p. 12.

particularly five Foot of Common Law, and seven of the best Civil'. Dummy books could often be used for this purpose, of course. A writer in *Notes and Queries* in 1849 (1st ser. 1. 166) reveals that a tradesman in S. Petersburg offered such 'books' at prices ranging from fifty to a hundred roubles per running yard, according to the binding, for the special benefit of courtiers of Catherine the Great, who could not win favour unless they possessed a library equipped with well-filled shelves of mahogany.

In another essay, *De Brevitate Vitae*, Seneca tilts at the vanity of much that passes under the name of research. This, he says, is a weakness of the Greeks that has infected the Romans. How many oarsmen had Ulysses? Which was written first, the *Iliad* or the *Odyssey*? Were they by the same author? This much ado about nothing, this virtuous passion for useless knowledge, makes you seem a public nuisance rather than a scholar. Here Seneca is on dangerous ground. We have been trained to believe that no knowledge is without potential use, that all scientific discovery is built on the development of apparently valueless knowledge, transforming the useless into the essential. Today, however, the researcher in literary and historical fields is growing sceptical about this dictum, and is learning to be less uncritical in the facts that he accumulates and records. The requirement of a thesis based on original research for a higher degree is not an unmixed blessing, and if Seneca is pleading for a sense of proportion in literary research, he is surely to be commended.

It was indeed only the idle vanities of research and book-collecting that Seneca condemned; he had too good a training in rhetoric from his father to be ignorant of the true value of books. In the dialogue *De Otio*, writing of the blessings of leisure and privacy, he stresses the chance it gives you to make friends with the great men of the past through their books, choosing thereby some favourite model for the conduct of your own life. But he rightly insists that it is far more satisfying to give yourself to a few authors, than to wander aimlessly through the multitude of books that are published and collected in libraries. Again, in the *De Consolatione* addressed to Polybius, who was the Emperor Claudius' secretary *a libellis*, Seneca is consoling Polybius on the loss of his brother. It is, he says, when you relax from your duties and retire to your home that you will feel your loneliness. Then your books, so long and so loyally your friends, will return your favour. Let them claim you as their high priest and worshipper. And recalling that Polybius had translated Homer into Latin and Virgil into Greek, he advises him to linger long in their company; your love for them, he says, will bring you comfort and peace of mind.

Seneca, quoting from one of Livy's lost books (Book CXII) the statement that the Alexandrian libraries were the finest fruit of royal taste and culture, is led to wonder whether the fire which Caesar started in the dockyard in 47 BC, was not after all a blessing in disguise. He is not the only scholar to whom this doubt has occurred. Sir Thomas Browne echoed the thought in *Religio Medici*. 'I have heard some,' he wrote, 'with deep signs lament the lost lines of Cicero; others with as many groans deplore the combustion of the library of Alexandria: for my own part, I think there be too many in the world; and could with patience behold the urn and ashes of the Vatican, could I, with a few others, recover the perished leaves of Solomon. I would not omit a copy of Enoch's pillars, had they many nearer authors than Josephus, or did not relish somewhat of the fable. Some men have written more than others have spoken. Pineda quotes more authors in one work [the *Monarchia Ecclesiastica*, in which 1,040 authors are cited] than are necessary in a whole world. Of those three great inventions in Germany [i.e., guns, printing and the compass], there are two which are not without their incommodities. 'Tis not a melancholy *utinam* of my own, but the desires of better heads, that there were a general synod—not to unite the incompatible difference of religion, but, for the benefit of learning, to reduce it, as it lay at first, in a few and solid authors; and to condemn to the fire those swarms and millions of rhapsodies, begotten only to distract and abuse the weaker judgments of scholars, and to maintain the trade and mystery of typographers.'

The good Sir Thomas Browne, who knew his Seneca well, is in some ways a gentler and milder version of Seneca himself, though without Seneca's human frailty. In more recent years, Dr Gilbert Norwood has argued that the burning of the library at Alexandria was a veritable boon, and Lord Grey of Falloden dreamt of a glorious holocaust of books, thinking of the pleasure one would take in stirring the fire. Wise men will not be lacking who are minded to agree with them. If books are powerful weapons of aggression (as indeed many are and always have been), then a disarmament campaign is as necessary (and as unlikely to succeed) as with those less dangerous weapons that are termed conventional. It is now generally believed that the fire of 47 BC did little actual damage to the Alexandrian library.[1] Seven centuries later, when the Arab armies captured Alexandria, legend relates that the volumes in the libraries were distributed to the four thousand baths in the city, where they were used as fuel for the furnaces; and so great was their number that six months elapsed before they were consumed. History lends no support to the story, but anyone who has ever tried to burn a book will not be surprised at the length of time that elapsed before they were finally reduced to ashes.[2] A more ingenious, if less commendable, use of literary fuel is reported from Constantinople, where Leo the Isaurian in the eighth century is credited with setting fire to the University Library. Rumour has it that he not only burnt the books, but projected the professors into the flames. This practice is not to be imitated today.[3] But Lord Grey, however vigorously he stirred the fire, would have difficulty in making much impression on the world's books now that printing has distributed copies of them everywhere. Ovid, in despair at the news of his banishment, threw the fifteen books of his *Metamorphoses* into the fire, but copies had been made, and by this happy accident the poem was saved. The printing press has made survival certain of nearly everything that matters; even the losses of the last war have been made good to a surprising extent in a comparatively short period. The Rev J. C. Cox once imagined the destruction by fire of all our libraries, and suggested that in this event the main facts of English history since the Reformation could be gleaned from our parish registers. This may be true, but

---

[1] See p. 36 *supra*.
[2] Gibbon gave no credit to this fairy tale. Pope, however (*Dunciad* III. 80) accepts it, comparing it with the action of Chi Ho-am-ti, who, in addition to building the Great Wall, destroyed all the books and learned men in China. Warburton's note to this passage wrongly ascribes to the Alexandrian Library the famous inscription ψυχῆς ἰατρεῖον, the dispensary of the soul. This was on an Egyptian library at Thebes.
[3] See p. 50 *supra*. The story about Leo the Isaurian and the professors whom he threw into the bonfire of books can be capped by a French schoolchildren's rhyme quoted by Iona and Peter Opie (*The Lore and Language of Schoolchildren*, 1959, p. 299 n.):—

'Vivent les vacances
Pour de pénitences,
Les livres au feu
Les maîtres au milieu.'

they could not give us back Shakespeare and Wordsworth; and as any sort of selective incendiarism would seem difficult to organize, Lord Grey's dream must be regretfully abandoned.

However legendary, the story of the use of books as fuel in Alexandria seems to have set a bad example. In the parish of S. Mary, Beverley, in 1856, the volumes in the parish library are said to have been used to light the church fires; only 32 books out of some 450 survived this outbreak of incendiarism.[1] Then at Luddington, in Warwickshire, early in the nineteenth century, a certain Mrs Pickering, housekeeper to the curate, being anxious to hasten the boiling of her kettle, burnt beneath it the parish registers (which might, for all we know, have contained the record of the marriage of Shakespeare and Anne Hathaway; there is an unconfirmed tradition that the wedding took place at this church). If any doubt remains about the inflammability of books, a recent experiment in the United States may be of interest. A practical demonstration proved that a bookstack containing 14,000 volumes was almost entirely ruined by fire within ten minutes. In another experiment with sprinklers working, hardly any volumes were damaged either by fire or water beyond repair.[2]

About a hundred years later than Seneca, another prophet was castigating the sins of the book collector. Lucian (c. AD 125-95) was a Syrian Greek who, though he travelled widely, wrote most of his works in Athens. The dialogue *Adversus Indoctum* ('Remarks addressed to an illiterate bibliophile') is a mordant satire on the person who buys up all the best books in order to pass for a man of taste. How, he cries, can such a person distinguish between the book of genuine value and the book that is worthless? His only guide is the activity of moths and worms: the accuracy of the copyist is beyond him. And even if he gets hold of fine editions and true works of scholarship, what use are they to him? He will be no nearer culture at the end of it. Books would indeed be precious if the mere possession of them guaranteed culture; the millionaire and the second-hand book dealer would then have absolute power. But the only purpose of this empty display of wealth is political and social advancement.

---

[1] See *The Parochial Libraries of the Church of England*, 1959, p. 68; also *Notes and Queries*, 3rd series, vol. 5, 1864, p. 51 and 6th series, vol. 6, 1882, p. 294.
[2] *Wilson Library Bulletin*, 1960, 34. 6.

Later still Ausonius, the fourth-century poet of Bordeaux, in one of his epigrams, asks a certain Philomusus if he imagines himself a learned professor of literature simply because his library is stuffed with purchased books; you might as well say that if you buy up a collection of musical instruments, you will immediately become a musician. Ausonius may have had Lucian in mind when he wrote this, but the sentiment is older than Lucian. When Socrates learnt that the young Euthydemus had amassed a great collection of the works of poetry and philosophy, imagining himself thus to be a prodigy of wisdom, he administered punishment of true Socratic type. Euthydemus sat down beside him, and Socrates enquired, 'Tell me, have you really collected all these books?'—'Indeed yes, and I am still collecting; I shall keep on till I have as many as I can possibly get.'—'Good gracious,' said Socrates, 'I admire you for preferring wisdom to money. Evidently you think the thoughts of wise men more valuable than silver or gold.'—Euthydemus was flattered at this, and Socrates noticing it said, 'What particular art are you hoping to learn from all these books? Medicine? Doctors have to study a great many books.'—'No, not medicine.'—'Do you want to be an architect then? Books are needed for that, too.' —'No.'—'Well, then, a mathematician? Or an astronomer? Or a rhapsodist? For I hear your library includes all Homer.'—'No, for the rhapsodists are fools even if they do know their Homer.'— 'Perhaps then, you want to be a politician or an administrator?'— Euthydemus admits this to be his ambition. 'My goodness,' says Socrates, 'you're flying high. It's the art of kings, the royal art. Have you ever wondered whether it's possible for a dishonest man to be a good politician? If not, do you yourself claim to be an honest man?...' And so the argument progresses, and poor Euthydemus becomes more and more entangled, discovering that he never understood the meaning of the Delphic inscription 'Know thyself' and is, in fact, a complete ignoramus. Finally he went away in despair. But unlike some of the people cross-examined by Socrates, Euthydemus had the good sense to return in humility, and Socrates then tantalized him no further, but told him clearly what he ought to know and what he ought to study.[1]

Seneca and Lucian taken together reveal the extent to which private book-collecting had reached in the first two centuries of the

[1] Xenophon, *Mem.* IV. 2. 6.

Empire; and they show, moreover, that the second-hand market had taken full advantage of the demand, collectors' pieces and fine editions being sought everywhere by the discriminating and the uncritical alike.

Chance has not preserved for us the details of any of the private book displays so scorned by the satirists; modern examples are, of course, not far to seek in eighteenth and nineteenth-century England. Two libraries of unusual size are indeed recorded. Epaphroditus of Chaeronea was the slave and pupil of an Alexandrian scholar in the first century AD; after obtaining his freedom, he set up as a schoolteacher in Rome, where he collected a library of 30,000 books, and a reputation as a grammarian. He is not to be confused with S. Paul's friend of the same name, nor with Nero's secretary, nor with the man to whom Josephus dedicated his *Jewish Antiquities*. An even larger collection of 62,000 books was amassed by Serenus Sammonicus (the younger of that name, whose father was murdered by Caracalla, AD 212). Serenus was tutor to the younger Gordian, and he bequeathed his great library to the Emperor. Gibbon's reference to this imperial windfall is typical: 'Twenty-two acknowledged concubines, and a library of 62,000 volumes, attested the variety of his inclinations, and from the productions which he left behind him, it appears that the former as well as the latter were designed for use rather than ostentation.' The explanation is, as one might guess, in a footnote which informs us that each of the concubines presented him with three or four children, and his literary productions were by no means contemptible.

One point of interest can be noted. The English collection of the eighteenth century was sometimes the work of a scholar nobleman, and as such is worthy of profound respect. Where this was not the case, it was often nevertheless something more than an idle display of wealth; it was, in fact, part of the internal decoration of the house. The new squirearchy that built our great houses decorated some of the walls with French or Chinese wallpapers or old masters; others were adorned with books in noble bindings. We may raise our eyebrows at those who regard books mainly as decoration; as a sort of academic wallpaper, in fact. But they do provide an attractive background for a room intended for their use, if not by the owner himself, at least by visiting guests and scholars. The physical beauty of a library is something that we have been able to appreciate only since printed books were finely bound and displayed in elegant presses. The medieval reader knew that a book in itself could be beautiful, but he never saw the beauty of a great library of well-bound volumes, framed in oak or walnut and ranged round three sides of a well-lit room. It is even more difficult to associate any beauty with a collection of papyrus rolls, however resplendent they may have been in their parchment covers of gold or purple, with bosses of ivory or bright colours, and the papyrus new and snow-white.[1] Normally the rolls would be kept in a storeroom (the small room that has survived at the Piso villa in Herculaneum is an example), whence they could be brought out for reading either to a study or more probably into one of the courtyards. The younger Pliny kept only his special favourites in the cupboard built into the wall of his study, and he describes the situation of this room minutely. From the portico, he says, you enter the hall, with windows and doors all round it. On the left is the parlour, and beyond that a smaller room, with windows facing east and west, and a view over the sea. Next is a room forming the segment of a circle, and open to the sun all day, and it was in the wall of this room that his book press was fitted.[2] But the villa libraries that roused Seneca's wrath were obviously something different from this. Here the volumes were not stored away, but were on show, decorating that most public of all rooms, the dining room. They were in presses of citrus wood and ivory up to the ceiling, and their titles were visible, so that presumably the rolls lay in pigeon-holes, with the title-labels showing. It is difficult to visualize the general appearance of such a library; perhaps it resembled the dusty untidiness of a solicitor's office, with its racks of files and documents; and its ugliness may have contributed to Seneca's anger.

As long as the papyrus roll was the standard form of book, beauty could only be achieved by hiding the rolls in closed armaria; this method was indeed adopted in the Octavian and Palatine libraries founded by Augustus, both of which were magnificent buildings relying for their beauty on their colonnades and pavements and their sculptures of marble and bronze. When the codex began to replace the roll in the third century, the books

[1] See, e.g., Tibullus, III. 1. 7; Catullus, XXII. 6.
[2] Pliny, *Ep.* II. 17.

themselves must, at least, have gained something in appearance, even if their bindings were at that date primitive. Boethius, while he languished in prison, conjured up a picture of his library, its walls decked with ivory and crystal.[1] And the villa libraries described by Sidonius Apollinaris in the fifth century were obviously pleasant places.[2] But for its main decorative features a library continued to depend for many centuries on its portrait busts and sculptures and inscriptions, rather than on the books themselves. This is evident in the case of the library described by Rusticus, Bishop of Lyons, in the fifth century[3], and in that of Isidore, Bishop of Seville, in the seventh century.

No small part of our interest in the Roman villa libraries arises from the fact that they were probably the main channel through which the texts of classical Latin were handed down, till they eventually found a precarious refuge in the monastic libraries. There is no reason to think that the Roman temple libraries made any substantial contribution to this task. They carried out no editorial or bibliographical tasks such as the Alexandrian libraries had performed. No scholars of distinction were associated with their work. Caesar was dead and Varro outlawed before the great library they planned could be established; and Ovid, who might perhaps have filled the part played by Callimachus at Alexandria, was instead banished to the farthest corner of the Empire. Ovid's friend, Hyginus, the first librarian of the Palatine, did, it is true, write a commentary on Virgil, but he is scarcely comparable with the Alexandrian editors. And so far as the preservation of the texts is concerned, the villa libraries were probably much safer repositories than the temple libraries, most of which were damaged in the fires of AD 64 and AD 191; and late in the fourth century Ammianus Marcellinus describes them as sealed forever like the

---

[1] De consolat. 1. 5. 20.
[2] *Heritage*, pp. 83-4; also *infra* p. 89.
[3] J. W. Clark, *Care of Books*, pp. 43-5. The writer calls to mind what he had read as a boy in the library of a learned scholar. There were portraits of orators and poets in mosaic or coloured plaster, and beneath each the owner had placed inscriptions describing their characteristics. For a portrait of Virgil he had chosen a quotation from the *Aeneid* itself (1. 607):—

> As long as rivers run into the deep,
> As long as shadows o'er the hillside sweep,
> As long as stars in heaven's fair pastures graze,
> So long shall live your honour, name and praise.
> (Conington's translation).

tomb. He wrote in troubled times when thousands of books were being confiscated and burnt, and thousands more were burnt by their owners in panic, for 'we were all at that time creeping about in Cimmerian darkness, with the sword of Damocles suspended over our heads'.[1] Ammianus exaggerated, of course, for the Ulpian library was still open in the next century, when the works of Sidonius Apollinaris and his statue in bronze were installed there; and by this time, too, the provinces (particularly Southern Gaul) were taking charge of the traditions which Rome herself was forgetting.[1]

There is, however, little doubt that the main traditions of Latin literature were passed down through the grammarians and schoolteachers and the private collections of individual scholars, rather than through the public libraries. In both classical and medieval periods, the real stabilizing influence in both language and literature was not the library, but the schools which the libraries served. The Alexandrian libraries would have lost half their significance if their directors had not been teachers as well as librarians. And in Rome, which had no true university of its own, and where none of the public libraries was associated with a long tradition of teaching, the private library was developed on a far wider scale than it ever had been at Athens or Alexandria, spreading as time went by wherever Roman civilization penetrated—into North Africa, Spain, Southern Gaul and the Eastern Mediterranean, and becoming thereby the true vehicle of the Latin literary tradition.

[1] *Heritage*, pp. 80-4.

CHAPTER V

In Roman Britain

I SUPPOSE that the average historian of libraries would omit any chapter on the libraries of Roman Britain, for there is no direct evidence that any existed. That is not the whole of the story, however, as I hope to show.

It is worth remembering that, leaving aside such famous institutions as the Alexandrian museum, the direct evidence for most of the Greek and Roman libraries is extremely slender, and often entirely circumstantial.¹ Consider the university libraries for example. We can assume that any corporate academic institution owning endowments and land must almost certainly have had a library attached to it. This assumption is reinforced by the fact that, through the chance survival of inscriptions, libraries are known to have been associated with at least three of the Greek universities: Athens, Rhodes and Cos. Of the four Athenian schools of philosophy, the library at the Lyceum, is of course, well documented; the Epicurean library is supported by a single reference in Diogenes Laertius; the library of the Academy is a matter of surmise, though an academic institution that survived nearly a thousand years could scarcely have failed to have one; and as for the Stoics, they owned no land or property, and cannot, therefore, have had a library. We can fairly argue from this that any classical university of recognized standing is at least likely to have had its own library. The argument is strengthened still further, of course, if research of the kind that involves the use of a library is known to have been carried out there. Centres of legal or medical education, for example, inevitably need a library, and an institution such as the famous school of Roman law at Berytus must have been so equipped. Or again, the existence of the Imperial and Patriarchal libraries at Constantinople is well attested. If it were not, however, we could guess the existence of a great

¹ On this see *Heritage*, pp. 43–53.

library at Constantinople from the production of such works as the Suidas lexicon, which could not possibly have been compiled without wide bibliographical resources.

In other cases the existence of a library is attested only by a single, quite incidental reference. Suidas mentions casually that Euphorion of Chalcis was appointed to the charge of the public library at Antioch by Antiochus the Great. This is the only authority, though in fact few places are more likely to have had a library than Antioch, both in its earlier days and in the time of Julian the Apostate and Libanius. Or again at Smyrna, the only reference is in Strabo, who, after describing the appearance of the city and its buildings, adds 'And there is also a library'. In still other cases, archaeological evidence survives which identifies a particular building as a library, such as for example at Trajan's settlement of Thamugadi (Timgad) in Numidia, and at Ephesus. For several centuries Ephesus was not only a university town, but a banking, commercial and administrative centre, and we should certainly expect to find a library. There is a lively account of life there in Acts xix, where we are told of the great purge of the libraries of those who practised 'curious arts' (i.e., sorcery and magic) to the value of 50,000 pieces of silver. On the other hand Thamugadi was a new settlement, not unlike the Romano-British towns in the provision of public buildings; and if this had its public library, so might other such towns. Chance allusions and survivals of this character make it plain that libraries were certainly not confined to Alexandria, Pergamum and Rome, and indeed that they were a fairly general feature of provincial life under the Empire; and the possibility of their existence in Roman Britain is at least worth investigation. For four centuries Britain was Roman. It is as easy to underestimate as to overestimate our debt to Roman culture, but it would surely be a grave mistake to ignore it in any history, either of our civilization in general or of our libraries in particular.

Indirectly the influence of Rome had made itself felt on the south-eastern part of England, even before Caesar's invasion. The period that archaeologists know as Iron Age C was already well advanced when Caesar landed, and the Belgic tribes who not long before had migrated to this country from North-eastern Gaul were very far from being illiterate savages. Gaulish kings had held sway over the neighbouring part of England, and Kent was thickly populated, rich and the most civilized part of the country. At the time of the invasion, the La Tène culture had spread over most of the Home Counties. There were trading relations between Kent and Gaul, but if town life existed at all, it was very rudimentary. Caesar suggests that the nearest approach to towns was the fortified forest encampment: *oppidum autem Britanni vocant, cum silvas impeditas vallo atque fossa munierant*.[1] There was no native Celtic alphabet or system of writing, but the Latin used in Gaul must have been familiar to the Belgic traders, who had indeed an inscribed coinage of their own in the Roman alphabet. It is worth bearing in mind that inscribed coins are not merely a certain indication of commercial activity and of at least the slight element of literacy which that presupposes; they are themselves one of the earliest forms of literary (and in a sense of printed) record to appear in the history of a country. Belgic coins from Gaul are found throughout South-eastern England, and it is at least possible that their coins were being struck in Britain before Caesar's invasion. Mediterranean coins, the result perhaps of the tin trade with the Cassiterides, have also been found in the south-west. It is of interest to note that, according to Caesar, the Druids in Southern Gaul used Greek characters for business purposes, borrowed probably from the Greek traders at Marseilles.[2]

Between Caesar's raid in 55 BC and the Claudian invasion in AD 43, there was considerable development. Cunobelinus at Colchester (whom Suetonius calls *rex Britanniae*) was not unfriendly to Roman ways, and a certain amount of Romanization took place; Strabo records a peace treaty between the British rulers and Augustus which made the whole island practically a Roman province.[3] Town life of a primitive sort began at centres such as Verulam, Colchester, Chichester, Silchester, Winchester and Canterbury; and there was quite possibly a pre-Claudian trading centre on the site of London. Nowhere however, did it reach the more advanced stage of organization of some of the Gaulish towns such as Bibracte, and none of the British towns offered any resistance to the Roman troops.

[1] Caesar, *De Bell. Gall.* 5. 21.
[2] Caesar, *op. cit.*, 6. 14.
[3] Strabo, 4. 200.

The encouragement of urban life was a marked feature of Imperial policy, and under Roman rule British towns developed rapidly. Where a Celtic hill-top town existed, this was replaced by a 'new town' in a neighbouring valley; Augustodunum in Gaul, and Verulam, Dorchester and Caerwent in Britain are examples. Where the Celtic town occupied a valley site, it was merely replanned in Roman style, as at Silchester, Winchester and Chichester. Two of the five Roman municipalities in Britain were established almost immediately by Claudius: the colonia at Colchester and the municipium at Verulam. Most of the rest followed in the Flavian age and under Hadrian towards the close of the first century and early in the second.

The character of these Roman towns is of interest to us because it is here that we might expect to find libraries. Their population is a matter of guess-work, but none of them was large by modern standards. The largest in area was London with 325 acres; London was, in fact, one of the largest cities in the Western Empire. Next in size was Cirencester (240 acres), Verulam (200 acres), Wroxeter (170 acres), Colchester, Leicester, Silchester, and possibly Caerleon (all about 100 acres) and Caerwent (40 acres); there were, in addition, several towns whose size is uncertain. The Numidian town of Timgad, with its library and other public buildings, had only 30 acres, though it grew later beyond its walls.

All the Romano-British towns were planned in the normal chess-board pattern, with regular *insulae* or blocks separated by streets at right angles, though for geographical reasons the outline of the walls was irregular. Most of them were provided with public buildings on a generous, and indeed on a quite extravagant scale, far beyond the needs of the available population, and far beyond the provision in any modern towns. Forum, basilica, baths, temples and amphitheatres were all lavishly built. At Silchester, the basilica covered 14,000 square feet, and was probably 60 feet high; under modern conditions it would have seated 4,000 people, or more than twice the estimated population of the city, though no basilica was, of course, intended for a seated audience. The baths at Wroxeter had hot and cold rooms each measuring 2,800 square feet, with the rest of the building on an equally magnificent scale; here, indeed, the Roman surveyors over-reached themselves, for the baths were never finished, being replaced by a large forum with new baths on a fresh site.[1] Shops were built and also (judging from the example at Silchester) even hotels. But the private houses were, compared with the scale of the public buildings, surprisingly few; there were only 80 in Silchester. They were not town houses of the type found in Roman Italy, but country villas, mostly single-storied and with gardens. Their equipment was, however, wholly Roman in character; their wall-paintings and mosaics may have been poorer in quality than would be expected in Italy, but the hypocausts (as befitted the climate) were more numerous. The plans of at least two towns, Silchester and Caerwent, are fairly complete, and it is interesting to compare them with that of Timgad.[2] Only a few of the *insulae* can be identified as serving any special purpose; as has already been mentioned, the assignment of one to the library at Timgad is due to the chance survival of an inscription.[3] There is, indeed, scarcely any means of identifying a library from its foundations, in the absence of inscriptions, unless the walls remain (as at Pergamum) sufficiently high to reveal pigeon-holes. The normal situation of a Roman town library was close to or adjoining the curia, and at Silchester there are unidentified sites on either side of the curia, and between the basilica and the western colonnade of the forum, where it might have been placed. This is, of course, guess-work, but it is more than probable that towns so handsomely provided with public buildings, as, for example, Wroxeter, should have had a library included.

We may perhaps guess from Matthew Paris' account of Abbot Eadmar's discoveries at Verulam in the eleventh century that a domestic library of Roman times, had actually survived to that date. The collection was apparently found in an armarium in the ruins of a private house, and the rolls must surely have been of parchment if they survived a thousand years in that situation. We can only take the story for what it may be worth, and assume that it was based on a genuine discovery of early manuscripts, either Roman or more probably post-Roman.[4]

[1] R. G. Collingwood and J. N. L. Myres, *Roman Britain and the English Settlements*, 1936, Ch. XII.
[2] F. Haverfield, *The Roman Occupation of Britain*, 1924, pp. 298–312.
[3] There is a useful account of the Timgad library in the *Bulletin of the Board of Celtic Studies*, XVI, Pt. II, May, 1955. See also the French official guide to the Roman town.
[4] The passage is quoted in R. E. M. Wheeler and T.V. Wheeler, *Verulamium*, 1936. See also Stuart Piggott in *English historical scholarship in the sixteenth and seventeenth centuries*, ed. L. Fox, 1956, p. 97. The description of the other discoveries (mosaics, pottery,

The Romano-British towns were artificial implantations in a country that was not yet accustomed to the urban life on which Graeco-Roman civilization was built. They were without economic justification, for the surrounding countryside was too thinly populated to support them, and although some were associated with special local industries, such as Wroxeter with its ironworking, none of them was the centre of a system of villages like the modern country town. Nevertheless they endured for two centuries or so, with all the external trappings of Roman civilization, and we must enquire what sort of culture they represented.

That there was a reasonable level of education is beyond doubt. Tacitus tells us how Agricola deliberately fostered the arts of peace, encouraging with official grants the erection of temples, public buildings and private villas. He arranged for the sons of the leading Britons to be trained in the liberal arts, and he noted the superiority of native ability in Britain over the trained skill of the Gauls. As a result, the first reluctance to learn Latin was replaced by a general anxiety to acquire it. Roman ways and Roman dress became the fashion, and (as Tacitus dryly observes) the Britons were tempted by all those frills which make vice pleasant, and quickly came to regard the new ideas as civilization, when they were really nothing but a mark of their enslavement.[1] This was the routine policy of Romanization, which balanced so successfully the policy of using the native magistracy for local administration. And in the province of Britain it was, indeed, completely successful.

Latin became almost at once the normal language of both rich and poor in the towns, and at least of the wealthier classes in the country. How far the Celtic dialects survived in the villages is unknown, but they may well have borne the same relation to Latin as Gaelic does to English in the Highlands today. A very few Celtic inscriptions from the Roman period remain in Gaul, but not a single one in Britain; the inscription in Ogams found at Silchester is post-Roman, the result probably of the Irish migration in the fifth century. A Greek inscription occurs in mosaic flooring at

---

glass, funeral urns, etc.) is circumstantial and convincing, and it is difficult to discount entirely the description of the documents. For more recent information on Verulam see S. S. Frere, *Verulamium, three Roman cities*, Antiquity, 1964, 38, pp. 103–12.

[1] Tacitus, Agricola 21.

Aldeburgh, but apart from this, Latin was universal. The Latin phrases scribbled by workmen on bricks, tiles or Samian ware suggest that this was their customary language.[1] These workmen were probably British; some may have come from Northern Gaul, but there was no immigration from Italy.

Schools must have been common in the towns throughout the period. There is a casual reference in Plutarch to the fact that a certain Demetrius of Tarsus had just returned from a lecture tour in Britain; this would have been during Agricola's term of office as legate, and he may conceivably have been commissioned by Agricola himself.[2] It so happens that in 1840 on the site of York railway station two bronze dedicatory tablets, inscribed in Greek and bearing this name, were discovered, and they quite possibly refer to Plutarch's schoolmaster.[3] Juvenal, writing early in the second century, has a reference to British lawyers learning their profession from Gaulish masters, and to the teaching of rhetoric in the far north.[4] In the third century Bonosus, who was proclaimed emperor at Cologne and was finally vanquished by Probus, AD 280, was the son of a British schoolmaster and a lady of Gaul. It is evident that Romano-British culture was an importation from Gaul. Geographically, South-eastern Britain was in effect part of Northern Gaul; the same tribes and the same dialects were found, and, as Caesar tells us, the same chiefs often ruled on both sides of the Channel.

The suggestion has been made that in the later Empire a purer and more 'classical' Latin was spoken in Britain than in Gaul, and that this was due to the fact that the Roman Briton learnt his Latin mainly in school, from professional grammarians, while the Gallo-Roman tended to pick it up orally in the course of his daily life at work, in the army or in his home.[5] The stabilizing influence of school discipline, particularly in the field of rhetoric, is a very marked feature of the medieval period, both in the Western Church as regards the Latin language, and at Constantinople as regards Greek.

Martial, writing soon after Agricola's return to Rome, boasts

[1] Haverfield, *The Romanisation of Roman Britain*, 1923, Ch. III.
[2] Plutarch, *De Defectu Oraculorum*.
[3] A. R. Burn, *The Romans in Britain*, 1932, p. 67.
[4] Juvenal, 15. 112.
[5] Kenneth Jackson in *Medieval Studies in Honor of J. D. M. Ford*, 1948, pp. 83-103.

that his poems were not only read by city idlers, but thumbed by the hard-boiled centurion, 'and even Britain is said to sing my verses.'[1] Presumably he was thinking of the Roman troops in Britain, rather than the Britons themselves. In the first thirty years of the conquest, most of the legionaries came from North Italy; in Martial's day and afterwards, however, both legionaries and auxiliaries were drawn from many parts of the Empire, Gaul, Spain, the Rhine, the Danube and even Syria, with a proportion from Britain itself in the later period. The influence of these troops on civilian culture was perhaps limited, for they served on the frontiers, not in the new towns. But they were Latin speaking, and they represented the centrally organized machine that was the Roman Empire. They imported books from Rome, if Martial can be credited, and the official gazette (*acta diurna*) circulated amongst them.[2]

That Roman Britain had its bookshops is, at least, a possibility. There is no architectural evidence; indeed, few Roman shops have left any trace of their wares. There is literary evidence for many bookshops in Italy, Athens and Gaul. As we noted in the previous chapter, Pliny and Martial testify to the existence of bookshops in Lyons and Vienne.[3] And if in Lyons and Vienne, why not in Silchester, Verulam or Wroxeter, where elegant shops, some displaying luxuries such as Samian ware from Gaul, are known to have existed? An inscribed tile found at Silchester bears the Virgilian tag *conticuere omnes*, which suggests that somebody there at least knew his Aeneid.

In the third century urban life throughout the Empire began to decay. Under Septimius Severus, Imperial policy, which previously had encouraged the Romanizing influences of town life, transferred its interest to the army as the basis of its power. Taxation, forced levies and currency inflation crushed the towns out of existence, and the urban population began to drift back to the land, where a self-contained existence on villa farms offered more chance of security.[4] In Britain towns such as Silchester, Wroxeter and Verulam were deserted, or abandoned to squatters who knew none

---

[1] Martial, *Ep.* 11. 3.
[2] Tacitus, *Ann.* 16. 22.
[3] Pliny, *Ep.* 9. 11.; Martial, 7. 8.
[4] Rostovtzeff, *Social and Economic History of the Roman Empire*, p. 422; Collingwood and Myres, *op. cit.*, p. 203.

of the graces of Roman life. Forum, walls, theatres and houses fell to ruin. Sometimes, as at Wroxeter, they were never repaired. At Verulam, there was some reconstruction under Constantius Chlorus about AD 300, but decay had gone too far, and within fifty years Verulam was again despoiled, though not entirely abandoned.

This did not signify the end of Romano-British culture, but merely its transference to the villa estates, which reached their highest standard of prosperity in the third and fourth centuries. For the most part these were independent farms, occupied by Romanized British farmers, and producing most of what they needed within their own boundaries. The villa civilization of these two final centuries has been described as a second period of Romanization, apparently quite spontaneous, for there was no influx of settlers from abroad, although there may well have been a movement outwards from the abandoned towns.[1]

About 500 villa sites are known, nearly all in Southern and Eastern England. Most belonged to the corridor-type common in northern Europe, but some of the largest and most elegant were built on the courtyard plan. There is no literary evidence about the life of their inhabitants, and even the archaeological evidence is scanty, but although they were in many ways quite different from the villas that Cicero and Pliny owned, yet their furnishings and equipment were fine and often magnificent, suggesting a completely Romanized standard of life. The scale on which some were planned, the number of their rooms and colonnades, make it more than likely that they were provided with libraries. Remembering Haverfield's dictum that Britain belongs geographically to northern Gaul and that what occurs in one area may, therefore, be expected to occur in the other,[2] we can perhaps find a parallel in the life of fourth- and fifth-century Gaul. This was of course a period when Western scholarship tended to move away from Rome to provincial cities such as Milan, Carthage and Ravenna, and this movement also brought a very considerable renaissance in Gaul. There were many Gallo-Roman university cities. Tacitus, himself possibly educated at Marseilles, mentions the Schools of Augustodunum, and these again became famous in the fourth century.

---

[1] Collingwood and Myres, *op. cit.*, p. 215.
[2] Haverfield, *The Roman Occupation of Britain*, p. 172.

There were other universities at Lyons, Nîmes, Vienne, Toulouse, Bordeaux, Poitiers and Narbonne. One of the most attractive of the fourth-century writers, Ausonius (his *Mosella* is still worth study by travellers in that river valley) was educated at Bordeaux and Toulouse, and for thirty years he taught, first as *grammaticus* and later as *rhetor*, at the University of Bordeaux, where his uncle was also a professor. In his *Commemoratio Professorum Burdigalensium* he lists twenty-five of the Bordeaux professors, of whom all but six were natives of the district. Bordeaux also supplied professors for the chairs of rhetoric at Narbonne, Poitiers and Toulouse. In the 'little renaissance' of the fifth century, both Narbonne and Lérins became centres of brilliant scholarship, and Narbonne in particular was one of the last active centres of Greek studies in the West. One of Ausonius' most famous pupils at Bordeaux was Paulinus of Nola who, after a brief but successful career in the Imperial service, was baptized, together with his wife Therasia, and both vowed themselves to the religious life.

Sidonius Apollinaris, the fifth-century Bishop of Auvergne, was perhaps a trifle pedestrian as a writer, but his letters show that he lived in a thoroughly cultured society. He has many references to his own library, and to the villa libraries of his friends: particularly those of Consentius at the Villa Octaviana, near Narbonne; of Magnus Felix at Narbonne; and of Tonantius Ferreolus at Prusianum, in which (as we are told) the Roman classics were arranged on one side of the room, and the Church Fathers on the other, much as the Greek and Latin collections were kept separate in the Roman temple libraries. Sidonius himself was much more than a scholar and a poet; he was a brave and resolute leader who guided the fortunes of the first resistance movement in Gaul against the invading Visigoths. One of his friends was S. Lupus of Troyes, who accompanied Germanus on his first visit to Britain.

The collocation of pagan and Christian writings at the villa of Tonantius illustrates one feature of Gallo-Roman scholarship, which was founded to a striking degree on the marriage of classical and orthodox learning. A natural result of this marriage was the birth of heresies such as Pelagianism and Priscillianism, which were the outcome of classical learning in general, and of Stoic philosophy in particular, as seen through Christian eyes. Pelagianism is claimed as British in origin; and it may be noted that some of the adherents of Priscillianism, including Bishop Instantius, were exiled to the Scilly Isles, AD 384.[1]

The renaissance mainly affected the southern part of Gaul, but its influence must have extended northwards to the Romanized areas of Northern Gaul and Britain, wherever archaeological remains testify to a respect for the graces of living. We can indeed picture what biologists call a 'cline' of culture, weakening gradually as one travels northwards. For three centuries Britain had been the most peaceful of all the frontier provinces, and in the southern part of the island, the standard of civilization may well have remained high.

In the first quarter of the fifth century, the Roman troops and administrative officials were withdrawn from Britain. It is unlikely, however, that there was any immediate change in the character of the villa civilization; the probability is that the villa farms, threatened on all sides by raiding Picts, Saxons and Irish, as well as by wandering bands of peasants of the same type as the Bacaudae who at this time were harassing Gaul, were thrown back still more on their own resources, losing gradually the slight contacts they had enjoyed with the outer world. A self-supporting farm can carry on for a considerable time under such conditions, but inevitably the graces of civilization fall away and the standard of living falls. But the fall must have been gradual. There was at least some contact with Gaul and Rome, mainly ecclesiastical, till the middle of the fifth century. By this time the Church was beginning to take charge of the tradition of literary record, a responsibility which she shouldered successfully for a thousand years. After AD 455, such civilization as survived in the western parts of Britain and in Ireland was entirely due to the missionary endeavour of the Celtic church; and it is appropriate to add that the inspiration behind the Celtic Church was neither Irish nor Pictish, but Romano-British. If the villa civilization of Roman Britain is to be judged by its fruits, this is perhaps the noblest of them.

S. Ninian was a Romano-Briton who in his youth made a pilgrimage to Rome and remained there to complete his education. At the end of the fourth century he was despatched on a missionary

---

[1] For a discussion of the relations between Gaul and Britain in the fifth century, see Mrs N. K. Chadwick's *Poetry and Letters in Early Christian Gaul*, 1955, and her contributions to *Studies in Early British History*, 1954, and *Studies in the Early British Church*, 1958. For Ausonius and Paulinus, see Helen Waddell, *The Wandering Scholars*.

enterprise to Northern Britain, and in 397 (probably a few years after the Wall had been abandoned) he established his Candida Casa, the whitewashed stone church or monastery at Whithorn, dedicated to S. Martin of Tours. His influence extended beyond Galloway into the Border country, and a church of S. Martin was founded within the fort of the Roman wall at Brampton. S. Ninian is said to have died in 432, but his tradition may well have endured almost to the time when the Irish missionaries arrived from Iona in the seventh century. A late fifth-century Christian tomb at Chesterholm, another fort in Northumberland, suggests that his influence extended all along the Celtic settlements on the Wall; and the many dedications in his honour show that his fame spread far beyond this. The most remote of these dedications is on S. Ninian's Isle on the west coast of Dunrossness in Shetland, where a valuable hoard of silver bowls and brooches was recently discovered.[1] He was known also in the west of Ireland, for S. Enda of Aran is said to have visited him.

S. Ninian had several contemporaries who provide evidence of the standard of education in the Britain of his day. Pelagius may have been a heretic, but he was a cultivated scholar with a graceful literary style. He spent his life wandering through the Mediterranean countries, and his *Expositions of Thirteen Epistles of S. Paul*, written in Rome about 405, ranks as the earliest surviving work by any writer of this country. His friend and colleague Caelestius was perhaps the first of the long succession of Irish scholars who roamed the continent during the early middle ages. The first book to have been written in Britain may have been the devotional work *On the Christian Life*, by another cultured British churchman, Fastidius.[2]

More important perhaps than any of these, and equally British, was S. Patrick, who was born towards the end of the fourth century at an unidentified place called Bannavem Tabernae, near the west coast. Dumbarton has been claimed as his birthplace, and also Bewcastle in Cumberland;[3] but the fact that both his father and grandfather were deacons, and that his father was also a *decurio municipalis* or town councillor, suggests that his villa farm was in

---

[1] *Antiquity*, 1959, 38.
[2] R. S. T. Haslehurst, *The Works of Fastidius*, 1927.
[3] M. P. Charlesworth, *The Lost Province*, 1949, p. 30.

the Romanized part of Britain, and so somewhere in the West Country. At the age of fifteen he and his two sisters were carried off by Irish raiders to Antrim, where he worked for many years as a slave. In due course he escaped and returned to his family, and then becoming aware of his vocation he went south for his training, studying possibly at Lérins and at Auxerre under S. Germanus. In 432 he was consecrated bishop, and spent the remaining thirty years of his life in Ireland, where he had as his colleague another British bishop, named Palladius. During this period he laid the foundations of the Celtic Church with its monastic organization, which a century later produced its two great missionary enterprises in Iona and in Central Europe, with the libraries and scriptoria associated with them[1]

S. Germanus of Auxerre was one of the greatest of the fifth-century bishops of Gaul: a little earlier than Sidonius Apollinaris, and with a much more definite vocation. Sidonius' main interests were those of a country squire and a rather pedantic poet, and his greatest ambition was realized when his portrait was placed above his works in the Ulpian library. His own villa library probably contained all the standard Latin authors, and some Latin translations of Greek works. S. Germanus on the other hand was a high Imperial official in central Gaul who underwent a genuine conversion at the age of forty, and became a convinced Christian and a great teacher. He was well known in Britain, where there are twelve pre-Norman dedications to him. His first visit was in 429 with Bishop Lupus of Troyes, some years after the Roman administration had been withdrawn, when he led a campaign against the Pelagians; he also took command of the militia in a successful battle against the Picts and Scots. During this visit he met the chief magistrate at Verulam: a fact which suggests that Verulam still survived as a town with a local administration. The anti-

---

[1] It is perhaps worth adding that, according to a tale that is, alas, probably apocryphal, the first Irish saint was Saint Ciaran, said by Ussher to have been born AD 352, but more likely about AD 500. The story tells that the saint spent twenty years studying in Rome and collecting books, and was then ordained bishop and sent back to Ireland. On the road through Italy he met Saint Patrick; this was before Saint Patrick was made bishop by Pope Celestine. And S. Patrick bade Ciaran go before him to Ireland, as a sort of S. John the Baptist, and appointed a meeting place, at a well called Fuaran, where he would join him in thirty years' time. These and similar stories at least suggest that there was traffic between Ireland and Rome in the fifth and sixth centuries, and that books were reaching Ireland from Rome in that period.

Pelagian mission was equally successful, and they preached everywhere, 'filling the island of Britain with their learning and virtues'. In 446 the British leaders sent a fruitless appeal to Rome for military help, and in the following year they made a more successful appeal to S. Germanus, who paid his second visit to Britain in 447, and is said to have found the people constant in their faith.[1]

S. Patrick had two fellow students at Auxerre, in S. Illtud and Paulinus, who themselves became the teachers of S. David, the apostle of Wales, and the founder of the early Welsh monastic houses.

In 455 the British Church accepted the date of Easter as settled by the Council of Arles and modified by Leo I. That is the last known contact with the continent till the coming of S. Augustine in 597. For a century and a half there are no real facts to guide us. Under Saxon pressure, such civilization as remained withdrew to the west, and, in R. G. Collingwood's words, 'men lived on the relics of Romanity in a pervading medium of Celticism.' The silence in this period is broken only by Gildas, who wrote in the middle of the sixth century, either in Western Britain or in Brittany. Gildas' book is not a history, but an ecclesiastical lamentation on the state of Britain. Indeed, it is so violently anti-British that it has been suggested that he was a foreigner. In any case his ignorance of Roman Britain is surprising. Whatever his failings, his work indicates that Latin of a sort was still being read at this time in Celtic Britain as well as in S. Columba's Ireland. It shows also that memories of Roman Britain had grown dim, and that written records were scanty. Gildas himself says that he did not obtain his material from local sources, because none had survived; he obtained his information *transmarina relatione*, which may well mean from current gossip in Brittany. There is nothing to suggest, for example, that he had access to any of the continental historians of the late Empire, and any library on which he drew must have contained little but the scriptures, and perhaps a few pagan texts, such as Virgil. There is no reason to suppose that any books at all survived from the villa or town libraries of Roman

---

[1] For S. Germanus, see Mrs Chadwick's *Poetry and Letters in Early Christian Gaul*, 1955, Ch. IX. Many authorities believe that he made only one visit to Britain, in 429, the account of the second being an echo of the first.

Britain. If, as is probable, the town libraries were abandoned in the third century, they would have consisted entirely of papyrus rolls, which would have a very transitory life in our misty climate. Even by the fifth century, any books in codex form would have been mostly Christian works.

The sources used by the Irish monastic scriptoria in the sixth and seventh centuries are unknown. S. Patrick himself was not a scholar, nor was he entirely at home in the Latin language, which even in his later life he wrote with difficulty. Nevertheless, the impact of Latin on the Welsh language, and even through trading relations on the Irish language, was so marked that abundant traces of it survive to this day, and the prestige of Roman administration remained high in Celtic Britain long after the rest of the country had become Saxon. We can fairly assume, therefore, a tradition of Latin teaching at the monastic schools in Ireland and South Wales. The scriptorium at Iona probably confined itself to the scriptures and to service books of the kind that missionaries would normally carry with them wherever they went. The Bangor scriptorium, however, from which S. Columban went to found his chain of monasteries in central Europe, was on a different scale, for it could draw on a good array of classical texts. S. Columban's own writings suggest acquaintance not merely with the scriptures, with Christian authorities such as Eusebius and Jerome, Christian poets such as Sedulius and Prudentius, and contemporary writers such as Gregory the Great, Fortunatus and Gildas, but also with pagan writers, such as Virgil, Horace, Ovid, Ausonius, Juvenal and some others.[1] The isolation of the Celtic Church after 455 makes it difficult to explain the origin of these. S. Patrick and Palladius were certainly not the only emigrants to Ireland in the fifth century, and travellers from Armorica as well as from Britain may have brought books with them. The Irish Church certainly maintained contact with S. Ninian's mission in Galloway, and probably also with S. Illtud's houses in South Wales; while S. Cadoc the Wise, the friend of Gildas, is said to have travelled not only

---

[1] J. F. Kenney, *The Sources for the Early History of Ireland*, vol. I; J. W. Thompson, *The Medieval Library*, Ch. IX. See also the chapter by Kathleen Hughes on "The Distribution of Irish Scriptoria and Centres of Learning from 730 to 1111" in *Studies in the Early British Church*, 1958. An unpublished thesis by W. G. Wheeler, 'Libraries in Ireland before 1855, a bibliographical essay' (University of London, Postgraduate Diploma in Librarianship, 1957) contains a useful summary of our knowledge of early Irish monastic libraries.

through Scotland and Ireland, but to Rome and Jerusalem, in search of instruction. Even though formal contact with Rome was broken after 455 (and this is shown by the fact that news of the change in the date of Easter made at the end of the fifth century never reached the Celtic Church), it is probable that contact still existed between Ireland and Armorica, where indeed many Britons are known to have emigrated in the fifth century. Celtic Armorica, though itself an isolated part of Gaul, remained under Roman control longer than Britain; indeed, it was under S. Germanus' administration at Auxerre in the days before his conversion, and in his diocese afterwards; and it was during a mission to Ravenna in 448 to intercede with the emperor on behalf of the Armoricans (who were under sentence for rebellion) that he died.

A good case has been made for linking the rhetorical conventions of early Irish literature with the Gaulish schools of rhetoric at Bordeaux and elsewhere; and it is known that refugees from the advancing Visigoths fled northwards to Armorica, Britain and Ireland, as well as southwards to Spain and Africa.[1] Some evidence of intellectual contact between Gaul and Britain in the late fifth century can also be drawn from Sidonius Apollinaris. In one letter (ix. 9) addressed to Bishop Faustus of Riez (formerly Abbot of Lerins), he refers to a visit from the monk Riocatus, who was returning to Britain carrying copies of Faustus' works. It has been suggested that both Faustus and Riocatus were descendants of the British prince Vortigern.[2] Another letter (viii. 6) refers to a request from Namatius, the Gaulish commander of the *Classis Britannica*, the Roman fleet still apparently operating on both sides of the Channel, for copies of Eusebius and Varro.

Some contact must also have existed at the end of the fifth century in the time of Arthur, who, as a Romanized Briton, may have assumed the old title of *comes Britanniarum* in command of a mobile field army with heavy cavalry in the new Roman fashion. This interesting theory has been doubted, perhaps even discredited, but the probability of contact between Arthurian Britain and Gaul remains. That it survived through the sixth century is

---

[1] Mrs Chadwick, *op. cit.*, p. 327. See also her chapter in *Studies in Early British History*, 1954.
[2] *Studies in Early British History*, p. 226 and Appendix.

suggested by the work of Gildas, who may indeed have written in Armorica.[1]

If the historical evidence for contact between Ireland, Britain and France in the fifth and sixth centuries is slender, it is at least well established by legend. S. Enda of Aran, after visiting S. Ninian at Candida Casa, is said to have founded a house called Latinum (Irish *Letha*, signifying Armorica); he afterwards founded his monastery in the Aran Islands. S. Finnian (d. 550) is said to have visited Tours, and he also spent a long period at Mynyw (S. David's) where he met S. David and Gildas. S. Cainnech of Aghadoc (d. 598), who studied in Wales under S. Cadoc of Llancarvan, the cousin of S. David, and was well known also in Scotland, is said to have penetrated as far as Italy; authorities such as Dr Forbes (in his *Kalendar of Scottish Saints*) regard such a pilgrimage as by no means an uncommon incident in the lives of Irish saints of this period. Archaeological evidence suggests that wine and other commodities were being imported from Southern Gaul throughout the fifth and sixth centuries; the wine trade probably continued till the Arab conquest of Spain.

There is, therefore, a strong probability that S. Columban's library at Bangor, and the other Irish monastic libraries of which less is known, drew their books originally from the academic centres of Southern Gaul and perhaps also from Armorica and Britain. We must assume, however, that though this link with Roman civilization survived, it was too slender and uncertain to transmit the changes in the date of Easter to which the Celtic Church was not reconciled till the Synod of Whitby in 664.

Whatever doubt there may be about the Celtic contribution to the culture of the early middle ages, there can be no doubt at all about the contribution of Irish librarianship to the monastic houses of central Europe; and one can feel equally certain that the library of Bangor was built on a tradition that had its roots in Roman Gaul and Roman Britain.[2]

---

[1] Collingwood and Myres, *op. cit.*, p. 322. The argument against this theory is given by K. H. Jackson in *Arthurian Literature in the Middle Ages*, ed. R. S. Loomis, 1959, p. 9.
[2] On this see also *Heritage*, ch. VIII.

CHAPTER VI

In Saxon England

JUST as the historian of our libraries commonly ignores the four centuries when Britain was Roman, so also is he tempted to leap directly over the dark period that precedes the great Benedictine age in Norman times. In either case, he will thereby lose an important link in the uninterrupted chain of our heritage. The achievements of the Benedictine Rule in the twelfth century had their roots in the obscure and troubled years between Alcuin and Lanfranc.

R. W. Chambers has reminded us that it was not the Norman Conquest that made England part of continental civilization, as modern historians sometimes assert. Monk Wearmouth, Jarrow and York had, long before this, been centres of Western European civilization and learning. Britain had been part of the ancient Roman world, and in spite of a century and a half of Teutonic heathendom, the earlier Christianity of Britain had been passed on to sanctuaries like Glastonbury, Malmesbury and Iona. The mission of Augustine meant the return of Britain to Europe.[1] It meant also the very slow and gradual re-establishment of literacy in England after a period of unlettered paganism. The Saxon invaders were indeed pagans (*pagani*) in every sense of the word. Like the German peoples described by Tacitus, they never lived in cities. They had no use for towns, or for the civilization which the Greeks and the Romans had built on the foundation of urban life. The few towns which may have enjoyed a nebulous continuity of occupation (such as Canterbury, Lincoln and Carlisle), have yielded no evidence of a continuity of culture. Even the abandoned Roman villas were ignored and left to decay. Alone amongst the invaders, the Jutes of Kent and Hampshire may have been subject to some slight degree of Roman influence in the Rhineland whence they are believed to have come. By and large, how-

[1] R. W. Chambers, *Thomas More*, 1935, (Epilogue).

ever, the slate had been sponged clean, and England had to start afresh on its laborious journey in the direction of education and culture. Even in Western Britain, memories of Roman town life had vanished, and the Celtic Church was based on tribal territory rather than on the orthodox pattern of the episcopal see with an urban headquarters.[1]

In 597, when S. Augustine landed in Kent with his forty monks, the brief isolation of this country was finally broken. For some years there had been a Christian queen and a Frankish bishop worshipping in the ruined Roman church of S. Martin, outside Canterbury. In that city, which can perhaps claim a continuity of occupation longer than any of our towns except London, S. Augustine founded the monastery of Christ Church in a restored Roman basilica. It was destroyed by fire in 1067, and Lanfranc began the building of the present cathedral three years later. A second monastery, of SS. Peter and Paul, was founded outside the city; this became the modern S. Augustine's.

In 669 there arrived in Canterbury two far greater men than S. Augustine: Theodore and Hadrian. The former was Archbishop till his death in 690, and Hadrian was Abbot of SS. Peter and Paul. Both were scholars with a genuine knowledge of Greek. Theodore came from S. Paul's city of Tarsus, and had been educated at Athens, where apparently teaching continued in spite of Justinian's closure of the university in 529. In Bede's words:

'Both of them were well read in both sacred and secular literature, and they gathered a crowd of disciples, and there daily flowed from them rivers of knowledge to water the hearts of their hearers; and together with the books of holy writ, they also taught them the arts of ecclesiastical poetry, astronomy and arithmetic. A testimony of which is that there are still living at this day some of their scholars who are as well versed in the Greek and Latin tongues as in their own in which they were born.'

---

[1] The arguments for a much longer survival than commonly imagined of the rural life of sub-Roman Britain into the Anglo-Saxon period, especially in the West Midlands and the West country, are set out in H. P. R. Finberg, *Lucerna*, 1964. It is conceivable, for example, that in the Anglo-Celtic kingdom of Wessex, the British monasteries at Sherborne, Shaftesbury and Glastonbury maintained their corporate existence undisturbed, sometimes under abbots with British names. There is at least some evidence of continuity between Roman villa estates such as Withington in the Cotswolds, and the medieval parish boundary, though in this case the British name has been lost.

IN SAXON ENGLAND

From the seventh century onwards there was continuous contact between England and Rome: much closer contact than is sometimes realized. Many English kings, from Ina of Wessex to Alfred the Great and Cnut, visited the city that throughout this period remained the headquarters of Western civilization. King Ina during his stay in Rome is said to have founded the hospitium on the banks of the Tiber for Anglo-Saxon pilgrims to the Holy City. This was destroyed in 847 and refounded in 855 by Æthelwulf, who is also believed to have originated the annual payment of Peter's Pence. Alfred the Great spent three years of his childhood in Rome, where Leo IV formally dedicated him to the royal mission that awaited him. The flow of pilgrims to the Eternal City gathered weight steadily; Cnut's visit in 1027, was, in part, to ensure greater security for the humbler pilgrims on their long journey. Some penetrated even to Jerusalem, and the *Anglo-Saxon Chronicle* tells us that Alfred sent Sighelm, Bishop of Sherborne, as far as India, with gifts for the Malabar Christians: he returned with gifts of jewels and spices. Though Irish influence is not to be ignored, the main source of monastic inspiration and of books for the monastic libraries was continental. In return, England exerted its own influence on continental culture, through the missionary work of Boniface in Germany, and the educational work of Alcuin at the court of Charles the Great.

Theodore and Hadrian established a school at Canterbury[1] which included the teaching of Greek, and a library which included Greek books. This was indeed our first English library. To this time also we can date the introduction of the written records of the grant of land which we know as charters. They were based on the private charter of Roman Imperial times, and were designed to give security of tenure to monastic and similar foundations.

The best known of Theodore's pupils were Aldhelm, Tobias, Bishop of Rochester (whose Greek learning is commended by

---

[1] It is possible that S. Augustine's School at Canterbury was founded AD 598, a year after S. Augustine's arrival. Another school is said to have been founded AD 631 by Sigebert; during exile in Gaul he had become familiar with the Gaulish monastic schools, and he followed their pattern, drawing his teachers from Canterbury. This school may have been attached to a monastery founded by the Irish missionary S. Fursa at Burghcastle on land provided by Sigebert. The site is uncertain, but it was not at Cambridge as some have supposed. It is known that S. Felix, the Bishop of Dunwich, was a Burgundian. Song schools at York and Rochester followed soon after. See A. F. Leach, *The Schools of Medieval England*, 1916.

Bede and Aldhelm) and Albinus, who succeeded Hadrian as Abbot of SS. Peter and Paul, and gave Bede material on Kentish history for his *Historia Ecclesiastica*. Aldhelm's first teacher was the Irish scholar Maildubh who is said to have founded the abbey of Malmesbury, where four centuries later William of Malmesbury served as librarian. After a period under Theodore, he returned to Malmesbury as Abbot, and later became Bishop of Sherborne. Much greater than Aldhelm was another West Saxon of this period, S. Boniface, whose story belongs to the history of German rather than English libraries. After training at a monastery at Exeter, he became head of a monastic school at Nursling, near Winchester. Thence in 716 he set out on his great missionary campaign in Frisia and Germany, becoming Archbishop of Mainz in 732, and founding the monastery and library of Fulda in 744, planning it as the headquarters of Northern monasticism and a counterpart of Monte Cassino in Italy. His influence extended to the Irish foundations of S. Gall and Reichenau; English books were added to their libraries and English handwriting introduced into their scriptoria. His correspondence with his friends in Southern England (in which the need for books is frequently stressed) shows good evidence of literary culture on both sides. It was S. Boniface's custom to carry a travelling library in the form of a chest of books on his journeys. On his final journey to Frisia, he packed a linen shroud with his books; and it was with one of these volumes that he tried to defend himself at his martyrdom. Three of the volumes were recovered and brought back to Fulda, including a damaged codex of the Gospels, said to have been the same volume that he had used as his last weapon.[1] Later Archbishop Cuthbert and a synod of English clergy decreed that S. Boniface should be ranked with S. Augustine and Gregory the Great as one of the three patrons of the English Church. There is no doubt that much of the effectiveness of the Carolingian renaissance can be ascribed to the preliminary work of the English missionaries in Germany in the early eighth century.

Meanwhile in Northumbria the great houses of Wearmouth and Jarrow had been founded by Benedict Biscop, who between 663 and 690 made five visits to Rome, partly to obtain books and furniture for his new foundations. In these years he built up the

---

[1] See G. W. Greenaway's *Saint Boniface*, 1955.

first great monastic library in England: the library which made possible the work of Bede in the following generation. Bede himself describes the large and noble library which the founder brought from Rome, and which was necessary for the edification of his church; he had ordered it to be kept entire and neither injured by neglect nor dispersed. Benedict's successor, Ceolfrith, doubled the library in size, and completed a purchase which Benedict had planned by giving a 'beautiful volume of the Geographers' to Aldfrith, the learned king of Northumbria, who had been educated at Iona. Later Adamnan of Iona presented him with one of his books, and Aldhelm also dedicated a treatise to him, so we may credit Aldfrith with the first English royal library.

Ceolfrith's pupil, Bede (673-735), is far too mighty a figure for summary treatment. There is no evidence that he ever travelled beyond York or Lindisfarne, and yet his writings show beyond doubt that he was familiar with an astonishing range of historical, classical and patristic literature, all of which must have been in the libraries of Wearmouth and Jarrow. The probable contents of these libraries have been studied in detail by Dr Bressie;[1] Bede's reputation spread immediately through Western Europe and to Rome, and his works were being copied in continental scriptoria down to the fifteenth century. The fact that most of the MSS are continental is no doubt partly due to the destruction of English libraries by the Danes in the ninth century.[2] The monastic library tradition was well established in Bede's day, and he himself describes a numerous and noble library collected by Acca at Hexham.

Bede's *Church History* was dedicated to one of his last pupils, Egbert, who became Archbishop of York, where he founded the school made famous by Alcuin. It was more than a merely religious seminary, for it had a wide range of subjects, including the classics (especially Virgil), the sciences, arts and grammar. The library was established by Egbert's successor, Æthelbert. Alcuin began teaching in the school in 767, and became its headmaster in 778.

[1] J. W. Thompson, *The Medieval Library*, pp. 109–12. The two-storied porch and west wall of the original church founded in 674 still survive, and excavations have revealed the foundations of the nave and choir of Bede's church. Parts of about ten parish churches dating from this period still remain, the most complete being that at Brixworth, near Northampton. See article in *The Times*, October 31, 1964. Bede's complete dependence on his library is illustrated by the fact that his account of the Roman Wall, which was only ten miles from the cell in which he wrote, is based on literary sources.

[2] R. W. Chambers, *The Lost Literature of Medieval England*, 1925.

Some time during these years he wrote the carmen which includes the well-known hexameters describing the library and its contents. He had good reason for his pride, for it must have been the best equipped library in Western Europe, outside Italy; its nearest rivals would have been Wearmouth and Jarrow, and perhaps Malmesbury. The school and its library flourished till the middle of the ninth century.[1]

Alcuin joined the court of Charles the Great in 782, and the rest of his life belongs to France rather than to England. Just as S. Boniface brought English books to the Fulda library, so Alcuin replenished the library of S. Martin of Tours with books from York. Alcuin himself was undistinguished both as a scholar and a writer, but he was beyond doubt a great teacher. To read his works, or the works of the other teachers of this period such as Rabanus Maurus of Fulda, is to realize the elementary and childish simplicity of the pupils they were dealing with. Europe had sunk abruptly into a slough of ignorance and illiteracy, but in every generation there were a few patient souls to keep the light of knowledge burning.

Alcuin's contemporary Nennius, the Welsh chronicler who is thought to have flourished about 800, based his *Historia Brittonum* mainly on Gildas, but he apparently had access also to Jerome's Eusebius, Prosper and Isidore, together with certain Irish and Northern annals. His method was the uncritical one of assembling all the traditions and legends he could lay hands on; 'I have,' he says, 'made a pile of everything I have found.' He seems to have heard nothing of Bede, but his chronicle suggests that libraries of some sort existed in Wales at this time, and that contact with scholars in Ireland and Scotland was still being maintained.

Alfred the Great (849–901) was faced in England by the same darkness that Alcuin had found in France a century earlier; and he set himself not only to gather round him a circle of scholars as Charles the Great had done, but to attempt in England the educational reforms that Alcuin had instituted in France. His own pic-

---

[1] This was a secular cathedral school. Its original founder may have been Paulinus, the first holder of the see (*d.* 644). That the library survived into the ninth century is suggested by a letter from Lupus of Ferrières to the Abbot of York, *c.* 850, asking for books, including a copy of Quintilian. It is said to have been finally destroyed by fire during the hostilities in 1069. See Leach, *op. cit.*, pp. 58, 64, and P. M. Tillott, *ed. A History of Yorkshire:* the city of York, 1961, pp. 6–7 (V.C.H.).

ture of the state of England is given in the letter to Bishop Werferth of Worcester, prefixed to his translation of Gregory's *Cura Pastoralis*. Here he suggests that the trouble was due not so much to the lack of books, as to plain ignorance of the Latin in which the books were written. He looks back to the time

'when men came from oversea in search of wisdom and instruction, which we should now have to get from thence if we would have them.... Few there are on this side Humber who understand the English of their service, or can translate a letter from Latin, nor are there many, I know, beyond Humber more learned.... I cannot remember one south of Thames when I first began to reign. God Almighty be thanked that we have any teaching among us now... I remembered how I had seen, before the land was ravaged and burnt, how its churches stood filled with treasures and books, and with a multitude of His servants, but they had very little knowledge of the books, and could not understand them, for they were not written in their own language.'

Later he adds that though the knowledge of Latin had decayed, yet many could read English. So he outlines his plan for the translation of Latin works into English, and the education of 'all the youth in England of free men rich enough to devote themselves to it, first in English, and later in Latin for those destined for high office.'

It seems likely that Alfred underestimated the learning of Mercia at least, for four of the scholars at his court were Mercians, including Bishop Werferth and Plegmund, Archbishop of Canterbury. Three others came from distant parts: Grimbald, a monk from St Bertin's at St Omer, a Saxon named John who was set in charge of the new monastery at Athelney, and Asser, from St. David's, who became his friend and biographer, helping him with his Latin studies, and with his translation of Gregory, Orosius, Bede and Boethius, all of which were rendered into the untried medium of English prose. To Alfred's reign we owe the beginning of the *Anglo-Saxon Chronicle* in its existing form; the earlier part was possibly based on a set of West Saxon annals in Latin. This great national undertaking was unique among the literary records of its time.

From S. Benedict's day to the coming of the universities in the thirteenth century, an educational programme meant inevitably the foundation of monastic houses with schools and libraries attached to them. Alfred founded at least two houses: one at Shaftesbury for women, and one at Athelney for men. His own daughter became the first Abbess of Shaftesbury. There were no English recruits for the Athelney house, and it began with foreign monks under John the Old Saxon. A third house planned by Alfred was established by his son Edward, with Grimbald as its abbot. None of these lasted long, though the Shaftesbury nunnery survived till Æthelstan's day.[1]

By the time of S. Dunstan's birth in 909, organized monastic life had practically disappeared in England. Cathedrals such as Winchester and Worcester were served by secular communities of *clerici*, of which only a small proportion were priests, and even these seem to have been living in a regrettably lax way. When S. Oswald went to Worcester he found there a 'family' of seventeen clerks, including two priests and one deacon. At Glastonbury a secular school survived, ruled probably by a lay abbot or local thegn; it still attracted Irish scholars, and there were books in its library from which S. Dunstan could profit.

Æthelstan, the grandson of Alfred, reigned from 925 to 939, and this period saw at least the beginning of the great monastic revival and reformation of the tenth century. Æthelstan's court was a migratory institution, but it was notable not only on account of its magnificence (which was famous throughout Europe) but because there is the first certain evidence that a permanent writing office was attached to it: a body of clerks engaged in the collection of revenues and the preparation of charters in formal Latin to perpetuate the record of royal grants or confirmations of land. The tradition of an English royal library dates back to Alfred, and perhaps to Aldfrith, but Æthelstan was a collector of books and relics on a relatively grand scale, and his gifts to the communities at Canterbury, Bath and Winchester are recorded; the Æthelstan Psalter was given by him to the Old Minster at Winchester.

---

[1] There appears to be no certain evidence of schools at Winchester or elsewhere in Alfred's time. The establishment of strongholds with collegiate churches and schools by Æthelflaed (d. c. 918) at Tamworth, Warwick, Stafford and Bridgnorth is however probable, and by Æthelstan at Beverley, Ripon and Chester-le-Street is certain. See Leach, *op. cit.*, p. 79.

S. Dunstan was educated at Glastonbury, and when his uncle Athelm, the Bishop of Wells, became Archbishop, he accompanied him to Canterbury and was introduced to Æthelstan's court. He became in due course a monk, and later, with his friend Æthelwold, a priest; and after Æthelstan's death he was chief adviser to the young King Edmund, who made him Abbot of Glaston. There, with his brother Wulfric and with Æthelwold, he began to rebuild and reform the abbey, introducing a discipline that was strict, though not of the full Benedictine pattern. Under his rule, which lasted for fifteen years, the abbey became famous as a great teaching institution; indeed it was the only school of true monastic life in England, and a training ground for the abbots and bishops who were to lead the coming revival. In addition the abbey was at this time not only the repository of the national treasury, but the national record office in which the royal charters and deeds were kept. In 955 there was a reaction against S. Dunstan's influence, and he was driven into exile, finding refuge at the religious house of Blandinium in Ghent. About the same time, the other great figure in the English revival, S. Oswald, having become dean of the secular community at Winchester, was so scandalized by their mode of life that he turned his back on it, crossed the Channel and entered the community at Fleury with the avowed object of learning the pure Benedictine rule. To Fleury also S. Æthelwold, now Abbot of Abingdon, sent one of his monks, Osgar, with the same purpose. The origin of the movement for Benedictine reform was French, and these three were mainly responsible for its introduction in England.

The original rule of S. Benedict was designed for a simple community of uninstructed lay monks, mostly agricultural labourers, in central Italy.[1] It provided for about four hours in the day to be devoted to services, the *opus Dei*, a similar period to reading and meditation, and the rest to manual work. The duty of reading involved necessarily the duty of copying manuscripts, and on these two primary functions the whole edifice of monastic librarianship is built. By the eighth century the manual work was being carried out increasingly by lay servants, and still greater emphasis was being placed on the scriptorium and library. The first great revision of the rule was the work of S. Benedict of Aniane, the 'second

[1] But see *Heritage*, p. 127.

founder', and was confirmed by a Council in 817 under Louis the Pious; but the break-up of the Empire made it impossible to reorganize and centralize the Benedictine system, and the movement lapsed. The reformation made a fresh start at Cluny, which was founded in 910. Cluny was governed from the start by the Customs of S. Benedict of Aniane, and it was, moreover, given direct papal protection. Its second abbot, Odo (927-41), was more than anyone else responsible for the spread of the reformed discipline. Odo, who was not only a great abbot but a good Virgilian scholar and a founder of schools at Liège, Rheims, Paris and Metz, reorganized many houses in France and Italy, including Fleury on the Loire, where S. Oswald was a monk. Two other movements for reform ran a parallel but independent course: one among houses in Lorraine, and the other inspired by Gerard of Brogne, who studied at the monastery of S. Denys at Paris and founded or reformed many houses, including Blandinium (where S. Dunstan spent his exile) and S. Bertin's at St Omer, from which the existing monks were expelled, finding a refuge at the abbey of Bath.

In 957 S. Dunstan was recalled to become Archbishop of Canterbury. S. Oswald also returned to the see of Worcester, and S. Æthelwold became Bishop of Winchester. At Winchester the secular clerks were forcibly replaced by monks from Abingdon; and a similar, though more gradual, change was effected at Worcester.[1] S. Oswald founded the small house of Westbury-on-Trym, and the much larger one of Ramsey; and many others were restored or reformed, including Ely, Peterborough, Thorney, Malmesbury and Bath. King Edgar, who had recalled S. Dunstan, died in 975, and at some date before his death there was held the important Synodal Council of Winchester, at which the *Regularis Concordia* was issued. This was a revision of the Benedictine Rule drawn up by S. Æthelwold, probably with S. Dunstan's active help, and it was intended as a basis for discipline at all English houses. Its distinguishing feature is the daily prayers for the royal family, especially the King and Queen who respectively were regarded as patrons of the houses for men and women, and it plays

---

[1] The secular clerks were apparently allowed to remain at Canterbury. Eadmer, *c.* 1100, describes the old Saxon cathedral, which had a secular school in its north tower. See A. F. Leach, *op. cit.*, p. 34.

an important part in the unification of England and in the complete co-operation of Church and State throughout the country. The reformed Benedictine discipline, instituted at Cluny in 910, held sway for two or three centuries, growing gradually more and more elaborate, till the Cistercian reaction came in the twelfth century under Stephen Harding and S. Bernard of Clairvaux, when a fresh return was made to the purity of the original rule.

The *Regularis Concordia* brought a renewal of close contact between the English and continental houses. This period also saw the introduction of Caroline minuscule writing into this country, where it assumed its special English characteristics. The Benedictional of S. Æthelwold and the Bosworth Psalter (probably written for S. Dunstan's use at Canterbury) belong to this time, as does the Exeter Book in the older insular hand. The *Regularis Concordia* does not refer directly to the monastic library, but it directs that the *lectio* and *meditatio* are to be carried out in the cloister at the customary times in the Benedictine horarium. The hours devoted to *lectio* included writing and illumination of the type that made the Winchester school famous, and the main times for this were before Sext and after None. It was one of the duties of the *circa*, the brother appointed to patrol the cloister, to confiscate books which had been left there on his rounds after Compline; these were exhibited next day at Chapter.[1]

The end of the tenth century is marked by the work of at least three distinguished scholars at English houses. The most learned of the Fleury monks, Abbo, taught at the school at Ramsey for two years, and one of his pupils was Byrhtferth, who later became head of the school. He was a mathematician and scientist of a surprising calibre for his age; his classical learning suggests, moreover, that Ramsey possessed no mean library. His best known work is his commentary on Bede's four astronomical and mathematical treatises. The third scholar of this time was Ælfric Grammaticus, pupil and biographer of S. Æthelwold, and abbot probably of Eynsham. He was the author of school books,[2]

---

[1] Dom Thomas Symonds, *Regularis Concordia*, 1953; J. Armitage Robinson, *The Times of S. Dunstan*, 1923.

[2] The school books were a translation of Priscian's grammar, a glossary, and a *Colloquy*; his school, as described in the *Colloquy* seems to have been a Sunday school attended by boys of every sort, free and otherwise. See A. F. Leach, *op. cit.*, pp. 85–90.

including a grammar dedicated to the boys of England, but he is chiefly famous for his homilies and scriptural translations into Anglo-Saxon, and for his slightly unorthodox views on transubstantiation which seem to have been accepted by the English church authorities of his day. These naturally caught the attention of Archbishop Parker in post-Reformation times, and Ælfric's *Paschal Homily* was indeed one of the first productions in the series of Anglo-Saxon works printed for him by John Day to strengthen the case for the continuity of Ecclesia Anglicana. Ælfric's homilies were compiled and rendered into English for the benefit of the many who in the eleventh century found Latin unintelligible; there was little gospel light, Ælfric explained, for any except such as could read Latin, save what was contained in King Alfred's translations. It is important to note that some of Ælfric's works, especially the lives of the saints and translations from the Bible, were definitely written for laymen. This was a period of rapid monastic extension, and we can infer that laymen as well as clerics were in some degree being educated at the monastic schools. The abbots of as many as eighteen English houses are known to have attended Æthelred's court towards the end of the tenth century. Most of these were in the south and east; in the north there were none at all. S. Wilfrid's house at Ripon had failed, and even by 1066 there were no monasteries north of Crowland and Burton on Trent.

In the eleventh century England drew still closer to the continent; the Norman Conquest indeed began many years before 1066. The stream of pilgrims to Rome was increasing, and as has been mentioned, Cnut himself journeyed there in 1027, partly to attend the coronation of the Holy Roman Emperor, and partly to ensure greater security for the humbler pilgrims. On his way he distributed rich gifts to the monasteries he passed. These may well have included English service books, for several are known to have been sent abroad at this time: benedictionaries from Ramsey and the New Minister went to Fleury and Rouen, and a Peterborough sacramentary went to Cologne, whence it was later brought back by Ealdred, Bishop of Winchester.

At the time of the Conquest there were about sixty religious houses in England, all independent and all following the Benedictine rule.[1] Many were clustered round the Severn valley, where scholarly traditions had been preserved since Alfred's day, and where S. Wulfstan was now bishop at Worcester. The monasteries of Normandy, which at this time were at the height of their fame and prosperity, supplied many abbots and bishops to the English church. The foundation of the first houses in the north, however, was due to the efforts of two English monks who set out from the abbey of Evesham, with their vestments and their library carried on the back of an ass. Whitby was restored, and the new house of S. Mary at York was opened about 1078. Jarrow and Wearmouth were reopened, and with the help of monks from these two houses, a monastic community was re-established at Durham under the Norman bishop William de St Carilef, who also built a great part of the cathedral. He gave many books to the monastic library, and its first fragmentary catalogue is written on the first folio of a Bible which was one of his gifts.

The greatest of the Norman religious leaders was, however, Lanfranc. Greek influences from Constantinople were now strongly making themselves felt, and in Italy there was increasing contact with the Greek world; Greek as well as Latin was being used in the services at S. Peter's in Rome. Both Lanfranc and his successor Anselm had felt the impact of this new influence, and had at least some knowledge of the Greek language. Lanfranc was a lawyer from Pavia who, impressed by the contrast between his secular learning and his religious ignorance, entered the Norman house of Bec, where he in due course became prior and head of the Abbey school. In 1070 William brought him to Canterbury as his right-hand man in the building of the new nation and the new national church. At Canterbury he compiled the *Monastic Constitutions* which bear his name, primarily for the community of his Cathedral of Christ Church, but they served also as a general guide to English Benedictine practice. They were based in part on the Customs of Cluny as revised in 1067, and they thus replaced the *Regularis Concordia* of S. Dunstan's time. They give a complete and detailed picture of English monastic life at the beginning of the great Benedictine period.

[1] Dom David Knowles gives the number of large religious houses in England in 1066 as 52, including 12 nunneries. At the end of the previous century the total was 37, including 7 nunneries. See his chapter in *Medieval England*, ed. A. L. Poole, 1958, vol. II, p. 400.

The careful directions for the annual redistribution of books on the first Monday of Lent have often been quoted. This took place in Chapter, and the librarian (*armarius* in Bernard of Cluny, *custos librorum* in Lanfranc) is instructed to have all the books, other than those issued the previous year, arranged on the carpet. The proceedings begin with the reading of the passage in the rule regarding the observance of Lent, and a sermon, after which the librarian reads out the list of books issued to the brethren the previous year. Each brother on hearing his name returns his book, and if he is conscious that he has not read the book in full, he confesses his fault prostrate and asks for pardon. Then a new distribution of books is made and a new list compiled. These directions have been cited as revealing the narrow compass of the monastic library if all the books could be assembled on a carpet, and the limited part it played in the daily life of the brethren. It seems clear, however, from Bernard of Cluny that the books on the carpet were a deliberate selection, corresponding to the number of the brethren. One such list has survived, containing sixty-four titles and the names of the recipients. Most of the volumes were long treatises, such as S. Augustine's *De Trinitate*, Isidore's *Etymologiae* and Eusebius's *Historia Ecclesiastica*. The choice was, however, adjusted to the recipient's abilities, and Brother Henry received the Book of Kings, and Stephen (who perhaps found reading difficult) was merely handed his own psalter.[1] It should not be imagined that this annual distribution comprised all the study carried out by the brethren. Those engaged on special tasks would have access to the library as often as might be necessary.

The care of the library was usually placed in the hands of the Cantor or the Precentor, who was also responsible for the service books used in the church, for the archives of the house, its registers and necrology and for the official seal. Lanfranc, describing the duties of the Cantor, notes that he has charge of all the books of the house, and has them in his keeping, if his interests and learning are such as to fit him for this task. As a result the Precentor often developed into the annalist or chronicler; Eadmer,

---

[1] Dom David Knowles, *The Monastic Constitutions of Lanfranc*, 1951, pp. 19, 150; *Monastic Order in England*, p. 522. Dom Bruno Albers, *Consuetudines Monasticae*, I, pp. 185–6. R. W. Southern, *The Making of the Middle Ages*, p. 189.

IN SAXON ENGLAND

Symeon of Durham and William of Malmesbury are examples.[1]

The monastic horarium in Lanfranc's period assigned about five periods each day, both in the summer and winter timetable, to study, talk and other tasks in the cloisters, the main period for reading being in the afternoon. There would also be reading aloud in the refectory, and during tasks in the cloisters. The only reference which Lanfranc makes to manual labour directs the Cantor to arrange for such reading during tasks, either by himself or by one of the children; by the eleventh century, all laborious work had been passed over to the servants of the house.

This, then, is briefly the stage which the monastic library reached in the greater English houses at the beginning of the Norman period. The important period of the chroniclers was still to come. Though the inspiration for reform and reorganization came largely from France and Normandy, the foundations had been laid in earlier centuries by S. Columba and Bede and Alfred and S. Dunstan; and the Anglo-Saxon traditions of the English houses survived far into the Norman period. The libraries and scriptoria of the Benedictine houses of later days played their part in preserving, re-copying, and transmitting to future generations, not only the texts of classical paganism,[2] but the great works of Anglo-Saxon history, biography and theology which the Elizabethan antiquarians so anxiously strove to reassemble from the wreckage of the suppressed monasteries.

The story of Anglo-Saxon libraries may conclude with the mention of two quite new forms of literary record at the beginning of the Norman period. The first is the Bayeux tapestry, which is in effect a contemporary pictorial chronicle or strip cartoon of the conquest, with occasional Latin captions such as *Hic Harold Rex interfectus est*.[3] The second, and more important, is the Domesday Book of 1086, a national economic survey which was unique for its time. It forms a prelude to the long series of English charter, patent and close rolls; no comparable survey was attempted till the Hundred Rolls of Edward I. The clerical work involved in the

---

[1] At the Norman secular cathedrals the schoolmaster (later termed the chancellor) might also be the librarian. This was the case at S. Paul's, *c.* 1111. A. F. Leach, *op. cit.*, p. 110.

[2] The golden age of monastic classical studies was 1150–1200. Interest in classical texts declined when the recruitment of children ceased, after which little fresh copying was done. See Knowles, *Religious Orders in England*, 1955 II, p. 338.

[3] See *The Bayeux Tapestry*, ed. by Sir Frank Stenton, 1957.

tabulation and analysis of the returns is a tribute to the efficiency of the French civil service which was responsible for its production, and it has been said that the work was as competent and accurate as that of any modern government department working with all the apparatus of card indexes and typewriters.[1] The survey was preserved in the Treasury at Winchester, which thus replaced Glastonbury as the national record office.

[1] Lady Stenton, *English Society in the Early Middle Ages*, 1951, p. 63.

CHAPTER VII

Colonnade and Cloister

No man who studies the history of classical and medieval libraries can fail to notice the fact that in both periods the colonnade or cloister forms a conspicuous feature of their architecture. Two questions arise at once: what was the purpose of this special feature that so recommended itself to librarians over so long a period? And was the monastic cloister directly descended from the classical colonnade?

Let us first of all record the facts. The typical institutional library of classical times appears to have consisted of a series of store-rooms fitted with either pigeon-holes or cupboards in which the rolls were kept, and a range of covered walks where they were consulted by readers. It was not usual for books to be both stored and read in the same room, but we have no knowledge of how the reader obtained the books from the store. Nor do we know what steps were taken to prevent books being taken away from the library. This was indeed usually prohibited; an inscription found at Trajan's library in Athens explicitly forbids it,[1] though the colonnade system may well have made the rule difficult to enforce. A letter from Marcus Aurelius to his tutor, Fronto, suggests that it was necessary to lubricate the wheels in order to get books out of the Palace Library of Tiberius.[2] The story recorded by Aulus Gellius about a book which was obtained from the library at Tibur[3] is of little help, because the incident may have taken place within the temple precincts.

The earliest example of such a colonnade was at Aristotle's Lyceum in Athens, founded about 335 BC, where it formed so striking a feature of the college that his school of philosophy (the Peripatetics) took their name from it. It was from the library at the

---

[1] *Hesperia*, 1936. 5. 41-2.
[2] Fronto, *Ad M. Caes.* 4. 5.
[3] Aulus Gellius, 19.5.

Lyceum that Demetrius of Phalerum drew his inspiration for the great library at Alexandria. Demetrius was himself an old student of the Peripatetic school. While governor of Athens (318–07 BC) he had helped Theophrastus to purchase an estate for the school and to endow it; and when a few years later he arrived in Alexandria, his head was full of ideas as to how a philosopher-king could organize the scholarship and learning of his kingdom. The result was the famous Museum and Library, with its colonnade and its seats and its great refectory for the research fellows.[1] When, fifty years later, Ptolemy III founded the Serapeum with its 'daughter library' (as Epiphanius termed it[2]), the great colonnaded court of the temple of Serapis and Isis had the temple proper at its northern end, and the library at the southern end under a vast marble staircase. The library rooms were built in a trench cut from the rock, and were heated by a hot air furnace; we may guess, therefore, that these were store-rooms, and that the colonnades were used for reading.[3]

The library at Pergamum was for long famed as the rival of the Alexandrian library. In fact it was probably not fully established till the time of Eumenes II, a clear century after the foundation of Ptolemy's Museum. The surviving remains suggest that the court of the temple of Athena had on its northern and eastern sides a two-storied cloister, and that the upper story of the cloister led to four rooms used by the library.[4] These from their small size (the largest had space for less than 20,000 rolls) must have been little but store-rooms, though one contained a statue of Athena and a series of plaques inscribed with the names of great writers, belonging possibly to the portrait busts which often ornamented classical libraries. They can, therefore, have formed only a fraction of the storage accommodation needed by any rival to the Alexandrian Museum.

The temple and library were still new when in 168 BC, Crates of Mallos, the head of the Pergamene School, visited Rome, and when the Macedonian Royal Library was brought back to Rome after the battle of Pydna. At Rome, the Octavian Library was

---

[1] Strabo, 17. 1. 8.
[2] Epiphanius, *De Pond. et Mens.*, 9–10.
[3] Alan Rowe and E. Drioton, *Discovery of the Famous Temple and Enclosure of Serapis*. (Supplément aux Annales du Service des Antiquités, Cahier 2.) Cairo, 1946; *J. Hellenic Studies*, 1945. 65. 106–9.
[4] Hansen, *The Attalids of Pergamum*, 1947; J. W. Clark, *The Care of Books*, 1901.

adapted by Augustus from a temple built by Quintus Metellus, who had fought at Pydna and may well have known the Pergamene temple. All the Roman temple libraries of which we have any knowledge were equipped with colonnades. The siting of the Greek and Latin department of the Octavian Library, close to the colonnaded temple court, is clearly described by Clark.[1] The Palatine Library, also founded by Augustus, followed a very similar plan. The Ulpian Library repeated the same general arrangement. This library survived well into Christian days, and as late as AD 455, Sidonius Apollinaris, Bishop of Auvergne, describes how his own statue was erected in the Ulpian portico between the Greek and Latin libraries.[2] Both these departments were small, measuring only 60 by 45 ft., which again indicates that they must have been mainly storage rooms. Nevertheless, it is evident that the public had direct access to them, for a reference in the *Historia Augusta*[3] directs attention to a particular volume bound in ivory in the sixth press (*in Bibliotheca Ulpia in armario sexto librum elephantinum*).

Let us turn now to monastic days. The typical conventual plan of the Benedictine period provides for a great church, with the subsidiary buildings ranged round a cloister garth at one side of it. In England the cloisters would usually be on the south of the church, which to some extent sheltered them from the weather. Along the eastern walk of the cloister garth, the south transept of the church would lead to the vestry, chapter house and parlour, and this protected corner of the cloisters would be used for library purposes. The books (other than those needed for special purposes in the church, refectory and school) were housed either in presses in the cloister itself, or in a small store-room opening off it. In a few cases, some of the arched bays of the cloister were fitted with carrels for individual study. The individual cells in the Dortor were in some houses equipped with a reading desk under the window, where at least some private study was carried out; and in the fifteenth century, special library rooms were installed at Durham, St Albans, and Canterbury. These were, however, comparatively late developments, and throughout the Benedictine period the cloister remained the normal place for teaching and reading. In

---

[1] J. W. Clark, *The Care of Books*, 1901, p. 13.
[2] Sid. Apoll., *Ep.* 9. 16; *Carm.*, 8. 7.
[3] Vopiscus, *Tacitus*, 8. 1.

a very real sense it was the heart and centre of the life of the whole monastery. Here took place all the communal activities of the house: not merely reading and writing, but the internal administration of the community, the instruction of the novices and much of the permitted conversation and recreation. Indeed, the words 'cloister' and 'religious life' are often interchangeable. And to the medieval mind, the term 'cloister' suggested inevitably 'books': *claustrum sine armario est quasi castrum sine armentario.*

Is it possible then that the monastic cloister was a lineal descendant of the classical colonnade? No certain answer can be given, but it is improbable that there was any conscious imitation of classical models in the design of the monastic cloister. It is more likely that the same circumstances and the same needs chanced to produce similar results.

It is important to remember that the colonnade was a prominent architectural feature of almost all classical buildings of any size. It is very commonly associated with temples and basilicas, either as an internal or external feature, and its use for temple libraries (as at Alexandria and Pergamum) may well have been accidental in origin. It is common again in all collegiate or corporate buildings such as the Atrium Vestae in Rome, the police barracks at Ostia and at the garrison headquarters of permanent military stations. It appears also in the atrium and peristyle of the larger Roman villas; and it may be noted that while the private villa library would be kept in a small store-room, a sheltered corner of the colonnade would normally be used for reading. There were quite obvious reasons for the popularity of this form of architecture. No other method gives such welcome shelter from hot sun and cold wind. Nor is the plan found only in classical buildings. The Great Mosque at Mecca, for example, is an open courtyard surrounded by four walls, each 180 feet long, with an arched colonnade down each side and a canvas extension o give extra protection for the crowds; the shrine, sanctuary and granite pulpit stand in the centre of the courtyard. Gibbon surely did not understand the reason for this feature when he expressed himself as shocked by the windowless rooms of Diocletian's palace, which he described as 'repugnant to our modern notions of taste and conveniency'.[1]

Both Greeks and Romans were intensely social in all they did.

---
[1] *Decline and Fall*, Ch. XIII.

They were never so happy as when walking and talking with their friends, and they lived in a genial climate where for a great part of the year it was pleasanter outdoors than in closed rooms. They rarely spent long hours in solitary study. There were indeed few, if any, scholar-recluses among them. Although they all knew their country's literature perhaps better than we know ours, their study of philosophy and rhetoric (which made up the normal academic curriculum) was a matter of lectures and debate rather than private reading.

Nevertheless, protection both from the weather and from intruders was needed. Although glazed windows were in use in Roman times, they were never large enough to light a hall of any size. Nor would the lamps in common use have been of much value for reading in a large and probably dark hall. These facts alone would have made the provision of anything like the British Museum Reading Room out of the question in classical times. Trajan's library at Athens (the only institution where we know the times of opening) was open in daylight only, from the first hour to the sixth, that is, from dawn to midday.

If, therefore, protection, security, privacy and light were required, what was more natural than to turn the eyes of the house inwards, presenting blind walls to the outer world, and enclosing a colonnaded courtyard sheltered from wind and rain, and warmed and lit by the sun at least on two sides. Even in northern climes, or in the Roman winter, the sunny side of the court would often be warm enough for strolling, and light enough for reading. The courtyard plan, with covered ways, gave easy access from one point to another, and easy defence against enemies. This basic plan is met with wherever the Romans penetrated. The Romano-British villas show either this courtyard plan, or alternatively, a corridor plan with a verandah. The courtyard system has such obvious advantages that it was adapted for many types of buildings in the middle ages and in more recent days. It can often be seen in the medieval fortified manor house, in the colleges at Oxford and Cambridge (which in some cases were directly adapted from monastic buildings), in many large Renaissance mansions such as Sir Thomas Gresham's first Royal Exchange, and in the large farmhouse with its outbuildings grouped round a central yard. Indeed, this general arrangement of farm buildings has persisted with little interruption from the time of the Romano-British villa-farm to the present day, though the covered ways may be missing or only present in part, in the form of open sheds. The continuity of the courtyard pattern in farmhouses is revealed clearly by two illustrations given by M. S. Briggs in his *English Farmhouse* (1953), first of a reconstruction of the Roman villa at Chedworth, near Cirencester, showing its colonnades, and second, of the large moated farmhouse of Markenfield Hall, near Ripon, built between 1310 and the sixteenth century.[1]

The 'rows' at Chester and perhaps some other medieval towns were intended not, of course, for readers of books, but to shelter promenaders and shoppers. Lydgate, in *The Troy Book*, called them 'alures' and 'deambulatories'.[2] Though they occur at Chester, they are medieval, not Roman. But Roman shops did, in fact, take advantage of the colonnades in much the same way. Martial writes of a bookshop in the Argiletum where the pillars were plastered with advertisements of poetry: *scriptis postibus hinc et inde totis*.[3]

Nevertheless, the links which prove its direct descent from Roman times are missing. The monastic plan was first formulated in Gaul and Italy, but there is nothing to show that it was deliberately based on classical models. We can guess that the designers were familiar with the Roman colonnade and its uses; indeed it must have formed one of the most conspicuous features of the Roman buildings that were still, in early medieval days, thickly scattered over Italy and Southern France. It is indeed probable that the ruins of Roman colonnades were sometimes appropriated for the building of religious houses. This was done, for example, at Cluny, where Odilo was Abbot from 994 to 1049. Odilo is said to have found Cluny wood and left it marble. Roman columns of marble were sought out and brought by water up the Rhône and the Saône to adorn the new cloisters at Cluny.[4] Three centuries earlier, Benedict Biscop had, according to Bede, built his

---

[1] There is a useful discussion of the development of the quadrangular plan in English domestic architecture in A. Hamilton Thompson's chapter on *The English house;* in *Social life in early England,* ed. Geoffrey Barraclough, Historical Association, 1960.

[2] For the structure of the rows at Chester, see *Medieval England*, ed. A. L. Poole, 1958, vol. I, p. 70. Defoe in the *Tour through England and Wales*, had nothing good to say in favour of the rows, considering that they served only to make the city look old and ugly.

[3] *Ep.* I. 117.

[4] R. W. Southern, *The Making of the Middle Ages*, 1953, p. 165.

new foundation of S. Peter's, Wearmouth, 'in the Roman style', using masons and glaziers from Gaul. Benedict had made many journeys to Rome, and was familiar with the Roman architecture of Gaul and Italy. At Wearmouth even the cloisters were glazed: a remarkable fact at so early a date. The passage in which this statement occurs in *The Lives of the Holy Abbots* is, so far as I know, the first reference to cloisters in England. But neither Wearmouth nor Cluny can have known anything of the classical association between libraries and colonnades. There is no reference to it in Isidore, from whom the medieval world derived what little knowledge it possessed regarding classical libraries.

There is the further point about the colonnade and cloister libraries: namely, that they must have been of special advantage in times when all reading and all writing meant reading and writing aloud; a habit which would be intolerable in a closed room occupied by many students. All children as they learn to read, instinctively speak the words aloud; and indeed this is the natural method for all who read only occasionally, or find it a laborious task. Even today, if you watch a man reading silently, you will often see his lips moving, and there is some evidence that the voice muscles tend to move even if the lips are still. Similarly in writing, if the task is unfamiliar, the words are commonly pronounced as the pen moves; much as Sam Weller, struggling to compose his valentine at the Blue Boar, 'formed with his tongue imaginary characters to correspond.' So also Swift, in writing his 'little language', would make up his mouth as if he were speaking, putting on what Austin Dobson describes as 'a kind of grimace, resembling nothing so much as the imitative motion of the lips which one makes in speaking to a pet bird.'[1] It must have been in much the same way that Hannah in the Old Testament (1 Samuel 1.13) moved her lips in anxious but silent prayer, so that Eli thought she must have drunk wine too freely.

In just this way the medieval scribe (and probably also the scribe of classical times) pronounced the words aloud as he wrote. An eighth-century scribe added the following comment to his book: 'Ignorant people regard the scribe's profession as easy. Three fingers are engaged in writing, the two eyes in looking.

---

[1] *Eighteenth Century Vignettes: the Journal to Stella.*

Your tongue pronounces the words and the whole body toils. But all labour comes to an end, and its reward shall have no end.'[1] By way of contrast, Thomas Hoccleve, who was a clerk in the privy seal office early in the fifteenth century, in his well-known description of the scribe's profession,[2] makes no mention of the part played by the tongue. He admits that writing is 'wel gretter labour than it seemeth', but he says that the three things on which the scribe must depend are 'mynde, ee and hand', and that with these members

> ... we laboure in traveillous stillnesse
> We stoupe and stare upon the shepes skyn,
> And keepe must our song and wordes in.

Hoccleve, however, had been at his clerical work for twenty-four years, and had perhaps got past the oral stage of writing. In the same century the Paston Letters show plainly that writing was still a laborious task for the members of a well-to-do family, and there was even greater illiteracy in high places at a later date than this.

As for reading aloud, there is considerable evidence that this was for long a normal habit from which only after long practice could an experienced reader escape. S. Augustine, noting with surprise how S. Ambrose read without sound or movement, exclaimed, 'His eyes were led along the page and his heart sought into the meaning, but his voice and tongue were silent.' The evidence for this widespread habit has been fully discussed by J. Balogh.[3] It is strong enough to convince one that in classical and medieval times a crowded reading room would have been as murmurous as a hive of bees, and ill adapted for profound study. The open air, or at least an open colonnade, would at least have been more tolerable

---

[1] Quoted by Wattenbach, *Das Schriftwesen in Mittelalter*, 1896. I am indebted to Dr G. S. Ivy for this reference.

[2] *De Regimine Principum*.

[3] *Philologus*, 1926. 82. See also H. J. Chaytor, *From Script to Print*, 1945. There are many classical and medieval allusions which suggest this habit. For example, the whole point of Ovid's story in the *Heroides* of Acontius and Cydippe lies in the latter's reading aloud the message written on the apple: 'I swear by Artemis that I will marry Acontius.' (L. P. Wilkinson, *Ovid Recalled*, 1955.) Note that medieval punctuation was intended mainly to guide those reading aloud, rather than to point the grammar of the sentences. The sad effect of faulty punctuation on the reader is illustrated by Quince's prologue in *A Midsummer Night's Dream* (V. 1. 108–17).

in this respect. The familiar library notice requiring silence is a modern invention. That a library might at times become too noisy, however, may be guessed from one of the inscriptions[1] in the library of Isidore, Bishop of Seville, a couplet which may be rendered:

> *Loquacity the studious writer shocks,*
> *And so be gone from here, Sir Chatterbox.*

But this is pointed *ad interventorem*, at the intruder or idle visitor, not at the reader of books.[2]

It may be noted that under Rabbinic law the Jewish scribe, when writing on the parchment scroll for use in the synagogue, is still bound to pronounce aloud every word he intends to write before committing it to the parchment.[3] A similar practice was suggested in the Qurān which Muhammad is said to have transcribed from the heavenly records. Muhammad's call to rise as a prophet in Sura 96 ('Recite thou in the name of the Lord...') may equally mean 'read aloud', which was the normal method of reading. On the other hand dervish ritual in the Naqshabandi order requires the notice to impress on his soul the declaration of his belief in Allah by shutting his eyes and mouth, pressing his tongue against the roof of his mouth, clenching his teeth and holding his breath, while he recites with his heart but not his tongue the words of the *shayk* instructing him.[4]

The modern student may well think that any advantages of the open cloister from this cause would have been counterbalanced by

---

[1] Migne, 83. 1107.

[2] The question of how books were copied by scribes—whether by dictation, which would involve one man reading aloud, or individually from exemplars, which might involve each scribe reading aloud to himself—is a complicated problem. Almost certainly both methods were used. There are a few instances where internal evidence suggests dictation, e.g. the Codex Sinaiticus; this and the Codex Vaticanus may well have been rejected copies from the 50 vellum Bibles prepared for Constantine the Great at Caesarea— an enormous undertaking, done probably in a hurry. The inclusion of officials described as expert readers (*anagnostae optimi*) in addition to a large copying staff (*plurimi librarii*) in the publishing house of Cicero's friend and agent, Atticus (see Cornelius Nepos, *Atticus* 13) does not necessarily imply dictation, as the *anagnostae* may have been employed for proof-reading. Cicero's own staff seems to have included only *librarioli* and *glutinatores* (copyists and binders), and this suggests individual copying. On this whole problem see T. C. Skeat, *The use of dictation in ancient book production* (Proc. of the Brit. Academy, vol. XLII) and Robert Devreesse, *Introduction à l'étude des manuscrits grecs*, 1954.

[3] I am indebted to Miss R. P. Lehmann of the Jews' College Library for this information.

[4] A. Guillaume, *Islam*, 1954, pp. 59, 150.

the discomforts arising from other causes. There are indeed plenty of complaints from scribes of the hardships of writing in the cold of northern winters. Even Sidonius Apollinaris, in the comparative comfort of his villa library, complains of the difficulty of writing in the bitter winters of Gaul, when the ink froze to his pen.[1] The hardships must have been far more acute in the exposed cloisters of a monastery in the bleak and lonely north. It was comparatively late before glazing was possible in the cloister windows (the glazed cloisters at Wearmouth, already noted, were exceptional), and if wooden screens were used, they must have shut out much of the light. Little wonder, however, that at a few houses, such as Gloucester and Durham, the cloisters were partitioned into carrels to mitigate the worst of these difficulties.

The earliest known reference to monastic carrels in England occurs in the Augustinian Chapters, AD 1232. They were indeed a thirteenth-century development, along with the provision of bedside lockers; and they had a marked influence on monastic life by providing places where private, and possibly illicit, property could be kept. The appropriation of carrels by individual monks who kept them locked was the cause of many complaints, and there were frequent episcopal orders that they should be regularly inspected three or four times a year. But properly used (as they doubtless were in general) they must have been a very desirable aid to study.[1]

Let us, therefore, summarize the argument. The architectural problems of building and lighting a large enclosed hall were not adequately solved till Renaissance times. The natural alternative of the open colonnade was successfully adopted in the Mediterranean region for large institutional buildings of every type in classical times, and in medieval times particularly for monastic houses. Such a colonnade proved a convenient and reasonably sheltered meeting place for those whose business took them to the building in question; and where a temple or a religious house had a library, it proved also the most satisfactory place for readers to consult the books and discuss them. There is no proof of any con-

---

[1] Sid. Apoll., *Ep.* 9. 16. 15.
[2] J. R. H. Moorman, *Church Life in England in the Thirteenth Century*, 1945, pp. 328, 341. Moorman, quoting H. E. Salter's *Chapters of the Augustinian Canons*, 1922, corrects the statement by J. W. Clark that the first mention of carrels is at Westminster between 1258 and 1283.

scious imitation by monastic designers of the classical association between colonnades and libraries; but there is abundant evidence that in both periods the covered ways were found useful by readers, and that book store-rooms were placed where they would be easily accessible either from cloister or colonnade.

CHAPTER VIII

The Dispersal

THE great turning point in the history of English libraries occurred in the fourteen years between 1536 and 1550, when the contents of the monastic libraries were scattered to the winds, and when the few remaining libraries were purged of what the Act defined as superstitious books. The losses arising from the Act of 1550 were far greater than in the earlier dispersal; wanton destruction is indeed always a graver matter than the mere neglect to preserve. The forbidden service books were to be seized by officials in each district, and surrendered to the diocesan 'to be immediately burnt or otherways defaced and destroyed.'

The volumes in the Royal Library were ordered to be stripped of their garniture of gold or silver, and much that was more precious than silver or gold perished in the destruction that followed. At Oxford, Duke Humphrey's library closed its doors, and at Cambridge the losses were equally disastrous. The destruction at the Guildhall was complete. Stow in his *Survey* tells us what happened: 'Adjoining to this chapel [of S. Mary Magdalen, near unto the Guildhall] on the south side, was sometime a fair and large library, furnished with books, pertaining to the Guildhall and college [i.e., the College of our Lady, Mary Magdalen and All Saints, called London College]. These books, as it is said, were in the reign of Edward VI sent for by Edward, Duke of Somerset, lord protector, with promise to be restored: men laded from thence three carries[1] with them, but they were never returned. This

---

[1] Carry = cart or two-wheeled barrow. At the most, three carts would contain 900 volumes. A Durham chronicler estimated that Richard de Bury's library would have filled five carts, i.e., perhaps 1500 volumes. The library of a rural dean of Worcester in the thirteenth century, which was impounded at a tollgate, was in two carts (Moorman, *English Church Life in the Thirteenth Century*, 1945, p. 99n.). On the other hand, when in the last century the Phillipps library was removed to Thirlestaine House, Cheltenham, well over 100 wagon loads were needed.

library was built by the executors of Richard Whittington, and by William Burie: the arms of Whittington are placed on one side in the stone work, and two letters, to wit, W. and B., for William Bury, on the other side: it is now lofted through, and made a storehouse for clothes.' At Eton the losses were less severe, and are ascribed to disuse rather than destruction, but only 60 or 70 out of perhaps 500 MSS in the library in 1535 have survived.[1]

The value of the books that perished can be guessed from the quality of the few volumes that survived, having been either hidden away in safety by the faithful or sent abroad: volumes such as the Lindisfarne Gospels, the Golden Gospels, the Luttrell Psalter and others which for us today are some of the chief remaining glories of medieval art. The number of service books destroyed at this time has been put at a quarter of a million: a guess, no doubt, but it indicates the scale of the destruction. One result of this is the dearth, as Cardinal Gasquet pointed out, of English Church music books of the period. 'That the choral schools were in full swing at the time of the destruction cannot be doubted. And yet practically nothing is known of the compositions of later English musicians or their works, so complete has been the destruction of this manuscript music.'[2]

The dispersal of the monastic libraries took place in 1536–40.[3] Though the losses were great, much of their contents was not beyond recovery. The muniments passed to the Crown, and afterwards to the purchasers of the monastic property. The service books were abandoned, except where an abbey church became a cathedral or parish church, in which case they probably survived till 1550. Less is known of the fate of the libraries, but it is certain

---

[1] R. Birley, 'The History of Eton College Library.' *The Library*, 1956, pp. 231–61.

[2] Gasquet, *Henry VIII and the English Monasteries*, 7th ed. 1920, p. 418. Dom David Knowles studies the monastic contribution to the history of English music, especially in the period between John Dunstable (d. 1453) and the suppression, in *The Religious Orders in England*, vol. III, 1959, pp. 15–21.

[3] On the general subject of this chapter see especially Dom David Knowles, *The Religious Orders in England*, vol. III, 1959, and Dr C. E. Wright's two important chapters on the Dispersal, and on the Elizabethan Society of Antiquaries and the formation of the Cottonian Library, in *The English Library before 1700*, ed. Wormald and Wright, 1958. On monastic libraries in general see Knowles, *op. cit.*, vol. II, and Wormald and Wright, *op. cit.*, ch. II. The development and significance of these libraries is discussed in *The Heritage*, ch. VIII–X. For their contents see Wormald and Wright, ch. V and VII, and Neil Ker, *Medieval Libraries of Great Britain*, 2nd ed., 1964.

that many of the abbots and priors transferred to the cathedral posts or livings which they received in compensation, or to the manors they had secured in anticipation of the suppression, some of the monastic books, plate and vestments. Many books on the other hand were sold as waste paper; many were exported; many were abandoned, and used by the new owners of the property for binding account books and estate papers. Within a very few years, however, the re-collection of the dispersed books began; by the end of the century it was in full swing under the guidance of the Elizabethan antiquarians; and a substantial number of the books are now in our national libraries. Much research has been done on this aspect of the dispersal, but there is a rich field here for further study.'

The librarian who is interested in the fate of the dispersed volumes cannot help but be interested also in the causes that lay behind the dispersal. It was so sudden and so overwhelming a tragedy that it seems to require more explanation than is often given to it in the general histories. It was, of course, a comparatively minor incident in a great social change, and as such receives but little attention even in special studies such as Philip Hughes' *The Reformation in England* or Geoffrey Baskerville's *English Monks and the Suppression in the Monasteries.*

Henry's need for money, and the greed of his servants for land and power, account in part at least for the events of 1536–40. Indifference, rather than ignorance, may explain why most of the monastic books were cast aside and abandoned; Cromwell's Commissioners may have been blind, but they were neither ignorant nor uneducated. The positive destruction of 1550 was however an act of deliberate policy; there was no indifference here. The books of the old faith were replaced by those of the new, but the change was more radical and more comprehensive than this. Anthony à Wood noted that the burning of the books in 1550 was carried out to the sorrow of many as well of the Protestants as of the other party. C. S. Lewis describes the great purge as the climax of the battle between the humanists and scholasticism, adding that the conflict cut right across the divisions of religion. 'Men of the old religion, if they were humanists, might despise scholasticism; men of the new, if they were philosophers, might revere it. Thus we find Hooker strongly impregnated with Thomism, and More and

Erasmus among the mockers of the schoolmen.'[1] The impact of humanism on English thought, together with the coming of the printed book, meant inevitably that the old libraries seemed useless and out of date. This feeling had been gathering force for a century. Poggio, writing about 1422 from England, complained that he could find no good books here, and even fewer scholars; the convents (he said) were full of books of modern doctors that are not worth hearing, with very few works of the ancients. In 1497 Erasmus drew a very different picture of Oxford. 'There is so much erudition, not vulgar, but recondite, accurate, ancient, both Latin and Greek, that you would not seek anything in Italy but the pleasure of travelling.' But Erasmus was describing, not the monastic collections, but the university libraries, enriched by fifty years' intensive collecting in Italy on the part of the fifteenth-century humanists—the good Duke Humphrey, John Tiptoft, Earl of Worcester, William Gray, Bishop of Ely, Robert Flemmyng, Dean of Lincoln, and many others. In 1514 Corpus Christi College with its beautiful library was founded. This was the first of the academic foundations of the English Renaissance, and its library drew high praise from Erasmus, who said that its Trilinguis Bibliotheca would draw more students to Oxford than in old times had been attracted to Rome. But it was not to be a peaceful revolution. The enemies of scholasticism, combining with the enemies of the old faith, were too powerful, and the end was violent and indiscriminate. Five years after the purge, in 1555-56, the empty shelves and stalls of Duke Humphrey's library were sold by the University. Four years more, and Thomas Bodley had entered Magdalen College.[2]

There are always men ready to plunder and destroy. But no revolution succeeds unless the ground has been prepared and the nation as a whole is willing to accept the change. The old faith was

---

[1] C. S. Lewis, *English Literature in the Sixteenth Century*, 1954, p. 31. The critique of humanism in the introduction to this book can be balanced by a study of R. R. Bolgar, *The Classical Heritage*, 1954.

[2] See Knowles, *The Religious Orders in England*, vol. III, 1959, pp. 141-56, for a valuable assessment of the standpoint and influence of Erasmus. So far as we know, he was to the end a practising Catholic, though with a 'modernist' outlook. Criticism of the monastic system was already part of the mental climate of educated Europe, well before Luther launched his attack; and nothing had a stronger influence in forming this mental climate than the consistent and caustic writings of Erasmus which had been circulating throughout Europe since the beginning of the sixteenth century.

still supreme when the religious houses were suppressed. How was it that men acquiesced in the sudden ending of something that had been an intimate part of their religious life for five centuries? The daily work of the monastic houses, their almsgiving, their prayers, their social and educational services were profound realities to the ordinary man; yet all were swept away in four years with scarcely a protest from the laity beyond the unhappy Pilgrimage of Grace. How did this come about?

This question is obviously important to the historian of our libraries. To answer it fully would require a whole volume, but some points are worth noting briefly here.

The end had indeed been foreseen by many people for long enough. The monastic movement as a whole had lost its early vitality. Many of the houses were badly administered and gravely in debt.[1] Many were big landowners with the impersonality of all great corporations, and with a reputation for squeezing their tenants; even in More's *Utopia*, the Abbot is instanced as the type of the bad landlord.[2] The flow of endowments had been largely diverted during the past century to the foundation of chantries and schools; there were over 2,000 chantry chapels at the time of the dissolution. The population of the religious houses had dropped from 10,000 in the thirteenth century to 7,000 in 1536.[3] Anti-clericalism and anti-monasticism had been growing steadily for two centuries, and both could coincide with a genuine devotion to the orthodox faith. The Robin Hood of the popular ballads had no respect for bishops or fat abbots, but he had his own chaplain in Friar Tuck. The devout and pious peasant was often capable of raiding and sacking a rich monastery such as S. Edmundsbury.

The actual suppression of monasteries was far from being a new idea in 1536. Proposals for the dissolution of foreign houses had been made by the Commons in 1380, and again in 1410 the disendowment of the Church and the transfer of Church revenues to the landed nobility was suggested. The endowments had been

---

[1] It is probable that fewer houses were in any serious financial difficulty, and their administration was on the whole more efficient, than has often been supposed. See Knowles, *The Religious Orders in England*, vol. III, 1959, pp. 241-59.

[2] Dr Coulton (*Medieval Village*, p. 142) judged the monks to have been slightly better landlords than the laymen.

[3] This is Trevelyan's estimate. Dom David Knowles however computes that the number of religious at the end of Henry VII's reign was about 12,000—higher than at any time since 1348.

THE DISPERSAL

originally given by the nobility, and it was supposed that the nobles had every right to reclaim them if the Church misused its wealth. Actual suppressions were by no means uncommon. In 1312, the Order of Templars was suppressed by statute, and its property transferred to the Knights Hospitallers; in the absence of this transfer, the lands would have reverted to the various lords of the fees. In 1411 the small priories belonging to French houses were closed; some of their endowments went to the new Carthusian foundations, though most were used for new colleges and schools, such as Eton, Winchester, King's College, Cambridge, and All Souls College, Oxford.[1] During the fifteenth century there were many individual suppressions, particularly of small Augustinian priories and of nunneries which had become almost emptied of their inmates. The nunneries suffered much more from depopulation and poverty than the monasteries, and as many as eight were dissolved between 1500 and 1527.[2] At Cambridge for example, in 1496 the nunnery of S. Rhadegund, which then had only two nuns in residence, was dissolved, making way for the new foundation of Jesus College. Two nunneries were suppressed to aid the foundation of S. John's College, Cambridge. Twenty houses were with Papal authority suppressed to make possible Wolsey's Cardinal College at Oxford, besides some others intended for the endowment of his projected school at Ipswich. Trinity College, Cambridge, was largely endowed with abbey lands, and its endowments from monastic sources were indeed extended by Mary.[3]

The diversion of monastic revenues to educational foundations was thus an accepted policy in orthodox quarters. When Bishop Foxe in 1514 (over twenty years before the dissolution) was

[1] John Selden (1584–1654) noted in his *Table Talk* that Henry the Fifth put away the Friars aliens and seized to himself 100,000 l. a year; and therefore they were not the Protestants only that took away Church lands.

[2] Dickinson, J. C., in *Medieval Studies presented to Rose Graham*, 1950; Eileen Power, *Medieval English Nunneries*, 1922.

[3] For suppressions in the fifteenth century see Knowles, *The Religious Orders in England*, vol. III, 1959, pp. 13–14, and also p. 200 (the Austin canons at Christ Church Priory, London, 1532), and for European precedents, pp. 165–72. The suppression of religious communities in Switzerland which took place from 1524 to 1530 was well known in England. There is not the same certainty that the English government was familiar with events in Denmark and Sweden, where the suppressions were mainly directed by economic motives, and might have formed a useful object lesson to Henry VIII. For later Continental suppressions see p. 141 *infra*. As regards Wolsey's suppressions, there is a list of these in Knowles, *op. cit.*, Appendix II. There were 22 in 1524–5 and 8 in 1527–8, though one of the latter did not take effect while Wolsey was in power.

E

founding Corpus Christi College at Oxford, Bishop Oldham of Exeter, sensing even at that distance the shadow of the coming tragedy, warned him not to make it a monastic house 'whose end and fall we may live to see. No, no (he said) it is more meet a great deal that we should have care to provide for the increase of learning, and for such as who by their learning shall do good in the Church and Commonwealth'. Even Cardinal Pole declared that except for the Bridgettine nuns, the Carthusian monks and the Observant friars, the Orders were utterly degenerate, and that a completely fresh start should be made,[1] Bishop Latimer, on the other hand, was in favour of two or three houses remaining in each diocese, and the wealth of the remainder being devoted to education and charity. Henry himself had much the same good intentions. There exists a preamble to a projected Act, written by Henry himself, in which it is proposed to assign the monastic revenues to the establishment of schools, almshouses and new episcopal sees; the Act was, however, withdrawn before the suppression occurred. The preamble to the Act suppressing the chantries also used fine language about the devotion of their endowments to schools and hospitals, but little of this was in fact carried out. John Knox had similar plans in Scotland, but (as Scott describes in *The Abbot*) both Morton and the Regent Murray scoffed at his vain dream; they had no wish to set up 'new hives to sing the old drone.'[2]

The educational work of the monasteries themselves had been severely restricted since the thirteenth century, when the new universities took over the responsibility for higher education. The two great orders of friars, the Franciscans and the Dominicans, concentrated their teaching at the universities. Both the Cistercians and the Benedictines were constrained in self-defence to maintain their academic 'nurseries', but few of them profited in any degree from this chance of an Oxford education, and still fewer made any notable contribution to academic work. There were exceptions such as the Benedictine humanist and book-collector William

[1] Pole was one of the subscribers to the report, *Consilium de emendanda ecclesia*, made in 1537 by the papal commission of reform to the Pope, which recommended the gradual extinction of the conventual orders in Italy, and a prohibition on the future admission of novices. This report, which came too late to influence English policy, was rendered sterile by vested interests. See Knowles, *The Religious Orders in England*, vol. III, 1959, p. 171.

[2] The detailed scheme for school and university teaching which Knox outlined in *The Book of Discipline* makes no reference to libraries, although his quite enlightened curriculum would certainly have required them.

Celling, who became prior of Christ Church, Canterbury, and Richard Reynolds, the Cambridge scholar who was head of the monks of Syon and was martyred by Herny. On the other side, however, there is only too much evidence of unlettered ignorance in English religious houses of the period. In the twelfth century, for example, many a scholarly monk not only knew his Ovid and his Virgil, but was a master of three languages. Abbot Samson, as Jocelyn of Brakelond tells us, was fluent in Latin and French and could preach an eloquent sermon in the Norfolk dialect. And there is no better mental discipline than a knowledge of languages, as the Romans found when they welcomed Greek as their second tongue. Such accomplishments must have been very rare in the houses that Henry suppressed. It had indeed been plain to many for long enough that the momentum of the monastic system in England was running down. If the spiritual value of the monasteries was still a reality to the faithful (and who can doubt this?) yet academically their inspiration had died and their function had passed into other hands.

The brilliant success of the Grey Friars at Oxford was confined to the first hundred years of their existence. Their fall from grace was rapid; within a century they had forsaken their founder's ideals. Chaucer's friar was no advertisement for his order, and in most people's eyes they came to be classed with rogues and vagabonds. Curiously, one of the reasons for their fall (and there were many) was the influence of Grosseteste, who was determined to add scholarship to their evangelism. Under his inspiration Oxford produced a succession of Franciscan scholars with a European reputation. But this was in a sense the undoing of the Grey Friars, for an intellectual life implies the security of settled houses, leisure for study, and the possession of great libraries; Grosseteste himself bequeathed his own library to the Oxford Franciscans. S. Francis had tried to guard against the failings of the monastic system. But in a few years the Grey Friars were gathering property and wealth, building a new monastic system of their own, and becoming, like the Dominicans, a learned order; so that Brother Giles was led to cry 'Paris, Paris' (he might equally have said 'Oxford, Oxford'), 'Thou has destroyed Assisi.' In the last half of the thirteenth century the flow of gifts to monasteries was largely diverted to the friars; but by Chaucer's time their reputation was gone, and gifts were being transferred to chantries and schools;[1] that good friars still existed however may be seen from *The Book of Margery Kempe*.[2]

Criticism of the monastic system was becoming outspoken even before the arrival of the friars. It can be found, for example, *c.* 1200, in Giraldus Cambrensis, and in the *De Nugis Curialium* of his contemporary Walter Map. The Cistercians were Walter Map's pet aversion, partly owing to a dispute with them over the rights of his church at Westbury. Giraldus says that Map always excepted the Jews and the Cistercians from his oath to do justice to all men, since it was absurd to do justice to those who were just to none. This was over a century before Boccaccio was fulminating against the Italian, and Richard de Bury against the English, houses for their neglect of learning. The monks, said Richard, were busying themselves in emptying cups rather than in correcting codices, and attending to their sheep and corn and gardens rather than their studies. And Grosseteste did not mince his words about monastic abuses such as the appropriation of benefices. Another hundred years passed, and Thomas Gascoigne, the Chancellor of Oxford University, was writing, 'In olde days the kings had in the monasteries they founded excellent writers of the books of great doctors and of chronicles; but now alas in our monasteries more books are spoiled and perish than those which are written afresh.'[3]

At many houses the once famous scriptoria had become idle. Monastic accounts often show the trifling sums spent on parchment annually. At Abingdon and Norwich over a period of fifty years the amount averaged only fourpence a year, and even this was for account books, whilst the accounts themselves were drawn up by professional scribes. Gradually indeed all the famous monastic crafts were being taken over by independent craftsmen or by London firms. The copying of MSS and the binding of books was being entrusted to professional scriveners and binders; the painting of miniatures for books, the carving and gilding of figures and can-

---

[1] On Grosseteste and the Franciscans see *Heritage*, ch. IX and references there quoted.
[2] Knowles, *The Religious Orders in England*, 1955, II, pp. 198–202.
[3] Many other illustrations could be given of medieval attacks on the monastic system, e.g. the satire by Nigel Wirecker, *Speculum Stultorum*, narrating the adventures of the ass Brunellus, written towards the end of the twelfth century, and the French satire "*The Order of Fair Ease*" at the end of the thirteenth century.

opies, the making of the *opus Anglicanum* (the famous embroidery produced by English nunneries) and many other crafts were handed over to outsiders. Thus William More, who was Prior of Worcester 1518-35, ordered his vestments, goblets, carpets and books (including a complete set of S. Augustine) from London shops, and engaged a Worcester firm to gild and paint the figures in one of his chapels.

The climax of monastic culture had come with the chronicles in the twelfth and thirteenth centuries, especially in the great period when Henry II was ruling from Scotland to the Pyrenees. These were indeed their main contribution to scholarship, apart from their somewhat precarious preservation of the Latin classics. The age of the chronicles probably reached its peak with William of Malmesbury, the librarian of the famous Wiltshire house which even in his day had four centuries of history behind it, and with Matthew Paris, the superintendent of the St Albans scriptorium, who proved himself an exact and critical historian of his own age. The debt we owe to the monastic chroniclers for preserving the records of three centuries is enormous, and the contribution of St Albans is particularly noteworthy; indeed, as Professor Galbraith has observed, it outweighs all the rest put together.[1] After the thirteenth century, however, the monastic contribution declines. The greatest chronicler of the fourteenth century was not a monk, but a secular—the wandering scholar Froissart who flourished in the time of Chaucer and Petrarch. In the fifteenth century there were still monastic chroniclers of a pedestrian kind, but they were not of the standard of Matthew Paris. Thomas Walsingham (d. 1422) was the last of the superintendents of the St Albans scriptorium, and our chief authority for the period of the Peasants' Revolt, during which St Albans suffered severely losing many of its court rolls and charters. Later in the same century, Abbot Whethamstede of St Albans was not only a copious writer, but something of a humanist as well. He built new libraries both at St Albans and at Gloucester College, Oxford, and spent much money on book-collecting for them; his acquisitions included some of the productions of Italian humanism, both ancient classics and con-

---

[1] V. H. Galbraith, *Historical Research in Medieval England*, 1951. See also the short but admirably clear survey of English monasteries and monastic chronicles by Rose Graham in G. Barraclough *ed.*, *Social Life in Early England*, 1960.

temporary translations of Greek works into Latin. He was one of Lydgate's patrons, paying him £3 6s. 8d. for translating the life of S. Alban into verse. Another of Lydgate's patrons was incidentally the good Duke Humphrey, for whom he wrote among other things an epithalamium on his marriage with Jacqueline. Lydgate was a monk of Bury, and may possibly have attended Gloucester College, the Benedictine nursery at Oxford. As a poet, he was prolix and dull, but his patrons deserve some credit for picking out one of the very few English monks of the fifteenth century who had at least some creative ability, and some leanings towards humanism.[1]

Whethamstede, Celling and even Lydgate were exceptional in their period. But although creative work in the monastic houses was fast dying, nevertheless the books in their libraries were multiplying to such an extent that both historical and theological studies were in danger of becoming unmanageable. In the absence of modern techniques of research and arrangement, the only way of reducing the accumulation of details to reasonable limits was by summarizing and epitomizing; and this was in fact the main task of the few fifteenth-century monastic scriptoria, such as Durham, which were still producing books. Professor Galbraith gives some illuminating examples of how the medieval editor was fast becoming overwhelmed by his material, and of how epitomes such as Higden's *Polychronicon* tended to survive, while the originals disappeared. The introduction of alphabetic indexes and arabic pagination were important bibliographical developments, but they did not suffice to reduce the material to order.[2] The problem was all the greater as the monastic libraries (all of which were small by modern standards) were scattered far and wide through the country, and were often in remote and inaccessible spots.

The complications of the problem can be judged to some extent from the work of the monastic bibliographer John Boston of Bury. Boston was an Augustinian monk attached to the abbey at Bury St

---

[1] Whethamstede, during his first abbacy, spent large sums on buildings and repairs, including £170 on books for the library and choir. For Whethamstede and Lydgate, see Knowles, *The Religious Orders in England*, 1955, II.

[2] The earliest recorded references to Arabic numerals in the West seem to be in a work produced at a Syrian monastery on the Upper Euphrates, AD 662, and again at the court of al-Mansūr at Baghdad, AD 773. They did not reach Europe till the twelfth century; by the fourteenth century they were becoming familiar in European MSS. For the arguments for and against an Indian origin of Arabic numerals, see G. T. Garratt, *The Legacy of India*, 1937, pp. 357 ff.

Edmunds. He flourished c. 1410 in the time of Abbot Curteys, who built the abbey library; and it is possible that Boston acted as its librarian. He is known to us mainly from his *Catalogus Scriptorum Ecclesiae*, which listed about 700 authors in English monastic libraries; the authors were arranged alphabetically, and each work was marked with a location number showing the library that possessed it. The *Catalogus* was unknown to Leland, and also to Bale when he issued the first edition of his *Scriptores Britanniae* in 1548 though he used it for his enlarged edition published on the continent in 1557. Bale assumed that Boston travelled through England visiting the libraries and noting the titles of their books, with their opening words, and he describes him in the *Catalogus* as 'making one library out of many'—a union catalogue in fact. It is however believed that the *Catalogus* is based on the thirteenth-century Franciscan *Registrum librorum Angliae* which used with few exceptions the same location numbers for the libraries. To this list Boston added 9 new libraries; 4 of these were friaries (there were no friaries at all in the *Registrum*), and 8 of the 9 were in East Anglia, within easy reach of Bury. He increased the list of authors however from 94 to 673, and he added the titles of their works and some biographical information. It is known that Boston was interested in biographical and bibliographical matters, both from some annotations probably in his hand that have survived, and from other work with which Bale credits him, the *Speculum Coenobitarum*, a chronicle of monastic life with bibliographies. The *Catalogus* may therefore be, not a catalogue, so much as a dictionary of Church literature, and it may well have been compiled as a guide in the reorganization of the Bury library. In this case, it is probable that he did not travel through England at all, as Bale suggested. The use of the same location numbers for the different libraries suggests that the *Registrum* was widely known in monastic circles.[1] Many problems regarding Boston still await solution, but the *Registrum* and the *Catalogus* contain useful clues to the contents of our monastic libraries. And they both illustrate the difficulties in the path of the medieval student (e.g., the diversity and variety of the libraries, the distance between one library and another, and

---

[1] E. A. Savage, *Notes on the Early Monastic Libraries of Scotland*. Edinburgh Bibliographical Society, 1928, vol. 14. See also Professor Mynors' chapter on the Latin classics known to Boston in *Fritz Saxl, 1890-1948*, ed. D. J. Gordon, 1957.

the accumulation of elaborate, composite works) which were never satisfactorily overcome under the monastic system. While the rise of the new universities concentrated academic study in the two centres of Oxford and Cambridge, the impact of humanism on the age of Erasmus involved an even more drastic change. Not only were the old educational tools and methods out of date; the new tools needed by the schools were printed editions from the presses, rather than manuscripts from the monastic scriptoria: new editions of Cicero, Horace, Ovid, Homer and Euripides, the Greek Testament, new Latin grammars (even if they were only old Donatuses refurbished and set up in type) and new Bibles and service books printed either in Latin, or presently in the vernacular.

The monastic houses met this challenge with a dogged conservatism. They belonged to the medieval world which the flood of humanism was destined to submerge, and like all big and impersonal corporations they could not trim their sails to the changing wind. The message of humanism was conveyed in no small measure by the printed book, and it was perhaps the printing presses more than any other factor that finally killed the monastic libraries. Rowland Phillips, who was Vicar of Croydon at the time of the dissolution, exclaimed, 'We must root out printing, or printing will root out us.' This was a die-hard view that must have been expressed and repeated in many a monastic cloister. The rejection of the new and powerful weapon of the printing press was indeed fatal. If the great Benedictine houses had seized their opportunity, and set up active presses beside their scriptoria, the history of the sixteenth century might well have been different. How many presses were directly associated with monastic houses? Very few indeed. Caxton's press was set up within the precincts of the Abbey of Westminster, probably in a house rented from the Abbey, but there is no reason to think that his venture was sponsored by the Abbey.[1] The St Albans printer who produced eight books between 1480 and 1486 is supposed to have been the Abbey schoolmaster. The monastery of S. Scholastica at Subiaco housed the press of Conrad Sweynheym and Arnold Pannartz in 1465; it was a Lactantius from this press that Gerard, the calli-

---

[1] See L. E. Tanner, *William Caxton's Houses in Westminster*, The Library, 1957, pp. 153-66.

THE DISPERSAL

graph in *The Cloister and the Hearth*, saw to his consternation in a Roman bookshop, being greatly disturbed by this threat to his own profession. A few German Benedictine houses set up presses. One in England, at Tavistock, produced two books in 1525 and 1534.[1] On the other side the Abbot of Sponheim in 1492 produced his tract *De Laude Scriptorum*, in which he maintained that the written work on parchment would last a thousand years. 'How long,' he asked, 'would a work on printed paper last?' It would be lucky if it survived two centuries. And he urged his scribes to copy out even those volumes already printed. This is, of course, the normal and understandable reaction of the craft-worker to the machine-made novelty.

Certainly there were printed volumes, especially amongst the service books, in many religious houses early in the sixteenth century.[2] Bishop Foxe of Winchester in 1516 translated the Rule of S. Benedict for the ladies of three nunneries in his diocese 'who were utterly ignorant of Latin', and had it printed by Richard Pynson. There was a Caxton edition of the Rule in English in 1491, and there must have been many printed breviaries, horae and similar works in the monasteries. Between 1478 and 1517 there were 144 editions of the Sarum Prymer in Latin, and between 1534 and 1547 there were twenty-eight in English. There was indeed no shortage of printed religious works; out of 349 books

---

[1] For English printing presses associated with monastic houses, see Dom David Knowles, *The Religious Orders in England*, vol. III, pp. 25-7. Apart from Caxton's press at Westminster there were three, viz.

St. Albans. On this see H. R. Plomer in *VCH. Herts*, IV, 1914, pp. 258-61, and E. G. Duff, *Fifteenth Century English Books*, 1917. The connection of the St. Albans schoolmaster with the Abbey is uncertain. A later press (1526-38) was managed by a professional printer, John Herford, working under the patronage of the Abbey.

Tavistock. See H. P. R. Finberg, *Tavistock Abbey*, Cambridge, 1951, Appendix D, pp. 290-3. The printer-monk was Thomas Richard, and his patron was Robert Langdon, who chose the first title known to have been printed (a translation of Boethius by John Watts, a canon of Oseney, in 1410). This was produced in 1525, and in 1528 Richard became prior of Totnes. The press remained at Tavistock, where the only other recorded work was printed, in 1534. The press is believed to have left the Abbey at the dissolution with one of the monks, and was still in his family thirty years later.

Abingdon. A monastic breviary was printed in 1528 by John Scolar, who had produced earlier five books at Oxford. Scolar's connection with the Abbey however is said to have been accidental.

[2] Dom David Knowles (*Religious Orders in England*, 1955, II, p. 333) states that almost the only printed books in the monastic libraries not duplicating MSS were volumes of the Statutes of England, which in Tudor times were as essential to Abbots as works on the canon law.

produced by the English presses between 1468 and 1530, slightly more than half were religious. It is curious, however, that the first half century of English printing produced no English Bibles. By contrast there were twenty complete translations in Germany between 1466 and 1522, and in France there were seven reprints of the translation by Jean de Rèly between 1487 and 1521. In this period the English presses produced only a single Latin text of the Sunday epistles and gospels. English law forbade nothing but the unauthorized translation, and More was expressing the orthodox view when he told Tyndale that 'no good man would be so mad as to burn a Bible in which they found no fault'.[1]

The few printed volumes in the sixteenth-century English monastery were indeed mostly service books, and so not part of the library proper. Only a handful of the monastic libraries can have acquired printed books for their libraries in any quantity. In 1525 Wynkyn de Worde published the *Image of Love* by an Observant friar named John Ryckes, and though this was condemned as heretical, it is known that the nuns of Syon purchased 60 copies. The Synon library was probably at this time one of the most modern and best equipped of any English monastic foundation. It was indeed an exceptional institution in many ways. The chaplains and religious directors to the Bridgettine nuns were largely of a scholarly and academic type; many had been fellows of colleges at Oxford or Cambridge. These brought their books with them, to add to the great library of Syon at their death. The largest of these contributions was the collection of 94 volumes left to the community by Richard Reynolds, who had been a Fellow of Corpus Christi College, Cambridge and the friend of Erasmus, More and Reginald Pole. The latter regarded him as the ablest of the religious of his day, combining the best qualities of the old learning and the new. He met his end along with the Carthusian martyrs at Tyburn in May, 1535. The Syon Library was for the use of the brethren; the nuns would have had a smaller collection of their own.[2]

William More, Prior of Worcester (1518-35), is known to have spent money on printed books, but as he was accused of misappropriating the priory funds, he may merely have been feathering

---

[1] Philip Hughes, *The Reformation in England*, 1952, vol. I, pp. 98-111.
[2] Knowles, *The Religious Orders in England*, vol. III, 1959, pp. 212-21.

his own nest; he resigned in 1535 and retired to a private house which he had secured at Crowle.[1] The Prior of Reading brought 60 volumes of the new learning from Oxford to the abbey library; he was put into the Tower, and the other monks infected by the new learning were forcibly discouraged. Understandably a few monks at certain houses surrendered to the appeal of the 'new learning': the source of infection was usually Oxford or Cambridge however, not their own monastic library. And in this context the noble phrase 'new learning' meant, not the doctrines of humanism in general, but rather the teachings of Martin Luther, William Tyndale, Simon Fish and John Frith, while in some cases it seems to have implied little besides an impatience of the discipline of the Church, especially in the matter of fasting.[2] The apparent alliance between humanism and the new religion made it all the more difficult for the monastic libraries to welcome the new printed books on their shelves.

And so by 1540 the common view was probably that the monastic library had been superseded, and was in fact dead and therefore useless. The age of reverence for things past had not yet arrived, and men who saw no shame in using monastic ruins as barns or stables found nothing unworthy in using monastic vellum to bind their account books. So far as the spoliation had any intellectual basis, the issue was three-sided, as between scholasticism, humanism and the new religion. The identification of scholasticism and the old faith was of course as mistaken as the identification of humanism and the new faith, but the humanists and the Lutherans found some common ground in their attack on scholasticism. Both were in some degree represented in Cromwell's Commissioners (those ruffians of the reformation, in Johnson's words) who supervised the destruction. By and large the Commissioners were, however, time-servers intent on lining their pockets with plunder while the opportunity lasted. Perhaps the arch-ruffian under Cromwell was the Chancellor of the Court of Augmentations, which handled the revenues of the suppressed houses, Sir Richard Rich, the unscrupulous lawyer who trapped the betrayed More and Fisher and had a hand in the ruin of most of the prominent

---

[1] See Dom David Knowles, *The Religious Orders in England*, vol. III, 1959, pp. 108–26 and 342–4.
[2] G. Baskerville, *English Monks and the Suppression of the Monasteries*, 1937, pp. 138–43.

men of his time, including Wolsey, Cromwell, Somerset and Northumberland. The chief Visitors were Richard Layton, John London, Thomas Legh and Sir John Prise (or ap Rice). Layton, who afterwards became Dean of York, was a relative of Cuthbert Tunstall and also (curiously enough) of Robert Aske, the leader of the Pilgrimage of Grace. He had a part in the interrogation of the monks of Syon in 1533, and of Fisher and More in 1535. His visitations included Oxford, where he was responsible for the first purge in that city. He typified the anti-scholastic reformer; it was he who boasted to Cromwell that they had utterly banished Duns Scotus from Oxford for ever, with all his blind glosses, and that he was 'now made a common servant to every man, fast nailed up upon posts in all common houses of easement: *id quod oculis meis vidi*'. This disgraceful treatment of the last and one of the ablest of the schoolmen shocks us today. But to many at Oxford at the time of the purge his work must have seemed as outdated as a pre-Darwinian textbook of biology would to us. And the English people lightheartedly surrendered many works of equal value to the salvage authorities during the recent war.

Dr John London, the Warden of New College, was another unsavoury character. Matthew Parker spoke of him as 'that fat and filthy prebendary', and modern writers have had even worse names for him. Sir Thomas Legh was a lawyer who made a fortune out of visitations. Sir John Prise, also a lawyer, was a quite different type, much more moderate in his dealings with the houses he visited, and the only member of the team who had any real pretensions to scholarship. He was the author of four historical works, including a history of Wales, and he seems to have had a genuine interest in the medieval histories of Britain. He evidently was at pains to preserve the historical works in the monastic libraries which he visited, and he gave some of his finds to Hereford Cathedral and left others to Jesus College, Oxford. Most, however, remained in his own family, finding their way later to Balliol and the Cotton collection. Neil Ker observes that Prise had two important merits as a collector: he did not disdain MSS outside his own particular subject, and he did not rebind his MSS. He was one of the pitifully small group of genuine collectors in this period, the others being John Leland, Henry's library keeper and antiquary, John Bale, bishop of Ossory and prebendary of Canterbury, and Leland's intimate friend Robert Talbot, who can claim to be our first collector of Anglo-Saxon MSS.[1]

This, then, was the inglorious end of the libraries whose traditions carry us back to Bede, Benedict Biscop and Theodore of Tarsus. I have given none of the unhappy details of the spoliation: the curious can find in Bale and Fuller and Aubrey glimpses of the shameful events that took place.[2] They managed things better in France in 1789 and 1794, when the libraries of the émigrés and the religious houses were expropriated, their books passing into the care of the State in a comparatively orderly way.

It is notable that the monastic houses met much the same end everywhere in Western Europe, either through the wave of Protestantism that spread through Northern Europe in the sixteenth century, or the so-called enlightenment of the eighteenth century, or the rationalism and liberalism of the nineteenth century. In the fifteenth century the end came in Scandinavia, Germany, Scotland and Ireland, as well as in England. In the eighteenth century, almost all the monastic orders were suppressed at the time of the French Revolution, or by Napoleon or Joseph II. A rebirth followed early in the nineteenth century, but between 1834 and 1903 religious houses were expropriated in many countries: first in Spain and Portugal, then in Italy (1866–1870), then in Germany under Bismarck, as well as under Nazi rule later; and in France in 1903 all monastic communities were expelled. These suppressions were not entirely successful, of course. In most of the later suppressions, the libraries were appropriated systematically for the nation.

Thus in France the monastic books went to the Bibliothèque Nationale. In Spain in 1835 they were divided amongst the university and public libraries. In Portugal (1834) they went to the Biblioteca Nacional in Lisbon. At Rome, the Vittorio Emanuele was founded in 1875 from the libraries of the suppressed religious

---

[1] For Richard Layton, Thomas Legh and the other visitors, and for a detailed account of the visitation of 1535–6 see Knowles, *The Religious Orders in England*, vol. III, 1959, pp. 268–90. For Dr John London (who does not come into the picture till 1538) see Knowles, *op. cit.*, pp. 354–6. See also Neil R. Ker, "Sir John Prise," The Library, 1955, p. 1. There are useful studies of Leland, Bale, Prise and Talbot, in T. D. Kendrick, *British Antiquity*, 1950.

[2] See especially Dr C. E. Wright's chapter on "The Dispersal" in Wormald and Wright, *The English Library before 1700*, 1958. H. F. M. Prescott's novel *The Man on a Donkey*, 1952, gives a restrained and accurate picture of a nunnery at the time of the suppression.

houses of Rome and the Papal States. If monastic houses must be dissolved, Europe has apparently learnt, perhaps from our own mistakes in the sixteenth century, how it can be done without gravely risking the destruction of their treasures and the heritage of the past. The transfer may indeed yield direct benefits to scholarship and research. When for example, about 150 Bavarian monastic libraries were expropriated early in the nineteenth century, the Bavarian State Library gained the largest collection of incunabula in any library, and Ludwig Hain was enabled to compile his *Repertorium bibliographicum* (1826–38), thus achieving the first scientific survey of early printed books on a large scale. Questions of property apart, the concentration of rare books at centres where they will be cared for and made generally accessible has obvious advantages. It is not, of course, always easy to determine whether these outweigh the disadvantages of closing down a library with a long history behind it. This is a problem which arises today in regard to the occasional sale or transfer of English parochial libraries, for which a faculty from the Consistory Court is required, though some sales have taken place without a faculty. The decisive factors are the safe keeping and accessibility of the books, and if these can be assured without alienation, then it is surely in general, wise to leave them in their original home.[1]

[1] *Heritage*, p. 260.

CHAPTER IX

Physical Handicaps

MOST people, if asked to account for the literary and scholarly achievements of the human race, would think either of the divine inspiration which is supposed to guide the poet's pen, or the transcendent capacity of taking trouble, which Carlyle said was the first mark of genius. It is a chastening experience, however, to remember how closely our literary endeavour has been dependent on economic and material conditions. If the seed is to bear fruit, not only must the good ground be tilled and made ready, but there must be a market for the fruit when it is harvested. And since the contents of libraries are books, these flourish only under the same conditions.

The first need of the writer has always been paper, pen and ink. These are his raw materials and, unless paper (or some substitute for paper) is plentiful and cheap, few will think it worth while to record their thoughts, and few will be led to read those that are recorded. Not only must there be a durable and cheap material on which many copies of his work can be produced, but there must be some even cheaper material on which he can make his notes and jottings. With most people, rough notes are an essential part both of creative writing and scholarly research. For temporary scribbling, nothing is quite so attractive, to grown-ups as well as to children, as sand, whether on the seashore or in the sandtray. There is classical authority for this. Plato found the court of Dionysius overcome by the fever of geometry, with all the palace tracing figures in the dust; and Archimedes, when his friends urged him unwillingly to the baths, whiled away the time of waiting by drawing diagrams in the ashes. For less transient notes, however, the whitened or waxed tablet, scratched by the point of a stylus, served tolerably from Homeric days to the Renaissance. Victorian children were accustomed to the rather similar slate and slate pencil; and indeed, not children only. The habits of Miss Jenkyns in *Cranford*, with her literary reputation, may be recalled. 'Epistolary writing, she and her friends considered as her *forte*. Many a copy of many a letter have I seen written and corrected on the slate, before she "seized the half-hour just previous to post-time to assure" her friends of this or that.'

But both tablets and slates were cumbersome, and the black wax with which tablets were coated needed frequent renewal—at least monthly in the schoolroom. If used for letters, they must have been more expensive than our modern notepaper. They could be laced together and sealed for privacy. Ovid used them for his letters home from his lonely place of exile on the Black Sea. In Martial's Rome, lovers used a fancy variety called Vitellian tablets for their loveletters; and in Egypt Cleopatra (as might be expected) chose tablets set with onyx and crystal for her messages to Antony. You might, of course, erase the writing and reply to your letter on the same tablet, but not if you valued the original message. The tablet, indeed, can never have been as handy for any of these purposes as paper: either scraps of waste paper for rough notes, or more elegant sheets for formal use.[1]

For finished literary work, only four materials have proved really satisfactory: stone, parchment, papyrus and paper.[2] Stone, incised by the chisel, is the most durable of all. Though used today mainly for inscriptions, in Greek temples it was not uncommonly used for quite long dedicatory poems and paeans. But stone, though durable, is not portable; it is laborious to inscribe and of little use for lengthy texts. Papyrus was cheap and abundant in the Greek world, and it solved the problem admirably for several centuries. It suffered from two handicaps, however. Except in the dry climate of Egypt, it was very perishable. Damp ruined it, and in Rome, and still more in Gaul, texts had to be constantly recopied to preserve them. The Emperor Tacitus, for example, wishing that the works of his imagined ancestor, the historian of the same

---

[1] Tablets continued in use till the eighteenth century, and slates till the present century. Leigh Hunt in his *Essay on Pocket-books* and *Keepsakes* traces the evolution of the tablebook or tablets of old into pocket-books, books of paper being found more convenient to the pocket than tablets. Tablets (tavolette) came to us, he says, like almost everything else, from Italy, and are still to be purchased, made of the same materials as of old—slate, ivory, etc.

[2] These and other aspects of book production in the classical period are considered in some detail in *Heritage*, ch. VI.

name, should be in all the Roman libraries, felt it necessary to order ten copies to be made by his official copyists every year and delivered to the libraries.[1] And Martial in his epigrams frequently reminds his readers that a shower of rain would damage his books, while to use them (as some apparently did) for wrapping fried fish, produced immediate disintegration. The other difficulty was that papyrus was weakened by even a single fold. It was really satisfactory therefore only for the roll form of book. This was indeed the normal format for seven centuries or more, but it had several disadvantages. It was wasteful of library space, for a large number of rolls were required for any substantial work, and it was cumbersome to handle. Both hands were always needed for reading, and the task of referring backwards or forwards to particular passages in a long book was extremely laborious: all the more laborious because for a great part of this period Greek texts lacked such elementary aids to intelligibility as pagination, punctuation and the separation of one word from another.[2]

Parchment was much more durable, and it could be folded several times without risk. But compared with an easily manufactured material such as papyrus, it was naturally scarce and expensive. As long as papyrus was plentiful, the use of parchment was restricted to the cattle raising districts of Asia Minor, and even there most scribes must have used imported papyrus as long as it was available. There were at least two reasons for its disappearance as a writing material. The plant (*Cyperus papyrus L.*) from which it was made had flourished in the swamps of the Nile delta, but for some reason unknown, it ceased to be plentiful there. Except for plants in the Cairo Botanical Gardens, it has vanished from Egypt. It still grows wild in the Sudan and Abyssinia, and at Palermo in Sicily, where it was introduced by the Romans.[3] More important than this was the demand for a stronger material that could be folded into codex form. This new form was Roman in origin; indeed, Caesar is said to have adopted it for his

---

[1] Vopiscus, *Tacitus*, 10.3. One may infer that there were not more than ten libraries of any importance at this date (AD 275).

[2] 'The idea of an ancient library perplexes our sympathy by its map-like volumes, rolled upon cylinders. Our imagination cannot take kindly to a yard of wit, or to thirty inches of moral observation, rolled out like linen in a draper's shop.'—Leigh Hunt in *My Books*. But an average roll would be ten yards long, not one; and much longer rolls than this are known.

[3] J. Černý, *Paper and Books in Ancient Egypt*, 1952.

despatches to the Senate,[1] and it was certainly in limited use in Rome in the time of Martial. In Christian circles it came into use in the second century, and possibly in the first; for pagan literature it was not employed to any extent till the third or fourth century. These economic facts had a direct effect on literature and book production. The import of papyrus into Greece began to increase substantially about the middle of the sixth century BC. The great flowering of Greek literature in the fifth century followed quickly. The dates of Aeschylus were 525-456 BC, and he was followed immediately by the long series of lyric and dramatic writers and historians that together make up the wealth of classical Greek literature. Before 550 BC the number of writers diminishes abruptly; there were few besides Sappho and Alcaeus, and in a still earlier century, Hesiod, Homer, and the Epic Cycle. In Rome, the literary output of the Augustan age was similarly preceded by a rise in the imports of papyrus in the first century BC. There is at least a possibility that papyrus was also used for the earlier Hebrew literature; in later times the Torah was written on papyrus, and it has always preserved the roll form which is specially suited to that medium.[2] Not only did the import of papyrus affect the amount of classical book production; it influenced also the extent and form of literary compositions. Rolls varied as much in size as modern books do, but for convenience in handling, the average height for a Greek roll would be eight or ten inches, and the sheets would be fastened into strips between fifteen and thirty feet long, giving a cylinder $1\frac{1}{2}$ or 2 inches thick. Few compositions were short enough to be transcribed on a single roll of normal size; the *Iliad*, for example, would have required about a dozen rolls. Perhaps the most important contribution to scholarship made by the Alexandrian Museum was the editorial work carried out on the Greek literary texts in the library. This involved the division of works into 'books', the recopying of texts on rolls of suitable size for storage, and the preparation of the great bibliography of Greek literature which Callimachus superintended. Thus Zenodotus, the first head of the library, undertook the recension of Homer, and was responsible for the arrangement of the *Iliad* and the *Odyssey*

---

[1] Suetonius, *Div. Jul.* 56. Professor Cerny interprets the passage differently, but I think mistakenly. See *Heritage*, p. 98.
[2] Černý, *op. cit.*, p. 4.

into twenty-four books. Aristophanes of Byzantium carried out similar tasks on Pindar (of whom he produced the first complete edition, arranged in seventeen books), on Plato (whose fifteen dialogues he arranged in trilogies), and on Euripides. He also began the work of supplying punctuation and accents for the Greek texts which the Museum was copying. It is a fair guess that this work was governed partly by the need for new rolls of a standard pattern which could be stored conveniently in bins or pigeon-holes.

The change to the codex form, first on papyrus, and then, when that proved unsatisfactory, on parchment, was momentous. It has been well described by Sir Frederic Kenyon.[1] The demand for it came first from the primitive Church, which not only needed books urgently and abundantly for missionary work and services, but needed them for quite different purposes from the pagan world. There was nothing in pagan literature comparable to the Scriptures or to church service books. Obviously such works were safer and easier to use when gathered between the covers of a vellum codex. The change made it immediately possible to produce the Gospels and the Acts, if not the whole New Testament, in one volume, and, as Kenyon remarks, both Irenaeus and Origen may have used them in this form. Origen's great library consisted at least in part of rolls, however, for after his death the damaged rolls were replaced by copies on vellum. The parchment codex must have been a gradual development, extending over three or more centuries. It is noteworthy that the great reference works, lexicons and encyclopaedias of early times, such as 'Suidas', for which the codex form is almost essential, belong mainly, if not entirely, to the Byzantine period. Papyrus remained in some use for a considerable time, and S. Augustine felt it necessary to explain his use of vellum for a letter, as neither papyrus nor his tablets were at hand.[2] Profits were being made from the Egyptian papyrus industry as late as AD 272, when Firmus financed his rebellion against Aurelian from this source. Similarly, the roll remained in use for special purposes for a long period. For genealogies, cartularies and certain legal documents it had evident advantages, displaying a large amount of matter on one side of a single sheet. There is, for example, a pedigree

---

[1] Kenyon, *Books and Readers in Ancient Greece and Rome*, 2nd ed., 1951. See also C. H. Roberts, *The Codex*, Proc. Br. Acad. 1954, pp. 169–204, and *Heritage*, pp. 95–101.
[2] Migne, 33. 80.

roll of the Shirley family in the Staunton Harold archives at Leicester, thirty feet long and dating from *c.* 1640. It had advantages also for verse and music; a fifteenth-century vellum roll at Trinity College, Cambridge, six feet long, contains thirteen carols with music.[1]

Over a thousand years after the introduction of the codex, there came another momentous change, or rather two: the replacement of parchment by paper, and the introduction of printing. Both were equally important, and indeed complementary, for if the printing presses had been restricted to the use of parchment, they would, to say the least, have been gravely handicapped. Both these changes belong in the main to the fifteenth century. Paper proved an even stronger rival to parchment than papyrus, for it was not only much cheaper, but (despite the doubts of some fifteenth-century writers) quite as durable. It is worth remembering that one sheep yields no more than a single sheet (two leaves) for a folio book. The production of a single copy of a folio volume therefore may involve the sacrifice of a very large flock of sheep. No material so extravagant as this could compete with fine hand-made rag paper. Sheep were, of course, comparatively plentiful in fifteenth-century England, particularly in the Cotswolds and East Anglia and on the Cistercian farms in the North; and the custom of salting down meat in the autumn provided ample material for the scribes in the winter months. But this source could never have provided the vellum needed for the production of large editions of printed books. The market value of a parchment volume in medieval days was always high, and usually far beyond the reach of an ordinary university student. In the catalogue of William of Wykeham's books at New College, Oxford, for example, quite normal textbooks are priced at the equivalent of £50 or £100.[2]

The structure of a text is often affected by its purpose. The length and plan of a play by Euripides or Shakespeare, for example, is governed by contemporary fashions of play production, and the length of a school book may be influenced by the course of

---

[1] Unlike the papyrus roll, the medieval parchment roll normally has its text in one column down its whole length. Two forms are distinguished: the Chancery type, in which the membranes are sewn together end to end, and the Exchequer type, in which a number of membranes are sewn together at one end and then rolled. The parchment roll has proved an excellent medium for documents which need safe preservation, but are not likely to be consulted frequently.

[2] Strickland Gibson, *Some Oxford Libraries*, 1914, p. 5.

instruction for which it is designed. It is fairly certain that the textual structure has also at times been influenced by the nature of the material used and by current methods of book production, and this would indeed be a fruitful and interesting field for research. Stone and wood must inevitably influence the length and design of inscriptions; papyrus, paper and parchment each have their special influence on the character of the handwriting used by the scribe. There is little doubt that the division of a text into 'books' by an institution such as the Alexandrian Library had some relation to the standard size of roll in use. When tablets were the common medium in use for notes or verses, their normal dimensions must often have controlled the length of a poem by Catullus or Ovid or even Sappho. In the middle ages the verses of Baudri, the abbot of Bourgueil in the Loire valley, were fashioned to suit the elegant tablets of green wax, with space for no more than eight hexameters, which were presented to him by the abbot of Séez, who later became Archbishop of Canterbury.[1]

As with the introduction of papyrus into Athens, so the introduction of paper and printing was followed by the finest flowering of English literature. The Elizabethan period came a full hundred years later. It had been preceded, and perhaps delayed, by the sterility of the years between the martyrdom of Sir Thomas More and the accession of Elizabeth: a sterility due almost entirely to religious and political causes. The new printing presses had, however, a much more immediate result. The beginning of the sixteenth century produced a full tide of quite astonishing genius in the fields of art and letters and scholarship. In England there were Erasmus and More and Colet and Fisher, to name only a few. Abroad this was the age of Leonardo da Vinci, Machiavelli, Budaeus, Copernicus, Rabelais, Savonarola, Julius Caesar Scaliger and S. Ignatius Loyola, not to mention Michaelangelo and Raphael. The European reputation of men such as Erasmus was built firmly on the printing press. If Henry had remained true to his early love of scholarship and to his title of Defender of the Faith, and had gathered the great scholars of his time about him, as Charles the Great or the Ptolemies had done in earlier centuries, the course of history would indeed have been different. No English king ever had such an opportunity in his grasp. Supposing, for example, he

[1] Helen Waddell, *The Wandering Scholars*, 7th ed., 1934; *Heritage*, p. 97.

had taken Erasmus into his service and given him a printing press; it is not hard to imagine the magnificence of the result, or the kind of Royal Library that might have ensued. Instead, Henry wantonly destroyed practically every library in the country. The setback, tragic though it was, could not be anything but temporary. The pen is not only more dangerous than the sword; it is cheaper to buy and easier to wield, and the printing press is simply a pen multiplied a thousandfold.

There is an interesting example of the dependence of art and letters on economic factors in the history of Iceland, which was first settled by Norwegians between AD 860 and 930. Unlike Scandinavia and Ireland, where the visual arts flourished, Iceland was empty not merely of any native population, but of the materials which the artist needs. There was neither wood nor stone suitable for carving, nor any metal for moulding. Yet the settlers were men of good birth and breeding, artistic, self-reliant, vigorous, with a strong tradition of culture behind them. In consequence their art came to be expressed mostly in words. The long Northern winters gave them the leisure for creative work; the need to kill off each autumn most of their cattle gave them an abundant supply of young calf skins for vellum; and the coming of Christianity brought them a practicable alphabet and an acquaintance with books in the conventional codex form. On the estates of the great chieftains and bishops, and in the monasteries and later even among the farmers, there was a tremendous outpouring of original work in history, poetry and saga, and in translating, adapting and copying. There are still extant, either entire or in fragments, some 700 MSS on vellum, all that remains of perhaps ten times that number of works —the remnants of great libraries that have perished, not for the most part through wanton destruction or dispersal, but simply from the ordinary wear and tear of use and reading.[1]

Let us now view the problem from the angle of the reader, rather than the writer. If the author is stimulated by an abundance of writing material, so is the reader by the abundance and accessibility of books, and by the conditions under which they can be read. Subject to certain conditions, the supply creates the demand. There must be first of all the means of education at school and university, and that recognition of the economic value of literacy which always

[1] G. Turville-Petre, *Origins of Icelandic Literature*, 1953.

accompanies the development of commerce. There must be collections of books maintained by corporate endowed institutions, such as universities, monasteries and churches. There must be shops where books can be bought and literary gossip enjoyed, and there must be homes where there is security and leisure and room for private reading. All these conditions have operated to a varying extent from classical times onwards, and their relations to literary culture in the different periods would repay study. It is of interest to note, for example, how a period of creative activity is succeeded by a period of research, criticism and library development; the two rarely coincide. Again, we can often trace an association between literary renaissance and commercial prosperity; and this is not necessarily a mere coincidence. Apart from these general considerations, there are other more particular factors which need investigation. We have already mentioned the physical form of the book. The codex is far easier to handle and consult than the roll. Martial, who made the earliest comments of all on the codex form, noticed this. Unlike the roll, it could be held in one hand, or it will lie open on the table before you while you play dice.[1] Some have assumed that Martial in these passages was referring merely to toys or epitomes,[2] but there are strong reasons for doubting this. Some were big enough to occupy a traveller's time on a long journey;[3] and though at least one is described as massive, he is constantly marvelling at how much can be compressed into a single small codex. These are the very features which have recommended the codex form ever since.

The animal kingdom provided the scholar with both parchment and pen. It is not without interest to note that, if the difficulties of handling these materials became unduly irksome, legend often arranged for nature to co-operate even more actively. Irish tradition is particularly rich in such stories. Thus while S. Cainnech of Aghaboe was studying in a forest, a stag offered him his antlers to serve as a lectern for his heavy volume. S. Colman was assisted by a variety of animals, including a mosquito which thoughtfully settled on his page to mark where he left off reading. And S. Molaisse of Devenish, needing a pen for his writing, was con-

---

[1] *Ep.* 1. 2; 14. 185.
[2] Kenyon, *op. cit.*, p. 94.
[3] *Ep.* 14. 188.

veniently served by a bird that dropped a quill at his feet. (In a similar predicament, Locksley in *Ivanhoe* brought down a passing goose with an arrow.) Such stories testify not only to the problems of primitive scholarship but to the aura of magic which surrounded it.[1]

There are still other physical factors which have had a greater effect on reading than is often realized. In an earlier chapter I have pointed out how in classical and medieval days, most study was carried out alfresco, in colonnade or cloister: a pleasant enough custom in the Mediterranean summer, but a formidable handicap in the Northern winter. One reason for this was the architectural difficulty of building a large hall sufficiently well lit for comfortable reading. Windows of any kind were a rarity in the ancient world, and where they existed, they were intended to let in air rather than light. If the structural problems raised by large openings in a wall are surmounted, there still remains the difficulty of making them weatherproof. Glazing was adopted in Roman Imperial times, but the large sheets of glass and the wide window openings needed for good natural lighting did not begin to make their appearance till the end of the sixteenth century. The gloom of a Gothic cathedral was a structural necessity rather than a religious virtue. The recognition of this fact doubtless confirmed the designers in their policy of utilizing windows as picture books in stained glass rather than as sources of light for reading. In the perpendicular and decorated periods, windows grew wider, and in the best Tudor architecture we find for the first time glazed windows large enough to light a room well. One of the earliest examples of a great mansion really well supplied with windows was Holdenby House in Northamptonshire, built by Sir Christopher Hatton about 1580. It was full of windows in a way no previous English house had been. Every room was well lighted, and nearly all had bay windows and fireplaces.[2] The new fashion seemed strange to contemporary eyes. Bacon may well have had Holdenby House in mind when, in describing his ideal mansion, he warned his readers to beware of 'fair houses so full of glass, that one

---

[1] For these tales, see Eleanor Duckett, *The Wandering Saints*, 1959, p. 15.
[2] The plan of Holdenby House is reproduced in *Shakespeare's England*, vol. II, p. 55. A surviving example of another such great house of the same period, equally 'full of glass', is Hardwick Hall in Derbyshire, built by Bess of Hardwick (Elizabeth Talbot, Countess of Shrewsbury).

PHYSICAL HANDICAPS

cannot tell where to become to be out of the sun or cold'.[1] Not till the eighteenth century did the smaller English house enjoy natural lighting as good as this.

The other problem of artificial lighting was not solved till a much later date. It is only within fairly recent times that it has become possible to light a large hall safely and effectively. Till late in the nineteenth century, the normal form of domestic lighting was by wax or tallow candles. Those who know their *Cranford* will remember that Miss Matty's chief winter occupation was the making of candle-lighters. And candles were expensive; she was never happy if more than one were alight at a time. When early in the Crimean War, the Royal Naval Hospital was opened on the Bosphorus, the surgeon in charge demanded 3,000 lb. of candles, claiming that candlelight was more brilliant than lamplight. The Board of Admiralty reproached him for this extravagant idea, and he had to be content with candles for the officers' quarters only.

The reader of *Vanity Fair* may remember that Sir Pitt Crawley used a rushlight in a tin candlestick at his town house; this was in the teens of the nineteenth century. And during Becky's first night at Queen's Crawley, he broke into her room 'in his night-cap and dressing-gown, such a figure!... "No candles after eleven o'clock, Miss Becky," said he. "Go to bed in the dark, you pretty little hussey".'

Sir Pitt Crawley's rule would however have seemed extravagant to some. Aubrey[2] tells a pleasant tale of the mathematician William Oughtred, the author of the *Clavis Mathematicae* (1631). His wife, says Aubrey, 'was a penurious woman, and would not allow him to burne candle after supper, by which meanes many a good notion is lost, and many a probleme unsolved; so that Mr Henshawe, when he was there, bought candle, which was a great comfort to the old man'. (This was Thomas Henshaw, the brother of the physician, Nathaniel Henshaw; both were early members of the Royal Society). It is fair to add that Oughtred was a man of peculiar habits which may well have annoyed his wife. He used to lie abed with his doublet on till eleven or twelve o'clock; according to his son Benjamin, he 'studied late at night; went not to bed till 11 a clock;

[1] Bacon, *Of Building*.
[2] *Brief Lives*, vol. II, 1898, p. 110.

had his tinder box by him; and on the top of his bed-staffe, he had an inke-horne fix't. He slept but little. Sometimes he went not to bed in two or three nights, and would not come downe to meales till he had found out the *quaesitum*.'

Candles indeed seem to have offered a favourite means for economy to the miserly. Nollekens provides another example. With him a candle 'was a serious article of consumption: indeed so much so, that he would frequently put it out, and merely to save an inch or two, sit entirely in the dark, at times too when he was not in the least inclined to sleep.' This fancy caused him to scold his maid for causing the candle to flare when she opened the yard door, and his man Dodimy for lighting himself to bed with a candle. ' "Why don't you go to bed in the dark, you scoundrel?'—"It's my own candle," replied Dodimy. "Your own candle! well, then, mind you don't set fire to yourself." '[1]

Candles, of course, were not merely costly; they were dangerous, and those in charge of our great libraries have always been nervous about them. Candles may have been used occasionally in medieval libraries; indeed, the fifteenth-century code of the Canons Regular of the College of S. Mary at Oxford permits a student to enter the library at night with a candle if he has some urgent reason.[2] Bodley, however, set his ban on all forms of fire and flame, and this practice was followed generally. Artificial heating caused as much apprehension as artificial light, and the installation of a heating system at the Bodleian in 1845 caused dire consternation until the pipes were safely insulated.[3] Leibniz did his best to secure a separate room which could be heated and lit at Wolfenbüttel when this library was rebuilt in 1706-10, but this did not materialize till 1835. As late as 1872, the will of Sir Thomas Phillipps contained the express provision that 'no hot air flues or gas pipes shall be ever lighted or used in Thurlestaine House'. Warmth and light (as well as his unfortunate daughter Henrietta, his offending son-in-law James Orchard Halliwell and all Roman Catholics) were thus carefully excluded from his great library.[4] Lack of heating has indeed had its tragedies, as well as its inevitable discomforts. Descartes met his death in 1650 as a result of Queen Christina's peculiar habit of wanting to discuss

[1] J. T. Smith, *Nollekens and his Times*, ch. XIV.
[2] Strickland Gibson, *Some Oxford Libraries*, 1914.
[3] Sir Edmund Craster, *History of the Bodleian Library, 1845-1945*, 1952, p. 134.
[4] A. N. L. Munby, *Phillipps Studies*, vol. II, 1952, p. 109.

philosophy with him in an unheated library at 5 o'clock in the morning during the Swedish winter.

The result has been that very few libraries have till quite recent times been open except in the hours of daylight, and for much of the year students were compelled to work in unheated gloom. Candles could, of course, be used in the domestic library. But neither candlelight, nor its humbler companion the rushlight (so attractively described by Gilbert White in *Selborne*) makes a good illuminant, and only the most persevering of readers would continue their studies into the night. There were, naturally, a few obstinate exceptions. Johnson's friend, Elizabeth Carter, the poet, being determined to overcome her natural incapacity for learning, 'read both late at night and early in the morning, taking snuff, chewing green tea, and using other means to keep herself awake'. By this method she acquired a knowledge of almost every known language, dead or living. But in the process she injured her health, suffering from frequent and severe headaches all her life.[1] Horace Walpole was another midnight scholar, preferring to write between 10.0 p.m. and 2 a.m. 'when I am sure not to be disturbed by visitants'.[2]

Candlelight might well have had a chapter to itself, for in the long history of English reading it has given more comfort and delight, and weakened more eyes, than anyone can estimate. There was a time when the word served as the happy synonym for 'twilight'; a man might write 'In the evening about candlelight'—as we might say 'about dusk'.[3] Elia, who spent thirty-six years of his life in the counting-house of Boldero, Merryweather, Bosanquet and Lacy in Mincing Lane, working eight or ten hours a day with no holidays but one day at Christmas, one at Easter, a week in summer, and of course his dismal London Sundays, describes how through these years he had no time of his own but candlelight time, when he used to weary out his head and eyesight with his reading. His firm, with surprising generosity for the period, retired him at fifty with a pension of two-thirds his salary, so that ever after he might read, write or scribble as the mood seized him.[4]

Constance Holme in *The Splendid Fairing*, pictures aptly the gloom of candlelight in a lonely farm-house. 'The candle,' she writes, 'as

[1] *D.N.B.*
[2] J. Pinkerton, *Walpoliana*, 1799.
[3] As indeed someone did in one of the queries printed by the *Athenian Mercury*.
[4] *The Superannuated Man*.

always drove the impression of utter darkness home. No other light produces that same effect of a helpless battle against the dark. No other is so surely a symbol of the defiant human soul, thinking it shines on the vast mysteries of space. No other shows so clearly the fear of the soul that yet calls its fear by the name of courage and stands straight, and in the midst of the sea of the dark cries to all men to behold that courage and take heart.' And again: 'A candle may shine like a good deed in a naughty world, but anyone who is used to candles must often think the good deed very puny and the naughty world very large.' Portia indeed seems to magnify its radiance when she exclaims 'How far that little candle throws his beams.'

Good oil lamps were not available till the last years of the nineteenth century. Gas lamps with incandescent mantles were not in common use till even later, and for long of course, they were confined to towns. R. L. Stevenson had a curious enthusiasm for gas lamps. Oil lamps, he says, are hard to kindle, easy to extinguish, pale and wavering in the hour of their endurance. But of the coming of gas lamps he writes, 'The work of Prometheus had advanced by another stride. Mankind and its supper parties were no longer at the mercy of a few miles of sea-fog; sundown no longer emptied the promenade: and the day was lengthened out to every man's fancy. The city folk had stars of their own; biddable, domesticated stars.' He concludes with an awful warning of the horrors of electricity: 'To look at it only once is to fall in love with gas, which gives a warm, domestic radiance fit to eat by.'[1]

The inevitable price of nocturnal study was damaged eyesight. Chaucer complained that it would make 'A-night ful ofte thyn heed to ake', and Elizabeth Carter would have agreed with him heartily. Spectacles were of course a medieval invention; that painstaking civil servant Thomas Hoccleve in the fifteenth century, confesses that he should have worn them to prevent eyestrain, but his vanity forbade it, as indeed it has forbidden others since. But they were neither generally effective nor widely used till late in the nineteenth century, when indeed better forms of illumination were being developed. It cannot be a gross exaggeration to say that, before that time, nine-tenths of all the studious reading that was done was carried out in the hours of daylight. Gibbon tells us that

---

[1] R. L. S., *A Plea for Gas Lamps*.

'Happily for my eyes, I have always closed my studies with the day, and commonly with the morning'. Most wise readers must have followed a similar rule.[1]

John Selden must have provided himself with spectacles in generous measure. When in 1659 the library of over 8,000 volumes which he bequeathed to the Bodleian reached Oxford, several pairs were discovered marking places in various books he had been studying. Swift, purchasing spectacles for Stella on Ludgate Hill, gave her the warning 'Preserve your eyes if you be wise.' Both Bach and Handel probably owed their blindness to the writing of crabbed music script. Bach's boyhood feat of copying out a forbidden manuscript of organ composition by moonlight may well have begun the damage to his eyes. Milton's blindness, whether due to cataract or glaucoma, must have been aggravated by his writing, and he is said to have finished the *Defensio Secunda* (1654) against his physician's advice and at the expense of his eys.[2]

But let us remember what this means. If any protracted course of study must be undertaken mainly in the daylight hours, the only people free to accept such conditions would be, first, professors, tutors and students at the universities; secondly, clergymen, and lastly those men of wealth and leisure whose interests extend beyond administrative business or rural pursuits. Everyone can think of a few exceptions to prove this rule, but before 1850 the number of such exceptions was infinitesimal. When hours of work were long and holidays rare, when nothing but candlelight could illumine the darker hours, then only the leisured few could well afford the means of study.

Reading, of course, serves other ends than systematic study, and the great increase in the reading population since the beginning of the eighteenth century testifies to this. I have described elsewhere,[3] how in the time of Pepys the gentleman's study began to assume its modern shape, with book-lined walls clearly lit by bay windows. A hundred things may combine to tempt the reader to surrender

---

[1] According to Pope, both Addison and Dryden confined their study and their writing to the mornings; their afternoons were spent, the one at Button's and the other at Will's. Dryden came home earlier than Addison, who was inclined to stay at Button's far into the night. See Joseph Spence, *Anecdotes, etc., Collected from the Conversation of Mr Pope*, 1820.

[2] Amongst devices to preserve eyesight may be noted the *conserves* mentioned by Naudé (see p. 166 *infra*). These according to Diderot were spectacles fitted with plain (not convex) lenses to reduce glare. John Locke in his will refers to his 'silver screen to preserve the eyes in reading by candlelight.' (J. Harrison and P. Laslett, *The Library of John Locke*, 1965, p. 9.

[3] *Heritage*, ch. XIV.

himself: the choice of one favoured volume from a great company of its fellows, the comfort of the chair by the fireside or in the window, the mellow odour of calf bindings, the very atmosphere of the room and its furnishings. More important still, the chosen book will be not merely pleasant to handle and the product of an artist in paper, type and binding; it will be light enough to carry from its shelf to your chair, and to balance easily on your knee. In other words, it must be portable, neither too large nor too weighty. In the thirteenth century the wandering friars had little use for massive folios chained to monastic shelves; they needed portable volumes that they could carry in their scrips, and small Bibles and service books on fine vellum were made for them. So also in the eighteenth century, though for less pious reasons, Lydia Languish needed editions of *Peregrine Pickle* and her other favourites which she could read in comfort on her sofa, and fling under the toilet on the approach of Sir Anthony Absolute; even the volume of James Fordyce's *Sermons to Young Women*, which she thought proper to leave lying open on the table, was a duodecimo. Most of the novels in the circulating libraries at the end of the eighteenth century, including nearly all of the Minerva Press novels, were in fact, duodecimos, though they tended to grow larger in the nineteenth century. It is strange, however, to note that the really small book, such as we now call a pocket edition, is also something of an acquired taste, not at first commending itself to the new reader, who commonly desires an appearance of more meat on the bone, even if some of it be fat. There is perhaps a slightly sophisticated air about the pocket edition, with its India paper and its tooled binding. But the Penguin and its relations satisfy a modern demand for extreme portability in unsophisticated garb, being designed for the restless readers of today who must needs sacrifice some of the graces of living for the sake of what they hope is a higher standard of life. There is a change in values here which, whether we frown upon it or not, must at least be recorded. For those who must travel in crowded trains or live in miniature flats, this type of book has obvious uses. It is not a new type; there have for long enough been continental paper editions equally compact and sometimes better in design. There is good reason for a frown if a flat, equipped with every conceivable new luxury, lacks only the older luxury of a bookcase. But to what extent are such editions given a permanent home on a bookshelf beside their better dressed cousins? How many of them are discarded with last month's popular magazines? In other words, are they *temporary* books, expendable, to be read and thrown away, and so not books at all but mere ephemeral shadows of the real thing? And yet they are certainly not 'biblia a-biblia', for Elia would have delighted in these little books; his pockets would have been stuffed with them. It was that other sort of book for which he reserved his scorn—the indigestible volumes 'which no gentleman's library should be without'.[1] There are surely no grounds for anxiety here. A live library in your pocket is better than a dead library in your bookcase; and in every age literature has had its ephemeral fringe, both in form and content. Leaving this aside, the demand for portability is having a happy effect in book production in general. The day of the almost immovable folio is over, and even our most ponderous works of reference are assuming a format that is easier to handle and carry about.

[1] *Last Essays of Elia:* Detached thoughts on books and reading.

CHAPTER X

Gabriel Naudé and the Problems of Mass Production

THE introduction of paper and the invention of printing in the fifteenth century were followed not only by a great increase in the number of books published, but by a steady, though more gradual, increase in the size of the libraries needed to accommodate them. For the first time since the days of the Alexandrian Library or the equally large Arabian libraries at Cordova and elsewhere, librarians were faced by the problem of the mere quantity of books, with all its new implications of selection, classification and storage. In England, the growth of libraries was delayed owing to the troubles of the sixteenth century, and the problem scarcely made itself felt till the Restoration; in France the change was felt earlier.

It is well known that the medieval library was invariably small by modern standards. A glance at Appendix C in Dr Savage's *Old English Libraries* will show how small indeed they were; except for Christ Church and S. Augustine's in Canterbury and Bury St Edmunds (each with about 2,000 volumes), and Syon Monastery (1,450 volumes) few had more than 1,000 volumes, and the great majority were much smaller than this.[1] Before the seventeenth century, the normal English private collection rarely amounted to more than a few score volumes, probably stored in an oak chest, or laid flat on a table, or possibly kept on a shelf or two fastened to a wall. The occasional larger collection, such as those of John Fisher, Bishop of Rochester, Lord Lumley (who acquired many of Cranmer's books), Sir Thomas Smith, Dr John Dee, Sir Robert Cotton and Robert Burton, would be stored on fixed shelving, either sloping or horizontal. John Fisher's library, which was plundered by

---

[1] As many volumes were composite, the number of separate works would be much larger than this. There is a useful discussion of the size of monastic libraries in Knowles, *The Religious Orders in England*, Vol. II, 1955, p. 350.

Cromwell just before his martyrdom, was described by a contemporary as 'the notablest Library of Books in all England, two long galleries, the Books were sorted in stalls and a Register of the names of every Book at the end of every stall'.[1] Where a library of the larger sort was kept in a room rather than in a gallery, fixed wall shelving can perhaps be assumed. During this period a gradual change in binding fashions reveals how the growing size of libraries compelled a change in arrangement. Graham Pollard in a recent article of considerable importance has shown how bindings with cameos or bosses or elaborate designs on their sides, intended for storage on sloping shelves, gave place in the seventeenth century to bindings with ornaments or lettering on the fore-edge or the spine, in order to save shelving space.[2]

It is unlikely that any English libraries in the sixteenth century rivalled in size the great collection of the historian Jacques de Thou in France, which amounted to 8,000 printed books and 1,000 MSS. The 3,000 volumes in Grolier's collection might however, have been matched by the library of Dr John Dee at Mortlake (which was famous enough to draw a visit from Queen Elizabeth), and that of Lord Lumley, (partly inherited from his father-in-law, the Earl of Arundel, and purchased after his death in 1600 for the ill-fated Prince Henry). Other notable collections such as the 2,000 volumes belonging to Robert Burton, the library of John Donne with its '1,400 authors besides his own papers and sermons', and the original Cottonian collection of about 1,000 volumes, must be regarded as exceptional in size for English libraries at the beginning of the seventeenth century. Later in that century the library of the jurist John Selden must have equalled De Thou's collection in size; over 8,000 of his books reached the Bodleian after his death in 1654. From Selden onwards a steady rise in numbers took place.

The famous collection of Samuel Pepys amounted to about 3,000 volumes, now displayed at Magdalene College, Cambridge, in the elegant presses in which he himself arranged them, all in double rows with large books behind and short ones in front.

The next sixty years was a period of brilliant scholarship and

---

[1] W. Y. Fletcher, *English Book Collectors*, 1902.

[2] Graham Pollard, 'Changes in the Style of Bookbinding, 1550–1830', *The Library*, 1956, pp. 71–94. See also pp. 175–6 *supra*.

aristocratic munificence, so that libraries grew rapidly in size. Bishop Stillingfleet's collection of 10,000 volumes was purchased mainly by Narcissus Marsh for his new public library in Dublin.[1] Bishop Moore's library, occupying eight chambers at Ely Place, held 29,000 printed books and 1,790 MSS; it was bought by George I for the University of Cambridge. Sir Hans Sloane's great collection at Chelsea included some 40,000 printed books and 3,516 MSS. And the even greater collection made by Robert and Edward Harley, the first and second Earls of Oxford, was estimated in 1741 at about 50,000 printed books, 350,000 pamphlets, 7,639 volumes of MSS, with 14,236 charters, rolls and deeds and 41,000 prints.

It is, of course, foolish to confuse quality and quantity. Figures are always deceptive, and in nothing so much as in the world of books. But the appearance of collections of this size meant that the new and difficult problem of their management had to be solved systematically. A man can carry in his head everything that matters about the contents and arrangement of his library if this amounts to five hundred volumes; with five thousand volumes, this might be difficult; with fifty thousand it would be quite impossible. The principles of arrangement and the routine of management must consequently be worked out, and the birth of what came to be called 'library economy' follows.

In 1627, when few English libraries possessed more than a thousand or so books, Gabriel Naudé published in France his *Avis pour dresser une Bibliothèque*, the first serious attempt at an outline of library organization. In 1642 Naudé was given by Cardinal Mazarin the task of collecting and arranging the great library which bears his name; and he had soon gathered from England, Germany, Flanders and Italy some 40,000 volumes for what he regarded with some justice as the eighth wonder of the world. He

---

[1] For the public library founded by Narcissus Marsh (1638–1713) in Dublin, see the account in Maura Tallon's *Church of Ireland Diocesan Libraries*, Dublin, 1959. It was a library of considerable size and importance for its period. Its three basic collections were (1) that of Bishop Stillingfleet, which Marsh acquired for £2,500 in 1704; (2) Marsh's own library of about 3,000 printed books, mainly Oriental, but including some seventeenth century science and mathematics; (3) the library of Marsh's first Keeper, the Rev. Elias Bouhéreau, a French Huguenot, which is strong in early French literature and in Huguenot volumes; and (4) the library of Bishop John Stearne of Clogher, bequeathed in 1745 and amounting to 3,000 volumes. With other more recent acquisitions the library now contains about 25,000 volumes, including 300 MSS and 80 incunabula.

was not without experience, for his own private collection amounted to 8,000 volumes; but the speed and efficiency with which he brought together the Bibliothèque Mazarine was remarkable. All the volumes were bound in morocco and stamped with the Cardinal's arms; and with surprising tolerance the library was dedicated 'à tous ceux qui y voiloient aller estudier'.[1] Naudé's greatest contribution to library economy is that for the first time he took scholarship and practical use as his main criterion, both in selection and in classification, setting it above considerations of rarity or prestige. A translation of Naudé's work by John Evelyn was published in London in 1661 under the title of *Instructions concerning erecting of a library*; and Evelyn must be credited with considerable foresight, for at that date the increase in size of English libraries was only just beginning.[2] The modern librarian will find much interest and some profit in a closer analysis of this pioneer work in library management.

Naudé begins with an emphatic declaration in favour of quality in books, rather than quantity. This is illustrated by a quotation from Seneca '*Quo mihi innumerabiles libros et Bibliothecas, quarum dominus vix tota vita sua indices perlegit*', and an epigram from Ausonius which Evelyn translates pleasantly:

> *That thou with Books thy Library hast fill'd,*
> *Think'st thou thy self learn'd, and in Grammar skill'd?*
> *Then stor'd with Strings, Lutes, Fiddle-sticks now bought;*
> *Tomorrow thou Musitian may'st be thought.*

'Quality' is defined in a tolerant and catholic manner; it is something that goes beyond personal tastes, and neither the works of the heretics, nor trivial pieces ('Libels, Placarts, Theses, Fragments, Proofs, and the like') are excluded. In this Naudé is far in advance of the restrictive policy that Bodley adopted at Oxford. With quality must go comprehensiveness. 'There is nothing which renders a Library more recommendable, than when every man findes in it that which he is in search of, and could nowhere else

---

[1] L. C. F. Petit-Radel, *Recherches sur les Bibliothèques Anciennes et Modernes*, Paris, 1819; Edwards, *Memoirs of Libraries*, 2nd ed., 1901; Hessel, *History of Libraries*, trans. R. Peiss, 1955.

[2] Evelyn's dedication of his translation of Naudé's book to Clarendon is notable because it contains the first known reference in print to the name of The Royal Society. It is not known how the name first originated. For his own library see p. 203 *infra*.

encounter; this being a perfect Maxime, that there is no Book whatsoever, be it never so bad or decried, but may in time be sought for by some person or other.' This is of course an echo of the elder Pliny's dictum, '*Nullum esse librum tam malum ut non ex aliqua parte prodesset*'.

After developing this general principle, Naudé turns in Chapter VI to the planning and situation of the library. He is evidently thinking here of the private library in a great house, not of a public or institutional library. We are warned to place the library 'in a part of the house the most retired from the noise and disturbance, not onely of those without, but also of the family and domesticks, distant from the streets, from the kitchen, the common hall, and like places; to situate it (if possible) within some spacious Court, or small Garden, where it may enjoy a free light, a good and agreeable prospect; the air pure, not too near to marshes, sinks, or dung-hills, and the whole disposition of its edifice so well conducted and ordered, that it participate in no kind of indecorum or apparent incommodity'. We are further to avoid dampness of the ground by raising the library up by at least a few steps, and the 'intemperature of the air' by building garrets and chambers above it. 'But all these difficulties... are nothing to those which are to be observed for the giving light, and conveniently placing the windows of a Library, as well for being of so great importance, that it be fully illuminated to the very farthest corners.' The provision of good natural lighting has always been a problem in library planning. Even Pepys was not satisfied with the lighting in his carefully planned library: 'So I think,' he wrote, 'it will be as noble a closet as any man hath, and light enough—though indeed it would be better to have a little more light.' Montaigne on the other hand claimed to have plenty of light in the round room at the top of the tower which he used as his library.[1] Naudé makes no reference to either artificial lighting or heating; both would have been judged at this time to be foolish and dangerous.[2]

In Chapter VII he discusses the order and disposition of the books. 'Without this, doubtless, all inquiring is to no purpose, and our labour fruitless... be the collection of Books whatever, were it of fifty thousand Volumes, it would no more merit the

---

[1] Montaigne, *Of Three Commerces*. See p. 199 *infra*.
[2] See p. 154 *supra*.

name of a Library, than an assembly of thirty thousand men the name of an Army, unless they be martially in their several quarters, under the conduct of their Chiefs and Captains. . . .' In regard to the arrangement itself, 'I conceive that to be always the best which is most facil, the least intricate, most natural, practified, and which follows the Faculties of Theology, Physick, Jurisprudence, Mathematicks, Humanity, and others, which should be subdivided each of them into particulars, according to their several members, which for this purpose ought to be reasonably well understood by him who has charge of the Library.' The principle is illustrated by a classification of Divinity as follows:

1. Bibles, 'according to the order of the tongues.'
2. Councils, Canons, Ecclesiastical constitutions, 'forasmuch as they retain the second place of authority amongst us.'
3. The Fathers, Greek and Latin.
4. 'The Commentators, Scholasticks, Mix'd Doctors, Historians.'
5. 'The Heretiques.'

In all the faculties, certain cautions are to be observed:

(a) 'That the most universal and antient do always march in front.'
(b) 'That the Interpreters and Commentators be placed apart and ranged according to the order of the Books which they explicate.'
(c) 'That the particular Treatises follow the rank and disposition of their matter and subject, in the Arts and Sciences.'
(d) 'That all books of like argument and subject be precisely reduced, & disciplined in their destined places,' so that any desired book can be found 'in a moment onely', however great the library.

Books too small to be bound alone should 'be joyned onely with such as treat upon the like or very same subject; and yet it were better to bind them also single. . . .'

The 'difficulty of handsomly reducing and placing certain mix'd Books in any *Classes* or principal Faculty, and the continual pains which attends the disturbing of a Library when one is to range a thirty or fourty Volumes into several places thereof' is noted.

There are two answers to this: (1) 'That there are but very few Books but what are reducible to some order, especially when one has many of them'; (2) the 'mix'd books' might be set apart at the end of each 'faculty' (i.e., in a miscellaneous class). It would be better to reserve a special place for new acquisitions, sorting them into the general classification at the end of each six months. The books would thus be 'dusted and handled twice a year'.

The proposed systematic arrangement is thought to be superior to the fixed shelf location of the Ambrosian library and some others 'where all the Books are indifferently ranged *pell-mesle*, according to the order of their Volumes and Ciffers [ciphers], and onely distinguished in a Catalogue, wherein every piece is found under the name of its Author'. There would also be need in this case for a 'Catalogue faithfully compiled according to the Classes, and each Faculty subdivided to the most precise and particular of their parts'.

In Chapter VIII, we are told, 'As to the binding of Books, there is no need of extraordinary expense; it were better to reserve that money for the purchasing of all the books of the fairest and best editions that are to be found.' It is noted that they do not now 'place their Books upon Desks, as the antients did; but upon Shelves that hide all the Walls'. This leaves more room for the museum objects which seem always to have been Evelyn's chief interest when he visited the libraries of Oxford and Cambridge, or that of Sir Thomas Browne at Norwich. In lieu of costly adornments, one may supply 'Mathematical Instruments, Globes, Mapps, Spheres, Pictures, Animals, Stones and other curiosities as well Artificial as Natural'. The shelves should be protected with 'searge, buckrom or canvas, fitted on with nails' (glass is not mentioned). And there should be 'Tables, carpets, Seats, Brushes, Balls of Jasper, Conserves[1], Clocks, Pens, Paper, Ink, Penne-knifes, Sand, Almanacks, and other small moveables....'

Chapter IX discusses the duties of the librarian, and the need for catalogues. 'In vain does a man strive to put in execution any of the aforesaid Expedients, or be at any notable charge for Books, who has not a design to devote and consecrate them to the publick use, or denies to communicate them to the least, who may reap any benefit thereby.'

[1] See p. 157 *supra*.

For this purpose there is need for 'some honest person, learned and well experienc'd in Books, to give, together with the charge and requisite stipends the title and quality of Bibliothecary unto ...'. There is need also 'to make two Catalogues of all the books contained in the Library, in one whereof they should be so precisely dispos'd according to their several Matters and Faculties, that one may see and know in the twinkling of an eye all the Authors which do meet there upon the first subject that shall come into one's head; and in the other, they should be faithfully ranged and reduced under an Alphabetical order of their Authors, as well to avoid the buying of them twice, as to know what are wanting, and satisfie a number of persons that are sometimes curious of reading all the works of certain Authors in particular ...'.

There should be 'free accesse to the Bibliothecary, who should introduce him with the least delay or difficulty' and 'persons of merit and knowledge might be indulged to carry some few ordinary Books to their own Lodgings, nevertheless yet with these cautions, that it should not be for above a fortnight or three weeks at most, and that the Library-keeper be careful to register in a Book destin'd for this purpose, and divided by Letters Alphabetically, whatsoever is so lent out to one or other, together with the date of the day, the form of the Volume, and the place and year of its impression; and all this to be subscribed by the Borrower, this to be cancel'd when the Book is returned, and the day of its reddition put in the margent, thereby to see how long it has been kept; and that such as shall have merited by their diligence and care in conserving of Books, may have others the more readily lent to them'.

That Naudé's book was an important landmark is plain. He was feeling his way towards a rational system of library organization. Nothing similar had so far appeared in England. Sir Thomas Bodley, who was an able administrator as well as a scholar, might have produced such a work, but none of his earlier librarians (except perhaps John Rous) were men of wide vision. Moreover, in the seventeenth century the Bodleian scarcely experienced the problem of quantity (as distinct from space); beginning with 2,000 volumes, it reached 16,000 in 1620, but it was 1714 before the total number of printed books reached 30,000. At Cambridge, the University Library in 1649, before the arrival of the Lambeth collection, possessed only 1,000 books and 400 MSS; by 1710 it had 14,000 books. The Royal Library was equally limited, so far as the number of books is concerned; when it finally reached the Museum, it had no more than 9,000 printed books.

It was, nevertheless, a Royal Librarian who made the first written contribution to library economy in England. John Durie, a moderate Protestant divine, was Keeper of the Royal Library from the death of Charles I to the Restoration, though for much of this time he was travelling abroad. In 1650 he published *The Reformed Librarie Keeper*, which includes an account of 'one of the chiefest libraries in Germanie', namely Wolfenbüttel, where in 1691 Leibniz was to become librarian. Durie had a more tolerant and scholarly view of the work of a national library than was common at this time; he may well have based it on Naudé's book. His ideal was to expand the Royal Library into a truly national collection, whose function should be 'to keep the publick stock of learning, to increase it, and to propose it to others in the way which may be most helpful to all'. This ideal was far in advance of the times. Probably neither the Royalists nor Puritans would have supported it in practice; if the more extreme Puritans, including Hugh Peters, had had their way, the library would indeed have been sold and dispersed. The credit for saving it belongs probably to Bulstrode Whitelocke, the keeper of the great seal (to whom Durie owed his appointment as librarian) and perhaps to Selden, who was also responsible for arranging the transfer of Archbishop Bancroft's library to Cambridge. As has been mentioned, the major part of Selden's own great library went to the Bodleian after his death, so he must be accounted one of the principal benefactors of English libraries in the Commonwealth period.

Richard Bentley, the classical scholar and a much greater man than Durie, took charge of the Royal Library in 1694. His plans for expanding and reorganizing the library received scant encouragement from the authorities, mainly perhaps because funds were not available. He embodied them in a broadside *Proposal for Building a Royal Library*, 1697, in which he urged the establishment of a genuine national library in a new building, to be built out from S. James' into the Park. Three years later however, the Cotton collection was purchased for the nation, and in 1707 when Cotton

House was also acquired, the Royal Library was moved there. The Cotton and Royal Libraries went later to Essex House, to Ashburnham House (where the famous fire occurred) and to Westminster School, before finally reaching the British Museum.[1]

The greatest librarian of this period, Leibniz, owed much to Gabriel Naudé's work, and something also to John Durie and Richard Bentley. Leibniz visited England in 1673 and again in 1676, but he spent most of the four years 1672-76 in Paris, at the time when Colbert was vigorously expanding the Royal Library. In 1676, Leibniz became librarian and historiographer to the Duke of Brunswick-Lüneburg at Hanover, and in 1681 he also took charge of the important library at Wolfenbüttel, with its 30,000 volumes. He was perhaps the first scholar-librarian to have a real vision of an organized, comprehensive, scholarly reference library, adequately endowed, with regular acquisitions, and with all the emphasis on quality, rather than on variety or cost. Like all good librarians of earlier days, Leibniz was much besides a librarian; he was a great philosopher, a great mathematician and no mean historian. And to this—particularly perhaps to his historical researches which began in France under the guidance of the Jesuit and Maurist scholars—he no doubt owed his conception of what a great research library should be able to offer to the student. Indeed, there is nothing more likely to produce an able librarian than hard experience of the problems of research in a major subject, and the vision to comprehend the resources which other students need in other fields. This was certainly true in 1700, and it is not without truth today.[2]

If Wolfenbüttel owes some of its fame to the philosopher Leibniz, it gained perhaps a different sort of notoriety from a later visitor in the person of that brilliant scoundrel Casanova de Seingalt, who spent a week there in 1764 studying Homer; he called it the happiest week of his life. Unexpectedly, Casanova himself became a librarian during his declining years, when he was in nominal charge of Count Waldstein's library at Dux in Bohemia, (this was the brother of the friend and patron to whom Beethoven dedicated his sonata). At Dux he spent his time trying to recapture his youth

---

[1] The development of the idea of an English national library is sketched in detail in *Heritage*, ch. XII.

[2] See A. L. Clarke, 'Leibniz as a Librarian,' *The Library*, 1914, pp. 140-54, and A. Hessell, *A History of Libraries*, trans. R. Peiss, 1955, p. 71.

by writing his memoirs, and pouring forth in addition, a multitude of treatises on every subject under the sun.

Two characteristics especially distinguish the Restoration period in library history. These are, first, the rapid accumulation of printed books and pamphlets and their concentration, together with great stores of MSS from both Western monastic and Oriental sources, mainly in the aristocratic private libraries of the day; and secondly, the impulse given by the accessibility of these collections and by the more scientific approach of the new age, to carry out systematic research and to analyze and collate the wealth of material now for the first time available to the student. It was no accident therefore, that the Restoration period produced an unprecedented array of scholarly work in many fields, particularly perhaps in mathematics, history and classics. Names such as Newton, Bentley, Dugdale, George Hickes, Humfrey Wanley, Henry Wharton, Thomas Hearne, William Nicolson, Thomas Tanner, Thomas Rymer, and Thomas Madox in our own country, and on the Continent Baronius, Jean Mabillon, Du Cange, Descartes, Leibniz and the Bollandists—these call to mind some at least of the new and important work that was proceeding. These circumstances were both unprecedented and compelling; and it would have been strange indeed if scholars had not been driven to study for the first time the principles governing the organization of research material in libraries. If the main contribution to these studies came from Gabriel Naudé in France and Leibniz in Germany, the work of Durie, Evelyn and Bentley in England is not without importance. And the special interest of English scholars of this period in Anglo-Saxon and medieval studies turned attention perhaps to literary and bibliographical studies rather than to library economy. In this field the pioneer work of Bale and Pits in the sixteenth century was developed by Thomas Tanner in his *Bibliotheca Britannico-Hibernica*, 1748, by William Nicolson in his *Historical Library*, 1696, by William Oldys in his *British Librarian*, 1737, and by many cataloguers from Humfrey Wanley downwards. Their work, which lay with the material for research rather than the library that housed it, is not merely a genuine tribute to the scholarship of the period, but is complementary to the ideas of Gabriel Naudé which Evelyn made accessible to English book collectors.

Part Two
The English Domestic Library

CHAPTER XI

The Beginnings

THE term 'private library' means different things to different people. To the bibliographer or the bookseller it may suggest a collection gathered together by a bibliophile in much the same way as porcelain or glass or clocks are sometimes collected. A private library of this kind (the great collection amassed by Sir Thomas Phillipps in the nineteenth century is an obvious example) may be of prime importance to the bibliographer, whatever the methods or motives of its collector. The world owes an immense debt to the aristocratic collectors of Tudor and Restoration times, if only because so much that is beyond value was preserved by their efforts, and because in most cases their collections sooner or later came into the public keeping, either in the university or national libraries. But these private collections were not for the most part working libraries gathered for the purpose of individual study or personal enjoyment. This type of collection may be distinguished from the former by the word 'domestic', because in general it is inseparable from the word 'home', being so often the nucleus round which family life at its best is established. Domestic libraries in this sense also have their special importance, not so much perhaps for the bibliographer as for the social historian and the literary historian; they are the bricks and mortar out of which our literary and intellectual heritage is built.

The domestic working library in this sense is something much more than the shelf or case of books which it comprises. It cannot be fully considered in isolation from its background. It is its owner's workshop; and to understand its significance one must know something not only of the works themselves, but of their owner, his purpose in collecting them, the sources from which they came and the use he made of them. The works in such a library are tools, and indeed more than tools. They have a vitality breathed into them by their owner as well as by their author: a vitality which transcends their material qualities of paper and ink and binding. They each have their birth and their begetting; they each have their destined history, whether it be triumphant or inglorious. Like their owners or readers they may be busy or idle, bad or good, companionable or unfriendly, productive or sterile. They each have their parents and grandparents, their guardians, their lovers, and perhaps their own children and grandchildren. In short, they are living things, and the library in which they live is their city and their motherland; they are members one of another. And mark this: they are influenced, as we are, by the society which they keep; by their owners and guardians, by their readers and admirers; and by their own shelf-companions. This city of books which is the working library has a life and a reality that is absent from any other sort of collection; for the life of a book is not realized, its heart is not set beating, till it is read and loved and made at home among its fellows. Till then it sleeps, awaiting the touch that will raise it from the dead. The full creation of a book is a labour in which many must share: owner and reader as well as author. It is a seed which brings forth fruit only if it falls into good ground; and the good ground is the home into which it is adopted, and where it is nourished and enriched and enjoyed.

This then is the sense in which I use the term 'domestic library'. What is the story of such libraries in England? You would find examples in the Roman world, in the villa libraries of the time of Cicero and the younger Pliny. They flourished for five centuries or so, but with Sidonius Apollinaris and Boethius they come to an end, and are almost completely absent till they reappear in fourteenth-century Italy and fifteenth-century England. There are certain special conditions of life which favour the growth of domestic libraries, and without which they will rarely prosper. There must be a certain degree of literacy among at least a section of the population. There must be an adequate corpus of national literature, including a fair proportion that may be characterized as non-professional. There must be an appreciation of the value of books, both for their own sakes as objects of art, and for their contents. There must be an active book market, with publishers, scribes or printers, booksellers and perhaps fairs and pedlars. And there must be a class of people with settled homes and with sufficient security, leisure and wealth to enable them to enjoy books and

THE BEGINNINGS

to build up the habit of reading. These conditions obtained in the time of Cicero and Atticus. They disappeared with the fall of the Empire, but began to re-establish themselves in the time of Petrarch, Boccaccio and Chaucer.

In pre-Chaucerian England literacy was all but confined to the clergy. A few Saxon kings (Aldfrith of Northumbria, Alfred the Great and Æthelstan) took some interest in book production, but there were no lay scholars, and all the students at Oxford and Cambridge were destined at least for minor orders. There were privately owned libraries amongst the clergy of course, but these were in the main professional collections, hardly to be classed as domestic libraries. Even these were limited in number and scope. The first English collector on a large scale, Richard de Bury, Bishop of Durham (1281-1345) was unique in his zeal for amassing books, and his collection was far larger than any others of his day; it may have amounted to 1,500 volumes. It was a more personal (and therefore a more domestic) collection than most episcopal palaces could boast, for the Bishop had literary and humanist interests in advance of his time, and we are told that it was piled so thickly in his own chamber that he had to climb over the volumes to reach his bed. It was bequeathed to Durham College, Oxford, but it never reached its destination as the Bishop died in debt. Rather earlier, Robert Grosseteste, Bishop of Lincoln and first Chancellor of Oxford, (d. 1253) had left his collection to the Oxford Franciscans: doubtless a smaller library than Richard de Bury's, but Grosseteste was a greater man both as scholar and writer, and his library must have been outstanding.[1]

There were other scholar bishops in this period, but their collections would have been small by comparison, and mainly professional in character. One of them, Robert Kilwardby, Archbishop of Canterbury (d. 1279) is known to have carried off some Canterbury books and registers to his retirement in Rome.[2] The largest episcopal library known in any detail belonged to Richard de Gravesend, Bishop of London (d. 1303) whose catalogue lists eighty volumes valued at £116 14s 6d. The unsettled conditions

---

[1] On Grosseteste and Richard de Bury see *Heritage*, ch. IX and X.
[2] Tout in *D.N.B.* Others would include the Archbishops Thomas Bradwardine (d. 1349) and Simon Langham (d. 1376); also Adam Easton (d. 1397), William Rede, Bishop of Chichester (d. 1385) and William of Wykeham, Bishop of Winchester (d. 1404).

made it well nigh impossible for substantial libraries to be collected. Both bishops and nobles were still living a largely nomadic life, travelling from manor to manor as food and supplies were exhausted. For the more conscientious bishops travelling was further increased by the need for diocesan visitations. Moorman quotes the case of Richard de Swinfield, Bishop of Hereford, (d. 1317), a fragment of the roll of whose household expenses has survived. During 296 days covered by the fragment he moved his household 81 times; in the 51 days between April 10th and June 5th he slept at 38 different places.[1] No scholarly work or book collection could be expected under such conditions; it is likely that most bishops who are known to have produced books did most of their writing before their elevation to episcopal rank.

Religious houses with large estates imposed a similar burden on their administrators. Dom David Knowles quotes the case of a Prior at Durham; in 1298-9 he spent 119 days in travelling round his manors and in 1310-11 as many as 249 days.[2]

Only one instance of the library of a parish priest in this period is known in detail: that of Geoffrey de Lawarth, rector of S. Magnus, London. This contained 49 books, chiefly on theology, dialects and grammar, but including three medical works. Moorman also quotes the case of a rural dean of Worcester, whose two carts carrying his books were impounded for six weeks by the men who farmed the toll at Wychbold, causing him loss to the value of 100s.[3] In ecclesiastical collections at this time, the demarcation between official and personal books must often have been shadowy. It was the parish priest's responsibility to supply and maintain the service books, together with the ornaments and vestments, in his church, but after the thirteenth century this duty was to some extent transferred to the laity, and the churchwardens began to assume responsibility for the provision of books.

With Chaucer the scene begins to change, and the lay scholar, or at least the lay booklover, begins to appear. One of the first was perhaps Chaucer himself, in his home over the gatehouse at Aldgate, or in the country house described in the prologue to *The Legend of*

---

[1] J. H. R. Moorman, *Church Life in England in the Thirteenth Century*, 1945, p. 176.
[2] *Religious Orders in England*, vol. II, 1955, p. 325.
[3] Moorman, *op. cit.*, p. 99. The S. Magnus inventory occurs in a *Liber Decretorum* at Pembroke College, Cambridge.

Good Women. And in *The Hous of Fame* he tells us of his anxiety to get home from business to his books:

> *For whan thy labour doon al is,*
> *And hast y-maad thy rekeninges,*
> *In stede of reste and newe thinges,*
> *Thou gost hoom to thy hous anoon.*
> *And, also domb as any stoon,*
> *Thou sittest at another boke,*
> *Till fully daswed is thy loke,*
> *And livest thus as an hermyte,*
> *Although thyn abstinence is lyte.*

And back in his library over the city gate, he wearies his eyes with midnight composition:

> *Wherfor, al-so god me blesse,*
> *Joves halt hit greet humblesse.*
> *And vertu eek, that thou wolt make*
> *A-night ful ofte thyn heed to ake,*
> *In thy studie so thou wrytest,*
> *And ever-mo of love endytest.*

We know how deeply versed Chaucer was in Latin, Italian, French and English works, and can guess that his library was rich in the sources he used. Of all his books, perhaps he loved his Ovid most. In *The Hous of Fame* the *Metamorphoses* is referred to as 'thyn owne book', and in *The Book of the Duchesse* he seeks to cure his sleeplessness with the tale of Seys and Alcyone:

> *So whan I saw I might not slepe,*
> *Til now late, this other night,*
> *Upon my bedde I sat upright,*
> *And bad oon reche me a book,*
> *A romaunce, and he hit me took*
> *To rede and drive the night away.*

'Ovydes Art' was part of the curious volume in which the Wife of Bath's fifth husband used to read nightly of 'wikked wyves'; and a very substantial part of *The Romaunt of the Rose* came straight from Ovid.

From Chaucer's day onwards there was a steady increase in

literacy, especially in the south-eastern half of England.[1] That this increase did indeed take place can hardly be doubted, though its extent has been queried. Sir Thomas More's estimate, made in his *Apologye* (1933) is well known:

'If the having of the scripture in englyshe, be a thyng so requisite of precyse necessite, that the peoples soules shoulde nedes peryshe but if they have it translated into their own tongue: then must there the most part perishe for all that, excepte the preacher make farther provision besyde, that all the people shall be hable to reade it when they have it, of which people, farre more than fowre partes of all the whole divided into tenne, could never reade englishe yet, and many now too olde to begynne to goe to schole.'

H. S. Bennett[2] is inclined to dismiss this as little more than a rhetorical flourish; and it must be admitted that the estimate is expressed in peculiar terms. What precisely does 'far more than four-tenths' mean; and if 'the most part' are to perish, why say four-tenths rather than one half? More was never guilty of dishonest propaganda (indeed, he had no need to twist his arguments) nor did he commonly use loose phraseology. Respect for his integrity and judgement would lead one to guess that, of the people he was accustomed to meet in London, between forty and fifty per cent were illiterate. In other words, perhaps half the Londoners of his day could read to some extent. One must remember that there is no sharp line between the literate and the illiterate, and the ability to read may mean much or little; moreover the percentage would obviously be very different in the north or west of England. H. S. Bennett quotes some further evidence of an even more inconclusive nature on both sides of the question; and one concludes that More's estimate is as reasonable a guess for the London area as can be expected.

Over a century earlier in 1407, a remark by Master William Thorpe during his examination by the Archbishop of Canterbury gives us some slight basis for a further estimate.[3] Thorpe said that he had often tested the knowledge of parties of pilgrims, and had found that in any batch of twenty pilgrims, less than three could

---

[1] On the general question of literacy see *Heritage*, ch. XI.
[2] H. S. Bennett, *English Books and Readers, 1475–1557*, 1952, p. 28.
[3] A. W. Pollard, *Fifteenth-Century Prose and Verse*, 1903, p. 139.

repeat one of the Commandments, or say their Pater Noster, Ave Maria or Credo readily in any language. We can fairly guess that most men of this date who could read at all would pass this elementary test; and Thorpe's remark suggests therefore that 85 per cent of his pilgrims were illiterate. Both figures were admittedly rough guesses, but the decrease of illiteracy is beyond doubt. It is supported by evidence from many sources, and the case has been argued in two admirable articles in *The Library*.[1]

Though Latin was to remain for a long time as the language of the Church, and of law, medicine, science and scholarship in general, English established itself rapidly as the language of the ordinary educated layman. The vernacular preaching of the friars and parish priests kept it alive, and both Chaucerian and Tudor English owes not a little to the way in which our native language had been crystallized in the pulpit.[2] During the fourteenth century the religious plays produced in churches and churchyards were secularized, and were increasingly done in the vernacular.[3] Chaucer, Gower and Lydgate all helped to give shape and form to the new language; Gower, indeed, tried all three current languages for his three chief works, the *Speculum Meditantis* being in French, the *Vox Clamantis* in Latin and the *Confessio Amantis* in English. The development of English as the normal medium for correspondence and business documents was even more rapid, as the great series of Paston, Stonor and Cely letters show. The fifteenth century was a notable period for the foundation of schools, Eton being only the most famous of a large number. English was not, of course, taught as a subject in pre-Reformation schools. A large number of petty schools were, however, opened for teaching the ABC and reading; and some schools gave special attention to the needs of boys who did not wish to enter the Church but might desire training in the arts of writing and accountancy. Archbishop Rotherham, in founding his school at Rotherham in 1483, provided for a third master to give such boys instruction 'in the mechanic arts and other worldly affairs'. Another new departure occurred at Sevenoaks in 1432, where a London grocer, William

---

[1] J. W. Adamson, 'The Extent of Literacy in the Fifteenth and Sixteenth Centuries', *The Library*, 1930, 10. 163; H. S. Bennett, 'The Production and Dissemination of Vernacular MSS in the Fifteenth century', *The Library*, 1946, 1. 175.

[2] G. R. Owst, *Literature and the Pulpit in Medieval England*, 1933.

[3] Moorman, *op. cit.*, p. 143.

Sevenoaks, endowed a school whose headmaster was to be 'by no means in holy orders'.[1]

Some apprentices were provided with the necessary education by their masters. A record of one such case tells how a merchant, Robert Chirche, took an apprentice in 1442, and bound himself to send him to school for a year and a half to learn grammar, and for half a year to learn to write. The boy's friends complained that this had never been done, to his great harm and loss, but Chirche replied that the charge was false, and that the boy had been sufficiently instructed for his work.[2]

The custom of using posters and handbills for public information became common in this century: one must assume that there was sufficient literacy to justify it. And certain changes in the parish churches imply that the ability to read English and Church Latin was becoming more general. Clerestory windows were being added to many churches to provide more light in the nave; and a tendency began for all the windows to grow wider and taller. After the Reformation, the replacement of figures and paintings by inscriptions giving the Creed, the Lord's Prayer and the Ten Commandments implies a further advance in literacy. More important than this, the fifteenth century was notable for the installation of pews with book rests in the naves of many churches. This was indeed a revolutionary change, for before this period there was rarely any seating in the nave, except perhaps for stone benches along the walls of the aisles, intended for the aged and infirm. Pews would have made the nave unsuitable for the many secular purposes for which it was commonly used, such as church ales, feasting, and fairing, play-acting and dancing, and as a warehouse for goods placed in sanctuary or received in pledge by the churchwardens.[3]

Further confirmation comes in the kind of books that were most popular in the fifteenth century, and in the quantity in which these were sometimes issued. It was the age of the first great translations into English. These began with Chaucer himself, and with Ranulf Higden's *Polychronicon*, which was translated in 1387 by John de Trevisa, who, in the following year, also translated Bartholomaeus

---

[1] A. F. Leach, *The Schools of Medieval England*, 1916.
[2] Quoted by C. L. Kingsford, *Prejudice and Promise in Fifteenth-Century England*, 1925, p. 35; *Stonor Letters*, Intro, p. xlvi.
[3] On this see A. R. Powys, *The English Parish Church*, 1930.

Anglicus' *De Proprietatibus Rerum*; thus giving to the world in English the most popular universal history and the most popular encyclopaedia of the age. To these must, of course, be added many others, including the Wyclif translations which even though they were forced underground, so to speak, had a surprisingly wide circulation, especially in the West Country, East Anglia and London. Many anxious to read them were illiterate; others could not afford them;[1] but there seems usually to have been someone who could read them aloud; four centuries later, the *Rights of Man* was to achieve a very similar sort of underground circulation, and both cases testify to a fair degree of literacy among the humbler people. Wyclif apart however, translations formed a substantial and significant part of our literature in the fifteenth century—significant, because they indicate that people were reading who were not so familiar with the Latin tongue. During the fifteenth and sixteenth centuries, most of the classics became available in English translations: Virgil, Horace, Ovid, Seneca, Cicero, Pliny, beside some Greek; most of the other classical writers could be read in French or Italian.

If translations suggest the reading of books by ordinary people in their own homes, this is implied even more strongly by other types of book which were popular in this century: the courtesy books and manuals of etiquette and behaviour. To these must be added the commonplace book or scrapbook, which was a miscellaneous collection of pieces bound together, forming a whole library as it were, in a nutshell.[2]

The rising interest in personal religion gave a wide circulation to another type of book which seems to have found most of its readers in the homes of the newly appearing middle class. The devotional works of the contemplatives and mystics of the fourteenth and fifteenth centuries have survived in comparatively large numbers, and must have been produced in quantity; they were copied largely by the Bridgettine nuns of Syon and by the Carthusians of the London Charterhouse, Sheen and Mount Grace. One of the most

---

[1] A Norwich heretic deposed at his trial, *c.* 1428, that he had to pay four marks and forty pence (about five pounds) in London for a copy of the New Testament.

[2] H. S. Bennett, *Chaucer and the Fifteenth Century*, 1947, p. 164, quotes as an example a British Museum volume, MS Egerton 1995 (*c.* 1470–80) which combines in 450 pages some 15 items of romance, history, medicine, etiquette and sport, with various lists and notes for quick reference.

popular was Richard Rolle (*d*. 1349); over 400 of his MSS are extant. Another was Nicholas Love, Prior of Mount Grace, whose translation of the *Meditationes Vitae Christi* was produced *c*. 1410 under the title of the *Mirror of the Blessed Life of Jesus*. Not only was it one of the most widely read books of the century, but, as H. S. Bennett points out, it contains some of the most beautiful English prose of the century, too. Over 100 copies of the *Mirror of Christ* have survived, compared with eighty-two of the *Canterbury Tales*, fifty of *Piers Plowman* and forty-nine of Gower's *Confessio Amantis*. Still another was Walter Hilton's translation of the *Scala Perfectionis*, a work which continues to this day to give comfort and inspiration to the faithful.[1]

There were many other fifteenth-century works of this class, all testifying to the spread of the new habit of personal reading. The most famous of them all maintained its popularity unabated through the centuries of religious dissension, and is as well loved today as it ever was. Thomas à Kempis, the Augustinian monk from Kempen, near Cologne (*d*. 1471), was a foreigner, but he may almost be regarded as English by adoption, for his *De Imitatione Christi* had become firmly established in its English translation before the close of the fifteenth century. There can be no better evidence of the confirmed habit of private reading than the popularity of such a book, for the *Imitation* can only be read fruitfully in solitude and with the world shut out. We may call to mind the author's own words, inscribed on his portrait at Zwolle in Holland, where he lies buried, and said to have been written by him in a copy of the *Imitation*: 'In omnibus requiem quaesivi et non inveni, nisi seorsum sedens in angulo cum libello'; a significant sentiment which, however greatly it appeals to us today, would have seemed peculiar to most people living in any earlier period than the fifteenth century.

By the middle of the century, it is evident that MSS were being copied in fairly large numbers for domestic and lay readers. John Shirley the translator and scribe (1366–1456) was producing work of this kind in some quantity at his publishing office in London; he rented a large house and four shops from S. Bartholomew's Hospital for the purpose. The prefatory verses in one of his miscellaneous collections (B.M. Add. MS 16165) suggest that he was prepared to lend volumes to his customers, for the reader is exhorted

[1] On this see also *Heritage*, pp. 139–44.

to return the book to Shirley when finished with.[1] And there must have been many jobbing scribes such as William Ebesham, who was hired by the Paston family.

One more relevant feature of this century must be mentioned. Changes were occurring in domestic architecture in consequence of the new fashion whereby the lord and lady preferred to dine in private apartments, rather than to take their meals along with their retainers in the great hall.[2] The Norman house or castle provided little or no private accommodation for the lord and lady except a comparatively austere and unheated sleeping room. Langland noted the change in *Piers Plowman*; the lord and lady, he says, now dine by themselves 'in a chambre with a chymnye'. So also did that acute observer, John Selden, in the Commonwealth period, though without approval:

'The Hall was the Place where the great Lord used to eat, (wherefore else were the Halls made so big?), where he saw all his Servants and Tenants about him. He eat not in private, except in time of sickness; when once he became a thing cooped up, all his greatness was spilled. Nay, the King himself used to eat in the Hall, and his Lords sat with him, and then he understood Men.'

One sees Selden's point. But privacy seems an almost essential condition of culture. The Greeks managed without it; Euripides was unique in choosing a retired life in a cave or a cottage by the sea. But to us an element of privacy and seclusion appears a *sine qua non* of the intellectual life. Certain it is that without it, the private domestic library is not to be expected. The great castles of Norman and Plantagenet days were large and complicated organizations. They had their administrative records doubtless, but the only books they are likely to have possessed were any used by the chaplains who taught the boys in the lord's entourage. The coming of private apartments may have widened the gulf between lord and commoner, but it helped to make possible the culture of the Elizabethan age, by fixing the habit of reading and all that goes with it in the educated half of the population.

[1] H. S. Bennett, *op. cit.*, pp. 116–17.
[2] For the development of the Hall. see A. W. Clapham, 'The Origin of the Domestic Hall', in *Some Famous Buildings and Their Story*, and H. M. Colvin, 'Domestic Architecture and Town Planning', in *Medieval England*, ed. A. L. Poole, 1958, vol. I, pp. 37 ff. See also *Heritage*, p. 268.

Bearing all these points in mind, we might legitimately assume that domestic libraries were being collected by those who were acquiring the reading habit. There is, indeed, some confirmation of this; and the evidence, though scattered, is quite sufficient to support the assumption. Apart from direct histories of libraries (which do not occur before the Reformation[1]) the most fruitful source of such evidence can usually be found in letters, table-talk, diaries and essays, such as for example those of Cicero, the younger Pliny, Aulus Gellius and Athenaeus in the ancient world, and Pepys, Lamb and Leigh Hunt in later times. Fifteenth-century evidence of this kind is limited, but definite.

Apart from clerical libraries, it is likely that the earliest collections were made by prosperous merchants and civil servants. Chaucer's books have already been mentioned. It is in Chaucer that we first meet with the word 'study'[2]; the history of the study and the history of the domestic library after all, are much the same thing. John Carpenter, Common Clerk of the City, 1417–38, who was one of Richard Whittington's executors and was mainly responsible for applying part of Whittington's estate to the foundation of the Guildhall Library, is known to have been the owner of many books, which were left in his will to various friends; these included some Latin translations of Aristotle and a copy of the *Philobiblon*. He is remembered particularly as the compiler in 1419 of the *Liber Albus*, a collection of the laws and customs of the City extracted from the archives. Commercial success and literacy commonly go hand in hand, and there must have been many such collections in the City. No doubt there have often been business men who were not ashamed of their inability to write; Shakespeare's father, who was a general merchant in Stratford, is an example. But trade and commerce depend so closely on written records and speedy communications that the standard of education is always likely to be higher where trade is prosperous.

Much evidence of the ownership of books can be found in wills; and further research in this field would be fruitful. From the

---

[1] The first histories of English bibliography and libraries are to be found in the works of Leland, the Protestant John Bale (d. 1563), the Catholic John Pits (d. 1616), Thomas Tanner, Bp. of S. Asaph (d. 1735), the author of *Bibliotheca Britannico-Hibernica*, William Nicolson, Bp. of Carlisle (d. 1727), the author of the *Historical Library*, and William Oldys (d. 1761), the author of the *British Librarian*.
[2] On this word see *Heritage*, pp. 262 ff.

beginning of the fifteenth century books appear with increasing frequency in wills: sometimes single volumes, and sometimes larger collections. They were rightly regarded as valuable pieces of property, and it was often thought necessary for their sale or transfer to be properly authenticated. There is a note on a fly leaf of a manuscript at Gonville and Caius College, Cambridge, which reads: 'I bought this book from John Barclay on the Vigil of the Apostles Saints Simon and Jude, in the house of William Nessfield, stationer, before the following witnesses...', and the names of eight people are appended, ending with the words *cum multis aliis*. This was in 1309–10. There may have been some special reason in this case for so formal a ceremony; but the difficulty and expense of obtaining copies compelled a due regard for their value. The books in John Carpenter's will have already been mentioned. C. L. Kingsford quotes several instances of wills in the early years of the fifteenth century in which books are specified.[1] That of Henry le Scrope, third Baron Scrope of Masham (1376–1415) mentions nearly eighty volumes of French and Latin, and this was part only of his library. Dr Walter Crome, Rector of S. Benet Shorhog, left ninety-three volumes to the Common Library at Cambridge, his will being proved in 1452. Many similar records exist, and not all testators were aristocrats or ecclesiastics; some belonged to commerce or the crafts. A London draper, Thomas Walyngton, in 1403 left ten volumes, all concerned with religion. A mason of Southwark in 1411 bequeathed several books, including the Sunday Gospels in English, to S. Olave's Church. In 1474 Stephen Preston, of Sylton in Dorset, left a larger collection, including works of grammar, logic, sophistry and law, Boethius' *De Consolacione*, the *Prick of Conscience*, and a volume of S. Bonaventura. A merchant named Robert Skrayngham in 1467 left a copy of the *Polycronicon* to another merchant.[2]

One of the most interesting of fifteenth-century domestic libraries is revealed by the Paston letters. In these we see the owners of an ordinary and not very large Norfolk manor beginning to collect a small library of their own: the first instance of the kind of country-house library which becomes familiar in later centuries.

[1] C. L. Kingsford, *Prejudice and Promise in the Fifteenth Century*, 1925.
[2] The practice of mentioning specific books in wills survived, of course, till a much later date. On this see Sears Jayne, *Library catalogues of the English Renaissance*, 1956, p. 9; most of his lists of private collections came from this source.

There were over fifty volumes in the collection, including English and French romances, devotional works, some classical, historical and heraldic works, some composite works, and a few printed volumes. There are details too, of the similar library of their neighbour Sir John Fastolf at Caister. All the Pastons could read without difficulty, including the women members of the family,[1] and the men evidently knew some Latin and French. In addition, all could write, though there are signs that for the women writing was still a rather laborious task. When the family chaplain, Sir James Gloys, died, Sir John Paston did his best to get hold of his books, but he was too late; the best had been claimed by others and he lost interest in the remainder. Sir John occasionally hired a scribe, William Ebesham, to undertake copying for him. One of his productions was the *Great Book*,[2] a miscellaneous collection for which he charged 31s 1d, partly at 2d and partly at 1d a leaf. This was not a very rewarding occupation, and it is not surprising to find the scribe begging for any old clothes they have to spare: 'I have great need ... God knows, whom I beseech preserve you from all adversity. I am somewhat acquainted with it.'[3] Adversity there was in plenty both for the Pastons themselves and their scrivener; but there was also a new feeling of security and prosperity which survived the civil commotions and the political disturbances of that troubled century.

The Paston letters and other family correspondence surviving from the fifteenth century, leave us with the definite impression that the habit of writing as well as reading, had become firmly established not only in the new professions of law and medicine, but among merchants and shopkeepers in the towns and the squires and landowners in the country.

It would be impossible to write of English libraries in this century without mentioning the great humanist collectors who by a flight of fancy were said to have 'despoiled the libraries of Italy to enrich those of England': 'potential Maecenases' in R. R. Bolgar's phrase, such as Humphrey, Duke of Gloucester and John Tiptoft, Earl of Worcester, and ecclesiastics such as William Grey, Bishop of Ely, Robert Flemmyng, Dean of Lincoln, and (perhaps the most

---

[1] Anne Paston had her own copy of Lydgate's *Siege of Thebes*.
[2] B. M. Lansdowne MS. 285.
[3] H. S. Bennett, *The Pastons and Their England*, 1932, App. I. See also the same author's *Chaucer and the Fifteenth Century*, 1947.

scholarly of all) William Celling, Prior of Christ Church, Canterbury. Their activities however scarcely affected the domestic libraries of the period; and their influence on the academic curriculum and libraries of Oxford and Cambridge was slight. Moreover, the great majority of the books they imported from Italy were lost or destroyed in the troubles of the following century. The real age of humanism in England was to come later; and domestic interest was still largely confined to the type of books to be found in the Paston collection.[1]

[1] On the English collectors in Italy see R. Weiss, *Humanism in England during the Fifteenth Century*, 2nd ed. 1957. Though their immediate influence may have been slight, they marked the beginning of English interest in Italian culture which was to grow steadily in succeeding centuries. The young Lord Falconbridge (*Merchant of Venice*, I. 2. 73) who had 'neither Latin, French, nor Italian', so that Portia could neither understand nor be understood by him, must surely have been untypical of Elizabethan visitors to Italy.

CHAPTER XII

From Sir Thomas More to Samuel Pepys

THE first personal working library of any substance collected by an English lay scholar belonged to the statesman and martyr, Sir Thomas More. We can guess the nature and significance of this library from circumstantial evidence only: from More's background, from his written works, from his personal interests, from the esteem with which his friends, and especially Erasmus, regarded him, and from the reasoned and thoughtful consistency which governed all the actions of his life. No man of his time owed so much to that happy combination of wide reading and wide experience of men and things which is characteristic of the scholar-statesman. None lived in an atmosphere so permeated by the sense of learning in action; if his spiritul anchorage was the orthodox faith, his material anchors were the volumes on his library shelves. It is possible to argue that English home life as we know it today had its roots in the fifteenth century when it first began to reveal the security and stability and leisure which are its basis. There is no better illustration of this than the home life of More himself, which the homeless Erasmus regarded with wistful admiration, and of which his library and garden at Chelsea were in a special sense the heart and core. This picture of the sweetness and sanctity of More's home at Bucklersbury and later at Chelsea comes from the evidence of so many witnesses—Vives, Colet, Whittinton as well as Erasmus—that it cannot be doubted. The view of Robert Whittinton, the grammarian, is typical:

'More is a man of angel's wit and singular learning. I know not his fellow. For where is the man of that gentleness, lowliness and affability? And, as time requireth, a man of marvellous mirth and pastimes, and sometime of as sad gravity. A man for all seasons.'[1]

More's household was described by Erasmus as a Christian ver-

[1] Quoted by R. W. Chambers, *Thomas More*, 1935, p. 177.

sion of the Platonic Academy; by Chambers as a 'small patriarchal, monastic Utopia which came into existence first in the City, and then on Thames side'. At Chelsea William Roper tells us how his father-in-law, being 'desirous for godly purposes some time to be solitary, and sequester himself from worldly company; a good distance from his mansion house builded he a place, called the new building, wherein was a chapel, a library, and a gallery, in which as his use was upon other days to occupy himself in prayer and study together, so on the Fridays there usually continued he from morning unto evening, spending his time duly in devout prayers, and spiritual exercises'. This new building was in truth the cornerstone and heart of his home. Perhaps the library was in the gallery itself: a convenient place for books which lay flat on sloping shelves, as was the custom then. Doubtless, however, the children's schoolroom, their *Academia*, was in the mansion house itself, and it would have been there that they kept their own books and learnt their Latin, Greek, logic, philosophy, theology, mathematics and astronomy.[1]

More had tried without much success to educate both his first wife, Jane, and his second, Alice. Dame Alice however knew where his heart lay. When she visited her husband as he lay in the Tower, she pretended to upbraid him for his obstinacy, bidding him 'do as all the bishops and best learned of this realm have done. And seeing you have at Chelsea a right fair house, your library, your books, your gallery, your garden, your orchard, and all other necessaries so handsome about you, where you might in the company of me your wife, your children, and household, be merry, I muse what a God's name you mean here still thus fondly to tarry'.[2] More's reply was quiet and kindly, but her appeal was in vain.

We can only guess at the contents of More's library. He was born in 1478, the year when the first book to be printed in England made its appearance.[3] The books belonging to his father, John More, were presumably all in manuscript; and it was in a manuscript copy of Geoffrey of Monmouth that John entered the details of Thomas' birth; the volume still survives at Trinity

---

[1] There is a pleasant picture of the house at Chelsea in Anne Manning's *The Household of Sir Thomas More*.
[2] William Roper, *The Life of Sir Thomas More*.
[3] R. W. Chambers, *Thomas More*, 1935, p. 49.

College, Cambridge.¹ Thomas' education, at S. Antony's School, in the household of Cardinal Morton, and at Canterbury College, Oxford, was austere and exacting, and it left him a profound Latin scholar and a trained thinker. In later life More was intimate with all the great humanists of the day: with Fisher, Tunstall, Colet, Grocyn (who taught him Greek), and Linacre, and with Erasmus, Budé, Vives and Cranevelt. The library of such a man cannot help but have reflected the humanism of his circle.

The year 1516 was perhaps the high-water mark of pre-Reformation humanism in England. Lutheranism, with its distortion of the term 'new learning', was still at least a year in the future. Erasmus published his *Novum Instrumentum*, the great version of the New Testament in Latin which crowned his life's work, and the *Institutio Christiani Principis*. More published his *Utopia*. And the first Renaissance college at Oxford, Bishop Foxe's foundation of Corpus Christi College with its beautiful *trilinguis bibliotheca* which won Erasmus' lavish praise, was open. There is no record of More using any library but his own; probably no English library could have given him much that he did not find on his own shelves. In those happy days when printing was but a generation old, and before the mere quantity of authors had multiplied excessively, as it did a century later, the coming of the printed book had already solved some of the student's problems. No longer was there so great a need for the scholar to wander from one monastic or academic library to another in search of his manuscripts. The printing press had brought many of the fruits of learning within the reach of a man such as More; only the homeless Erasmus was forced to use other men's libraries.² To More therefore, the printed book was the answer to a problem, not the problem in itself which it became in the seventeenth century under the sheer quantity of production. The need for a great national collection had not yet arisen. There was no national library in Utopia, as there was in the New Atlantis a century later. But More's reference to humanism and printing is of interest. On his fourth voyage, Ralph Hythloday

---

¹ MS O. 2, 21.
² Erasmus had, of course, his own collection of books which travelled about with him. When he reached More's house from Italy in 1510-11, he filled the time before the arrival of his books by writing the *Praise of Folly*. Ten years earlier, he tells how in Paris the little money he was able to beg or borrow, went in buying the Greek books he needed for his *Adagia*. (Ep. XXIX, LXXX).

took with him a library—a 'pretty fardel of books', consisting of Greek works, some in Aldus's small print. The Utopians had previously used skin, bark and reeds for their writing, but Hythloday showed them how to make paper and how to print.

More must have taken many of his books with him into the Tower, where he wrote his last works, the *Dialogue of Comfort* and the *Treatise on the Passion*. But before the *Treatise* was well finished, his books and writing material were taken from him, and for some of the time he was forced to use a piece of charcoal as a pencil. On June 12, 1535, Richard Rich, the Solicitor-General, who had already trapped Fisher by a promise of secrecy, visited More, with two attendants, Southwell and Palmer; the examination which he then conducted gave him the opportunity for the perjury which secured More's sentence. Rich appealed to his assistants to confirm his story, but they were brave enough to refuse: 'Master Palmer, upon his deposition, said that he was so busy about the trussing up of Sir Thomas More's books in a sack, that he took no heed to their talk. Sir Richard Southwell likewise, upon his deposition, said that because he was appointed only to look unto the conveyance of his books, he gave no ear unto them.'[1] So his books were taken away, and the end came.

The martyrdom of S. John Fisher, Chancellor of the University of Cambridge and Bishop of Rochester, (1459-1535) took place a fortnight before that of Sir Thomas More. He was an able scholar, a great theologian and a great humanist. His library, which Cromwell seized after his conviction, has been described as the 'notablest Library of Books in all England, two long galleries full, the Books were sorted in stalls and a Register of the names of every Book at the end of every stall'.[2] The Bishop had intended his collection to go to S. John's College, Cambridge.

In the dark period that intervened between the death of More and the accession of Elizabeth I there is little to record. An inventory made at Losely House in 1556 by Sir William More reveals the progress of the manorial library. The walls of the library were hung with maps of England, Scotland and France, a perpetual almanack and a small picture. The furniture included a globe, a counter-board and cast of counters, a slate for notes, a pair of

---

[1] William Roper, *op. cit.*
[2] W. Y. Fletcher, *English Book Collectors*, 1902, p. 17.

compasses, a pewter inkstand, a pounce box, pens of bone and steel, and a penknife. There were about 140 volumes of printed books and MSS. Nearly 100 of these were in English: several volumes of chronicles, some translations from the Latin, some devotional works, including the Bible and the *Scale of Perfection*, a collection of medical and veterinary treatises, a few volumes on surveying, geometry and cosmography, and a number of legal works of the kind that a country justice of the peace would need. For recreation there was Chaucer, Gower, Lydgate, Barclay and Skelton, and a copy of John Heywood's *The Spider and the Flie*, which had been published only that year. There were also many volumes in Latin, French and Italian, including Cicero, Juvenal, Horace, Caesar, Boccaccio, Petrarch, Machiavelli and Froissart. No mention is made of any wall shelving, and the books may have been kept in chests, or even laid on tables. This must have been a much richer collection than the average manor of the time could boast.[1]

Probably a more typical collection of this period would have been the one described in the papers of the Johnson family at Glapthorn. John and Sabine Johnson, had, in the parlour of their manor at Glapthorn, Northamptonshire, a single shelf of books, including a Froissart, a Bible, and some works of devotion. Glapthorn was an ordinary middle-class household belonging to a merchant of the Staple. The other furnishings of this parlour were comparatively luxurious; there were carpets from Antwerp, wainscot panelling, curtains, chairs, stools and a clock, and plenty of velvet or embroidered cushions to render more tolerable the box-type oak chairs; there was also a pair of tables with chess men, and an old Venetian lute.[2]

In the Elizabethan period book-collecting for the first time became more systematic and more extensive. Two influences were at work. Under the inspiration first of Matthew Parker, and later of the Elizabethan Society of Antiquaries, there was a deliberate attempt to rescue the manuscripts dispersed at the suppression of the monasteries. Secondly, the rising output of printed books made it necessary for scholars such as Hooker, Donne and Burton to assemble substantial working libraries of their own.

[1] H. S. Bennett, *English Books and Readers, 1475–1557*, 1952, quoting J. Evans, 'Extracts from the Private Account Book of Sir W. More', *Archaeologia*, 1855, 36. 284–92.
[2] Barbara Winchester, *Tudor Family Portrait*, 1955.

The history of the domestic library is perhaps but little concerned with the antiquarian movement. The motives behind this remarkably successful salvage operation were as much political and religious as scholarly; part at least of the intention was to recover the historical evidence of the continuity of Ecclesia Anglicana. The leaders of the movement included three keepers of the Records at the Tower: William Bowyer and his son Robert, and William Lambarde, the compiler of our first county history, the *Perambulation of Kent*, 1576; Laurence Nowell, Dean of Lichfield; John Stow, the author of the *Survey of London*; William Camden, headmaster of Westminster School and author of the *Britannia*; Francis Bacon; John Speed, the cartographer; Sir Henry Savile; Lord William Howard of Naworth; and the young John Selden and James Ussher. It was however Sir Robert Cotton, Sir John Doderidge, the judge, and Sir James Ley, afterwards Earl of Marlborough, who presented to the King on behalf of the Society the unsuccessful petition for a charter for an academy of historical studies, with a library associated with it. But the noblest outcome of their efforts was the magnificent collection which Cotton himself formed. The original Cotton collection included less than 1,000 volumes; and it can safely be stated that never has so rich a collection of treasures been assembled in such a comparatively small compass. A very large proportion of the manuscripts thus re-collected by the Elizabethan antiquarians were later to reach a safe anchorage in the British Museum or in one of the University libraries.

Certain notable collections of this period must be mentioned briefly. At the death of his father-in-law, the Earl of Arundel, in 1579, John, Lord Lumley (1534–1609) inherited a collection of about 1,000 printed books and 150 MSS, half of which had come originally from Cranmer's library. The Lumley library, which was especially rich in medicine and geography, had reached 2,800 volumes by 1596.[1] Thomas Wotton (152–187), the father of Sir Henry Wotton, gathered his famous collection of finely bound volumes, inscribed in a happy imitation of Jean Grolier with the legend THOMAE WOTTONI ET AMICORUM: an inscription which set a precedent for the hospitality offered to scholars by nearly all

---

[1] The catalogue of 1609, ed. by Sears Jayne and F. R. Johnson, was published by the British Museum, 1956. The catalogue of Cranmer's library was printed by Edward Burbridge in 1885, and reprinted in C. E. Duffield's edition of his Works, 1965.

the aristocratic collectors of the following centuries. The statesman and classical scholar Sir Thomas Smith had a collection of about 1,000 volumes. The library of Dr John Dee, the astrologer and mathematician, at his Mortlake house is said to have been three times as large. This was famous enough to have drawn a visit from the Queen; two visits in fact, for on the first occasion she arrived just after the death of his wife, and would not trouble him. Part of Dee's library was destroyed by a mob in 1583, and the rest was dispersed after his death.[1]

John Stow, whose *Survey of London* (1598) was inspired by Lambarde's *Perambulation of Kent*, began collecting books and charters and transcribing MSS in 1560, devoting all his fortune to the task, and in later years spending £200 annually on new material for his library. In 1568 his collecting instinct came near to getting him into trouble. He was accused before the council of possessing a copy of the Duke of Alva's manifesto against Elizabeth, but the charge was apparently dropped. In the following year however the Bishop of London was directed to have his library searched, and a list of 'old fantastical popish books' in his collection (including, incidentally, a translation of Bede, some medieval chronicles and medical works) was compiled. Nothing however came of the matter, and Matthew Parker's confidence in him was unshaken; he undertook much editorial work for the Archbishop, producing on his behalf editions of Matthew Paris, Thomas Walsingham and the *Flores Historiarum*. His own collection was well known to all the Elizabethan antiquaries. In the *Survey* he mentions that he possesses some of John Shirley's publications.[2] 'This gentleman ... amongst his other labours, painfully collected the works of Geoffrey Chaucer, John Lidgate and other learned writers, which works he wrote in sundry volumes to remain for posterity; I have seen them and partly do possess them.' In describing the tomb in S. Mary Overy, where John Gower is shown lying with his head pillowed on his three major works, Stow states that he possesses the *Vox Clamantis* and the *Confessio Amantis*, but had never seen the *Speculum Meditantis*.

[1] See M. R. James, *Lists of Manuscripts formerly owned by Dr John Dee, with Preface and Identifications*, Bibliographical Soc., Supp. to Trans. 1. 1921. There is a good popular account of Dee in Denis Meadows, *Elizabethan Quintet*, 1957. See also *Heritage*, pp. 233-4.
[2] See p. 155 *supra*.

There is a glimpse of the libraries of Richard Hooker and John Donne in Izaak Walton's biographies.[1] Shortly before Hooker's death, he was told of a fire at his house, and on learning that his books and papers were safe, he replied 'Then it matters not, for no other loss can trouble me'. After his death his estate, consisting mainly of his books, was valued at £1,092 9s 2d, and his collection must therefore have been substantial. We are given a view of John Donne's study before his death in 1631. His books included '1,400 authors, most of them abridged and analysed in his own hand', besides six score of his sermons and a great collection of business documents. There were pictures on the walls, but we are not told how the books were arranged. For so large a library, fixed wall shelving seems probable, with the books either standing upright or lying flat—perhaps a mixture of both. About 100 volumes from Donne's library have been identified. Some were bequeathed by Selden to the Bodleian, having presumably been bought at the sale after Donne's death. Others went to the Middle Temple library through the agency of Robert Ashley, who died ten years after Donne.[2]

Few books point so plainly to research in a library as *The Anatomy of Melancholy*. In this great work Robert Burton is said to have cited nearly a thousand different authors, thus all but rivalling Pineda, whom Sir Thomas Browne held up to ridicule for the 1,040 authors cited in his *Monarchia Ecclesiastica*; 'Pineda', he said, 'quoted more authors in one work than are necessary in a whole world.' For the *Anatomy*, Burton must have relied in the main on the resources of his own collection, which is said to have amounted to 2,000 volumes. His will provided that Bodley's Librarian should select what he needed, and John Rous chose 581 books; another large portion of his library went to Christ Church, where Burton had been librarian. The Bodleian thus acquired a valuable collection of English literature, including Shakespeare's *Lucrece* and *Venus and Adonis* (of which it had so far no copies), and an equally important collection of the ephemeral news-books, pamphlets,

---

[1] For Izaak Walton's own library, see Sir N. H. Nicolas' ed. of *The Compleat Angler*, 1836 or 1860, vol. I. Many of his books are now in the Winchester Cathedral library.

[2] See Sir Geoffrey Keynes, *Bibliography of Donne*, 3rd ed., 1956, pp. 204–22, and his *Books from Donne's Library*, Trans. Cambridge Bibl. Soc., vol. I, 1953, pp. 64–8; also John Sparrow's article in *The Times Literary Supplement*, July 29, 1955.

plays and jest-books which Bodley himself had determined not to touch.[1]

In this period it would be wrong to ignore the libraries of the poets, though we can only guess their nature and size from the sources they used. Chaucer gives us much more information about his library than Shakespeare does. But it is possible to draw up a conjectural list of the works which Shakespeare knew or consulted; and a very imposing list it is. One cannot, of course, assume that all such works were in his own library. In his London days he had access to the library of Henry Wriothesley, Earl of Southampton, at Southampton House in Holborn—probably a very fine collection. It is scarcely conceivable however, that the New Place at Stratford on Avon was not provided with a collection of his own books; there is an imaginary picture of him in his library there in Carola Oman's novel *The Best of his Family*. Shakespeare's will made no mention of his books. John Hall the physician (1575–1635) who married Shakespeare's elder daughter Susanna, inherited the New Place through his wife in 1616; and he in turn left his papers and his 'study of books' to his son-in-law, Thomas Nash, after which nothing further is known of them.[2]

Similar lists can be made of the books used by Sidney and Spenser, though with more difficulty, especially in Spenser's case. Though Spenser was a scholar, and had read widely, he was not an exact scholar; and, as C. S. Lewis remarks, 'the fruits of his reading met and mingled and transformed one another till they became unrecognizable.'[3] Ben Jonson's chequered career gave him less opportunity to collect a settled library of his own. That he had an outstanding collection in his earlier days is certain, but it was constantly being depleted to raise cash, and finally about 1622 it was destroyed by fire. Later, amongst the contributions he received from his patrons, was an annual gift of £20 from the Earl

---

[1] On Burton's books see A. N. L. Munby, *The Libraries of English men of letters*, 1964, p. 7 and references there quoted. Dr Munby also notes here the collection of about 1,100 volumes made by Lord Herbert of Cherbury (1583–1648), most of which went to Jesus College, Oxford.

[2] Anders, *Shakespeare's books*, 1904; *Shakespeare's England*, vol. I, p. 280. But the authoritative work is Geoffrey Bullough, *Narrative and Dramatic Sources of Shakespeare*, to be completed in seven volumes, of which five have so far been issued (1965). Though Shakespeare may have consulted some manuscripts, he seems to have worked mainly from printed sources popular in his day.

[3] C. S. Lewis, *English Literature in the Sixteenth Century*, 1954, p. 355.

by a lucky chance a manuscript catalogue of the library compiled in 1724 which came to light in Australia in 1908; this listed about 2,000 volumes, including many incunabula.[1]

It is of interest to note that the Master of Madertie, the founder of the Innerpeffray Library, was a college friend of Montrose's at Saint Salvator's. It was at Montrose's first battle with the Covenanters at Perth that Madertie was captured while carrying a flag of truce and imprisoned. Something is known of Montrose's own books at Kinnaird, and particularly of his interest in the first folio edition of Sir Walter Ralegh's *History of the World* (1614), which was a favourite of his throughout his life.

Just as Montrose carried about with him his copy of Ralegh's *History of the World*, so Sir Walter Ralegh himself is said to have kept as his constant companion Sir Thomas Hoby's translation of Baldassare Castiglione's *Il Cortegiano*. So also Thomas Cromwell had his manuscript copy of Machiavelli's *Il Principe* (written in 1513 but not printed till 1532, five years after his death); this, and the *Defensor pacis* of Marsiglio of Padua, accompanied him everywhere. A hundred years later Oliver (as Margaret Irwin notes in *The Proud Servant*) doubtless found this same volume of *Il Principe* in his uncle's library at Hinchingbrooke and absorbed its lessons. (Oliver's great grandfather, Morgan Williams, had married Thomas Cromwell's sister and adopted the family name). So also Alexander the Great kept a Homer under his pillow throughout his campaigns. So Petrarch carried about with him a pocket edition of S. Augustine's *Confessions*.[2] Napoleon, who did everything on a grand scale, took whole libraries with him on his campaigns, but he treated his books as expendable, discarding them through the carriage window as he tired of them; this bad habit persisted at St Helena, where he had a collection of 8,000 volumes, which he threw one by one on the floor after he had read them. Even more memorable is the picture of the young Gibbon, as a captain in the Hampshire Militia, reading his Horace while he rode at the head of his battalion; 'On every march, in every journey, Horace was

[1] Paul Kaufman, 'The Earliest Free Lending Library in Britain', *Library Association Record*, 1961, pp. 160–2.

[2] One occasion when Petrarch found his copy of S. Augustine useful was during his ascent of Mt. Ventoux, near Avignon—the first recorded instance of mountaineering for pleasure. During the climb he was both impressed and disconcerted by coming upon the saint's reference to men who explore the heights of mountains and the circuit of the stars, and neglect themselves.

of Pembroke for the purchase of books.[1] Milton's librar[y]
well have been large. Anne Manning in her imaginary di[ary of]
Mary Powell, his first wife, gives a picture of the lodgi[ngs]
which he brought the seventeen year old Mary; there wa[s a]
room, half of it occupied by the bed and the other half filled [with]
piles of books. There is a story—a servant's tale—that Mil[ton's]
'undutiful children' combined to cheat him over house[hold]
matters, and even to sell his books secretly.

Though we are mainly concerned here with English librari[es, a]
glance at Scotland and France in this period may be permitte[d. It]
is probable that in the late sixteenth and early seventeenth c[en-]
turies the great houses of Scotland were better equipped w[ith]
libraries than those in England. There were young and vigor[ous]
universities at Edinburgh, Glasgow, St. Andrews and Aberde[en,]
and the general level of culture was high even though moral sta[n-]
dards may have been low. Copies of the works of Sir Dav[id]
Lyndsay (1490–1555), poet and Lyon king-of-arms, are said t[o]
have been on the shelves everywhere, in castle and cottage alike[,]
and scholars such as the mathematician John Napier (1550–1617)[,]
the laird of Merchiston, who invented logarithms and the earlies[t]
calculating machine, may well have had a richer library than an[y]
contemporary English scientist enjoyed. David Drummond[,]
Master of Madertie, founded the Innerpeffray Library in 168[0]
"for the benefit and encouragement of young students"; for al[l]
practical purposes the oldest public library in Scotland, it still sur[-]
vives today in the building provided by Robert Hay Drummond[,]
Archbishop of York, in the mid- eighteenth century.[2] Not onl[y]
the library, but its complete records since 1747 survive, showin[g]
the use made of it by students of every class in the thinly populate[d]
area around Crieff. Its only possible rival in Scotland was th[e]
library at St Mary's in Dundee, the management of which passe[d]
in 1442–3 from the Abbey of Lindore to the Burgh of Dunde[e,]
becoming thereby a town library, rather than a monastic collection[.]
During the next four centuries a library of some 6,000 books wa[s]
built up; practically the whole collection was, however, destroye[d]
by fire in 1841. Only a handful of books survived the fire, includin[g]

---

[1] See Dr Simpson's ed. of Jonson, I, pp. 250–71, XI, pp. 593–603, and A. N. L. Munb[y,] *The Libraries of English Men of Letters*, 1964, pp. 5–6.

[2] Paul Kaufman, 'A Unique Record of a People's Reading, *Libri*, 1964, XIV, pp. 22[-]42; 'The rise of Community Libraries in Scotland,' *Bibl. Soc. of America*, 1965, LIX.

always in my pocket and often in my hand.' Lawrence of Arabia likewise was accompanied by Aeschylus and Aristophanes on his journey from Jeddah to Damascus.

A comparative study of such men and their books (Gibbon excepted, they were mostly men of action) would be fruitful. There is material for such a work in *The Anatomy of Bibliomania*, but it needs digesting and developing.

The growth of the great private collections at this time can be even better illustrated from across the channel. The increase in the number of printed books and in the size of private libraries proceeded faster in France than in England. There was nothing in the England of the mid sixteenth century to match the finely bound library of Jean Grolier (1479–1565); this is believed to have totalled about 3,000 volumes, of which 550 much-prized examples survived its dispersal in the seventeenth century. Still less could any English library match the great library of the historian and discriminating collector, Jacques Auguste de Thou (1553–1617), who acquired some 8,000 printed books and 1,000 manuscripts, with some of the finest French binding in the fanfare style. In this same period, the essayist Montaigne (1533–92) has given us in his essay *Of Three Commerces* the most detailed account we have of any sixteenth-century domestic library. Like Burton with his *Anatomy*, Montaigne obviously had the use of a substantial collection of books. Imagine a round room, perhaps 45 feet across, with five rows of shelving round the walls, broken only by three windows and his desk. This is his description of it:

'I never travel without books, either in peace or war; and yet sometimes I pass over several days, and sometimes months, without looking on them: I will read by and by, say I to myself, or tomorrow, or when I please; and in the interim, time steals away without any inconvenience. For it is not to be imagined to what degree I please myself and rest content in this consideration, that I have them by me to divert myself with them when I am so disposed, and to call to mind what a refreshment they are to my life. 'Tis the best viaticum I have yet found out for this human journey, and I very much pity those men of understanding who are unprovided of it. I the rather accept of any other sort of diversion, how light soever, because this can never fail me. When at home I a little more frequent my library, whence I overlook at once all the concerns of my family. 'Tis situated at the entrance into my house, and I thence see under me my garden, court and base-court, and almost all parts of the building. There I turn over now one book, and then another, on various subjects without method or design. One while I meditate, another I record and dictate, as I walk to and fro, such whimsies as these I present to you here. 'Tis in the third story of a tower, of which the ground room is my chapel, the second storey a chamber with a withdrawing room and closet, where I often lie, to be more retired; and above is a great wardrobe. This formerly was the most useless part of the house. I there pass away both most of the days of my life and most of the hours of those days. In the night, I am never there. There is by the side of it a cabinet handsome enough, with a fireplace very commodiously contrived, and plenty of light; and were I not more afraid of the trouble than the expense—the trouble that frights me from all business, I could very easily adjoin on either side, and on the same floor, a gallery of an hundred paces long, and twelve broad, having found walls already raised for some other design, to the requisite height. Every place of retirement requires a walk: my thoughts sleep if I sit still; my fancy does not go by itself, as when my legs move it: and all those who study without a book are in the same condition. The figure of my study is round, and there is no more open wall than what is taken up by my table and chair, so that the remaining parts of the circle present me a view of all my books at once ranged upon five rows of shelves round about me. It has three noble and free prospects, and is sixteen paces in diameter. I am not so continually there in winter; for my house is built upon an eminence, as its name imports, and no part of it is so much exposed to the wind and weather as this which pleases me the better, as being of more difficult access and a little remote, as well upon the account of exercise, as also being there more retired from the crowd. 'Tis there that I am in my kingdom, and there I endeavour to make myself an absolute monarch, and to sequester this one corner from all society, conjugal, filial, and civil; elsewhere I have but verbal authority only, and of a confused essence.'

Not till the Commonwealth period was there in England a private collection as large as that of Jacques de Thou. This was the library of John Selden, the jurist, who was keeper of the records at the Tower for a period, and the author of many legal and political works, but perhaps best known to the ordinary reader for his *Table Talk* (1689), which was edited by his secretary Richard Milward. He was one of the first collectors of oriental material on a large scale, and his knowledge of this field is revealed in his *De Diis Syris* (1617). Over 8,000 of his books, including his oriental MSS, came to the Bodleian after his death. His scholarly judgement and tolerating principles exercised a moderating influence over the Puritans at a critical time for English libraries. It was probably owing to his intervention that the Royal Library, which the extremists would have dispersed, was saved. Under the Lord Keeper, Bulstrode Whitelocke, the care of the Royal Library was given to the Protestant divine John Durie, the author of *The Reformed Library Keeper* (1650), who himself had ideas of toleration only too rare in the Puritan camp. Durie's conception of a national library, 'to keep the publick stock of learning, to increase it and to propose it to others in the waye which may be most helpful to all', would doubtless have aroused violent opposition if ever the chance had come to put it into practice. To Selden also was due the temporary transfer of the Lambeth Library to Cambridge, where it was safer from molestation.

The end of the formative period of the English domestic library, and the beginning of the new age, is marked by possibly the most famous of all our private libraries, and the only one that has survived to this day in its original state: the library of Samuel Pepys. The existing presses were made in 1666, when 'his books were growing numerous and lying one upon the other'; and they are the earliest known examples of the independent movable cases which are now so constantly a feature of every man's study. The following is the entry in his diary for August 24, 1666:

'Up and dispatched several businesses at home in the morning, and then comes Sympson to set up my other new presses for my books, and so he and I fell in to the furnishing of my new closett, and taking out the things of my old, and I kept him with me all day, and he dined with me, and so all the afternoon till it was quite dark hanging things, that is my maps and pictures and draughts, and setting up my books, and as much as we could do, to my most extraordinary satisfaction; so I think it will be as noble a closet as any man hath, and light enough—though indeed it would be better to have a little more light.'

These same presses, designed for elegance as well as for use, still hold his books at Magdalene College, Cambridge. Their value to us today is that they remain a perfect and complete specimen of the library of a cultured gentleman of the Restoration period. In its contents and its arrangement we have the most intimate picture possible of the able civil servant and diarist—more intimate than any other relic could give, apart from the diary itself. If a man's clothes represent an extension of his personality, how much more vividly is this true of the books with which he surrounds himself, living with them as his chosen companions. The Pepysian library numbers about 3,000 volumes, arranged in eleven cases of red oak,[1] the doors being fashioned with small panes of glass, and the lower doors made to lift up. The books are in double rows, the taller volumes at the back and the shorter in front, so that every title is plainly visible; some very small volumes are placed on blocks to avoid an irregular line. It was set up first at the Navy Office in Crutched Friars, and later moved to York Buildings (now Buckingham St., Strand).[2]

The Pepys Library today rightly commands universal admiration, but it has had its detractors. William Cory, in a letter to one of his *discipulae* who was visiting Cambridge, speaks of Magdalene College 'where the absurd Pepys has his memory and his vulgar tastes embalmed in a library.' But Cory, able teacher and elegant poet as he was, had peculiar views about many things.

This was the beginning of the age of elegance and taste. The new and wealthy landowners were building their great Renaissance mansions, and furnishing them elaborately with fine books and pictures. It would be surprising if Pepys were the only collector of his day to give his treasures a worthy and beautiful setting. It is

---

[1] Not mahogany, as stated by W. Y. Fletcher in his *English Book Collectors*, 1902. Red oak is a North American timber, probably *Quercus borealis maxima* or *Qu. coccinea*; both these oaks were first introduced in England in 1691, and Sympson therefore must have used imported timber. Mahogany did not come into use till about 1730. For other similar cases made by Sympson, see *Heritage*, p. 273.

[2] A full descriptive and annotated catalogue of the Pepys Library, giving special attention to the medieval MSS. and the prints and drawings, is now in preparation and will, it is hoped, be published at an early date.

not impossible that the inspiration came to him in part from Sir William Coventry (1628-86) whose own study was refurnished at about the same time. On July 30, 1666, he writes, 'To Sir W. Coventry, at St. James's, where I find him in his new closet, which is very fine, and well supplied with handsome books.' In earlier days the individual book might often be a thing of great beauty, but there had been no chance to appreciate the beauty of a great collection of books, elegantly housed. Now indeed the chance had come. Few experiences are at once so satisfying and so stimulating as the sight of a comely room, well proportioned and well lit, with three walls lined with books, that in their appearance seem to respond to the care and knowledge of their owner.

Pepys had contemporaries who must certainly, one feels, have had an eye for the elegance of their library. John Evelyn himself, who translated Gabriel Naudé's *Avis pour dresser une bibliothèque*, foresaw the growth in size and beauty of the private collection of books, and knew something of the problems of caring for it. And Sir Thomas Browne's library must surely have been arranged with loving care. Evelyn described it in 1671: 'His whole house and garden being a paradise and cabinet of rarities, and that of the best collections, especially medals, books, plants and natural things.' As at Oxford and Cambridge, the curios and museum objects appeared to interest Evelyn even more than the books. One might have guessed that the *Religio Medici* was almost as much a product of library research as the works of Burton or Montaigne; but the author tells us that it was composed in his earlier years, 'when I had not the assistance of any good book, whereby to promote my invention or relieve my memory.'[1]

Evelyn's own library was larger than that of his friend Pepys, but it probably did not receive the elegant care that Pepys gave to his collection. There were nearly 5,000 books at Sayes Court when the catalogue of 1687 was made; this included many French and law books acquired by young John, in which Evelyn had little interest. Two cartloads of books were removed to Wootton in 1694, and most of the remainder followed in 1701, packed in thirty large cases and barrels. Nearly 1,500 were sold however, mainly because there

---

[1] Sir Thomas Browne's library was sold in 1711 after the death of his son, Dr Edward Browne; four copies of the sale catalogue survive. See Sir Geoffrey Keynes' bibliography, 1924, pp. 182-4, and A. N. L. Munby, *The libraries of English Men of Letters*, 1964.

was not room on the shelves at Wootton for them. A catalogue made in 1707 lists only 3,700 volumes.[1]

One of Pepys' contemporaries was Sir Kenelm Digby (1605-1665), the son of one of the Gunpowder Plot victims and a confirmed collector of books. His special interest was in the new experimental science, and he was indeed the only man associated with Bolton's projected Academy of 1617 who was also connected with the Royal Society forty-five years later; indeed, he was one of the twenty-one members of the Royal Society's first Council. Digby collected at least two libraries: (a) an English library, based on his father's collection, which was probably confiscated and burned by the Parliamentarians in 1643 when he was forced to flee to France; (b) in France he collected a new library, mainly of French works, but including Italian, Spanish, Latin and Greek books in all subjects from poetry to theology, mathematics, medicine and science. This amounted to more than 3,500 volumes, mostly in red morocco, and stamped with his monogram, KD (or KVD, to include the name of his wife, Venetia), with a fleur de lys in gold or the family arms. After the Restoration he returned to England, leaving his books behind in Paris. He never returned to claim them, and they were appropriated by the French government after his death. Fifty of the choicest volumes were secured for the Bibliothèque Nationale, where they still survive. The rest were sold in London in 1680, a first edition of *Paradise Lost* fetching only 2s, and a second folio Shakespeare 14s. Earlier in his life Digby had made gifts both to the Bodleian and to the new Harvard Library, founded in 1638. To the former he gave a collection of 238 manuscripts bequeathed to him by the learned Oxford mathematician, Thomas Allen, who had once been a friend of John Dee: and to Harvard he sent forty volumes, mostly theological.

During the sixteenth and seventeenth centuries, the English gentleman's study was gradually assuming its modern appearance. In the majority of pre-Restoration houses (and in some later ones), the collection of books was small. In such cases by far the commonest method was to store them in an oak chest,[2] or even to leave them lying on a table. Massive oak chests, such as the one that

---

[1] See W. G. Hiscock, *John Evelyn and His Family Circle*, 1955, pp. 146, 167, 214, 217; Sir Geoffrey Keynes' bibliography, 1937, pp. 3-30; and A. N. L. Munby, *The Libraries of English Men of Letters*, 1964, p. 11.

[2] See *Heritage*, pp. 264-6.

figures in the Mistletoe Bough legend, were familiar storage receptacles all through this period, and as useful for books as they were for clothes. In parish churches they were (and still sometimes are) the recognized means of preserving the registers, vestry minutes, churchwardens' and overseers' accounts, as well as such copies of the *Paraphrases* of Erasmus, Foxe's *Actes and Monuments*, Calvin's *Institutions* and the works of John Jewel, Bishop of Salisbury as the church possessed. It was doubtless a chest of this type in which Milton's friend, Hugo Grotius, was smuggled out of prison; the jurist's wife had sent it into the prison, packed with his books. In some larger libraries, chests continued in use together with presses and lecterns.[1] Chests were also convenient for travelling. There is an early instance in the chest that S. Boniface used to carry his books during his missionary journeys in Germany. The Latin term was *capsa* or *capsula*, and something similar must have been used in Roman days; when for example Catullus travelled to Verona, he was able to take with him only one of his book chests (*una ex multis capsula*).

Simple wall shelving, sometimes fixed on brackets, was also used on occasion for small collections. Chaucer's clerk Nicholas kept

> *On shelves couched at his beddes heed:*
> *His presse ycovered with a falding reed*

his copy of Ptolemy's astronomical treatise (the 'Almageste'), his astrolabe and his counters ('augrym stones'); the 'falding reed' was a coarse woollen curtain. The Johnson family at Glapthorn Manor kept their few books on a single shelf in their parlour.[2] Shelves are depicted in some seventeenth century portrait engravings: William Marshall's engraving of Francis Bacon in the 1640 edition of *The Advancement of Learning* shows him at his desk, with a bracket shelf above him carrying four volumes, spines to the wall and clasps to the front. The engravings of Sir William Dugdale in *The Antiquities of Warwickshire*, 1656, and his *History of S. Paul's Cathedral*, 1658, place him in front of some plain wall shelving, littered with an untidy array of books, mostly unbound. On the other hand the bracket shelves in the Holbein portrait of the merchant George Gisze are carved and much more ornate.

---

[1] E.g., Hereford Chapter Library; see B. H. Streeter, *The Chained Library*, 1931.
[2] See p. 192 *supra*.

The evolution of lecterns, stalls and wall shelving can be studied in J. W. Clark and Canon Streeter. In the sixteenth and seventeenth centuries, the heavier and more valuable volumes would often be kept on sloping shelves, sides up. Bindings with elaborate designs on their sides, or with cameos or bosses, were intended for this method of storage. But it was extravagant in space, and as libraries grew in size, it became necessary to change the method and to arrange the books upright on shelves side by side, showing only their fore-edges or spines. Designs and lettering on the spine or fore-edge in the seventeenth century reveal this new arrangement.[1] Private libraries maintained primarily for use rather than beauty would probably adopt whichever method might be most convenient for the various items; heavy folios and bundles of papers would lie on their sides, perhaps on tables; any ornate bindings would be given special positions on a lectern or reading desk; and smaller, less valuable works would stand upright on shelves where they would take less room and be easier to consult. This might well be the method adopted by scholars such as John Donne or Robert Burton. On the other hand, in a collection devoted to fine bindings with ornamented front covers, such as that of Jean Grolier, the volumes would all lie flat on sloping shelves. The great collection of De Thou was the first large library to be shelved with the spine outwards.

There were not however many collections of the standard of Grolier's. The ordinary Englishman's study and library must be regarded as developing gradually and according to size and convenience rather than any systematic plan, from the day when Chaucer wrote:

> *In thy studie so thou wrytest,*
> *And ever mo of love endytest.*

Except for the occasional scholarly collection, such libraries remained small, at least till the Restoration, and no elaborate provision of shelves or desks was needed. In the Elizabethan period,

---

[1] For the evolution of the lectern and stall system at Oxford, see especially J. N. L. Myres' comments on B. H. Streeter (*The Chained Library*, 1931) in his chapter in Wormald and Wright *ed.*, *The English Library before 1700*, 1958. For the copying of the Bodleian method at Hereford Cathedral and at the Old Library at Christ Church, see *Nat. Lib. of Wales Journal*, 1949–50, VI, pp. 363–4 and *Bodleian Lib. Rec.*, 1952, IV, pp. 145–9. See also Graham Pollard's article in *The Library*, 1956, pp. 71–94, and *Heritage*, pp. 264, 273.

with the growing output of printed books, scholarly working libraries were tending to grow in size, and until more convenient arrangements were adopted, they must often have presented an untidy appearance, especially as many of the new productions were pamphlets or tracts. The contemporary ballad known as *The Old Courtier of the Queen's*[1] contrasts various fashions of the age of Elizabeth with that of James I, including the

> ... *old study filled full of old learned books,*
> *And an old reverend parson you may judge by his old looks.*

against which is set the

> ... *new study stuffed full of old pamphlets and plays,*
> *And a new pedagogue chaplain that swears faster than he prays.*

Richard Hooker's study in which scholasticism, theology and history must have been well represented, might stand for the first type. It would be unfair and inaccurate to make Robert Burton's study stand for the second type, but it did indeed contain a large collection of pamphlets and plays, which are always difficult to arrange satisfactorily on shelves; note the distinction between 'filled' with books, and 'stuffed' with pamphlets.

At this date however, the provision of a library as a necessary architectural feature of a large house had not been generally accepted. The ideal great house described by Bacon in his essay *Of Building* makes no mention of a library: a curious oversight by the author of the dictum 'Reading maketh a full man'. It is not likely that Bacon had ever read *Gargantua*, or had noticed that François Rabelais endowed the fantastic and magnificent Abbey of the Thelemites on the banks of the Loire with 'six fair great libraries, in Greek, Latin, Hebrew, French, Italian and Spanish, respectively distributed in their several cantons, according to the diversity of their languages'. He must surely however have read Florio's translation of Montaigne, with its account of the essayist's circular library; and one would have thought that the need for a library in his great house would not have escaped the notice of a man who had taken pains to equip the New Atlantis with a national library.

---

[1] Sir Walter Ralegh, in *Shakespeare's England*, vol. I, 1916, p. 41, quoting MS. Ashm. 38, fo. 113.

It is, of course, unlikely that Bacon had seen any shelving designed for decorative as well as practical purposes. As has been noted, movable presses of good design did not appear till the Restoration. Fine examples of fixed wall shelving are scarcely found before Sir Christopher Wren's work in the libraries of Lincoln Cathedral and Trinity College, Cambridge, at the end of the century, and at S. Paul's in 1708–9. One of the earliest examples of the decorative treatment of fitted wall presses is at the Kederminster Library at Langley Marish parish church, Bucks, where the presses are provided with doors painted with Old Testament figures and saints. A tablet in the Kederminster vault states that Sir John Kederminster of Langley Park made and gave to this town for ever, the adjoining library in 1623; he died in 1631.[1]

---

[1] E. C. Rouse, *The Kederminster Library*, Records of Bucks, vol. XIV, 1941–6, pp. 50–66; *The Parochial Libraries of the Church of England*, 1959, plate III.

CHAPTER XIII

From Samuel Pepys to Dr. Johnson

THE Augustan age was perhaps the most brilliant period in the history of our libraries. Never have there been so many new collections of such rich magnificence; never have they been used by so many scholars to such effect. The harvest was comparable to the bountiful yield of the prairies when first the good earth was brought under the plough; and it is our happy fortune that there were at hand able men to reap and store the bounty. Though much had been done by the Elizabethan antiquarians, great quantities of the dispersed manuscripts of medieval England remained to be gathered together, arranged and interpreted; and quantities of material were also being brought from Italy and from the East. An astonishing amount of this work was concentrated into the seventy or eighty years that followed the Restoration.

It was a task that demanded both wealth and scholarship, and both were forthcoming. No other period in our history has produced such an outburst of aristocratic fervour in providing the materials of research. The current interest in inductive science or 'experimental philosophy' led scientists, historians and philosophers to co-operate in the foundation of the Royal Society in 1662, and in the second Society of Antiquaries in 1717; and the zeal for research which inspired the birth of such institutions extended to the whole field of knowledge. Science was not yet separated into its myriad compartments, and the great collections of a man such as Sir Hans Sloane (both Secretary and later President of the Royal Society), embraced quantities of material that did not fall within his particular interests of medicine and natural history. The Sloane collection was destined to become the main foundation collection of the British Museum, and the Act of 1753 providing for this scarcely refers to its particular interest in the field of science. On the other hand, the Arundel collection, which had slight scientific value (as we should understand the term today) was given in 1666 by Henry Howard of Norfolk to the Royal Society, though it was in part transferred to the Museum in 1830.[1] It was an unspecialised age, and the Royal Society in its first period was based on a broad conception of scientific humanism. Earlier plans for a national academy, such as those of Sir Humphrey Gilbert in 1572, Sir Robert Cotton and Edmund Bolton in 1617 were definitely humanistic; Francis Bacon's scheme described in the *New Atlantis* was humanistic at bottom, though couched in scientific terms.[2] Later the second Society of Antiquaries drew off some of the humanistic element from the Royal Society. Although the Augustan age is distinguished by the development of experimental philosophy, particularly in the sphere of mathematics, the progress of humanism was equally important and equally brilliant. The age was rich in classical studies, in historical research, in palaeography and in art and architecture. In the first three of these there are two requirements: the material must be accessible for research, and scholars must be at hand to harvest it.

For the first time indeed, there are signs that scholarship is being valued for its own sake, needing no justification other than its own natural interest. Scarcely any of the antiquarian research carried out in the period 1558–1660 could be called disinterested; the zeal for learning was not merely restricted to a very few, but nearly all of it was inspired by political or religious motives. The desire to salvage material in danger of destruction no doubt existed, but far stronger than this was the anxiety to bolster up pre-conceived theories by tracing things back to their origins for specific reasons: to investigate for example the origins of institutions (such as the English Church, or the law) to establish their continuity and authority; the origins of the British people, for the greater glory of the Tudors; the origins of families and places, to establish (or to invent) genealogical claims for the new landowners; the origins of Parliamentary Government, the historical basis of Magna Carta or the theory of absolute sovereignty and divine right, to support either side in the time of Charles I.

It is worth noting that Dugdale had to pawn manuscripts to make possible the publication of his *Monasticon*, and that it sold poorly when published. But his *Baronage* sold handsomely, for

---

[1] Arundell Esdaile, *The British Museum Library*, 1946, pp. 31, 254.
[2] *Heritage*, ch. XII, discusses all these points in more detail.

the descents were officially accepted by the Earl Marshal's Court, and it had thus an immediate practical use, and quickly became one of those works which no gentleman's library should be without. Earlier in the century, Spelman's great *Glossary* (1626) had received as cold a reception as the *Monasticon*, even though its importance was recognised by the few contemporary scholars interested in Anglo-Saxon and legal studies.[1]

The debt which we owe to the private collectors of this period is beyond estimation. In those spacious days the great private libraries were in a real sense taking the place of our present national and public libraries. Scholarship is generally hospitable to scholarship, and the genuine student found little difficulty in gaining access to his material. Professor Douglas in his important book on this period[2] underlines this fact strongly. The correspondence of the time, and the diaries of men such as Humphrey Wanley, show a long succession of scholars successfully seeking admission to these great collections. Indeed, their owners commonly regarded them as a public trust on behalf of learning, so that their eventual transference to the nation made little immediate change in the use that was made of them. Professor Douglas adds that 'to assess the debt of medieval scholarship to the families of Cotton and Harley would be to trace the course of English historical research from the foundation of these collections to the present day, when they repose in the British Museum'. Scarcely less is our debt to the many other aristocratic families of the day: the Earls of Sunderland, of Cardigan, of Derby, of Carlisle, and Lord Somers, and ecclesiastics such as Bishop Moore of Ely and Bishop Stillingfleet of Worcester.

There was, of course, the occasional example of inhospitality. James Wright, in dedicating his *History and Antiquities of the County of Rutland*, 1684, to the nobility and gentry of the county, records the prized privilege of admission to the Cottonian library, but complains that many of the local gentry were 'very shy in discovering the Evidences and Conveyances of their several Estates'. And Hearne notes in the preface of his *Textus Roffensis*, 1720, that the Dean of Rochester feared that publication would reduce the value of the MSS[3].

[1] See H. A. Cronne in *English Historical Scholarship in the Sixteenth and Seventeenth Centuries*, ed. L. Fox, 1956, pp. 79–80.
[2] D. C. Douglas, *English Scholars*, 1660–1730, rev. ed. 1951.
[3] Quoted by D. C. Douglas, *op. cit.*, p. 265.

The great private collections completely overshadowed the institutional libraries of the day. The Royal Library could offer no comparable assistance to English learning. And they were beyond doubt more accessible, more fruitful and more truly 'public' than either the Bodleian or the University Library at Cambridge. William Nicolson, whose *English Historical Library* was published in 1696-9, writes of 'the laudable emulation which is daily increasing amongst the Nobility of England, vying with one another in their curiosities and other rich furniture of their respective libraries', and concludes that this gives 'cheerful hopes of having the long hidden monuments of ancient times raised out of the present dust'. It was the beginning of the age of elegant design, in architecture, in landscape work, in furniture and in silver; and while the 'Nobility of England' were content to decorate some of their rooms with French or Chinese wallpapers, or with the pictures that have now become 'old masters', others were deliberately and worthily decorated with books. And we must concede that books make an excellent decoration for a room; none better indeed, now that presses built for beauty as well as use were available, and fine bindings that were not only beautiful in themselves, but might proudly carry the owner's crest. It was our good fortune that so many of these aristocratic collectors had eyes to penetrate the decorative veneer of their libraries, and to see something of the wealth within. And following the precedent of Thomas Wotton, they made their friends free of this wealth.

Let us glance at some of the scholars who used these great libraries, and in so doing lent a greater brilliance to the age. The period was particularly rich (as one might indeed expect, knowing the nature of the libraries) in Anglo-Saxon studies, in palaeography and in history. One thinks for example of William Dugdale, the author of the *Monasticon*; of George Hickes, whose *Thesaurus*, or 'Treasury of the Northern Tongues' appeared in 1703; of Humfrey Wanley, the greatest palaeographer of his time, who was for a brief period on the Bodleian staff—later he worked for George Hickes and finally became Harley's library keeper; his catalogue of the Harleian MSS in his monument. There was Henry Wharton, famous for his *Anglia Sacra*, 1691, a collection of lives of English archbishops and bishops down to 1540. There was Thomas

Tanner, the author of the *Notitia Monastica* and the *Bibliotheca Britannico-Hibernica*; William Nicolson, Bishop of Carlisle, the author of the *English Historical Library*; and Thomas Hearne, (also for a time on Bodley's staff) with his long series of editions of the English chronicles. There was Thomas Rymer, the editor of the seventeen volumes of the *Foedera*, the collection of treaties and alliances since 1101; and Thomas Madox, author of the *Formulare Anglicanum*, a chronological collection of charters from the Norman Conquest onwards, and the *History and Antiquities of the Exchequer*, which included the first printing of the *Dialogus de Scaccario*. And in other fields also there were outstanding names: Richard Bentley the classical scholar for example, who made use of the libraries of Stillingfleet and Moore; and Thomas Hobbes the philosopher, who perhaps relied on books less than some scholars (he was fond of saying that if he had read as much as other learned men, he would have been as ignorant as they were), but he must have used the library of the Cavendish family, whose patronage he enjoyed. Thomas Hobbes' comment contradicts Bacon's familiar dictum, suggesting rather that reading maketh an empty man. In the same vein Hazlitt affirmed that 'The idle reader at present reads twenty times as many books as the learned one.' On the other hand starvation may have as dire an effect as over-feeding. Lady Hester Stanhope told Kinglake that her only food was milk, and that her abstinence from food intellectual was carried as far as her physical fasting: 'She never looked upon a book, nor a newspaper, but trusted alone to the stars for her sublime knowledge.' But an exclusively astral diet is as unsustaining and as unbalancing to the mind as a diet of polished rice would be to the body. Man cannot live successfully without some communication with other minds, and Lady Hester Stanhope's life illustrates this truth.

A less extreme illustration might be found in Samuel Richardson, the professional letter writer, who himself confessed that he wrote far more than he read. 'My nervous disorders will permit me to write with more impunity than to read". He was not a well-read man, and his limitations in this respect are betrayed by the character and content of his writing.

It is right to remember here that on the Continent the seventeenth century was equally brilliant. The Counter-Reformation had a scholarly as well as a repressive side.[1] Rome, with its libraries and archives and publishing facilities was well placed to become the headquarters of Catholic scholarship. The calendar was reformed; the texts of the Canon Law and of the Latin Vulgate were revised; and definitive editions of the Fathers and of the Councils were projected. Baronius, the Vatican librarian, began his great series of ecclesiastical annals based on the Vatican archives, and had completed twelve folio volumes by his death in 1607. In Antwerp the group of Jesuit scholars known as the Bollandists (from their founder, John Bolland, 1596-1665) were publishing the *Acta Sanctorum*, and applying genuinely scientific criticism to material that was often legendary. And in France, Jean Mabillon (1632-1707) founded the sciences of Latin palaeography and of diplomatics; his work on the Benedictine saints gave him profound experience of Benedictine charters and archives, and his *De Re Diplomatica Libri Sex* became the foundation of all later study in this field. About the same time his contemporary Du Cange was engaged with his dictionaries (or rather encyclopaedias) of medieval Latin and Greek (1677-78). Contemporary too were the philosophers Descartes and Leibniz, the latter being also the greatest of the Renaissance librarians. And at the beginning of the century Justus Lipsius had published his *De Bibliothecis Syntagma*, the foundation of all modern histories of libraries.[2]

Two important working libraries at the close of the seventeenth century can be usefully noted here. The first is the library of Sir Isaac Newton (1642-1727). Some of Newton's papers passed to the Earls of Portsmouth at Hurstbourne, by whom the scientific portion of them was given to the University of Cambridge in 1888. Newton however, died intestate and his actual library was sold in 1727, after which it was lost sight of for almost two centuries. De Villamil however found an inventory at Somerset House which revealed that he left '362 books in folio, 477 in quarto, 1,057 in octavo ... with above one hundredweight of pamphlets

---

[1] On this see Lord Acton's chapter on the Counter-Reformation in his *Lectures on Modern History*, 1906. It is noteworthy that Ignatian piety developed and expanded the interest in personal religion which had contributed much to the growth of literacy. From S. Peter Canisius onwards, the Jesuits rightly regarded books as the most powerful weapons in their armoury.

[2] This work was published in 1602. See J. L. Thornton, *Classics of Librarianship*, 1957, pp. 6-12.

and waste books'. John Huggins, a warden at the Fleet Prison, paid £300 for the collection in 1727, and sent it to his son Charles, who was rector of Chinner, near Oxford. Charles added his bookplate to each volume; he himself died intestate however, and the collection was sold for £400 to the succeeding rector, Dr. James Musgrave, who pasted his own bookplate over those of Charles Huggins, and catalogued and pressmarked the library. After 1778, when Musgrave died, the books were sent to Barnsley Park, whence many were transferred to Thorne Park. There they were sold at auction in 1920, with no indication of their origin. Many were pulped, but some were acquired by the Babson Institute Library in Massachusetts. De Villamil discovered Musgrave's catalogue, which dates from c. 1760, and also catalogued the volumes still remaining at Barnsley Park in 1928—about 860 items. Details of the collection are given in De Villamil's book.[1]

The second notable collection of this time is the library formed by John Locke (d. 1704)—philosopher, political theorist, economist, educationist, theologian and medical doctor. At its largest this consisted of some 3,210 titles (3,390 vols.). About 820 of the books survive in the possession of the Earl of Lovelace, final descendant of Locke's heir, Peter King (later Lord Chancellor). The remainder of the collection was dispersed at various dates after his death.

Locke's library was a working collection in constant use by its owner, and elaborately catalogued and pressmarked. For the catalogue he used an interleaved folio copy of Thomas Hyde's 1674 catalogue of the Bodleian. The titles he possessed are marked 'L', and the rest of his books are entered on the interleaved pages, together with annotations, extracts, comments, prices, and desiderata. A second copy, somewhat abbreviated, exists in his MSS now in the Bodleian. Every volume has a pressmark, on the inside front cover near his signature, and also pasted on the spine; this referred merely to the shelf or box in which the book was kept—most of his books seem to have been in boxes. It consisted of a fraction, the top number referring to the box, and the lower figure the serial number in that box. In addition he had a shorthand description of each book in his catalogue, obtained by underlining the last two digits of the title-page date (or three digits if before 1600); and by

---

[1] R. de Villamil, *Newton the Man*, 1931. See also J. L. Thornton, *Scientific Books, Libraries and Collectors*, 1954, p. 219.

adding the final page number, which was overlined in the book. The price was entered in many cases on p. 11 of the book, in the bottom margin.

The library contents have been analysed for subject. Theology has 743 titles (23 per cent), politics, medicine and classics, and travel, all about 9 or 10 per cent. There were only 115 books on economics and 19 on education, but very little in these fields had yet been published. Of the languages represented, 42 per cent were in English, over a third were in Latin, and 17 per cent were in French. There were 30 Greek books and 81 Italian.

The greater part of the Locke manuscripts were acquired by the Bodleian in 1946. The printed books (about 835 volumes) and 11 manuscripts were sold by Lord Lovelace to the American collector Paul Mellon, who has now given them to the Bodleian; the MSS, including two volumes containing Locke's herbarium, and also his weather diary, were transferred at once, but the printed books will be retained by the donor during his lifetime, though microfilm copies may be made available for the Bodleian.

Mr Peter Laslett of Trinity College, Cambridge, regards this collection, together with Sir Isaac Newton's library at Trinity, as the two most important collections of the books of an individual Englishman which survive. This dictum overlooks, a little unfairly perhaps, Pepys' library at Cambridge and the Evelyn library, now at Christ Church Oxford. All four are in their way equally distinguished collections of the period.[1]

Leaving aside the libraries of the great collectors, the period is distinguished by hundreds of lesser collections. A few, by reason of some peculiarity, are to be classed as oddities. Some, though very small (and perhaps because of their smallness) exercised a significant influence on the work of their owners. And some were the well-established working libraries of great scholars and writers.

It was a great period for eccentrics; and eccentricity may as well embrace book collection as any other personal habit. We can fairly instance Thomas Rawlinson (1681–1725), who gathered books much as a squirrel gathers nuts. Addison nicknamed him Tom Folio—'a learned idiot—a universal scholar so far as the title-pages

[1] J. R. Harrison and Peter Laslett, *The Library of John Locke*, Oxford Bibliographical Society, 1965. See also *TLS* December 27, 1957 and March 11, 1960.

of all authors go, who thinks he gives you an account of an author when he tells you the name of his editor and the year in which his book was printed'.[1] He lived for a time in Gray's Inn, where his rooms were stuffed so completely with books that he had perforce to sleep in the passage; he thus outdid our earliest bibliophile, Richard de Bury, who four centuries earlier had been compelled to climb over his books to reach his bed. Collectors should beware of his example. But Rawlinson's books, though congested, were not dead. They were accessible to his friends, though it cannot have been easy to track down the volumes they wanted. And his friends included Thomas Hearne, Joseph Ames, the bibliographer and antiquarian, and Michael Maittaire, the classical scholar and typographer, himself the owner of a large library. Another of his friends was the biblioclast and shoemaker, John Bagford, who collected not books but title-pages, and was thus not a keeper but a destroyer of books—not a *curator* but a *destructor*. The sixty-four folio volumes of his amputations, with his collection of broadside ballads, are now in the British Museum; he collected ballads for Robert Harley, first Earl of Oxford.[2]

Still another eccentric contemporary of Rawlinson's was Thomas Britton, the musical small-coal man. In his blue smock, and with his coal sack slung over his shoulder, he would set out on Saturday afternoons hunting books at Christopher Bateman's shop[3] in Paternoster Row. There he would rub shoulders with half the great aristocratic collectors of the day: the Earls of Oxford, Sunderland, Pembroke, and Winchelsea, the Duke of Devonshire, and probably the Lord Chancellor, John Somers, for the Somers Tracts are supposed to have been based on a collection bought from Thomas Britton for £500. Britton's home was in a converted stable in Jerusalem Passage. The ground floor was his coal shop, and upstairs he kept his collection of musical instruments and his library of about 1,400 volumes. Here also for almost forty years, were given his celebrated Thursday concerts.

[1] *Tatler*, 158. De Quincey a century later, was even more of a squirrel in this respect; and a more unprofitable one, for his nuts were both hoarded and forgotten; see p. 266 *infra*.

[2] Bagford's example was followed by Joseph Ames; several volumes of his title-pages were sold with his effects after his death in 1759.

[3] According to Nichols, it was a rule of this shop that nobody was allowed to look into the books. Austin Dobson, in his *Eighteenth Century Vignettes*, wonders whether the rule was ever enforced with Dean Swift, who was a regular customer; one may doubt equally whether his aristocratic customers paid much attention to it.

A quite different sort of eccentricity is represented by the books that Horace Walpole interred in his little Gothic castle of Strawberry Hill. The collection began with his 'bookery' of a thousand or so volumes at Arlington Street, mounting in size till it reached 8,000 at Strawberry Hill. He had it in him to be a greater writer than he was, but his books (like his curios and enamels, his coins, his pictures, perhaps also his friends) were toys to play with rather than the tools of his craft or the objects of his study. Wilmarth Lewis protests that, though Walpole was neither bibliographer nor bibliophile, yet his collection was a working library which he used 'as a quarry of information on the subjects of his choice, and a stimulus in his pursuit of them'. If so, the harvest scarcely justified so fine a display: *nascetur ridiculus mus*. But in the true aristocratic tradition, Walpole associated a printing press with his library, as Sir Thomas Phillipps did in the following century, and as the Ambrosian Library in the century before; much as the great collectors of an earlier age had their private scriptoria.

Gilly Williams, describing Walpole, said 'I can figure no being happier than Horry. *Monstrari digito praetereuntium* has been his whole aim. For this he has wrote, printed, and built'. Wilmarth Lewis would add 'and formed his library'. Yet, as Lewis shows clearly, 'He knew his library . . . he bought only the books that he wanted to read, and my guess is that he at least glanced through most of them as soon as they came to hand . . . for the most part he bought books to read and use, not to love. His library was a working library. He drew heavily upon it for his works and letters.'[1]

Another, and much less attractive, type of eccentric is satirized by Pope:

> 'His Study! with what Authors is it stor'd!
> In Books, not Authors, curious is my Lord;
> To all their dated backs he turns you round;
> Those Aldus printed, those Du Sueil has bound.
> Lo, some are Vellum, and the rest as good,
> For all his Lordship knows—but they are Wood.
> For Locke or Milton 'tis in vain to look,
> These shelves admit not any modern book.'[2]

---

[1] Wilmarth Sheldon Lewis, *Horace Walpole's Library*, 1958 (Sandars Lectures, 1957).
[2] *Moral Essays*, IV, 133-40.

Still another type would be represented by Snuffy Davie in *The Antiquary*, who esteemed his volumes for any peculiar distinction which could give them value, always provided that the indispensable quality of scarcity or rare occurrence was attached to it. And his creator, in a letter to Lady Louisa Stuart, confesses that value depends on anything rather than sense or utility.

All the manifold gradations between 'philia' and 'mania' in the world of collecting have been described and mapped adequately—indeed far too adequately—by Holbrook Jackson in his two volume anatomical compendium.[1]

The very small domestic libraries of the period are by comparison humble things, but sometimes curiously significant and revealing, for their direct influence on their owner's life and work may stand out more conspicuously. We learn from *Grace Abounding* that when John Bunyan married in 1649, his young wife brought him as her only dowry two books left her by her father: *The Plain Man's Pathway to Heaven*, and *The Practice of Piety*. The couple were, as Bunyan says, 'as poor as poor might be, with not even a dish or spoon between them.' These two volumes awakened in Bunyan the idea of his mission in life.[2] In later days he came to rely to a peculiar degree on two other works, Foxe's *Actes and Monuments* and the Bible; these through life were his constant friends and indeed his private library, and their influence on his own writing is too plain to be overlooked.

Consider another example. William Blake was brought up on an austere diet restricted largely to the Bible, John Milton, Lavater and Swedenborg. Here again the influence is plain. His upbringing lacked almost entirely the discipline of classical studies, and indeed he never learnt to read critically and with discrimination. In after days William Hayley tried to teach him Greek, in the library of his cottage at Felpham (which Blake had adorned with a frieze of the heads of poets, now in the Manchester Art Gallery), so that the two of them could compare the *Iliad* in the original with Cowper's translation. If this kind of discipline had come earlier in his life, it might not have been a case of 'another fine mind dethroned

---

[1] *The Anatomy of Bibliomania*, 2v. 1930-1.
[2] *The Plain Man's Guide to Heaven* (1692) was by the blind prebendary of Westminster, Richard Lucas (1648-1715), best known as the author of *Enquiry after Happiness*, 2v., 1685. *The Practice of Piety* was by Lewis Bayly, Bp. of Bangor (*d.* 1631); it was published before 1613, and by 1735 had run through 59 editions.

in a chaos of its own creating'.[1] Nor perhaps would he have cherished his strange views on writers such as Bacon and Locke. Discipline might have curbed his wayward genius, but it might also have introduced greater coherence and order into his writing; whether the reader would find this desirable or not is doubtless another question. It is fair to add that Sir Geoffrey Keynes has printed a letter from Frederick Tatham, June 8, 1864, which suggests that Blake had a much wider knowledge of books than is sometimes supposed.[2] He had, says Tatham, 'a most consummate knowledge of all the great writers in all languages. To prove that, I may say that I have possessed books well thumbed and dirtied by his graving hands, in Latin, Greek, Hebrew, French and Italian, besides a large collection of works of the mystical writers, Jacob Behmen, Swedenborg and others'. Tatham in his *Life of Blake*, 1906, also states that 'among the volumes bequeathed by Mrs Blake to the author of this sketch the most thumbed from use are his Bible and those books in other languages. He was very fond of Ovid, especially the *Fasti*. He read Dante when he was past sixty, although before he knew a word of Italian'. Keynes considers various books bearing what is possibly Blake's signature, and others where the name appears among the list of subscribers; and he lists seventeen works which 'are certainly known to have been in Blake's possession', with three other possibles.

Whatever the relationship may be between Blake's genius and the books in his library, the effect of classical discipline on the writer is in general beyond dispute. John Buchan notes[3] that Sir Walter Scott had little or no Greek, and that some acquaintance with the Greek masterpieces, some tincture of the Greek spirit, might have trimmed that prolixity which was to be his besetting sin. On the other hand, his profound knowledge of the Border Ballads served to purify his taste and develop economy of words.

The peasant poets of the eighteenth century were often similarly restricted, to their even greater harm. John Clare, the Northamptonshire poet, picked up at a Stamford shop in his earlier days a copy of Thomson's *Seasons* for 1s 6d; and this became not merely

[1] Osbert Burdett, *William Blake*, 1926.
[2] *The Times Literary Suppl.*, March 8, 1957, and November 6, 1959. See also Keynes' bibliography of Blake (1921).
[3] John Buchan, *Sir Walter Scott*, 1932, pp. 42, 65.

his one model, but his entire library throughout his unhappy life, except for a few presentation copies. The result was that he attempted to shape his writing to a style that was foreign to him, rather than to rely on his native dialect and local colour. That other and lesser peasant poet, Robert Bloomfield, the author of *The Farmer's Boy*, suffered from an even severer mental starvation; he seems to have owned little but a dictionary, which he needed to help him understand the hard words in the newspapers. When he married, he was forced to sell his fiddle, and the young couple were so poor that it was several years before they had even a bed of their own.

There were of course, countless small libraries of little consequence, except as indications of the normality of human interests. One cannot expect every man to place equal reliance on the ownership of books; in the eighteenth even more than in the twentieth century, politics, the administration of justice and 'rural pursuits' exhausted the interests of many a squire and many an ecclesiastic. The patient reader of *The Diary of a Country Parson* is surprised to discover that, after his death in 1803, James Woodforde's inventory included an amount of £30 for his library. The entries in the diary itself lead one to suppose that books played no part in his life whatsoever; his meals, the weather, the coldness of his church (which in later life he abandoned entirely to a curate on account of its lack of heating) the waywardness of his bored niece, and an occasional mild adventure with smuggled liquor, seem to have filled all his waking thoughts.

There must have been many eighteenth-century vicarages, and even more manors, in comparison with which Parson Woodforde's library would have appeared large. Squire Western, it is true, read newspapers and political pamphlets and his sister was a studious and erudite person who presumably had some well-stocked bookshelves. There was a book published in 1643 called *Baker's Chronicle*,[1] which was a popular, though rather inaccurate historical best-seller, intended by its author to replace all other English histories so far written. It became the fashion for country gentlemen to keep this work open in their hall window; being a folio, it perhaps rested conveniently on the sloping stone sill. Sir Roger de

---

[1] Sir Richard Baker, *Chronicle of the Kings of England from the Time of the Romans' Government unto the Death of King James*, 1643. At least ten editions had appeared by 1730.

Coverley is made to keep his copy in this position by Addison;[1] Sir Roger is indeed always reading and quoting it. Squire Boothby in *Joseph Andrews* also kept his Baker in his hall window. This curious fashion suggests that the house had no library or study where the book might more appropriately belong; in such cases Baker's *Chronicle* was in fact the manorial library. Squire Boothby did however, own two other books: both rather unexpectedly religious best-sellers, the *Whole Duty of Man* and the *Imitation of Christ*. The popularity of Baker did indeed last a long time. It figured as one of the items in Leonora's library in *The Spectator* (April 12, 1711)[2]; and as late as 1791, William Cowper writes to the Rev W. Bagot, 'I have not a history in the world except Baker's *Chronicle*, and that I borrowed three years ago from Mr Throckmorton.'

The hall window, or parlour window, was also regarded as the right place for the fashionable best-seller of the time. Tristram Shandy opined that his book would come to rest there: 'As my life and opinions are likely to make some noise in the world, and, if I conjecture right, will take in all ranks, professions, and denominations of men whatever—be no less read than the *Pilgrim's Progress* itself—and in the end, prove the very thing which *Montaigne* dreaded his Essays should turn out, that is, a book for a parlour-window..."[3]. A study of the changing fashions of parlour-window literature would be a revealing and rewarding task.

Cowper's own library seems to have been shadowy and unsubstantial. He had collected a library in his chambers at the Middle Temple, but on his removal to St Albans at the time of his illness, this was lost. Afterwards he appears to have relied largely on borrowed books. In 1765, on leaving St Albans for Huntingdon, he told Major Cowper 'I am much happier than the day is long, and sunshine and candlelight see me perfectly contented. I get books in abundance'. In 1780, he writes to the Rev William Unwin of having read Lord Clarendon's *History of the Rebellion* and Hume's *History*, and asks for secondhand copies of Virgil and Homer 'with a Clavis, for I have no Lexicon'. Seven years later he is telling Lady Hesketh of some of the books he has read: Savary's *Travels*

---

[1] *Spectator*, 269, 329.
[2] *Heritage*, pp. 218–19.
[3] *Tristram Shandy*, I, IV.

into Egypt, Barclay's *Argenis* and the *Memoires d'Henri de Lorraine, Duc de Guise*. But in 1792 he wrote to William Hayley that he was 'heinously unprovided; being much in the condition of the man whose library Pope describes as

> No mighty store,
> His own works neatly bound, and little more'.[1]

The last five years of his life Cowper spent in the home of his cousin, the Rev John Johnson, Rector of Yaxham with Welborne, Norfolk, who, in his diary explains how, in order to draw him out of himself, he persuaded the poet to go through his collection of about 400 volumes, writing his name in each. Nearly all his books are thus authenticated by his signature, in addition to his crest and bookplate. After his death in 1800, Johnson purchased the books, most of which went eventually to his three sons. Some of the books have since been dispersed, but it has been possible to reconstruct an almost complete list of the original collection, and this has been printed by Sir Geoffrey Keynes[2].

Two other libraries of this period are elegantly described by Austin Dobson in his *Eighteenth Century Vignettes*. The sale catalogue of Thomas Gray's books in 1851 depicts the wealth and variety of his collection, but his books come to life more vividly in the *Dialogue of Books*, dated 1742 and probably written by Gray himself; in this, while the poet sits quietly in his study, an argument breaks out amongst his books, each volume contributing its share to the hubbub. The sale catalogue of Goldsmith's library at Brick Court in 1774 is equally revealing, though in a different way. Goldsmith was not a booklover; he could with equanimity underscore passages with his thumb-nail, or tear out pages to save the trouble of transcribing them. His own works are missing from the catalogue, but it contains many of the French writers from whom he may well have derived some of his skill in handling both prose and verse.

Let us end this chapter by considering two libraries of outstanding interest on account of the special importance in English literature of the works to which they contributed. If a tree is to be judged by its fruits, then Dr Johnson's collection must be ranked as one of the

---

[1] I have not been able to identify this quotation. Professor Sutherland assures me that it is not from Alexander Pope.
[2] *The Library of William Cowper* (Trans. Cambridge Bibl. Soc., 1959, III, pp. 47–69).

great libraries of this country. That it was an unsystematic and haphazard collection we can easily guess. If we need to be reminded that the practical value of a private library does not depend on its meticulous arrangement, cataloguing and shelving, no better illustration could be found than this: a one-man library can yield its fruit in good measure with little or none of the technical apparatus which the professional librarian finds so necessary. Edmund Malone tells us that, apart from certain volumes given to his friends, 'Johnson's library, though by no means handsome in its appearance [we can well believe this] was sold by Mr Christie for £247 9s 0d, many people being desirous to have a book which belonged to Johnson.

Mr Christie's sale catalogue of Johnson's library was reprinted in facsimile by Unwin for the Johnson Club in 1892; a pamphlet of twenty-eight pages with 650 lots. It was in Gough Square that his work produced its richest harvest: the *Idler*, the *Dictionary*, *Irene*, *The Vanity of Human Wishes* and *The Rambler* belong to this period (1749–59). And it was here (as Austin Dobson remarks), when his room had grown to be dignified by the title of 'library', that Johnson received Dr Burney who found in it 'five or six Greek folios, a deal writing desk, and a chair and a half'.

Dr Johnson, writing to Dr Brocklesby from Lichfield not long before his death, speaks of the London he loved so well: 'There are my friends; there are my books, to which I have not yet bid farewell." Yet he was not by nature a good 'keeper'; he did not hesitate to cut the leaves with a greasy knife, or to read while he ate (and one knows how he ate, adds Dobson), or in a moment of rapture over the copy of Petrarch which Garrick reluctantly lent him, to fling it over his shoulders on to the floor. He was quite capable of knocking down Osborne the bookseller with a folio. ('Sir, he was impertinent to me, and I beat him. But it was not in his shop; it was in my own chamber'.) He rarely failed to adorn a borrowed book with marginalia; he rarely remembered to return it. Boswell wrote to Temple in 1763 that 'He has many good books, but they are all lying in confusion and dust'. And Hawkins adds that they were 'miserably ragged, defaced, and chosen with so little regard to editions or their external appearance, as shewed they were intended for use, and that he disdained the ostentation of learning. But Austin Dobson's delightful essay in the second series of *Eighteenth Century Vignettes* reveals how rich the collection really was.

Dr Johnson made good use of many libraries in Oxford (especially at Trinity College, where his friend Thomas Warton was) and London, including the Royal Library (where in 1767 Mr Barnard introduced him to the King, thus gratifying what Boswell calls his 'monarchical enthusiasm'), and Mr Thrale's library at Streatham gave him infinite happiness. On October 6, 1782, after Mr Thrale's death, he made his 'parting use of the library', pronouncing the beautiful prayer with which he bade farewell to the home he had shared for so many years:

'Almighty God, Father of all mercy, help me by thy grace, that I may, with humble and sincere thankfulness, remember the comforts and conveniences which I have enjoyed at this place; and that I may resign them with submission, equally trusting in thy protection when Thou givest and when Thou takest away.'

Consider now in contrast a very different sort of collection. We know a good deal about the library of Edward Gibbon, both from the wide range of erudite sources which he acknowledges in the *Decline and Fall*, and from the details he gives in his autobiography. We know that it reached a total of nearly 7,000 volumes, carefully and systematically acquired. 'I am not conscious' (he says) 'of having ever bought a book from a motive of ostentation ... every volume, before it was deposited on the shelf, was either read or sufficiently examined, and . . . I soon adopted the tolerating maxim of the elder Pliny, *'nullum esse librum tam malum ut non ex aliqua parte prodesset."'* We know, too, that this great collection was consciously and deliberately amassed to make possible his *magnum opus*, and though he made free use of the libraries of Paris, Lausanne and Geneva, by far the greatest part of the *Decline and Fall* was conceived and born within the confines of his own library. It would be hard to find any collection of books that has been so completely and adequately justified by its fruit.[1]

Yet we must beware of judging a library only by its visible and immediate fruits. The provenance of recorded thought is too

---

[1] Strictly speaking, the idea first came to Gibbon while he sat 'among the ruins of the Capitol and listened to the barefooted fryars singing vespers in the temple of Jupiter'. On his library in general see especially the introduction to Sir Geoffrey Keynes, *The Library of Edward Gibbon: a catalogue of his books*, 1940.

complex a web for us to unravel every thread to its source. The library of a great teacher, though he may have written nothing, will live in the work of his pupils. The purposive collection of a library by a Bodley or a Pepys may in itself be a creative act of faith, to be justified by future generations; as for example, Benedict Biscop's act of faith in founding the library of Monk Wearmouth, was justified half a century later by the labours of the Venerable Bede.

Or again, the fruits of research may be hidden or lost, perhaps to be disinterred by chance centuries later. There is a hapy illustration of this in the work of the seventeenth-century botanist John Goodyer, the friend of the apothecary Thomas Johnson;[1] his name is commemorated by the little orchid of Scottish pinewoods, *Goodyera repens*. Goodyer was the steward of a manor at Mapledurwell, near Basingstoke, and a student of botany for its own sake, without any of the preoccupations of medicine which marked most botanists of his period. His exceptional ability as a field botanist was tempered by modesty, and he published nothing; the importance of his work was however, revealed when his books and papers, which had been left to Magdalen College, Oxford, were examined by Dr R. T. Gunther not long ago;[2] and a surprisingly valuable collection it is of botanical works of the sixteenth and early seventeenth centuries.

It is admittedly the duty of the scholar to record the results of his research, as it is of the poet to express the mature fruits of his imagination. Uncommunicated, the poem and the research are dead. Sometimes they are better dead; time is perhaps the wisest judge of this. But the conscious erection of a *monumentum aere perennius* cannot be regarded as a necessary purpose of scholarship. Work that is worthy of independent life will live; the rest, though unrecognised, will mingle with the stream of human endeavour and will play its destined part.

---

[1] Author of the *Iter in Agrum Cantianum*, 1629 and the *Mercurius Botanicus*, 1634–41.
[2] R. T. Gunther, *Early British Botanists and Their Gardens*, 1922. The catalogue of the library is given in pp. 197–232.

CHAPTER XIV

The Infectious Habit

§1—THE EPIDEMIC BEGINS

IF England became literate in the fifteenth century, in the eighteenth it acquired the *habit* of reading: in part no doubt, of reading for instruction and enlightenment (it was the age of enlightenment); in part for political purposes (it was the age when party politics first came to the fore as a topic for everyday discussion); but still more for entertainment and for the sheer delight of books in themselves. For in this century, the discovery was made by thousands that books, which had previously been intended ostensibly for study and grave contemplation, could equally be designed for relaxation, as a means of passing, or even killing, time. The change came gradually, of course. There has always been the occasional book written mainly for amusement, even if it has sometimes worn an allegorical or satirical garb for the sake of respectability; but there had been nothing to compare with the great flood of what Coleridge called 'pass-time' books that are so striking a feature of this century. The new habit was indeed infectious, for it spread by contact wherever books were to be found, and by imitation, wherever people were seen to be reading and enjoying the political pamphlets, the journals or the novels that were being discussed at every kind of social gathering, at the coffee houses, the 'routs' and assemblies, and the circulating libraries. It was a social age; social meetings imply discussion and criticism, and in a literate society, discussion implies the reading of the books and pamphlets of the moment.

There is ample contemporary evidence of this development, both direct and circumstantial. The first signs of the new habit become noticeable in the closing years of the seventeenth century. In 1684, when John Evelyn was discussing the new parish library that Dr Tenison was founding at S. Martin's-in-the-Fields, he assumed that the demand for reading in London was still mainly clerical. But the scene was already beginning to change. In 1694 Parliament refused to renew the current Licensing Act, and the system of licensing books finally expired. The change was not due to any new belief in the freedom of the press. It was rather a question of expediency, for the Act had for technical reasons been ineffective; and prosecutions against seditious or libellous publications continued for some time through other channels. But a considerable increase in the number of books published followed the ending of the licensing system; and the next step logically came in 1709 with the 'Act for the encouragement of learning', usually known as the Copyright Act, which was later, to the great surprise of the booksellers, found to have abolished perpetual copyright in favour of protection for twenty-one years.[1] The widening interest in reading at this time also expressed itself in the activities of the S.P.G. in England and the General Assembly in Scotland in establishing parish libraries, and the ineffective but well-intentioned Act for the better preservation of Parochial Libraries in 1708 gave an official blessing to these; these libraries however, whether Anglican or Presbyterian, remained largely theological in content.

The expansion of the book trade had its effect on both booksellers and authors. Bookshops began to spread slowly beyond the confines of Paternoster Row and S. Paul's Churchyard, the University cities and the pedlar's pack. Dr Johnson's father was a bookseller in Lichfield at the turn of the century, and he travelled with his wares all through the surrounding district, including Birmingham, which had no bookshops of its own at that time.[2]

Charles P. Moritz, the young Prussian clergyman, in his *Travels, chiefly on foot, through several parts of England* (1795), writes with delight of the second-hand bookseller, at whose movable stall you could buy odd volumes 'so low as a penny: nay even sometimes for an half-penny a piece'. And he himself bought a copy of *The Vicar of Wakefield* for sixpence the two volumes at one such stall. Elsewhere he says 'In Germany the classics are read only by the learned, or at most by the middle class of pepole. The English national authors are in all hands, and read by all people, of which

[1] See Sir Paul Harvey, *Oxford Companion to English Literature*, 1946, App. II.
[2] William Hutton transferred his bookshop from Southwell to Birmingham in 1750.

the innumerable editions they have gone through are a sufficient proof.'[1]

One result of the rising demand for books was a change in the system of literary patronage. The author had perforce depended, first on court patronage and then on political patronage; but he now began to discover that this kind of support was no longer necessary to success. Political patronage ended with the government of Walpole in 1721, partly owing to the growing power of Parliament, and partly because Walpole preferred to use the direct labour of hacks for such propaganda as was still required. There was now a new market for books in the expanding middle class, and the able writer could safely dispense with aristocratic subsidies. Later in the century Horace Walpole was able to say that 'Patronage is an antiquated fashion, and at present means nothing . . . the public favour is deemed a sufficient recompense'.[2] And Goldsmith in 1760 noted that 'The few poets of England . . . have now no other patrons but the public'.[3] In other words, the law of supply and demand was taking control of the market for the first time, and the habit of reading was becoming sufficiently ingrained to support and stimulate the output of books.

How did the habit make its appearance with such apparent abruptness? This is not an easy question to answer. To some extent no doubt a freer supply created a wider demand. The truth of this is well known in both bookshops and libraries, for among a literate people the demand for books is often latent and unexpressed, awaiting the stimulus of a visible supply to realise itself. Booksellers, pamphleteers and pedlars, equipped with more abundant stocks, found it not too difficult to dispose of their goods, and the need to replenish their stocks kept the market lively. That literacy was increasing rapidly, especially in the commercially prosperous areas, and in the period of settled security that came with the reigns of William and Mary, and Queen Anne, is evident; and though literacy and the reading habit are not the same thing, nevertheless literacy provides the fertile ground from which alone, under the stimulus of an abundant supply of books, the habit can grow. The spread of provincial grammar schools during the seven-

[1] Berlin, 1783; English transl. 1795. On bookshops in general, see Dr Marjorie Plant, *The English Book Trade*, 1939, ch. XII, especially pp. 253-6.
[2] J. Pinkerton, *Walpoliana*, 1799.
[3] *The Citizen of the World*, letter 84.

teenth century was very marked indeed. Academic teaching was, it is true, at a low ebb, the Universities being handicapped by a series of proscriptions by Laudians and Puritans, and finally by James II. But on a humbler level grammar school education was flourishing, in quantity if not quality. Some counties had more grammar schools in proportion to the population than they have today, and the number of different schools sending pupils to the Universities increased to an extraordinary degree.[1] The grammar schools produced perhaps but a small handful of great scholars: men such as Sir Isaac Newton, who came to Trinity College, Cambridge, from Grantham Grammar school or Bishop Moore, who came from the free school at Market Harborough to Clare College, Cambridge. They did, however, educate a vast number of ordinary people who, though not scholars, could read easily and were sufficiently familiar with the cultural background to find pleasure in the books within their reach. Amongst such people the new spirit of free enquiry and the new interest in experimental philosophy awakened a curiosity to learn the facts of the world about them and the experiences of travellers in other lands, as well as the right principles of religion and government: a curiosity which could only be satisfied by the reading and discussion of books and pamphlets.

Reading is essentially a social habit, both encouraging and being encouraged by, the fashion of social gatherings which make possible the discussion and criticism of the books that are being read. This brings us to one of the chief developments of the period, for it was above all, the great age of criticism. The dates of John Dryden were 1631–1700. That systematic literary criticism did not exist to any serious degree before Dryden, is due partly to the fact that criticism (like the collection of libraries) always *succeeds* a period of literary renaissance, rather than coinciding with it; it is as it were, the aftermath of great creative activity.[2] More particularly, however, it is due to the fact that it requires for its nourishment an atmosphere or climate of intellectual discussion; an atmosphere which established itself in England after the Restoration, and steadily gathered significance during the hundred years that followed. Intellectual

---

[1] The evidence for this is set out by W. A. L. Vincent in *The State and School Education, 1640–1660*, 1950, p. 9. Essex for example had 56 grammar schools in this period.

[2] There is an example of this in classical Greece, in the period following the literary output of the fifth century.

conversation and the social and literary life of the age found its expression in the dinner parties, the coffee houses[1] and the bookshops of the period; in the magazines and pamphlets that flooded the country; and in the many national societies and institutions which had their birth at this time: the Royal Society, the second Society of Antiquaries, and the long progression of other learned societies which distinguishes the eighteenth century. The habit of criticism grows only in fertile ground such as this, and it implies the existence and circulation of books and journals which invite discussion.[2] Both good and bad books stimulate discussion, provided they are books which everybody is reading. Indeed, the main object and constant standby of all intelligent conversation is books: especially the books of the moment. Beyond the book, it may of course be religion or politics, but in an age when the book or the pamphlet was the principal channel of communication, it would be religion or politics as expressed in books. The only other fruitful media were the pulpit and the theatre, and both sermons and plays had a necessarily limited appeal till they were perpetuated in print. Side by side therefore with the progress of criticism from Dryden to Addison, Pope and Johnson, there goes a striking expansion of intellectual experience and of the habit of reading; and it is fair to argue that the healthiness of literary criticism in any age is a sure indication of the healthiness of the reading habit and the efficiency of the circulation of books.

The activity of the book market after the expiry of the licensing laws in 1694, is indicated by the series of current bibliographies which made their appearance for the first time: Robert Clavell's quarterly *Catalogue of Books Printed and Published at London*, 1670–1709; the monthly *History of the Works of the Learned, or an Impartial Account of Books Lately Printed in all Parts of Europe*, 1699–1712; and the catalogues issued by B. B. Lintot, 1714–15, and Wilford, 1723–30.[3] The increase was particularly noticeable with the

---

[1] Some at least of the coffee houses had circulating libraries attached to them. Thomas Gray in his retirement at Cambridge was rarely seen except on his visits to the Rainbow Coffee House to borrow books from the circulating library there.

[2] On this see Professor James R. Sutherland's lecture, *The English Critic*, 1952.

[3] R. M. Wiles, *Serial Publications in England before 1750*, 1957. This author's statement that the bulk of the population at the end of the seventeenth century could not read is however, open to doubt. Literacy is not likely to have decreased between Sir Thomas More's time and 1700, and it is probable that a substantial proportion could at least read at this date.

slighter and more evanescent productions of the literary world. Party politics were for the first time exciting high emotion, and the conflicts of Whig and Tory called forth a quite extraordinary spate of pamphlets; so many indeed that, according to Swift, it would have been a full-time occupation for a man to keep pace with them. The more popular of the pamphlets had astonishingly large sales of forty, sixty or eighty thousand copies: sales that today, with our population ten times as great, would be nearing a million. Part at least of this hunger for reading matter was diverted from political issues by Steele and Addison; and the *Tatler*, and the *Spectator* (1709–14) concentrated it on the more rewarding topics of manners, ethics and literature, their object being 'to enliven morality with wit, and to temper wit with morality'. The sales of the *Spectator* reached twenty or thirty thousand, and its success was confirmed by countless imitations.[1] A stream of fugitive material of less importance continued throughout the century, and chapbooks, ballads and execution broadsides often appeared in enormous editions.[2] On a different plane, Edward Cave's *Gentleman's Magazine* ran successfully from 1731 to 1754.

The *Tatler* was not, however, the first literary periodical to testify to the new interest in reading. Nearly twenty years previously the *Athenian Gazette* (afterwards *Mercury*) made its appearance in 1690–91 and continued for seven years. It was produced by what Dr Johnson termed 'a knot of obscure men'; not so very obscure really, for the leading spirit, John Dunton, the bookseller and author of *The Life and Errors*, was assisted by Richard Sault, the mathematician and Samuel Wesley, the father of John Wesley. It took the form of the 'Answers to Correspondents' column of a modern periodical, and was indeed the first example of this piece of journalistic technique: a very good example too, for most of the answers show abundant intelligence, considerable tact and some polish. It forms one of the earliest pieces of evidence of the spread of the reading habit among ordinary people. It had indeed a successful contemporary in the *Gentleman's Journal* (1691–94), which was more general in scope, including prose and verse as well as news. It was edited by P. A. Motteux, who is otherwise known

---

[1] Alexander Beljame, *Men of Letters and the English Public in the Eighteenth Century*, English ed. 1948, pp. 307–16.
[2] R. K. Webb, *The British Working-Class Reader, 1790–1848*, 1955.

mainly for his completion of Urquhart's translation of Rabelais.

However successful Steele and Addison were in diverting to other fields some of the current interest in political questions, the demand for books and pamphlets on history and politics continued to rise steadily. Professor Thomson quotes estimates suggesting that the number of pamphlets and memoirs for the period 1700–14 amounted to 8,000; for the period 1714–89, some 150,000 separates were published; and in 1751–1800 the number of separates amounted to perhaps 300,000.[1] This relates to historical productions only, and provides excellent evidence of the rising flood of publications that distinguishes the eighteenth century.

Still further evidence of the growth of the reading habit, especially in the period 1730–1750, is provided by Professor R. M. Wiles. During these years the issue of both new books and reprints in monthly and weekly fascicules—i.e. on the instalment system—reached surprising proportions. More than three hundred such works appeared between 1678 and 1750, mostly in the later part of this period, one of the first examples being Joseph Moxon's *Mechanick Exercises*, 2 vols., 1677–78 and 1683. It is evident that this new method often proved extremely profitable to the publisher, and supplied an increasing demand from readers who were unable to afford the price of a complete new book at one time. Many of the works so published were of course pot-boilers of little importance, but the list includes some which have an undisputed place in our literature. Johnson's *Dictionary* was for example, reprinted in weekly numbers, very soon after the publication of the original folio edition in 1755. Smollett's *History of England*, issued in weekly numbers by James Rivington and James Fletcher, produced a handsome return for both publishers and author.[2] We are reminded of George Crabbe's lines in *The Library* (1781):

> '*Our nicer palates lighter labours seek*
> *Cloy'd with a folio number once a week;*
> *Bibles, with cuts and comments, thus go down;*
> *E'en light Voltaire is* number'd *through the town.*'

---

[1] Professor W. T. Morgan, *A Bibliography of British History* (1700–15), 5 vols. 1939–42; Professors Pargellis and Medley, *Bibliography of British History* 1714–89, 1951, p. v; W. S. Lewis, *Collector's Progress*, 1952, pp. xxi–ii. These references are quoted by Professor M. A. Thomson, *Some Developments in English Historiography during the Eighteenth Century*, 1957, p. 22.

[2] R. M. Wiles, *op. cit.*, p. 5. See also p. 281 *infra*.

We have said that reading is a social habit, and this aspect of eighteenth century reading is of considerable importance. The coffee houses were no doubt places for talk and discussion rather than reading, and as such they played their part in the formation of the literary climate and in strengthening the habit of reading. You could not discuss a book or a pamphlet intelligently unless you had read it, and to listen to intelligent talk surely inspired you to read. Throughout the century there grew up everywhere a surprising multitude of local societies formed for the co-operative provision of books and reviews. They were of every degree of formality or informality. Many were small; many were short-lived; many vanished without trace; a few however survived for long periods, and a handful are still in existence. They ranged from small book clubs to non-profit subscription libraries, literary and natural history societies, institutional libraries and commercial circulating libraries. Very few of their records and registers have survived, but evidence of their work is now accumulating as the result of the researches of a small band of students, especially perhaps of Paul Kaufman of the University of Washington Library, Seattle, who is the leading authority on this type of eighteenth century library in England.

Book clubs seem to have been almost universal in England.[1] They had a largely middle-class membership, and were mostly small, with perhaps a dozen or twenty subscribing members. They often met for a monthly dinner and an exchange of books; some disposed of all their books annually acquiring a fresh collection each year, and some maintained a permanent basic library; some were probably restricted to men and some to women, but many were mixed. The earliest reference to a book club of the smaller sort occurs in a letter of Philip Doddridge in 1725; 'It is my happiness to be a member of a society in which, for little more than a crown a year, I have the reading of all that are purchased by the common stock, amounting to sixteen pounds yearly. They are generally some of the most entertaining and useful works that are published.' Doddridge at this time was at Kibworth, and he may well have referred to the Kibworth Book Society. This is known

---

[1] P. Kaufman, 'English Book Clubs and their Role in Social History', *Libri*, 1964, pp. 1-31; 'The rise of Community Libraries in Scotland,' *Bibl. Soc. of America*, 1965.

to have been in existence fifty years later in 1774. Some clubs were in effect proprietary libraries, with the members as shareholders. The Luddenden library was of this kind;[1] it was also a club however, with monthly meetings at the Lord Nelson Inn which, though there were stringent rules against intoxication, were often attended by Branwell Brontë. Apart from the small clubs, there were in many counties larger organizations devoted to literature, philosophy and natural history and possessing substantial proprietary libraries; the Cornwall Library and Literary Society, founded in 1792, is one example, and the Spalding Gentlemen's Society is another. The latter, which is still active, was established in 1710 by Maurice Johnson, who also founded the Society of Antiquaries (1717) and a number of other local societies. More important perhaps are the proprietary libraries in the larger cities such as the Bristol Library (1773), the Liverpool Lyceum (1758) and the Birmingham Library (1779). The Bristol Library is of special significance in view of the analysis of its registers during the closing years of the eighteenth century, when Southey and Coleridge made use of it.[2]

The cathedral libraries played a not unimportant part in eighteenth-century England. Like the academic libraries of the period, they doubtless had an air of somnolence and inactivity, but they possessed rich and scholarly collections, and in many cases they were the only learned libraries in their particular district open to students. Before 1700 their use seems in the main to have been restricted to the cathedral chapter, but later their hospitality was extended not only to the diocesan clergy but to local professional men and even some women, subject to the approval of a member of the chapter. Such records of their use as remain have been analysed in a delightful essay by Miss Elizabeth Brunskill for the York Minster library (where the borrowers included Laurence Sterne and his

---

[1] P. Kaufman, English book clubs, pp. 21–22.
[2] P. Kaufman, 'The Reading of Southey and Coleridge', *Modern Philology*, 1924, pp. 317–20; *Borrowings from the Bristol Library, 1773–1784*. Charlottesville, 1960. For the Birmingham Library see C. Paris, 'An Eighteenth Century Proprietary Library', Library Association Fellowship Thesis, 1964. See also F. Beckwith, 'The Eighteenth Century Proprietary Library in England', *Journal of Documentation*, 1947, and R. D. Altick, *The English Common Reader*, 1957.

uncle Dr Sterne), and by Paul Kaufman for eight of the English cathedral libraries.[1]

Neither the cathedral libraries nor the academic libraries were of course, available to nonconformists. It was largely this disability that inspired Dr Daniel Williams to establish the library that bears his name. Williams was a self-educated Welsh peasant who had the good fortune to marry in succession two wealthy widows. With the money of his first wife he purchased the library of the Presbyterian divine William Bates, and with that of his second wife he endowed it by his will. He died in 1716, and the library was opened in 1729 to serve in a measure as a nonconformist rival to Sion College. For a century and a half it slumbered quietly, though not unprofitably; then late in the nineteenth century it came to life, and grew steadily into the great theological, historical and classical collection that it is today, no longer competing with Sion College, but co-operating happily with this and other learned libraries.[2]

The commercial circulating libraries that sprang up everywhere in the middle of the eighteenth century were mainly, but by no means entirely, patronized by women, and are referred to more particularly below.[3] The reason for their sudden appearance was doubtless the flood of novels that followed *Tom Jones* and *Pamela*, but it is likely that the success of many small book clubs that had sprung up in the earlier part of the century inspired the idea that there was a profitable market for publishers here. The earliest circulating library is commonly ascribed to Allan Ramsay at his shop in the Luckenbooths in Edinburgh in 1726, but there is some doubt as to the exact nature of his activities in this direction. About the same time as this, the young Rousseau was borrowing books from Madame La Tribu's circulating library in Geneva, which provided him with reading of all sorts. 'Good or bad was alike to me. I did not choose; I read everything with avidity... I read till my head spun, I did nothing but read. My master spied on me, caught me, beat me and took away my books. How many volumes

---

[1] E. Brunskill, *Eighteenth Century Reading*. York Georgian Society, 1950; P. Kaufman, 'Reading Vogues at English Cathedral Libraries of the Eighteenth Century', *Bull.* N.Y. Public Library, 1963-4. See also B. Botfield, *Notes on the Cathedral Libraries of England*, 1844; and 'The Cathedral Libraries Catalogue' by Miss Hands (Mrs Macleod), *The Library*, 1947.

[2] S. K. Jones. *Dr Williams and his Library*, 1948. See also p. 263 below.

[3] p. 248. See also *Heritage*, pp. 274-8. The main authority for these libraries is Miss Hamlyn's 'Eighteenth Century Circulating Libraries in England', *The Library*, 1947.

were torn up, burnt and thrown out of the window! How many works returned to Mme La Tribu's shelves with volumes missing! When I had no money to pay her, I gave her my shirts, my ties, my clothes; my weekly pocket money of three *sous* was carried to her regularly every Sunday.' It was not till much later at Turin that he began to acquire a more discriminating and less omnivorous taste for books.[1] There were apparently frequent complaints to *le Consistoire* (the Protestant ecclesiastical authority in Geneva) about La Tribu's library.[2]

The origins of the commercial circulating library may be obscure, but there is little doubt that it developed from the natural inclination of good booksellers to lend to their trusted customers volumes which they wished to examine before purchase. This pleasant custom is fortunately not unknown today, though it is perhaps less frequent than it used to be. It was certainly well known to Samuel Pepys, who on November 28, 1663, borrowed the second part of *Hudibras* from his bookseller in S. Paul's Churchyard, to see whether it was worth buying; he thought poorly of the first part, but bought it finally on December 10th. This courtesy was evidently good business on the bookseller's part, and sooner or later an enterprising salesman would advertise this service on commercial lines. Thus in 1671 Francis Kirkman, the bookseller, advertised his readiness to sell or lend upon reasonable considerations the plays in his *Catalogue of all the English Stage-Playes* (1661, later edition 1671); and it appears that a lending library of plays, poetry and romances was combined with his bookshop.[3] The practice is probably almost as old as the bookshop itself.

As a powerful force however, the circulating library was an eighteenth century institution. It is certain moreover that all these various types of library-book clubs, proprietary libraries, society libraries, academic and ecclesiastical libraries as well as the commercial lending libraries, exercised a considerable influence on the literary climate of eighteenth century England—on the activity of the publishing trade, on the demand for books and on the spread of the reading habit amongst men and women of all but the lowest classes.

---

[1] *Confessions*, Bk. I and III. Trans. J. M. Cohen.
[2] Eugène Ritter, 'La famille et la jeunesse de Jean-Jacques Rousseau,' *Annales de la Société Jean-Jacques Rousseau*, 1924–5.
[3] D.N.B.

§2—SCANTY INTELLECTUAL VIANDS

If the epidemic began among the male subscribers to the *Athenian Mercury* and the patrons of Button's and Will's in Addison's time, it spread to their daughters and granddaughters a generation or so later. This extension was even more overwhelming than it had been amongst men. At the beginning of the century few, if any, women of leisure had developed any genuine habit of reading; fifty or sixty years later, the great majority of women were confirmed readers of novels, and some were enjoying other types of book as well.

Charles P. Moritz in the work mentioned above, notes that even his landlady studies her *Paradise Lost*, and indeed by her own account she won the affections of her husband (now deceased) 'because she read Milton with proper emphasis'. One must add however, that when Moritz himself was discovered by some rustics sitting under a hedge on his way to Oxford reading Milton, they concluded that he had taken leave of his senses[1].

Though the fashion was new, there had always of course been the occasional woman with a love of learning or letters: Sappho and Hypatia in the ancient world, Hroswitha of Gandersheim in the medieval.

Nearer home there is the charming picture of Leobgatha (Leoba, the Beloved), kinswoman and dear friend of S. Boniface, sending the Saint specimens of the hexameters she had composed on the model of S. Aldhelm's awkward verses, with a covering letter begging him to correct her Latinity. Later she became Abbess of Tauberbischofsheim. And one should doubtless add Marie de France, the contemporary of Wace and possibly the half-sister of Henry II, the author of the *Lai du Chevrefeuil*; she has been called the ancestress of the great women novelists. But the male conviction, or illusion, of superiority has tended to curb overmuch feminine curiosity about books. Knowledge is power, and man has striven in self-defence to retain this miracle in his own hands. Women of the Alexandrian age, and of the Augustan age in Rome could doubtless read verse well enough, but this was part of the game of romance; this is a game for two, and love letters need to be both read and answered. In more rough and ready ages

[1] Austin Dobson, *Eighteenth century Vignettes*, 1st series.

they have been denied even this accomplishment; letters after all are but a substitute, and love lyrics are not always in fashion.

There is little sign of any reading among the Italian ladies who exchanged their stories in the *Decameron*. Indeed the very fact of storytelling as a regular diversion points to the absence of recreative reading; story-telling wanes as the reading habit waxes. The *Decameron* doubtless was written for reading, but many of the tales are of the type composed for male, rather than female, delectation.

A century earlier than Boccaccio, Matthew Paris was writing his lives of S. Alban and other saints in Anglo-Norman French for lay men and women, and his own notes on the fly-leaf of one of these books suggest that they were of special interest to the aristocratic ladies whom he numbered among his friends. He set out however, to help those who found reading difficult, by illustrating his books copiously and skilfully with his own coloured drawings, and it appears that these ladies passed the volumes round in their circle from hand to hand.[1]

In the later medieval period, when the lady of the manor had a complicated household to administer, she had need of a knowledge of reading, writing and figures, and the new interest in personal religion enabled her to find satisfaction in the works of Richard Rolle and Nicholas Love. The Paston women could read and write well enough; and if Margery Brews could write so attractively to her 'right well beloved valentine, John Paston', we can guess that the charming letter from Thomas Betson to Katherine Riche in the Stonor collection, June 1, 1476, received the kind answer it deserved.[2] In the next century Petrus Godefridus was forbidding women to learn writing, so as to guard them from the temptations of love letters;[3] this naïve prohibition is sure evidence of a free indulgence in such temptations. The innumerable books of deportment published throughout this period were obviously intended for feminine reading.[4] None of these is more interesting or revealing perhaps than the domestic 'enquire within' which Le Ménagier de

[1] Richard Vaughan, *Matthew Paris*, 1958, p. 170.
[2] *Stonor Letters*, 1919, II, pp. 6-8.
[3] *Dialogue of Love*, Antwerp, 1554; quoted by Burton, *Anatomy of Melancholy*.
[4] For a survey of such works, see A. A. Hentsch, De la littérature didactique du moyen age s'addressant spécialement aux femmes, (Cahors, 1903). See also Eileen Power, *Medieval People*, 1924.

Paris wrote for his young wife (*Traité de Morale et d'Economie Domestique*) composed c. 1393, and published in Paris in 1846.

Eileen Power in *The Legacy of the Middle Ages*, pp. 430-1, quotes several 15th century wills in which books are bequeathed to women.[1] The works specified are 'my boke of the talys of cantyrbury', 'unum librum de Romanse incipientem cum Decem Preceptis Alembes', 'unum librum de Romanse de Septem Sages', 'unum librum de Anglico vocatum Gower pro remembrancia', and 'librum Angliae de Fabulis et Narracionibus'; this last was left by a priest of York in 1432 to a woman who had been his servant for many years.

In Tudor times some genuine claims to scholarship are found among women in high quarters, such as the unhappy Lady Jane Grey, and Elizabeth herself. Still better examples are the daughters of Sir Thomas More, Margaret, Elizabeth and Cecily, all of whom were well grounded in the subjects of the day: Latin, Greek, Logic, Philosophy, Theology, Mathematics and Astronomy. More's letters to them were always in Latin; they could reply (and a daily letter was expected when he was absent from home) readily enough in the same language, though they were advised to make an English draft first, and then translate. This was a revolutionary accomplishment at the time, (though Vives and other scholars supported it), and their father was rightly proud of his success with them; Margaret was evidently the ablest of the three, and her learning seems to have been profound.[2]

The seventeenth century set a few feminine stars in the literary firmament: Lady Winchelsea; Margaret Cavendish, Duchess of Newcastle, whom Dryden likened to Sappho and Sulpicia,[3] Pepys condemned with scorn,[4] and Charles Lamb worshipped; Dorothy Osborne, the wife of Sir William Temple, whose productions consisted only of the famous letters to her husband, and Mrs. Aphra Behn, who was not merely our first woman novelist, but the first to make a living by writing.[5]

There is no more charming, more thoughtful or more scintil-

[1] In E. J. Jacob and C. G. Crump, *The Legacy of the Middle Ages*, 1926.
[2] R. W. Chambers, *Thomas More*, 1935, p. 181.
[3] In the dedication to *An Evening's Love*.
[4] *Diary*, 1668, 18 Mar., where she is described as a 'mad conceited, ridiculous woman'. In early entries he had displayed a more flattering curiosity about her.
[5] Mrs Aphra Behn was perhaps the first woman to make a living by writing plays and novels. Over two centuries earlier, however, Christine de Pisan (1364-c. 1430) was

lating account of the way in which women have struggled to free themselves of some at least of their man-made fetters, and to gain independence in reading and writing, than Virginia Woolf's *A Room of One's Own*. The seventeenth-century girl, once married, was condemned to household drudgery: any deviation from the narrow path was unworthy of the proper ideals of her sex. In Lady Winchelsea's words (quoted by Virginia Woolf):

> *Alas! a woman that attempts a pen,*
> *Such a presumptuous creature is esteemed,*
> *The fault can by no virtue be redeemed.*
> *They tell us we mistake our sex and way;*
> *Good breeding, fashion, dancing, dressing, play,*
> *Are the accomplishments we should desire;*
> *To write, or read, or think, or to enquire,*
> *Would cloud our beauty, and exhaust our time,*
> *And interrupt the conquests of our prime;*
> *Whilst the dull manage of a servile house,*
> *Is held by some our utmost art and use.*

Margaret Cavendish complained that 'Women live like Bats or Owls, labour like beasts and die like Worms'; while Dorothy Osborne, writing to her husband about Margaret's book, traitorously declares, 'Sure the poore woman is a little distracted, shee could never bee soe rediculous else as to venture at writing book's and in verse too, if I should not sleep this fortnight I should not come to that.' The prejudice was long-lived. Even in the nineteenth century Currer Bell, George Eliot and George Sand were driven to veil their identity with masculine pseudonyms. Charlotte Brontë's own vigorous views about the fate that condemns the unmarried girl to a life of sewing and cooking and nothing else are voiced at length by Caroline Melstone in *Shirley* (ch. XXII). Sir William Hamilton adjured his niece Mary, 'Keep your knowledge of Latin a dead secret; a lady's being learned is commonly looked

---

supporting herself and her children by her writing. She was left a widow with three children at the age of 25, and she is notable particularly for her attack on the *Roman de la Rose*, and for almost the first genuine presentation of the woman's view of life and morals. In 1418 she left Paris and retired to a convent.

For the reading of women in the sixteenth and seventeenth centuries, see L. B. Wright, *Middle-class Culture in Elizabethan England*, 1935, pp. 103–18; also *Heritage*, p. 218.

upon as a great fault, even by the learned.'¹ Unable to repress the feminine desire for learning by direct attack, men sought to counter it by art, raising virtue to so dizzy a pinnacle as the highest goal of womanhood, that scholarship could safely be forgotten, or at least left to the less easily soiled hands of men; as if the practical could be a fair substitute for the theoretic, or the good for the true. So Charles Kingsley was led to issue his dire warning, 'Be good, sweet maid, and let who can be clever.'² Coventry Patmore was known to exclaim, 'If there's anything that God hates utterly, it is a clever woman;' a view that must not be taken too seriously however, as a practical judgement, being rather the theoretic standpoint towards which Patmore's ideas tended to drive him almost against his will. His poems, his admiration for women such as Alice Meynell, and indeed his three experiences of marriage, contradict apparently this Oriental view of the duties and functions of women.³

And Princess Ida, whose mission had been

> *To lift the woman's fall'n divinity*
> *Upon an even pedestal with men*

could only satisfy the sentiments of Tennyson's public by allowing her University to abandon academic teaching in favour of practical nursing:

> *So was their sanctuary violated,*
> *So their fair college turn'd to hospital.*

And Florence Nightingale took precedence as the feminine ideal over her contemporary, Sarah Emily Davies, who founded Girton College in 1873, twenty or so years after Princess Ida's college closed down. Even Virginia Woolf in our present century was constrained to lay a curse on a certain famous academic library, when her entrance was barred by a 'deprecating, silvery, kindly gentleman, who regretted in a low voice as he waved me back that ladies

---

[1] Quoted by M. G. Jones, *Hannah More*, 1953, p. 50.

[2] Roy Lewis and Angus Maude, in *The English Middle Classes*, 1949, observe that "It was the Victorian woman, too, who decided that woman's duty was not wholly expressed in the exordium "be good, sweet maid, and let who will be clever", though it may be doubted if she ever envisaged that it would be so completely reversed as it has been by her granddaughters . . .' But they misquote: 'will' should be 'can'.

[3] Basil Champneys, *Memoirs and Correspondence of Coventry Patmore*, 1900, vol. II, p. 78. See also Virginia Crawford's article in the *Fortnightly Review*, 1901, 75, p. 309, and J. C. Reid, *The Mind and Art of Coventry Patmore*, 1957, p. 140.

are only admitted to the library if accompanied by a Fellow of the College or furnished with a letter of introduction'.[1]

However this may be, it was in the middle of the eighteenth century that the habit-forming fashion of reading laid its grip on women; or at least on women with any leisure for such temptations. It is not an accident that *Pamela* and *Tom Jones* and the new circulating libraries all appeared about the same time. Before this time the darkness was still thick. Mrs Aphra Behn's *Oroonoko* was published about 1678; if this sturdy innovator achieved only partial recognition, she at least won the distinction of a tomb in Westminster Abbey. Novels were still regarded with suspicion, and twenty years later the *Athenian Mercury* informed its readers that, though romances might be lawful for persons of quality, they were 'not all convenient for the Vulgar, because they give 'em extravagant Ideas of Practice, and before they have Judgement to bias their Fancies, and generally make 'em think themselves some way King or Queen or other'.

As it happens, there is little evidence that women were reading the *Athenian Mercury*, though in an early number Dunton appealed expressly for questions from them. A very small handful of the printed questions can be definitely ascribed to women. On several occasions advertisements were included of a writing school that taught shorthand to ladies as well as gentlemen, and a certain Mr Switerday offered also to teach them French and Latin. The ambitious girl might however be deterred by the ungallant answer to one query, which has a distinctly medieval flavour. It takes the form of a catechism:

Q. Is it expedient that Women should be Learned?

A. Knowledge puffeth up the mind; therefore if Women were Learned, they would be prouder and more unsupportable than before. Besides, a good opinion of themselves is inconsistent with the Obedience they are designed for. Therefore God gave Knowledge to Adam, and not to Eve, who by the bare desire of Knowledge destroyed all.

---

[1] Milton's view is given in *Paradise Lost*, IV, 637-8:
God is thy Law, thou mine; to know no more
Is woman's happiest knowledge and her praise.
Any suggestion that Eve had her tongue in her cheek when she said this would have shocked the poet profoundly.

Q. Why are they not Learned as Men; are they not capable to become such?

A. They are too delicate to acquire Knowledge, which is not obtained but with great Fatigue. Besides, the moisture of their Brain hindereth solidity of Judgement, which is so necessary for the Sciences.

Q. Why have they not solidity of Judgement?

A. Because the Judgement is an act of the Understanding, which reflecteth upon its Knowledge, and this Reflection dependeth on a dry Temperature, which is contrary to that of the Brain of Women.

Q. Have none of them been Learned?

A. Yes, but 'tis extraordinary. Besides, if we consider their works, they are always accompanied with lack of Judgement. They acquit themselves pretty well in their first Essays, but not in their second Thoughts, which are always meaner than the first. On the contrary, Men's second Thoughts surpass their first, by reason of a stronger Judgement that is in Men than is in Women.

Between the *Athenian Gazette* and the novels of Fielding, the darkness is relieved by little but the eclogues and letters of the brilliant Lady Mary Wortley Montagu. Steele and Addison were, however, deliberately trying to interest their women readers in the pleasure of books, and Richard Steele in 1714 was complaining that no lady felt ashamed of her illiteracy. Austin Dobson, writing of Steele,[1] says, 'As the first painter of domesticity, the modern novel owes him much, but the women of his own time owe him more. Not only did he pay them a magnificent compliment when he wrote of Lady Elizabeth Hastings that 'to love her was a liberal education', but in a time when they were treated by the wits with contemptuous flattery or cynical irreverence, he sought to offer them a reasonable service of genuine respect.'

Swift, fearing perhaps their intuitive perspicacity, developed a high contempt for the learning of women, and was disgusted by the *Spectator's* interest in their advancement. In 1723 he was declaring that not one gentleman's daughter in a thousand could read or understand her own natural tongue.[2] Turn forwards to Dr

---

[1] D.N.B. For Leonora's library in *The Spectator*, see *Heritage*, p. 218.
[2] *Select Works*, 1825, II. 64.

Johnson. In his life of Swift, Johnson has a sentence to the effect that 'we were not then a nation of readers'. In 1778 however, Boswell reports him as saying, 'We have now more knowledge generally diffused; all our ladies read now, and that is a great extension.' The change evidently occurred in these fifty years. It may be noted that in 1737 Pope was observing that 'Our wives read Milton and our daughters plays';[1] a statement that could hardly have been made at any date much earlier than this. Swift's comment, quoted above, was doubtless an outrageous exaggeration, and it would be a grave mistake to imagine that every woman in the early eighteenth, or the late seventeenth, century was idle and illiterate.[2] The truth must lie somewhere between Swift's conclusion and Pope's.

From one point of view the eighteenth century may be regarded as a steady progress from Moll Flanders to Sophia Western; from Sophia to Lydia Languish; and from Lydia to Catherine Morland. This was mainly perhaps progress in refinement, but it was a cultural advance also. Moll Flanders in 1722 had few accomplishments doubtless, but she did at least acquire French, writing and music in her youth. Sophia's environment in 1749 was a trifle more cultivated, and she was surrounded by a certain sort of education. Miss Bridget Allworthy had read sufficient divinity to puzzle the neighbouring curates, and Jenny Jones was as good a Latin scholar as most young men of quality of the age. Sophia's aunt was an even more erudite woman: 'She had considerably improved her mind by study; she had not only read all the modern plays, operas, oratorios, poems and romances—in all of which she was a critic; but had gone through Rapin's *History of England*,[3] Echard's *Roman History*,[4] and many French *Memoires pour servir à l'Histoire*: to these she had added most of the political pamphlets and journals published within the last twenty years.'

By contrast, Miss Williams in *Roderick Random* (1748) had a surprisingly intellectual upbringing. At the age of fourteen, a friend boldly urged her to learn to think for herself, advising her to read 'Shaftesbury, Tindal, Hobbs, and all the books that are remarkable

---

[1] Pope, *First Epistle of the Second Book of Horace*, 172.
[2] See Lady Stenton's comments on this point in her *English Woman in History*, 1957.
[3] Paul de Rapin, *History of England*, French ed. 1723–5.
[4] Laurence Echard, *The Roman History*, 2v., 1695–8.

for their deviation from the old way of thinking'. Miss Williams followed this advice, studied them with pleasure and in a short time became a professed free-thinker. For this she was sent back to her father in the country, where she consoled herself with a good library, though, having more imagination than judgement, she addicted herself too much to poetry and romance.

Lydia Languish was the confirmed habitué of the Bath circulating libraries. Her intellectual diet, it may be noted, might well have been worse. The volumes she was anxious to hide from Sir Anthony Absolute (presumably the ones she took most pleasure in) included *Peregrine Pickle*, *Roderick Random* and an Ovid. The works she considered it discreet to leave on view were *The Whole Duty of Man* (into which *The Innocent Adultery* was thrust); Mrs Chapone;[1] the Rev James Fordyce's *Sermons to Young Women*, 1765,[2] which the hairdresser had apparently been using for his own purposes, the first part being torn away, but it was tactfully opened at the sermon on *Sobriety* (in which, as Lydia knew, the evils of novel-reading are condemned); and Lord Chesterfield's *Letters*. This last, (published in 1774) together with Mrs Chapone's book, must have been quite new from the press, for *The Rivals* was produced in 1775. And note that almost all Lydia's books, including Fordyce, were duodecimos; that is to say, they were small and light enough to read comfortably while reclining on a sofa (as Lydia was in this scene), and in case of alarm to throw under the toilet, into the closet, behind the bolster or beneath the sofa. Almost the first requisite of the circulating library novel is that it should be reasonably light and portable. In *Northanger Abbey* the girls were slightly more purposive in their reading. Miss Tilney, who was fond of history, thought it worth while to be tormented for two or three years of one's life, for the sake of being able to read all the rest of it. And Catherine Morland, between fifteen and sixteen, when she was in training for a heroine, 'read all such works as heroines must read to supply their memories with those quotations which are so serviceable and so soothing in the vicissitudes of their eventful lives.' The novels that Isabella Thorpe recom-

---

[1] Hester Chapone (1727-1801), the bluestocking friend of Dr Johnson and Elizabeth Carter. The book was probably *Letters on the Improvement of the Mind*, 2v., 1773.

[2] It was from a copy of Fordyce's *Sermons* that Mr Collins in *Pride and Prejudice* chose to read aloud to the Bennet family on his first evening at Longbourn.

mended to Catherine were doubtless those that Miss Austen herself had read and enjoyed and perhaps laughed over.[1]

Schools for girls were spreading fast at this time. Not the least famous was the boarding-school kept by Hannah More's sisters at Bristol, where Hannah herself acquired her Italian, Spanish and Latin.

One notable pupil at this school was Mary Robinson, the 'English Sappho'. If she had remained in Hannah More's hands rather longer, then the Prince of Wales might never have found his Perdita. When Mary's father deserted her mother, she was transferred to two successive schools in Chelsea, received at the age of 13 a proposal of marriage from a Captain, R.N., assisted her mother in running a school of her own, also in Chelsea, and finally went to a finishing school in Marylebone, where she met not only David Garrick, but Thomas Robinson, whom she married when she was sixteen. The Prince first saw her at a command performance of the *Winter's Tale* about four years later.

Another fashionable establishment was the Belvedere House School at Bath, founded by the four daughters of the actor John Lee, Sophia, Harriet, Charlotte and Ann, which Mrs Thrale went out of her way to praise. Sophia was the authoress of *The Chapter of Accidents* (produced in 1780), and with Harriet of the *Canterbury Tales* (5 vols. 1797–1805). Still another was the school at 22 Hans Place, Chelsea, kept by the French refugee Mrs St Quintin, where Lady Caroline Lamb, Letitia Elizabeth Landon ('L.E.L.') and Miss Mitford were educated.

It would be a grave mistake to imagine that the Lydia Languishes were reared on nothing but a diet of novels. Listen to Hazlitt on this question:[2]

'To say nothing of a host of female authors, a bright galaxy above our heads, there is no young lady of fashion in the present day, scarce a boarding-school girl, that is not mistress of as many branches of knowledge as could set up half a dozen literary hacks. In lieu of the sampler and the plain-stitch of our grandmothers, they have so many hours for French, so many for Italian, so many

---

[1] See Michael Sadleir's introduction to the World's Classics ed. of *Northanger Abbey*, and his *English Association Pamphlet* No. 68 (1927), *The Northanger Novels: A Footnote to Jane Austen*.
[2] *On the Conversation of Lords*.

for English grammar and composition, so many for geography and the use of the globes, so many for history, so many for botany, so many for painting, music, dancing, riding, etc. ... A girl learns French (not only to read, but to speak it) in a few months, while a boy is as many years in learning to construe Latin. ...'

This new fashion of feminine reading produced a steady stream of what Horace Walpole called 'novel-writers in petticoats', and in addition a constellation of brilliant women; not all of them bluestockings in the unkinder meaning of the term. Some at least were women of evident ability and taste. Lady Mary Wortley Montagu, whom Pope and Walpole libelled outrageously, surely deserves the blessing of every reader of her *Letters from Abroad*, and of everyone who has escaped the tragedy of smallpox, as a result of the practice of inoculation which she introduced. And there was Hester Chapone, whose book Lydia Languish found convenient for display, and the famous quintet that Johnson praised so gallantly: Mrs Carter, Hannah More, Fanny Burney, Mrs Lennox and Mrs Montagu, whose grandfather was Conyers Middleton, the Protobibliothecarius at Cambridge. And of these, Fanny Burney at least, loved a gossip in a circulating library as much as any woman.

Catherine Morland used to think that 'gentlemen read better books'. This charming illusion was broken when Henry Tilney proved an even greater authority on *The Mysteries of Udolpho* than Miss Morland herself. Hannah More, it is true, took up a more superior attitude towards novel-reading and the circulating libraries, attacking them by writing a novel of her own with an appropriate moral, namely *Coelebs in Search of a Wife* (1809). For a brief while it was a best-seller, but it had little merit, and Sydney Smith unkindly likened it to the 'brick and mortar novels of the Minerva Press' (which were, so to speak, the bread and butter of all the circulating libraries).

The circulating libraries were the direct result of the new and infectious fashion. The habit of reading had spread far beyond the circle of those with unlimited money to spend; and most of the novels published after about 1775 were bought, not by individual readers, but by the libraries. They were too expensive and too ephemeral for individual purchase. Those who have studied the history of these libraries are at pains to point out that they contained much besides fiction. This is very true of the society and subscription libraries, and to a more limited extent of the circulating libraries, which were all commercial ventures more concerned with their market than with any educational function. The staple diet of the commercial libraries was, however, the novel. The fame of *Pamela* and *Tom Jones* drew forth as dense a cloud of trivial and empty romances as any that we have experienced in the present century, and to these the libraries owed their profits. A storm of criticism arose, which doubtless contributed to their success. Libraries sprang up everywhere: in London, at the holiday resorts and in all the provincial towns; and the great majority of their patrons were women, for whom they served the same purpose as the coffee and chocolate houses had done for their husbands and fathers. Many were attached to the shops of milliners or drapers, and many served as much for social gossip and the meeting of friends as our cafés do today. Many were supplied by that astute business man William Lane and his Minerva Press.[1]

It is fair to regard the circulating libraries at the close of the eighteenth century very much as our similar libraries in the twentieth century: just as harmless, that is, and just as harmful, according to one's point of view. Novels were then a new sort of toy, and as innocent as most other adult toys. The trouble was that they might be mistaken for, or taken as substitutes for, something of higher value; *The Innocent Adultery* and *The Whole Duty of Man* both wore the same outer clothes, as it were. Ever since, the literary snob has tended to raise his eyebrows at this intrusion into his preserves. In the old days before George III came to the throne, when the world was simpler and more select, the word 'book' meant one thing only. Now it meant two quite different things, and the confusion was the worse because, different as these two things could be, there was no sharp boundary between them; on the borderline they shaded imperceptibly into each other, though further apart chalk and cheese were not more different.

Not all the cognoscenti were equally disturbed. Charles Lamb,

---

[1] On this subject see Dorothy Blake, *The Minerva Press, 1790–1820*, Bibliographical Society, 1939; H. M. Hamlyn, 'Eighteenth-century Circulating Libraries', *The Library*, 1947, p. 197; also Frank Beckwith, 'Eighteenth-century Proprietary Libraries', *J. of Documentation*, 1947, 3. 85. J. M. S. Tompkins, *The Popular Novel in England, 1770–1800*, 1932, has much information about the lesser novelists of this period and the market for their wares.

in his charity, and remembering perhaps his sister's predilection for books with a story, 'well, ill or indifferently told—so there be life stirring in it, and plenty of good or evil accidents,'[1] tempered his censure with such gentle understanding that there was little trace of censure left. He speaks of 'the common run of Lane's novels' as 'those scanty intellectual viands of the whole female reading public', but this is mildness itself compared with the attacks of the literary snobs; Lamb was never a snob. It would be tedious to quote all the more censorious verdicts of less charitable writers; the feeling that their own market was being threatened by these intruders may have had something to do with their censoriousness. Let us be content with one specimen. Coleridge, in one of his less elegant passages of prose, sums up the case for the prosecution:

'For as to the devotees of the circulating libraries, I dare not compliment their pass-time, or rather kill-time, with the name of reading. Call it rather a sort of beggarly day-dreaming during which the mind of the dreamer furnishes for itself nothing but laziness and a little mawkish sensibility; while the whole *materiel* and imagery of the doze is supplied *ab extra* by a sort of mental *camera obscura* manufactured at the printing office, which *pro tempore* fixes, reflects and transmits the moving phantasms of one man's delirium, so as to people the barrenness of an hundred other brains afflicted with the same trance or suspension of all common sense and all definite purpose. We should therefore transfer this species of amusement (if indeed those can be said to retire *a musis*, who were never in their company, or relaxation be attributable to those whose bows are never bent) from the genus, reading, to that comprehensive class characterised by the power of reconciling the two contrary yet co-existing propensities of human nature, namely indulgence of sloth and hatred of vacancy. In addition to novels and tales of chivalry in prose or rhyme (by which last I mean neither rhythm nor metre) this genus comprises as its species, gaming, swinging or swaying on a chair or gate; spitting over a bridge; smoking; snuff-taking; tête à tête quarrels after dinner between husband and wife; conning word by word all the advertisements of the *Daily Advertiser* in a public house on a rainy day, etc. etc., etc.'[2]

[1] *Mackery End.*
[2] *Biographia Literaria*, ch. III, note.

It is fair to mention that not all the novels that were being read at this time had their source in the circulating libraries. Some were being bought and collected, if rather misguidedly, by the wealthier sort of woman. That curious character Lady Lillycraft, in Washington Irving's *Bracebridge Hall*, was such a one:

'Much of her time was passed in reading novels, of which she has a most extensive library, and has a constant supply from the publishers in town. Her erudition in this line of literature is immense: she has kept pace with the press for half a century ... she evidently gives the preference to those that came out in the days of her youth, and when she was first in love. She maintains that there are no novels written nowadays equal to *Pamela* and *Sir Charles Grandison;* and she places *The Castle of Otranto* at the head of all romances.'

An earlier example occurs in Charlotte Lennox's novel *The Female Quixote* (1752). The heroine, Arabella, who was the daughter of a statesman, born after his retirement in disgrace, was educated in solitude at his castle in a remote province. 'The romances which she found in the library after her mother's death, were almost the only books she had read; from these, therefore, she derived her ideas of life; she believed the business of the world to be love, every incident to be the beginning of an adventure, and every stranger a knight in disguise'. Fielding held that this story excelled Don Quixote in some respects, as Arabella was a more endearing character than Don Quixote, and it is more likely that the head of a young lady than that of an old gentleman would be turned by reading romances.[1]

It was of course Lady Lillycraft in *Bracebridge Hall* who contributed to the education of the fair Julia, and 'enriched her mind with all kinds of novels and romances'. Mark also that *Bracebridge Hall* was published in 1822, five years after the death of Jane Austen, who apparently had made no impression on the good lady's mind. Even more striking is the fact that this was almost exactly a hundred years after the death of Lady Winchelsea, who had complained so bitterly of the sentence that condemned women to the 'dull manage of a servile house', and forbad them 'to write, or read, or

---

[1] Johnson's review in the *Gentleman's Magazine*, 1752, XXII, 146. See also Austin Dobson, *op. cit.*

think, or to enquire'. It may indeed be doubted whether Lady Lillycraft spared any time for thought or enquiry. But she had contemporaries who wrote and thought to good effect: Mary Wollstonecraft, the author of the *Vindication of the Rights of Woman*, 1792, and the mother of Shelley's second wife, who published her *Frankenstein* in 1818; and Harriet Martineau, whose works were mostly published between 1832 and 1849. It would be easy to find other women writers in the early part of this century who were by no means undistinguished. There is, for example, a pleasant story told by H. F. Chorley, of Felicia Dorothea Hemans in her youth at Gwrych, near Abergele, reading Shakespeare and writing her verses while perched in the branches of an apple tree. And later in the century William Cory had his band of *discipulae* whom he found so charming in his later years, devoted ones sitting at his feet and learning to enjoy the *Supplices* or the *Aeneid*. 'The two undying evergreen languages' (he wrote) 'have been for me made beautiful by this after-growth of girlhood'. They were, one gathers, apter pupils and more teachable than his boys at Eton.

And by this time, women were penetrating other fields than social science and economics. Natural history had become a fashionable interest, and while some women were studying the rock pools at Ilfracombe with Philip H. Gosse, others were botanising, and Anne Pratt was writing her *Flowering Plants of Great Britain* (5 vols., 1855); a work of weight and substance which has remained a popular guide almost to this day. It was very definitely the product of research in a library as well as in the field, for it contains references to over 500 authors, including ninety or more poets. An equally good example would be Marianne North (1830-90), the distinguished plant collector and flower painter, who travelled all over the world in search of her subjects. Several new species were honoured with her name. In her youth she was a friend of Sir William Hooker, the Director at Kew Gardens; her sister Janet married John Addington Symonds.

If it be wondered why so few women have written works of this magnitude, the answer may be sought in Virginia Woolf's *A Room of One's Own*. It is rarely that a woman even today can enjoy the luxury of a private study, in which she may work without interruption. This is possibly the reason why a woman writer takes most easily to fiction; it is less easily marred by the constant distractions that the normal woman must always endure in her daily life. All Jane Austen's books were composed under such conditions. 'She had no separate study to repair to,' we are told, 'and most of the work must have been done in the general sitting-room, subject to all kinds of casual interruptions. She was careful that her occupation should not be suspected by servants or visitors or any persons beyond her own family party.'[1] It is in these circumstances remarkable that of the comparatively few women writers of ability since Jane Austen, so many have contributed so much to English literature at its best. This is as true of the present century as of the last. What delight the Brontes would have taken in Constance Holmes' novels! And how Jane Austen would have recognized a fellow spirit in Miss E. H. Young, the best of whose novels are well worthy to stand beside *Pride and Prejudice* or *Emma*. David Garnett regarded Mary MacCarthy's *A Pier and a Band* as Tchehov's *Cherry Orchard* in an English setting. And then of course, there is Virginia Woolf herself, and not a few others.

§3—IN HUMBLER QUARTERS

Almost the surest evidence of the extent of the new habit of reading is the depth to which it penetrated in the social order. In the eighteenth century it spread below stairs almost as rapidly as it did in the parlour, the boudoir and the study; and by the end of the century most people who had any sort of contact with the ranks above them had caught the infection, and were learning to read, and even to write. There was a wealth of tracts and guides published in the eighteenth century for the instruction of servants, and many of them must obviously have been able to read and profit by them.[2]

Richardson's *Pamela* (1740) consisted of course of a series of letters from the young maidservant Pamela Andrews; it was based on the author's experience as a professional letter writer 'in the service of the young women of the neighbourhood, who made use of his equipments and his discretion to convey their written sentiments to their sweethearts'.[3] It would be a mistake however,

---

[1] J. E. Austen-Leigh, *Memoirs of Jane Austen*, 1871.
[2] See especially J. Jean Hecht, *The Domestic Servant Class in the Eighteenth Century in England*, 1956, which is a valuable source of information on these matters.
[3] Austin Dobson, *Eighteenth Century Vignettes*, 2nd series.

to conclude that these young women were unable to read and write, merely because they lacked the fluency and the experience needed to produce a satisfactory love letter. Indeed the warning of Petrus Godefridus (quoted earlier) might suggest a very different conclusion.

Swift in his *Journal to Stella* recounts how he had discovered his footman borrowing one of his volumes of Congreve. Footmen often had access to their masters' libraries, and some seem to have made good use of them. The classic instance is Robert Dodsley the publisher (1703–64)[1] who began life as a footman in the household of the Hon. Jane Lowther, daughter of the first Viscount Lonsdale. Here he seems to have had the run of the library, and to have met many literary celebrities, including Pope and Defoe. Thus encouraged, he published his poem *Servitude* in 1729;[2] *A Muse in Livery* in 1732; and his play *The Toyshop* in 1735. With the profits of the play he resigned his post and set up as a bookseller and publisher at 'Tully's Head' in Pall Mall; not only did he publish for Pope, Johnson, Goldsmith and Gray, but in 1758 he founded, in co-operation with Edmund Burke, the *Annual Register*.

The sensitive Hazlitt seems to have had a prejudice against all footmen. Quoting the saying 'All men are equal except footmen', he distinguishes 'literary footmen' as the lowest class of this genus: 'These consist of persons, who, without a single grain of knowledge, taste or feeling, put on the livery of learning, mimic its phrases by rote, and are retained in its service by dint of quackery and assurance alone.... They walk with a peculiar strut, thrust themselves into the acquaintance of persons they hear talked of, get introduced into the clubs, are seen reading books they do not understand at the Museum and public libraries, dine (if they can) with lords or officers of the Guards ... give themselves out as wits, critics and philosophers (and as they have never done anything, no man can contradict them), and have a great knack of turning editors and not paying their contributors....'[3]

Equally with the footman, the lady's maid was not without some culture; she often had to be an intelligent companion to her mistress. A contemporary guide explains that she was required to

---
[1] There is an attractive picture of Dodsley and his bookshop in Austin Dobson's *Eighteenth Century Vignettes*, 2nd series, in the essay 'At Tully's Head'.
[2] Later re-issued as *The Footman's Friendly Advice to his Brethren of the Livery*.
[3] Essay on 'Footmen' in *Sketches and Essays*, 1839.

be well educated, able to read well aloud, and familiar with the French language, modes and customs.[1] On the other hand the ladies' maids with whom Hazlitt was acquainted do not seem to have had any French or Italian; the type is described, in the essay already quoted, as 'not speaking a word of the language except what she picks up "as pigeons pick up peas".'

The under-servants, aspiring perhaps to higher rungs of the ladder, may also have acquired the habit of reading, though perhaps they contented themselves with simpler fare. Leigh Hunt, writing in 1816, but referring to the period twenty or thirty years earlier, gives an inventory of the contents of a maidservant's room.[2] His prying eyes seem to have noted her possessions down to the last comb. They included an odd volume of *Pamela* and perhaps a sixpenny play, a Bible, and in a box under stout lock and key amongst her clothes, the rest of her library. (What, one wonders, was the inquisitive essayist doing in this secret compartment?) However, among the treasures he unearthed were two or three song-books, consisting of nineteen for the penny; sundry tragedies at a halfpenny for the sheet; the *Whole Nature of Dreams Laid Open* together with *The Fortune-Teller* and *The Account of the Ghost of Mrs Veal*, and *The Story of the Beautiful Zoa*, 'who was cast away on a desert island, showing how ... etc.'[3]

Of the lowlier folk who were mounting the ladder in the eighteenth century, John Clare and Robert Bloomfield have already been mentioned. There were others however. Ann Yearsley (Lactilla, or the Bristol milkwoman) who helped her mother sell milk from door to door, came to the notice of Hannah More, who gave her a grammar, a spelling-book and a dictionary, and helped her to publish her poems. After falling out with Hannah More, she opened a circulating library at the Colonnade in Hot Wells, Bristol. Stephen Duck, the Wiltshire farm labourer and poet, began his literary pursuits by puzzling out *Paradise Lost* with a dictionary, progressing therefrom to the *Spectator*, translations of

---

[1] Anthony Heasel, *The Servants' Book of Knowledge*, 1773.
[2] Leigh Hunt, *The Maidservant*.
[3] One of the long line of servants employed by Jane Carlyle in Cheyne Row was discovered by her master one morning at breakfast time sitting by the unlighted, half-scoured grate, deep in Goethe's *Wilhelm Meister*. Carlyle was much impressed, in spite of his breakfast being late, but Jane could not tolerate such habits, and the girl was soon sent back to her home (Thea Holme, *The Carlyles at Home*, 1965).

Seneca's *Morals*, *Télémaque* and Josephus, Dryden's *Virgil* and *Hudibras*: a curious diet. His poems brought him some reputation, and in 1730 Lord Macclesfield was reading them to Queen Caroline; five years later he became keeper of the queen's library at Richmond. Mary Leaper, a cook-maid and the daughter of a Northamptonshire gardener, obtained at an early age copies of Pope and Dryden, and modelled her own poems on their lofty example. These were published in two volumes in 1748 and 1751, but before they appeared, she had died of measles, aged twenty-four.

If such as these were writing, thousands more were satisfied with the chance of reading. In 1791, the London publisher James Lackington made an entry in his diary, which confirms the expanding demand for books.[1] 'The sale of books in general (he writes) has increased prodigiously within the last twenty years. The poorer sort of farmers, and even the poor country people in general who, before that period, spent their winter evenings in relating stories of witches, ghosts, hobgoblins, etc., now shorten the winter nights by hearing their sons and daughters read tales, romances, etc. . . . and on entering their houses you may see *Tom Jones*, *Roderick Random* and other entertaining books, stuck up in their bacon-racks, etc. If John goes to town with a load of hay, he is charged to be sure not to forget to bring home *Peregrine Pickle's Adventures*, and when Dolly is sent to market to sell her eggs, she is commissioned to purchase *The History of Joseph Andrews*. In short, all ranks and degrees now read.'

Lackington was, to some extent, drawing on his imagination to present a colourful picture. A hundred years later, in the Derbyshire farm described so attractively by Alison Uttley,[2] they were still beguiling the winter evenings with tales of witches and hobgoblins, and the books read aloud to the assembled household were *Robinson Crusoe* and *East Lynne* rather than Fielding or Smollett. But the habit of reading or being read to, was firmly planted in the eighteenth, as in the nineteenth, century.

The cottagers that Thomas Bewick knew during his childhood at Cherryburn were for example no strangers to books, though their resources were limited perhaps to 'the Bible, local histories

---

[1] Quoted by S. H. Steinberg, *Five Hundred Years of Printing*, 1955.
[2] In *The Farm on the Hill*, 1941, and *Ambush of Young Days*, 1937.

and old ballads'. Will Bewick on the other hand had somehow picked up a knowledge of astronomy and of the universe, which he used to impart to the young Thomas, 'sitting on a mound, or seat by the hedge of his garden, regardless of the cold and intent upon viewing the heavenly bodies'. Thomas' fell-side neighbour, Anthony Liddell, whom he terms 'the village Hampden', was a 'great reader of history, especially those parts where wars or battles were described; and in any meetings with his neighbours he took the lead in discourses founded on knowledge of that kind. After the Bible, 'Josephus' was his favourite author, next the 'Holy Wars'—these and 'Bishop Taylor's Sermons' composed his whole library; and his memory enabled him nearly to repeat whatever he had read. The farmers themselves were, in Bewick's view, less intelligent than the cottagers, 'Their minds being exclusively occupied with the management of their farms, they read but little. They were mostly of a kind and hospitable disposition, and well-intentioned, plain, plodding men, who went jogging on in their several occupations as their fathers had done before them.'[1]

George Crabbe's lines in his *Parish Register* (1807) are perhaps apposite here:

> *On shelf of deal, beside the cuckoo-clock,*
> *Of cottage-reading rests the chosen stock;*
> *Learning we lack, not books, but have a kind*
> *For all our wants, a meat for every mind;*
> *The tale for wonder and the joke for whim,*
> *The half-sung sermon, and the half-groaned hymn.*
> *No need for classing; each within its place,*
> *The feeling finger in the dark can trace;*
> *'First from the corner, farthest from the wall'.*
> *Such all the rules, and they suffice for all.*

[1] See Thomas Bewick's *Memoir*, and Montague Weekly, *Thomas Bewick*, 1953.

CHAPTER XV

The Nineteenth Century

§1—THE SCHOLARS AND THE ESSAYISTS

WE have brought the story of domestic libraries down to the time of Dr Johnson and Gibbon. To continue the account into a century when every man of note had his personal collection would yield a wearisome repetition of names and figures, and we must illustrate by choosing here and there a few that seem particularly significant or interesting.

Scholarly libraries increased in number and size. While Miss Burney was gossiping in Brighton circulating libraries or under detention in France, her brother Charles was collecting the great library that has brought him fame. He died in 1817, and his family petitioned Parliament to buy it for the nation, suggesting a figure of £14,000. There was a lively debate in the House of Commons on the proposal, during which Sir James Mackintosh was so carried away by his enthusiasm as to cry out that 'a single passage in Demosthenes was alone worth the sum in the eyes of a free nation'. One may doubt whether he would get away with such a remark in the House today. Nevertheless Parliament agreed to the scheme, reducing the figure by only £500 for form's sake, and the collection passed to the British Museum. It consists of about 13,000 printed editions of classical authors, many bearing MS notes by earlier scholars such as Richard Bentley, and about 500 volumes of Greek and Latin manuscripts, including the Townley Homer. In addition, there was his great collection of newspapers of the seventeenth and eighteenth centuries, filling 700 volumes. They were bound not in separate files, but chronologically, so that those of any one week were kept together, and a careful index was prepared by Burney himself.

Three or four other outstanding collections came to the Museum in the period. Sir Joseph Banks, botanist, traveller and President of the Royal Society, left his great library and herbarium, with an annuity of £200, to his third librarian, Robert Brown; his earlier librarians had been Daniel Solander and Jonas Dryander. The reversion was to the Museum, and after Banks' death in 1820, Brown passed on the books to the Museum without delay and later joined the Museum staff himself. Another contemporary botanical library, equally rich, found a different resting place. Sir James Edward Smith (1759-1828), the son of a wealthy Norwich manufacturer, had the foresight at the age of twenty-four to buy the library and herbarium of Linnaeus in 1783. They had been offered to Sir Joseph Banks for a thousand guineas, but on Banks' advice they were purchased by Smith. A few years later in 1788, at a coffee house in Great Marlborough St. the Linnean Society was founded by Smith and his friends; and after his death, the library was bought by private subscription for £3,000 and handed to the Society. Smith is perhaps best remembered for his part in the production of Sowerby's *English Botany*, 36 vols., 1790-1814, the plates in this great work being by James Sowerby and the text by Smith. The possession of an outstanding library, combined with a natural interest in botany, had astonishingly fruitful results in Smith's output; besides his books, he is said to have written well over three thousand articles on botanical subjects.

Of the other private collections which the Museum received, three may be recorded here. One belonged to the merchant banker Henry Huth (1815-78), and a choice of fifty volumes from his library (important particularly in the field of early English, Spanish and German literature and in early voyages) was offered to the Museum. Another was the magnificent collection formed by Thomas Grenville. He had bequeathed his library to his nephew the Duke of Buckingham, but conscientious scruples led him to add a codicil transferring the bequest to the Museum. He had been the last holder of the sinecure office of chief justice in eyre south of Trent, which carried a salary of £2,000; and he felt that as his books had in great part been acquired from this profitable source, they should return to the nation after his death. There were over 20,000 volumes, most of them nobly bound (if mistakenly) in his own full morocco; the original binding of even the Shakespeare first folio was discarded.

A third acquisition by the Museum may be recorded, though it came at a later date: the Ashley Library collected by Thomas James Wise (1859–1937), bibliographer and forger, and not the less important in view of the deceptions which he practised on the bibliographical world. It was an outstanding collection of first editions of English poetry and drama; some have been shown to be skilful fakes, but most are genuine. Its catalogue was issued in eleven volumes, 1922–30. Whatever the real motives of its collector, there can be no better example of a collection of supreme bibliographical importance which nevertheless is not a domestic working library; it illustrates the difference that can exist between a collection (however systematic) and a library. This is not to question the scholarship of T. J. Wise, but it does throw doubt on the use to which he put his scholarship. When bibliography, and indeed forgery, becomes an end in itself, rather than an honest means to a worthy end, it forfeits any claim to rank as the basis of a genuine working library.

Another rather curious library belonged to William Beckford (1759–1844), that 'enthusiastic collector of expensive trifles', as he has been described, at his extravagantly furnished house, Fonthill, and at Lansdowne Terrace in Bath. He is said never to have parted with a book during his lifetime; his library however was dispersed in the auction rooms in 1882.

Two far more magnificent collections deserve mention here. One was the 150,000 volumes gathered by the classical scholar Richard Heber (1773–1833), brother of Reginald Heber, Bishop of Calcutta, who won a different sort of fame as the author of 'God that madest earth and heaven' and other well-known hymns. When Richard died, he left eight houses filled to overflowing with his books.

The other was the Bibliotheca Phillippica. Sir Thomas Phillipps began his collection at Rugby, where all his pocket money was spent on books. 'I commenced with purchasing everything that lay within my reach (he wrote), whether good or bad, and more particularly those on vellum.' Indeed he became a 'vello-maniac', determined to preserve whatever he could find on vellum from destruction by gold-beaters; and to do this he deliberately forced up the price of vellum manuscripts in the hope of raising their value in the estimation of scholars and collectors. His ideal was to become a new Cotton or a new Harley of the modern age, and in a sense he succeeded, though his great collection did not in fact pass into the nation's hands, most of it being dispersed at sales between 1889 and 1908. He was much more than a merely acquisitive collector, for he understood and loved his possessions, and great quantities of his notebooks are filled with his comments and observations on them. In the good tradition of earlier collectors on the grand scale, he established his private press at Broadway, and was always glad to welcome the visits of genuine students. In 1863-64 the library removed from Broadway to Thirlestaine House, Cheltenham. This was a gigantic operation in the days before motor transport; a hundred and three wagons were employed, drawn by two hundred and thirty horses in the charge of one hundred and sixty men; local memory still retails stories of the broken wheels and axles that marked the progress of the library across the Cotswolds.

Thanks to the scholarly labours of Dr A. N. L. Munby, the Bibliotheca Phillippica is more fully documented than any other great collection in this country.[1] The collection contained in all about 60,000 MSS, and 50,000 printed books. The printed books in general were not of great importance. The collection can, in Munby's words, be judged by the MSS alone, 'the greatest library of unpublished historical material ever brought together by one man, more than double the size, as Henry Bradshaw wrote in 1869, of the whole of our Cambridge University and College collections put together'. Four facts stand out: (1) It was a vast collection, rather than a true library. The books were kept in coffin-like box shelves which, at Middle Hill especially, were piled in solid heaps in almost every room and passage. Boxes sometimes remained unopened for months or years after delivery, and often the task of locating a particular volume was insoluble. He administered this great collection singlehanded, and his *Catalogus Librorum Manuscriptorum*, listing and describing 23,837 items was his unaided work. (2) He continued the tradition of hospitality to scholars, especially foreign scholars (provided they were not Roman Catholics), though serious work among the boxes at Middle Hill must often have been difficult and unrewarding. (3) Though devoted all his life to the cause of scholarship, he was not himself a scholar, and certainly not a palaeographer. He was vain and arro-

[1] A. N. L. Munby, *Phillipps Studies*, 5v., 1951-60.

gant, and, his whole life being dominated by his mania for collecting, his family relationships were embittered by his own meanness and obstinacy. Sir Frederic Madden's estimate of Phillipps, revealed in the privacy of his own journals ('he had the brains of a tomtit') was scarcely fair or just; Madden, himself a great palaeographer, had all the limitations of an expert specialist. Phillipps' own publications are of very unequal value, and are far too full of errors and inaccuracies, but the best are still of use to antiquarians and genealogists. However unpleasant his selfishness may have made him, one cannot help but admire the dogged determination with which he achieved his lifelong purpose. (4) There seems no doubt that Phillipps' deliberate policy of forcing up the prices of MSS on vellum and paper in a market that was then overstocked, resulted in the preservation from destruction of thousands of manuscripts and deeds, and we must indeed be grateful to him for this. He was well aware of the effect of his wholesale purchases. 'Nothing', he wrote, 'tends to the preservation of anything so much as making it bear a high price'.

The third volume of the *Phillipps Studies* includes useful notes on the booksellers and collectors with whom Sir Thomas had dealings. Amongst the latter was Robert Curzon, with whom he maintained a friendly correspondence for a long period. Curzon's interests were mainly in Greek, Syriac and Coptic MSS, and his *Visit to the monasteries of the Levant*, 1849, is one of the most entertaining travel books of the 19th century, notable particularly for his account of the libraries of the twenty-one monasteries of Mount Athos, and for the dramatic story of the books at Souriani in the Natron Lakes, north-west of Cairo, where in a disused oil cellar he discovered a closet filled with the loose leaves of Syriac manuscripts two feet or more deep. Scattered in this heap were the fragments of the famous quarto dated A.D. 411 which Curzon was forced to leave behind; the account of its later rescue and piecing together by Mr Cureton is given in Curzon's appendix (1916 ed.). It reached the British Museum in 1847, and Curzon describes it as the most precious acquisition to any library in modern times.

Let us note one other great library of the true scholarly type. We have recorded the library of seven thousand volumes collected by Edward Gibbon as the type and model of the scholar's library, gathered by a single owner for a single purpose, and nobly realised in that purpose. A historical library almost ten times as large as Gibbon's, equally systematic and equally purposive, was collected by Lord Acton (1834–1902), Regius Professor of Modern History at Cambridge, founder of the *English Historical Review* and architect of the *Cambridge Modern History*. His library of about 60,000 volumes was bought by Andrew Carnegie, as a gift to Lord Morley, who himself presented it to the University of Cambridge in 1903.

It is, of course, given to few men to collect on this scale. By the beginning of the nineteenth century, if not earlier, it was becoming plain that even a wealthy scholar could no longer hope to rely on his own collection for his researches. Knowledge was expanding, both in area and in depth, so rapidly that even in a specialized field no single worker could hope to gather all the material of value. It was precisely this that led to the reorganization of the British Museum Library, the foundation of the London Library at Carlyle's instigation,[1] and of many libraries maintained by the learned societies. The earlier foundation of Dr Williams's Library (1716) and its successful career testifies to the financial and political handicaps under which dissenting ministers had laboured since the Restoration.[2]

It is not surprising that the movement to found proprietary libraries in the latter part of the 18th century owed much to the anxiety of both liberal nonconformity and of the newly developing sciences to make provision for their own special needs, which were satisfied neither by contemporary Anglicanism nor by the Universities. This is illustrated clearly by Paul Kaufman in his paper *The Eighteenth-Century Forerunner of the London Library*.[3] The influence of Joseph Priestley in the growth of the circulating libraries at Warrington, Leeds and Birmingham is well known. The stock of the first London Library had a strong scientific bias, and its membership included a good proportion of fellows of the Royal Society and physicians as well as ministers of religion. Priestley himself observed that 'The Dissenters have always been foremost to promote these libraries'. One significant exception was the Bristol Library Society, which had a mainly Anglican atmosphere, due perhaps to its early origins in the 17th century with the gift of

---

[1] On this see the chapter by Simon Nowell-Smith in *English Libraries*, 1800–50, 1958.
[2] S. K. Jones, *Dr Williams and his Library*, 1948. See also p. 236 *supra*.
[3] Bibl. Soc. of America, 1960, vol. LIV.

books by Dr Tobie Matthew, Archbishop of York (d. 1626).

If eighteenth century libraries owe much to nonconformity, so does the literacy of the common people. Just as Wycliffism aided the spread of literacy in the 15th century, so did Wesleyanism in the 18th century, and to a far greater extent. John Wesley himself was a pioneer in the popularization of reading. He was fond of producing simplified versions of the masters: *Pilgrim's Progress*, 1743, in a pocket edition at 4d; and *Paradise Lost*, Young's *Night Thoughts* were issued in this way, and his *Collection of Moral and Sacred Poems*, 1744, had a similar end in view. He preached the spiritual necessity of reading, and circulated books and pamphlets in great quantities. Many of the works of John and Charles Wesley had surprisingly high circulations; the little tract *Swear not at all* for example, had a run of 21,000 copies in seven editions.[1]

Increasingly, everyone who made serious use of his own domestic library, from professor to peasant, found himself forced to supplement it from outside sources, and to depend on one of the many forms of co-operative provision. This was especially true of the young writer or scholar whose early days were a struggle with adversity. Chatterton, Coleridge, Shelley, Leigh Hunt and Ricardo are examples that come readily to mind. Coleridge's disputes with the Bristol Library Society about the overdue fine on his copy of Brucker's *Historia Critica Philosophiae*, are well known,[2] Southey, after exhausting the library of his aunt, Miss Tyler, at Bath, made good use of the Bristol Library; that, of course, was long before he had built up his own library of 14,000 volumes at Greta Hall. Keats who, in 1819, spent some time in the Isle of Wight for his health's sake, abandoned Shanklin because there was no library there, and moved to Winchester, 'chiefly for the purpose of being near a tolerable Library, which after all, is not to be found in this place.'[3]

The philologist Joseph Wright (remembered chiefly perhaps as the compiler of *The English Dialect Dictionary*) is said once to have remarked, with reference to his house in North Oxford, that he was compelled to provide generous accommodation for his books

---

[1] See William B. Todd, *New Adventures among Old Books*, Univ. of Kansas Library, 1958, pp. 16–17.
[2] See H. M. Hamlyn, 'Eighteenth Century Circulating Libraries in England', *The Library*, 1947, p. 197.
[3] Letter to his sister Fanny, 28 Aug., 1819.

because he could not afford the time to visit libraries. This feeling is not as out of date as it may seem; the using of strange libraries, scattered perhaps in many parts of the country or even of the world, is a time-consuming operation, and the use of even a single great library, however well organized, may waste hours or days. No system of national or public libraries will ever replace the collection which the scholar needs always to have in his own study. But the complicated specialisation of modern knowledge makes it possible for few to have everything they need at their elbow, and the student who is using original sources must always be prepared to go out in search of them.

In the early part of the nineteenth century the ordinary working libraries of which personal descriptions have survived are beginning to wear a thoroughly familiar aspect, conjuring up pictures not merely of hard study but of pleasurable tasks and family enjoyment in bookish surroundings. Here, for example, is De Quincey in his pleasanter mood:

'Paint me, then, a room seventeen feet by twelve, and not more than seven and a half feet high. This, reader, is somewhat ambitiously styled, in my family, the drawing-room; but being contrived "a double debt to pay", it is also, and more justly, termed the library; for it happens that books are the only article of property in which I am richer than my neighbours. Of these I have about five thousand, collected gradually since my eighteenth year. Therefore, painter, put as many as you can into this room. Make it populous with books; and, furthermore, paint me a good fire and furniture plain and modest, befitting the unpretending cottage of a scholar. And near the fire paint me a tea-table; and (as it is clear that no creature can come to see one, such a stormy night) place only two cups and saucers on the tea-tray; and if you know how to paint such a thing symbolically, or otherwise, paint me an eternal teapot—eternal a parte ante, and a parte post; for I usually drink tea from eight o'clock at night to four in the morning. And, as it is very unpleasant to make tea, or to pour it out for one's self, paint me a lovely young woman, sitting at the table. Paint her arms like Aurora's, and her smiles like Hebe's;—but no, dear M. not even in jest let me insinuate that thy power to illuminate my cottage rests upon a tenure so perishable as mere personal beauty; or that the witchcraft of angelic smiles lies within the empire of any personal pencil. Pass, then, my good painter, to something more within its power; and the next article brought forward should naturally be myself—a picture of the Opium-eater, with his "little golden receptacle of the pernicious drug" lying beside him on the table.'[1]

Poor De Quincey can have tasted little pleasure of this kind. He became afflicted with that purposeless hoarding which seems to be an occupational hazard of collectors. He would gather his papers and books about him in such overwhelming quantity that his lodgings became uninhabitable. When this stage had been reached, he would lock the door, take away the key and seek new lodgings, where the same process would be gradually repeated. After his death in 1859, as many as four separate lodgings were discovered by his executors, all in the same condition. Other treasures were found beneath the piles of books: little packets of money waiting to be cleaned and polished, and some Scottish banknotes being pressed to remove the creases. De Quincey himself confessed that he was a 'helpless sort of person who cannot even arrange his own papers without assistance'.

In spite of this, De Quincey was a gentle and lovable soul, very human in his attitude to his books. Contrast the mental disturbance and despair which overwhelmed him at the sight of the vast accumulation of books in a great library[2] with the affection with which he writes of his ideal domestic library, or of the two or three hundred books of Wordsworth's library at Grasmere, in the little homely painted bookcase in the recess by the chimney in his sitting-room.[3]

More attractive perhaps are the glimpses that Lamb gives us of his library, if only because the man is more attractive; there are few books whose authors live so vividly within their pages as Elia does in his. Here, from *Old China*, is the beginning of his collection. Bridget speaks, harking back to their early days of poverty:

'Do you remember the brown suit, which you made to hang upon

---

[1] *Confessions of an English Opium-Eater*, rev. ed., 1856, Pt. II. The earlier account, in Pt. I, of the library De Quincey found at Oswestry is also of interest.
[2] *Letters to a Young Man*, III.
[3] Masson's ed. II, 335.

you, till all your friends cried shame upon you, it grew so threadbare—and all because of that folio Beaumont and Fletcher,[1] which you dragged home late at night from Barker's in Covent Garden? Do you remember how we eyed it for weeks before we could make up our minds to the purchase, and had not come to a determination till it was near ten o'clock of the Saturday night, when you set off from Islington, fearing you should be too late—and when the old bookseller, with some grumbling, opened his shop, and by the twinkling taper (for he was setting bedwards) lighted out the relic from his dusty treasures—and when you lugged it home, wishing it were twice as cumbersome—and when you presented it to me—and when we were exploring the perfectness of it (*collating* you called it)—and while I was repairing some of the loose leaves with paste, which your impatience would not suffer to be left till daybreak—was there no pleasure in being a poor man? or can those neat black clothes which you wear now, and are so careful to keep brushed, since we have become rich and finical, give you half the honest vanity, with which you flaunted it about in that overworn suit—your old corbeau—for four or five weeks longer than you should have done, to pacify your conscience for the mighty sum of fifteen—or sixteen shillings was it?—a great affair we thought it then—which you had lavished on the old folio. Now you can afford to buy any book that pleases you, but I do not see that you ever bring me home any nice old purchases now.'

Here again, from *Mackery End* is a picture of Elia and Bridget at their reading together. 'While I am hanging over (for the thousandth time) some passage in Burton, or one of his strange contemporaries, she is abstracted in some modern tale, or adventure, whereof our common reading-table is daily fed with assiduously fresh supplies. Narrative teases me. I have little concern in the progress of events. She must have a story—well, ill, or indifferently told—so there be life stirring in it, and plenty of good or evil accidents.'

Later he adds in regard to Bridget (who of course is Mary), that 'her education in youth was not much attended to; and she happily missed all that train of female garniture, which passeth by the name of accomplishments. She was tumbled early, by accident or

[1] Possibly the folio edition of 1647.

design, into a spacious closet of good old English reading, without much selection or prohibition, and browsed at will upon that fair and wholesome pasturage. Had I twenty girls, they should be brought up exactly in this fashion. I know not whether their chance in wedlock might not be diminished by it; but I can answer for it, that it makes (if the worst come to the worst) most incomparable old maids'. And here, in *The Two Races of Men*, is Elia discoursing of the borrowing of books:

'To one like Elia, whose treasures are rather cased in leather covers than closed in iron coffers, there is a class of alienators more formidable than that which I have touched upon; I mean your *borrowers of books*—those mutilators of collections, spoilers of the symmetry of shelves, and creators of odd volumes. There is Comberbatch[1], matchless in his depredations!

That foul gap in the bottom shelf facing you, like a great eyetooth knocked out—(you are now with me in my little back study in Bloomsbury, reader!)—with the huge Switzer-like tomes on each side (like the Guildhall giants, in their reformed posture, guardant of nothing) once held the tallest of my folios, *Opera Bonaventurae*, choice and massy divinity, to which its two supporters (school divinity also, but of a lesser calibre—Bellarmine, and Holy Thomas), showed but as dwarfs—itself an Ascapart!— *that* Comberbatch abstracted upon the faith of a theory he holds, which is more easy, I confess, for me to suffer by than to refute, namely, that 'the title to property in a book (my *Bonaventure*, for instance), is in exact ratio to the claimant's powers of understanding and appreciating the same'. Should he go on acting upon this theory which of our shelves is safe?

The slight vacuum in the left hand case—two shelves from the ceiling—scarcely distinguishable but by the quick eye of a loser— was whilom the commodious resting-place of Brown on Urn Burial. C. will hardly allege that he knows more about that treatise than I do, who introduced it to him, and was indeed the first (of the moderns) to discover its beauties—but so have I known a foolish lover to praise his mistress in the presence of a rival more qualified to carry her off than himself.—Just below, Dodsley's dramas want their fourth volume, where Vittoria Corombona is!

---

[1] i.e. Coleridge.

The remainder nine are as distasteful as Priam's refuse sons, when the Fates *borrowed* Hector. Here stood the Anatomy of Melancholy, in sober state.—There loitered the Complete Angler; quiet as in life, by some stream side.—In yonder nook, John Buncle, a widower-volume, with 'eyes closed', mourns his ravished mate.

One justice I must do my friend, that if he sometimes, like the sea, sweeps away a treasure, at another time, sea-like, he throws up as rich an equivalent to match it. I have a small under-collection of this nature (my friend's gatherings in his various calls), picked up, he has forgotten at what odd places, and deposited with as little memory at mine. I take in these orphans, the twice-deserted. These proselytes of the gate are welcome as the true Hebrews. There they stand in conjunction; natives, and naturalised. The latter seemed as little disposed to inquire out their true lineage as I am. —I charge no warehouse-room for these deodands, nor shall ever put myself to the ungentlemanly trouble of advertising a sale of them to pay expenses.

To lose a volume to C. carries some sense and meaning in it. You are sure that he will make one hearty meal on your viands, if he can give no account of the platter after it. But what moved thee, wayward, spiteful K.[1] to be so importunate to carry off with thee, in spite of tears and adjurations to thee to forbear, the Letters of that princely woman, the thrice noble Margaret Newcastle?— knowing at the time, and knowing that I knew also, thou most assuredly wouldst never turn over one leaf of the illustrious folio:— what but the mere spirit of contradiction, and childish love of getting the better of thy friend?—Then, worst cut of all! to transport it with thee to the Gallican land—

> *Unworthy land to harbour such a sweetness,*
> *A virtue in which all ennobling thoughts dwelt,*
> *Pure thoughts, kind thoughts, high thoughts, her sex's wonder!*

—hadst thou not thy play-books, and books of jests and fancies, about thee, to keep thee merry, even as thou keepest all companies with thy quips and mirthful tales?

—Child of the Green-room, it was unkindly done of thee. Thy wife, too, that part-French, better-part Englishwoman!—that *she*

---

[1] James Kenney (1780–1849), author of the successful farce *Raising the Wind*, produced in 1803.

could fix upon no other treatise to bear away in kindly token of remembering us, than the works of Fulke Greville, Lord Brook— of which no Frenchman, nor woman of France, Italy, or England, was ever by nature constituted to comprehend a tittle! *Was there not Zimmerman on Solitude?*

Reader, if haply thou art blessed with a moderate collection, be shy of showing it; or if thy heart overfloweth to lend them, lend thy books; but let it be to such a one as S.T.C.—he will return them (generally anticipating the time appointed) with usury; enriched with annotations, tripling their value. I have had experience. Many are these precious MSS of his—(in *matter* oftentimes, and almost in *quantity* not infrequently, vying with the originals)—in no very clerkly hand—legible in my Daniel; in old Burton; in Sir Thomas Browne; and those abstruser cogitations of the Greville, now, alas! wandering in Pagan lands—I counsel thee, shut not thy heart, nor thy library, against S.T.C.'

Elia's tastes were catholic, but he had his short list of aversions (to which all of us indeed are entitled). These are the *biblia a-biblia* mentioned in *Thoughts on Books and Reading*; the anti-literature, as De Quincey termed it. And the list he gives is an odd one. The first items are understandable: Court Calendars, Directories, Pocket Books, Draught Boards bound and lettered on the back, Scientific Treatises, Almanacks, Statutes at Large. Then he adds the volumes which 'no gentleman's library should be without', and these include Hume, Gibbon, Robertson, Beattie, Soames Jenyns, Josephus and Paley. 'With these exceptions, I can read almost anything.' Some of these are intelligible aversions; but Gibbon? Is there any other eighteenth century historical work that still, after nearly two hundred years, remains so magnificently readable?

One feels that he had all but added Burton to this list; a page or two further on he is calling him 'that fantastic old great man', and (referring to a reprint of the *Anatomy of Melancholy*) he asks 'what hapless stationer could dream of Burton ever becoming popular?' But we caught Elia a few minutes ago at his table with Bridget, 'hanging over (for the thousandth time) some passage in Burton,' and we reflect that we must take these confident assertions with a pinch of salt. Dr Johnson once protested that the *Anatomy of Melancholy* was the only book that ever took him out of bed two hours sooner than he wished to rise. Why is it, by the way, that Burton never fails to fascinate the reader, while Holbrook Jackson as easily displeases him? The *Anatomy of Bibliomania* is like an interminable course of hors d'oeuvres; the very richness of the fare embarrasses the diner and cloys his palate. It wears the clothes of Burton well enough, but somehow all the charm has escaped.

One final picture from Elia. It is from *New Year's Eve*, and we are considering grave matters of life and death:

'Sun, and sky, and breeze, and solitary walks, and summer holidays, and the greenness of fields, and the delicious juices of meats and fishes, and society, and the cheerful glass, and candle-light, and fire-side conversations, and innocent vanities, and jests, and *irony itself*—do these things go out with life? Can a ghost laugh, or shake his gaunt sides, when you are pleasant with him?

And you, my midnight darlings, my Folios! must I part with the intense delight of having you (huge armfuls) in my embraces? Must knowledge come to me, if it come at all, by some awkward experiment of intuition, and no longer by this familiar process of reading?'

And yet, however fond Elia was of his midnight darlings, his bookish habits are not always to be recommended. Five centuries before Lamb, Richard de Bury in the *Philobiblon* was castigating the young student for his slovenly ways with books—his black fingernails, the straws he used as markers, the crumbs of fruit and cheese that fell into his book, and the violets, primroses and four-leaved clover that he pressed between the pages. Here is Lamb writing to Coleridge in November, 1802; he had sent to Coleridge by the Kendal wagon a box of books, including certain volumes of Milton, and he writes: 'If you find the Miltons in certain parts dirtied and soiled with a crumb of ripe Gloucester, blacked in the candle (my usual supper), or peradventure a stray ash of tobacco wafted into the crevices, look to the passage more especially: depend upon it, it contains good matter.' We must forgive Lamb for this, even if no other such offender can be excused; for the good Bishop of Durham's sake however, we can feel relieved that the undergraduates of his day knew nothing of tobacco. Incidentally, Richard de Bury was not the only collector who objected to finding crumbs of cheese in his books. It was one of Sir Thomas Phillipps' peculiarities that he would not allow a morsel of cheese to enter his house at Middle Hill, nor any vinegar.[1]

Let us take independent evidence, and view Elia's library through the eyes of Leigh Hunt. The passage comes from *My Books:*

'His library, though not abounding in Greek or Latin... is anything but superficial. The depths of philosophy and poetry are there, the innermost passages of the human heart. It has some Latin, too. It has also, a handsome contempt for appearance. It looks like what it is, a selection made at precious intervals from the bookstalls;—now a Chaucer at nine and twopence; now a Montaigne or a Sir Thomas Browne at two shillings; now a Jeremy Taylor; a Spinoza; an old English Dramatist, Prior, and Sir Philip Sidney; and the books are 'neat as imported'. The very perusal of the backs is a 'discipline of humanity'. There Mr Southey takes his place again with an old Radical friend; there Jeremy Collier is at peace with Dryden; there the lion, Martin Luther, lies down with the Quaker lamb, Sewell; there Guzman d'Alfarache thinks himself fit company for Sir Charles Grandison, and has his claims admitted.'

Of Hazlitt, Leigh Hunt speaks less flatteringly. 'William Hazlitt, I believe, has no books except mine; but he has Shakespeare and Rousseau by heart.' Later, he remarks that Hazlitt had gone off with some of his set of English Poets, and with his Philip Sidney (all in one volume) and divers pieces of Bacon; and 'he vows I never lent them to him; which is the unkindest cut of all'.

Leigh Hunt loved to talk about his own books. For his reading he preferred a room that was small and cosy, with everything he needed within arm's reach. In *My Books* he writes:

'I dislike a grand library to study in. I mean an immense apartment, with books all in Museum order, especially wire-safed. I say nothing against the Museum itself, or public libraries. They are capital places to go to, but not to sit in; and talking of this, I hate to read in public, and in strange company.... A grand private library, which the master of the house also makes his study, never looks like a real place of books, much less of authorship. I cannot take kindly to it.'

[1] A. N. L. Munby, *Phillipps Studies,* III, 1954, p. 140, quoting Madden's *Journal.*

And in *Autumnal Commencement of Fires*, he returns to this theme:

'... we like a small study, where we are almost in contact with our books. We like to feel them about us—to be in the arms of our mistress Philosophy, rather than see her at a distance. To have a huge apartment for a study is like lying in the great bed at Ware, or being snug on a milestone upon Hounslow Heath. ... The Archbishop of Toledo, no doubt, wrote his homilies in a room ninety feet long. The Marquis Marialva must have been approached by Gil Blas through whole ranks of glittering authors, standing at due distance. But Ariosto, whose mind could fly out of its nest over all nature, wrote over the house he built, "parva, sed apta mihi." However, it is to be observed, that he could not afford a larger.'

In the essay *My Books* he gives a closer view of his own study:

'Sitting, last winter, among my books, and walled round with all the comfort and protection which they and my fireside could afford me; to wit, a table of high-piled books at my back, my writing-desk on one side of me, some shelves on the other, and the feeling of the warm fire at my feet ... I looked sideways at my Spencer, my Theocritus, and my Arabian Nights; then above them at my Italian poets; then behind me at my Dryden and Pope; then on my left side at my Chaucer, who lay on a writing-desk; and thought how natural it was in C.L. to give a kiss to an old folio, as I once saw him do to Chapman's *Homer*. ... I entrench myself in my books equally against sorrow and the weather. If the wind comes through a passage, I look about to see how I can fence it off by a better disposition of my moveables; if melancholy thought is importunate, I give another glance at my Spenser. When I speak of being in contact with my books, I mean it literally. I like to lean my head against them. ... I do not like this fine large study. I like elegance. I like room to breathe in, and even walk about, when I want to breathe and walk about. I like a great library next my study; but for the study itself, give me a small, snug place, almost entirely walled with books. ...'

In *Earth upon Heaven* we hear of some of the books Leigh Hunt will look for in a future life: new works of Shakespeare and Spenser and Walter Scott; a new *Decameron* and a new *Arabian Nights*. And in *The Old Gentleman* and *The Old Lady*, both of whom one feels were drawn from life, we are given a comparative view of their small collections. Here they are in parallel form:

The Old Gentleman	The Old Lady
A commonplace book	The Spectator
Shakespeare	Guardian
Paradise Lost	The Turkish Spy
The Spectator	Bible and prayer book
The History of England	Young's *Night Thoughts*, with a piece of lace in it to flatten
Works of Lady M. W. Montagu, Pope, Churchill	Mrs Rowe's Devout Exercises of the Heart[1]
Middleton's Geography	
The Gentleman's Magazine	Mrs Glasse's Cookery[2]
Sir John Sinclair on Longevity[3]	Sir Charles Grandison
Several plays	Clarissa
Account of Elizabeth Canning[4]	
Memoirs of George Ann Bellamy[5]	
Poetical amusements at Bath-Easton	
Blair's Works[6]	
Elegant Extracts[7]	
Junius as originally published	
a few pamphlets	

To catalogue all the Victorian essayists and poets and their libraries would be wearisome and unrewarding. Let us choose two further illustrations. The first, Coventry Patmore, is an excellent one for our purpose. There are few other writers in any age of whom it can be said so plainly that their ideas, and indeed the

---

[1] Mrs Elizabeth Rowe (1674–1737). Her *Devout Exercises* (i.e., prayers) were revised and published by Isaac Watts, 1737, and ran through many editions to 1811.
[2] Hannah Glasse, *The Art of Cookery made Plain and Easy*, 1747.
[3] *Hints on Longevity*, 1802.
[4] Elizabeth Canning, 1734–73. There were many pamphlets about this famous imposter, including one by Fielding.
[5] An actress who played with Garrick. *The Memoirs*, by a Gentleman of Covent Garden Theatre, were published in 1785.
[6] Robert Blair, author of *The Grave*, a didactic poem contemporary with Edward Young's *Night Thoughts*.
[7] Vicesimus Knox, *Elegant Extracts*, 1789.

whole course of their life, were systematically and consistently built on their reading. Patmore's knowledge of theology, philosophy and mysticism, was of course exceptional among Victorian literary figures. His intellectual diet began with Plato, Aristotle, Emerson, Coleridge and Wordsworth; passed thence to Swedenborg; and in due course embraced S. Thomas Aquinas, S. Bernard of Clairvaux, S. John of the Cross, S. Teresa of Avila, S. Augustine, S. Catherine of Genoa, S. Ignatius Loyola, S. Francis de Sales, S. Catherine of Siena; and finally Dante and Newman. Most of these authorities were represented in his own library, though he also made good use of the British Museum Library while he was on the Museum staff. The catalogue of Patmore's library confirms to a quite remarkable degree the conclusions as to his reading which can be drawn from a careful analysis of his writings.[1]

And for a final illustration, consider Thomas Carlyle. The accumulation of his own books, and their various removals, till they finally came to rest in the 'sound-proof study' which he built on top of the Cheyne Row house, can be traced in Thea Holme's book. This sound-proof room, carefully planned by an amateur architect, proved a disappointment. 'I fear my room is irremediably somewhat a failure', he wrote, 'and that "quiet" is far off me yet.' Jane Carlyle was more dramatic. 'The silent room is the noisiest in the house' she declared. 'Mr C. is very much out of sorts.'[2] Many of the books that Carlyle used were, of course, borrowed. Mill sent him barrowfuls of books to help him with his work on the French Revolution; this was in 1835, when the British Museum was proving so unsatisfactory to him, and before the London Library was founded. The London Library (his own child in a sense) gave him much help, but in one respect he helped it very little in return. 'There was practically no rule', writes Simon Nowell-Smith, 'that he, or his wife, did not break'. Jane, on her way to visit the sickbed of Erasmus Darwin (the brother of Charles), was driven by a shower of rain into the library, and did not scruple to sign the register for some French novels which she borrowed with Erasmus' name; the entry still stands in the register. Carlyle's own principal sins as a member 'were his refusal to return books on demand (or, still worse, denying that he had borrowed what he had borrowed).

[1] See J. C. Reid, *The Mind and Art of Coventry Patmore*, 1957 (especially Pt. II).
[2] Thea Holme, *The Carlyles at Home*, 1965, pp. 77-98.

§2—THE NEW POPULATION

This, then, was the world of Elia and Leigh Hunt: a very small, though very important, part of nineteenth-century England. The increase in the reading population of the eighteenth century has already been noted; it occurred in a total population that was all but static in numbers. In the rapidly expanding population of the nineteenth century a further remarkable increase occurred. This was in part the result of all the social and economic changes which are commonly described as the industrial revolution. In part it was due also to the sudden increase in the actual population, which doubled during the reign of George III. This increase has never been fully explained, though various factors, such as improved medical care and the introduction of cotton clothing, played their part. It was not caused by the industrial revolution, for it was as marked in Ireland, where there was no such revolution, as in England. Whatever the reason, there were thousands, and in due course millions, of new readers, representing not merely a change from illiteracy to literacy, but still more the creation of a new population. Moreover the literacy rate, which so far had always been highest in South Eastern England, was now highest in the North. Indeed, between 1800 and 1850 it is said to have been nearly 75 per cent higher in the industrial North than in the still rural South, while in Lowland Scotland illiteracy was almost unknown.[1]

The story of this development in the seventy years or so before the first Public Libraries Act of 1850 can only be understood if the background is sketched in. It was a period of distress, disturbance and often of panic: a period in which England progressed from Tom Paine to Peterloo and from Peterloo to Chartism. Terrifying things were happening across the Channel, and the fear of similar trouble in England was never far away.[2] The undisputed rule of the Whig and Tory aristocrats had scarcely begun to crumble, and the new age of State interference in the lives of private citizens had not yet dawned. The word 'democracy' was still a term of opprobrium.

---

[1] R. K. Webb, *The British Working-class Reader, 1790–1848*, 1955.

[2] The attempted revolution of 1839–40, which is glossed over by many history books, came near to succeeding. Karl Marx ascribed its failure to the empirical methods of its leaders, who had, as he said, no theory behind them. Some of the failure may have been due to the accident of heavy rain at Newport, Mon., on the criticial night of Nov. 3, 1839; see the account of this event by A. M. G. in *Blackwood's Magazine*, April, 1956.

Gibbon, speaking of Charles James Fox, said, in horror, that 'his inmost soul was deeply tinged with democracy'. Even in 1850, the accepted function of the State was little more than maintaining peace and order, and keeping the taxes down. The idea of civilisation as progressive would still have been strange to most people. A very mild and reluctant beginning had been made in social legislation, but the work of Darwin, Mill, Engels and Marx was still in the future. Ruskin's proposals for social reform, and the bitter storm that greeted them, were still ten years or more ahead. The limited franchise of 1832 was not extended till 1867 and 1884. Although the Municipal Corporations Act had been passed in 1835, the machinery of 'municipal socialism' did not begin to turn seriously till the last quarter of the century. The first Education Act was in 1870; religious emancipation at Oxford and Cambridge came in 1871, and the County Councils in 1888. We are apt to forget how recent some of these developments are.

In the circumstances it is perhaps not so surprising to find how suspicious many people were of the movement for popular education. Fear was at the root of this feeling; the memories of the French Revolution were still vivid. It was fear that delayed the Reform Act till 1832. It was fear that suppressed the *Rights of Man*, banished those found reading it to Botany Bay, and prosecuted the noncomformists and the radicals who advocated reform. It was fear that repeatedly imprisoned the harmless little bookseller, Thomas Spence, who imagined that land nationalisation would provide the money for free schools and public libraries. It was fear that maintained the Stamp Duty, the Advertisements Tax and the Paper Duty till 1853-61, in the desperate hope of preventing the working classes from reading their cheaper newspapers, while still allowing the wealthier classes to enjoy four pages of *The Times* at sevenpence. By way of illustration, let us see this fear in action in orthodox and respectable quarters. There was a Bill to establish parish schools out of the rates in 1807, and in the Commons debate Davies Giddy (who later changed his name to Gilbert and became President of the Royal Society) put the orthodox attitude in a nutshell. 'However specious in theory the project might be (he said), of giving education to the labouring classes of the poor, it would be prejudicial to their morals and happiness; it would teach them to despise their lot in life; instead of making them good servants in agriculture or other laborious employments, instead of teaching them subordination, it would render them fractious and refractory, as was evident in the manufacturing counties; it would enable them to read seditious pamphlets, vicious books and publications against Christianity; it would render them insolent to their superiors; and in a few years the legislature would find it necessary to direct the strong arm of power towards them.'

Or consider Hannah More, who through her 'Cheap Repository Tracts' placed herself in a sense at the head of the official propaganda campaign against the Radicals. The plan was to divert the movement from radicalism to evangelicalism. No woman of her time worked harder in the cause of primary education; the laborious task she undertook with her Mendip village schools shows this. No woman of her time was abler, wiser, or, indeed, more misunderstood and maligned. This is her considered view: 'My plan of instruction is extremely simple and limited. They learn on weekdays such coarse work as may fit them for servants. *I allow of no writing for the poor.*' (The italics are mine.) She found the common farmers as illiterate as their workmen, but for their sons she allowed a different regimen, adding writing and arithmetic to reading, which was all she thought necessary for labourers' children. 'I had long thought that the knowledge necessary for persons of this class, was such as would qualify them for constables, overseers, churchwardens, jurymen, and especially tend to impress them with the awful nature of an oath; which, I fear, is too commonly taken without any sense of its sanctity. Further than this I have never gone.' She regards with scorn the theory that there is *nothing* which the poor ought not to be taught, that, indeed, they must not stop short of science. 'Now the absurdity of the thing is most obvious; supposing they had money to buy such books, where would they find time to read them, without the neglect of all business, and the violation of all duty?' We must (she says) steer the middle way between the scylla of brutal ignorance, and the charybdis of a literary education; the one is cruel, the other preposterous.[1]

For at least the first half of the nineteenth century, this was the orthodox conservative view: the traditional doctrine of subordination, upheld so vigorously by Dr Johnson, demanding contentment 'in that station of life in which it shall please (or rather,

[1] Letters to the Bp. of Bath and Wells (1801) and to Sir W. W. Pepys (1821).

"hath pleased") God to call you.' The opponents of the first Public Libraries Bill in 1850 used the same quite logical argument. Not only would the new libraries add to the burden of the taxpayer; they would become schools of agitation and discontent and revolution. Which, indeed, they did, though mercifully the revolution was peaceful and constructive.

There is a good example of this attitude in the considered warning given in 1859 of the extreme danger of educating the Russian peasantry, not by an unthinking diehard, but by one of the ablest Roman Catholic scholars of the period, Count Joseph de Maistre. Not only must enfranchisement be severely curtailed (he says) but education as well. Learning (*la science*) must not be declared necessary in general for any civil or military employment. The minimum amount of technical knowledge must be demanded for occupations such as engineering. All public teaching of cultural subjects must be suppressed, especially amongst the lowest classes, and any misguided endeavours of this kind must be curbed without betraying oneself. The Count had been ambassador in Russia for fourteen years.[1]

Hannah More's attitude may seem strange today, but it was the accepted view in certain quarters almost to the outbreak of the first world war. Marianne Thornton for example, agreed with it exactly, at the end of the century. The purpose of education, so far as she was concerned, was to produce servants and governesses of good quality; and her enthusiasm for the Whitelands Training College for Teachers arose from the desire 'to make them really humble unpretending Village Teachers, making them clean and cook and iron (not wash) that they mayn't fancy themselves fine ladies *because* they teach geography and history and so on'.[2]

Not everyone however, even at the beginning of the century, adopted Hannah More's view. Indeed, there were hundreds who, through the Bell and Lancaster Schools, and even earlier, devoted their lives to the cause of genuine education for the poor.[3] There is in *Adam Bede* a vivid picture of the village dominie, Bartle Massey, struggling with cheerful humour against desperate odds not only

---

[1] *Quatre chapitres inédits sur la Russie*, Paris, 1959; quoted by Coulton, *Medieval Village*, 1931, p. 52.
[2] E. M. Forster, *Marianne Thornton*, 1956.
[3] There is an interesting account of the beginning of the Lancaster schools in Graham Wallas, *The Life of Francis Place*, 4th ed., 1925, Ch. IV.

with the children, but with the young men in his evening school who hoped to pick up enough education to get them better jobs in the new towns. This was at the end of the eighteenth century; but Bartle Massey has been a familiar type ever since, and we owe him and his kind a great deal. Of the same pattern was Gilbert Gray, the bookbinder of Newcastle, who earlier had worked in Allan Ramsay's bookshop in Edinburgh. He was the faithful friend and mentor of Bewick, and of many young mechanics and craftsmen who spent their evenings in his workshop. The savings made possible by an austere life enabled him to print and circulate books cheaply, though his interest was perhaps in morality rather than education.[1]

The young men he taught were those who, a little later, joined the new Mechanics' Institutes, flocked to the lectures arranged by George Birkbeck and his colleagues in the industrial north and in London, and joined the libraries associated with them. It is more than coincidence that the Institutes were born during the period when Pitt's Combination Acts were in force (1799–1825), and when the Government was striving most actively to keep the working class in its proper station and to prevent its reading radical propaganda. One of the best authorities for the earlier years of the Institutes, and one of their staunchest friends, was Lord Brougham. Let us summarise his arguments in their favour.[2]

First he makes the point (here flatly contradicting Hannah More), that no class of the community is so occupied with work as not to have an hour or two every other day at least for reading, nor so poor as not to have the means of contributing something towards its cost. Then he emphasises (and he insists on this point repeatedly) that the people themselves must act on their own behalf. Nobody else will organise adult education for them; or if they do, it cannot be half so effective and fruitful as if it is organized by the people themselves. The two major difficulties are time and money. In trades where the work is hard and the hours long, there is, as he admits, a 'tendency to sleep immediately after it ceases'. Such occupations are, however, he rather optimistically believes, 'less

---

[1] Montague Weekley, *Thomas Bewick*, 1953, p. 38.
[2] *Practical Observations upon the Education of the People.* (An address printed in 1825 for the London Mechanics' Institution.) Lord Brougham, *Works*, 1872, 8. 417. For Birkbeck himself, see Thomas Kelly, *George Birkbeck*, 1957, and the lecture by W. G. Munford in *English Libraries 1800–1850*, University College, London, 1957.

unfavourable to reflection, and have a considerable tendency to enlarge the mind'. The money difficulty is perhaps easier to solve, and the first need is to encourage cheap publications, especially in Great Britain where books are particularly expensive. 'A gown which anywhere else would cost half a guinea can be made in this country for half a crown,' but a book priced at half a guinea in London would cost six francs, or less than five shillings, in Paris. One reason, of course, was the iniquitous duty on paper. Brougham even recommends lowering the cost by narrowing the margins and crowding the letterpress, and he gives instances of how economies can be effected by this means. Another method is the practice of 'publishing in Numbers', which is admirably suited to the wage-earner. Twopence a week is easily saved by any labourer, or sixpence by a mechanic; and examples are given of various books, from Bacon's *Essays* to *The Arabian Nights*, which can be purchased by this system. Periodicals, such as *The Mirror* and *The Mechanics' Magazine*, can similarly be bought, and he notes that the circulation of the former is sometimes over 80,000. This sort of publication, he thinks, is guiding us towards a classless society.

Publication by numbers was, of course, common. It had advantages for author and publisher, and it appealed equally to the wage-earner and to the impecunious ladies of Cranford; all, that is, except Miss Jenkyns, who, on the strength of her deceased father's library regarded herself as literary. 'I consider it vulgar, and below the dignity of literature,' she remarked, 'to publish in numbers.' She had already announced her preference for Dr Johnson over Mr Boz, so one can forgive the Captain for reminding her at this point about the *Rambler*. The poor Captain was immersed in the latest number of *Pickwick* when he met his sad fate on the railway.

Given cheap publications, there are other means by which the working man, in Lord Brougham's view, can help himself. Circulating libraries are not of great use to those whose time is limited, but book clubs and institutes are of the highest value; and there follows a detailed account of those that have been formed, with advice as to the best ways of organising them. Twelve neighbours paying 1½d a week to their own book club will, thereby, provide themselves with as many books as they have time to read in a year; more, indeed, than the average number borrowed from Mechanics' Institute libraries, where the annual subscription varies from 15s to £1. The libraries may well be assisted at the start by donations from wealthy individuals or firms; for example, at Glasgow the Gas Light Company provided free light on two evenings a week. But their management must at all costs remain in the hands of the men themselves. In some places where the work is quiet, time could be saved by arranging for a man or boy to read aloud during working hours: a curious device that calls to mind monastic customs in the refectory, as well as 'music while you work' in the modern factory. Another idea is the formation of study circles (or in Brougham's words 'conversation associations'), though caution is needed in the conduct of these. To assist in all this work there is urgent need for the publication of elementary textbooks of the right kind, and for good lecturers able to adapt their subjects to the special needs of their audience.

Brougham closes his essay with a reference to the objections to the diffusion of science among the working classes. The time is past and gone (he thinks) when any such objection could be seriously argued; the question no longer is whether or not the people shall be instructed, but whether they shall be well or ill taught. That the movement succeeded is beyond doubt; by the mid-century there were institutes in nearly every town in England.[1]

It is plain from Brougham's words that the institute libraries were intended to supplement, by co-operative purchase, the small domestic libraries which in his view every artisan and even every labourer should be able to afford. There is plenty of literary evidence for the part played by circulating libraries in the life of the middle classes, but the institute libraries figure very rarely in the literature of the time, and it is hard to estimate how the scheme worked out in practice and what its influence amounted to. The scholar naturally had doubts about the wisdom of any policy which favoured superficial learning or 'potted knowledge'. Dr T. D. Whitaker, the Lancashire topographer, advanced this view of library societies in his work on Airedale and Wharfedale in 1816: 'These institutions (he wrote) have almost created the character called a well-informed, as distinguished from a learned, man; and in proportion as they have exalted in the scale of acquired intellect

[1] J. W. Hudson, *History of Adult Education*, 1851, gives details of 610 institutes in England, 12 in Wales, 55 in Scotland and 25 in Ireland. The English institutes had over 100,000 members, and nearly 700,000 books; the smaller institutes were omitted in this survey. I am indebted to Mr M. L. Pearl for this reference.

men of no profession, they have a mutual tendency to depress to the same level those whose professions are denominated learned. Correctness of reasoning, exactness of style, the habit of getting to the bottom of every subject, and that pertinacious meditation by which real science alone can be acquired, are formed by the use of a small library well selected and well digested. For this reason circulating libraries have undone, I doubt not, many a hopeful scholar'.[1] This must surely be regarded as a warning of the dangers, rather than an absolute condemnation of the library societies. The self-educated man, whether he obtains his knowledge unaided or with the help of his neighbours, must always face this handicap. The single-mindedness of the true scholar is as much a matter of temperament and pertinacity, as of the kind of opportunity that is offered to him. Francis Place, for example, was a self-educated man who mastered his subject by sheer energy and perseverance, in the years just before the first institute libraries appeared in London. He tells us how in his boyhood he was often driven away from a bookstall when the owner objected to his standing there reading, and how he used to borrow books from a little shop in Maiden Lane, Covent Garden, leaving a small sum as a deposit and paying a trifle for reading them. Early in his married life he lodged with an old woman who had charge of chambers in the Temple, and she lent him many books which she abstracted from the rooms which she cleaned. The list of his reading at this time is imposing. In due course he built up a substantial library of books, pamphlets and Parliamentary papers behind his shop in Charing Cross: a library which became not only a place of study, but a famous meeting place for the Benthamites and the reformers. At the end of his life some of it had to be sold to raise money. When in 1851 he left his wife and went to live with his married daughter in Hammersmith, the remainder of it was brought in a wagon and stored there in a stable; he could then no longer read. Place had been naturally interested in the development of the Mechanics' Institutes; indeed he collected most of the funds required to start the London Mechanics' Institute in 1824. The scheme was viewed with suspicion both by some of the working men and by some of the wealthy subscribers. He tells of an interview with Lord Grosvenor, who announced naïvely that he wished to help the project, but he

---

[1] T. D. Whitaker, *Loidis and Elmete*, 1816, p. 86.

feared that the education the people were getting would make them discontented with the Government. Place replied that they already *were* discontented with the Government; teaching would not remove this, but it might make them less turbulent. The noble lord said, 'True, but *we* must take care of ourselves.' In the result he gave nothing.

Although Birkbeck had launched the institutes primarily for the benefit of mechanics who wanted more technical knowledge, the libraries, quite naturally, began to devote themselves to entertainment as well as vocational training. The rather sober Lord Brougham had warned them against 'cheap works of a merely amusing kind', but it was not to be expected that such a warning would be taken too seriously. Charlotte Brontë described the excitement in Haworth when it first became known that Currer Bell was the same person as their own Miss Brontë. 'The Haworth people' (she wrote) 'have been making great fools of themselves about *Shirley*; they have taken it in an enthusiastic light. When they got the volumes at the Mechanics' Institute, all the members wanted them. They cast lots for the whole three, and whoever got a volume was only allowed to keep it two days, and was to be fined a shilling per diem for longer detention. It would be mere nonsense and vanity to tell you what they say.'[1] The Brontë girls made some use of the library of the Keighley Mechanics' Institute,[2] but it is plain from Charlotte's letters that it could never have supplied more than a fraction of the books she wanted. She was lucky in having as her publishers Smith and Elder, who were prepared to send her regular parcels of books on loan. These gave her great comfort. 'What, I sometimes ask, could I do without them? I have recourse to them as friends; they shorten and cheer many an hour that would be too long and too desolate otherwise; even when my tired sight will not permit me to continue reading, it is pleasant to see them on the shelf or on the table. I am still very rich, for my stock is far from exhausted. Some other friends have sent me books lately . . .', and she mentions Harriet Martineau's *Eastern Life*, Newman's work on the *Soul*, and Froude's *Nemesis of Faith* (which she thought morbid).

---

[1] Mrs Gaskell, *Life of Charlotte Brontë*, Ch. XIX.
[2] The catalogue of the 2,000 volumes in the Keighley M.I. is reprinted in *Trans. of the Brontë Society*, 1952. There was no library at Haworth.

There is an entertaining account of a Mechanics' Institute library in Flora Thompson's *Lark Rise to Candleford*, an autobiographical study which incidentally gives a most valuable and detailed picture of social conditions in a rural district of the South Midlands in the last decade of the nineteenth century. It is evident that this library, which Flora Thompson had known and used herself, was doing good work in a limited sphere; the description might equally apply to many small-town public libraries of that period, and even to a few of more recent days. When Laura (we are told) had exhausted the books in Miss Lane's parlour at the Candleford Green post office, including *Don Juan* (devoured secretly in bed), Shakespeare and *The Origin of Species*, she took a ticket at the Mechanics' Institute in Candleford town. Within a year she had laughed and cried over Charles Dickens, finished the Waverley Novels and sampled Miss Austen and Trollope. The caretaker of the Institute acted as librarian: a one-legged man without manners or qualifications who bore a positive grudge against frequent borrowers. 'Carn't y'make up y'r mind?' he would growl. 'Te-ak th' first one y' comes to. It won't be no fuller o' lies than t'others.' And if that failed he would fetch his broom, and sweep round the borrower's feet till he was fairly brushed out of the room. 'But there was no dearth of books. After she left home, Laura never suffered in this way. Modern writers who speak of the booklessness of the poor at the time must mean books as possessions; there were always books to borrow.' Elsewhere she speaks of the Penny Readings which were still in vogue at Candleford Green in the nineties. At these she listened to passages from Dickens (always popular), *Uncle Remus* and other works. But the villagers would not borrow Dickens from the Parish Library. Although they liked to listen, they were not readers. They were waiting, a public ready-made, for the wireless and the cinema.[1]

Another contemporary writer, Michael Home pays a similar tribute in one of his autobiographical works. Towards the end of his time at Ouseland Grammar School, at the close of the nineteenth century, he sometimes spent an hour or two at the Mechanics' Institute in the market place:

---

[1] Flora Thompson, *Lark Rise to Candleford*, Ch. 31, 33. On the general question of popular taste in the mid-nineteenth century see Margaret Dalziel, *Popular Fiction 100 Years Ago*, 1957.

'The last time I was at Ouseland, I went there to renew my youth, but alas! it had gone. I owe it an enormous debt. Not only did it place at my disposal reference books which the school did not possess, but it had the daily papers to put me abreast of the times, and weekly illustrateds and *Punch*, even if it was to be a good time before I considered that latter the equal of my former *Comic Cuts*.'[1]

Throughout this century, working men in the industrial areas must have found help and encouragement in the institute libraries. Those living in remoter spots, if they felt the need for books, will often have met with disappointment and frustration. The smallest cottage library may make life immeasurably richer for the family that lives there, but it cannot provide technical or scientific information for the specialist. It is this factor more than any other that has made co-operative library provision a necessity. Consider one or two examples of legitimate frustration. Thomas Edward, the shoemaker naturalist of Banff, whose life was written by Samuel Smiles, faced the most extraordinary difficulties in prosecuting his studies and in identifying his specimens. He overcame these difficulties after many setbacks, and at long last was admitted to membership of the Linnean Society in recognition of his work. There was no library, either private or public, which was open to him, and although the University of Aberdeen was but forty miles distant, he derived no help from that quarter. Edward had little schooling; indeed by the age of six he had already been expelled from three schools owing to his inconvenient zoological interests, and he was even in trouble during his militia service for breaking ranks in pursuit of a butterfly. He had scarcely any friends, and no books. His natural history was learnt from observation alone except for some help he derived from the *Penny Magazine* (for which he subscribed from its inception in 1832) and from pictures in the Aberdeen bookshops and from stuffed animals in the taxidermists' shops. And yet he assembled more than one enormous collection of carefully arranged specimens.

Thomas Edward was not the only naturalist of his day who was similarly handicapped. He had a friend living still farther north in Thurso, Robert Dick, who was both a geologist and a botanist, and

---

[1] Michael Home, *Spring Sowing*, 1946. Ouseland is Thetford.

supplied Hugh Miller with much of the material which enabled him to revise *The Old Red Sandstone*, and to produce his *Footprints of the Creator*. 'He has robbed himself,' said Miller, 'to do me service.' Dick had access to more books than Edward, and, indeed, he was a wide reader; but he died in 1866, worn out by poverty and neglect. He himself had a friend in another famous geologist, Charles William Peach, who was in the revenue coastguard service, and was handicapped by financial difficulties almost as great.

The naturalist whose work lies for the most part in observation and identification of specimens needs a discerning eye and infinite patience, but comparatively few books, until, in due course, he reaches the stage of laboratory work and theory. Thomas Edward, who was perhaps unique, managed with none. The mechanic who needed more than the practical guidance that can be obtained from his apprenticeship (which, indeed, provided the national system of technical education from the Statute of Artificers in 1562 to the nineteenth century) usually lived in an industrial area and within reach of a Mechanics' Institute.

§3 — CHILDHOOD REMINISCENCES

There is an entirely delightful picture of a small domestic library in action in Alison Uttley's autobiographical sketches.[1] She writes of her childhood on a lonely Derbyshire farm, where life was self-contained and outside attractions were few. In the dark winter evenings the whole household would gather in the great farm kitchen, parents, children, the servant lad and girl, farm hands, relations and friends; and while the others worked, making rugs or quilts or whittling 'spells', her mother read aloud from Dickens, *Uncle Tom's Cabin, East Lynne, The Patchwork Quilt*, or, on Sundays, *Pilgrim's Progress*. The favourite, however, was *Robinson Crusoe*. Crusoe lived a life they could all understand,

'catching the food he ate, sowing and reaping corn, making bread, taming beasts, planting and fencing, and each one translated the tale into terms of his own experiences on the farm, and each shared that life of loneliness they knew. The bearded man dressed in his

[1] Alison Uttley, *The Farm on the Hill*, 1941; *Ambush of Young Days*, 1937.

goatskin clothes was their friend, known intimately to them, and each identified himself with the castaway.'

An earlier, and perhaps unexpected, example of the custom of reading aloud in a farming community occurs in *Don Quixote*. The innkeeper in ch. XXI tells how the reapers at harvest time came to refresh themselves at his inn in the heat of the day, and to listen to one of their number reading one of the romances that the landlord possessed. It was of course Don Quixote's fondness for these 'cursed books of errantry' that caused all his troubles. When (ch. VI) the curate and the barber came to examine and destroy the knight's library while he lay asleep, they found in his study over a hundred large volumes and many small ones. Some of these are identifiable in the tale, beginning with *Amadis of Gaul* (the 'first book of knight errantry ever printed in Spain'). Most of the volumes were sent flying through the window to be burnt in the yard. The smaller books, chiefly poetry, met the same fate, for fear that the knight, tiring of errantry, might turn poet, 'which they say is a catching and incurable disease'. *Don Quixote* dates from 1605.

Note that this custom of reading aloud to the family circle offers one very happy solution of the difficulties mentioned in an earlier chapter connected with candlelight or lamplight. In more primitive days the part of the reader was taken by the storyteller or bard. Today the reader has been replaced by the radio, with some gain and much loss.

Not every nineteenth-century farmhouse was, of course, quite as idyllic as Alison Uttley's, even in retrospect. Anthony Trollope spent some of his boyhood at a very different sort of farm at Harrow Weald. It was

'one of those farmhouses which seem always to be in danger of falling into the neighbouring horse-pond. As it crept downwards from house to stables, from stables to barns, from barns to cowsheds, and from cowsheds to dung-heaps, one could hardly tell where one began and the other ended! There was a parlour in which my father lived, shut up among big books; but I passed my most jocund hours in the kitchen, making innocent love to the bailiff's daughter....'

And there follows a grim picture of the austere poverty of the place, of the father struggling vainly to compile, in the hours snatched from farm-work and ill-health, his *Encyclopaedia Ecclesiastica*, of the lonely boy repeating his Latin grammar while his father shaved at six o'clock each morning, or sitting beside him with his lexicon while his father pored over his futile ecclesiastical researches. 'In those days he never punished me, though I think I grieved him much by my idleness; but in passion he knew not what he did, and he has knocked me down with the great folio Bible which he always used. In the old house there were the two first volumes of Cooper's novel, called *The Prairie*, a relic—probably a dishonest relic—of some subscription to Hookham's library. Other books of the kind there was none. I wonder how many dozen times I read those two first volumes.'[1]

For a pleasanter illustration, consider the boyhood of Robert Louis Stevenson: his grandfather at the manse of Colinton, silver-haired, but fierce, writing his sermons in his dark and cold study with its library of bloodless books; his mother reading to him in their home in Heriot Row, and introducing him to all that was best in literature; his father's library which, as he says, was a spot of some austerity, though it included in holes and corners a few things really legible—*Rob Roy*, *Guy Mannering*, Bunyan's *Holy Wars*, George Sand's *Mare au diable* ('how came it in that grave assembly?' he inquires) and *The Tower of London*; and, of course, the covenanting volumes of his beloved nurse Alison Cunningham, for whom cards were the devil's books and the novel and the playhouse alike anathema. 'It's *you* that gave me a passion for the drama, Cummie,' he cried—'Me, Master Lou,' I said; 'I never put foot inside a playhouse in my life.'—'Ay, woman,' said he, 'but it was the grand dramatic way ye had of reciting the hymns.'[2]

An insight into Stevenson's later development can be found in some of his essays, particularly *Popular Authors* and *Books Which Have Influenced me*; the latter is R.L.S. at his poorest, however.

Two more pictures of childhood reading at the close of the century may suffice. One comes from an autobiographical work by Douglas Fisher:

'But near-bedtime was lightened for us by our mother's nightly

---

[1] Trollope, *Autobiography*, Ch. I.
[2] Graham Balfour, *The Life of Robert Louis Stevenson*, 1901.

reading aloud. She would glance at the clock, see that we put our books and games away, and take down a red-backed book from a high shelf. We drew closer to the fire with our feet on the steel fender, to listen. The book was Ralph Boldrewood's *Robbery Under Arms*, and one reading of it lasted a winter. We loved it so much that we had it read to us for several winters in succession. It lived on a shelf in company with *Heart of Midlothian*, *The Lilac Sunbonnet* and *The Channings*. These were all the adult books in the house and we were not allowed to read them for ourselves as they were "too old for us". I discovered later that *Robbery Under Arms* contained a fair amount of strong language, which Mother naturally omitted as she read, though, as is the custom with the Victorian novels, swear words were printed with their initials before a dash.'

This writer's own youthful library was compounded of Sunday School Prizes (religious) and the annual gift to the choir boys of more secular books, such as *Peter Simple*, *Masterman Ready* and *Ungava*. 'My mother considered much reading a waste of time, and indeed, neither she nor my Father had the money to spare to buy books.'[1]

Another rather similar illustration can be found in Margaret Penn's *Manchester XIV miles* (1947) which is evidently based on the author's own recollections. In the Winstanley household which she described, the Bible, in padded black leather with locked clasps, lived on a table in the front room window. There was a pile of Sunday School prizes, (including *From Log Cabin to White House* and *The Basket of Flowers*), and copies of the *Family Herald* and the *Chatterbox* annual were available. In the period described (c. 1907) Hilda was the only member of the family who could read and write. She used to borrow novelettes from a neighbour, and a weekly book from the Co-op Library. Her borrowings from this included *Robinson Crusoe*, *Tess*, *East Lynne* and *The Pilgrim's Progress*, the cost being twopence a week. Her parents, unable to tell what she was reading, were suspicious of everything except the Sunday School prizes. 'What dost want to go and give t'Co-op tuppence a week for wi' all them prizes in t'house?' her mother asked resentfully. In its way Margaret Penn's book is as valuable

---

[1] Douglas Fisher, *Little World*, 1948.

a study of the first decade of this century as *Lark Rise to Candleford* is of the eighties and nineties of the last century.

Scraps of autobiographies such as these could no doubt be multiplied indefinitely. They are of interest if they reveal the formative power that a bookish environment can exert over a man's life and personality. We know something today of the way in which a man's character and happiness may be shaped by the experiences of early childhood: by the influence of food on his bodily growth, and of fear and love on his emotional health. Sometimes perhaps we are tempted to overestimate the strength of such influences, but there can be little doubt as to their existence. The influence of a child's intellectual environment is as potent as any other; and this influence is largely exerted, either directly or, at his mother's knee indirectly, through the medium of books. It may well often happen that the nursery, or at least the home, counts for more in establishing a man's reading interests and habits than later influences from outside the home. The reader may recall the passage in *Eothen* in which Kinglake describes how he learnt to love and know his Homer at his mother's knee, as other children learnt perhaps Watts's hymns or the collects for the day. 'It was not', he cries, 'the recollection of school or college learning, but the rapturous and earnest reading of my childhood which made me bend forward so longingly to the plains of Troy.' This is a truth which every good school librarian will appreciate; the earliest years of reading at home may fix habits that endure through life.

Consider another famous writer's childhood. Much of Sir Walter Scott's infancy was spent at his grandfather's farm at Sandy Knowe in Tweeddale, where 'on winter evenings his grandmother sat beside the fire at her spinning-wheel, and his grandfather opposite in his elbow chair, while he lay on the floor and heard his Aunt Janet read, or his grandfather tell of the Border merry men and their wild ways out of a memory in which they were a living tradition. In his aunt's reading the Bible was varied with one or two books from a pile on the window-seat—an odd volume of Josephus, that portentous author whom few Scottish children in older days escaped, and Allan Ramsay's *Tea-Table Miscellany*. From the latter he learnt by heart the ballad of "Hardicanute", which he shouted about the house'.[1] This was at three years of age.

[1] John Buchan, *Sir Walter Scott*, 1932, pp. 29-30.

By the time he was six, he was already dubbing himself a virtuoso and reading like a Garrick. 'I cannot', he wrote to Lockhart, 'at the moment tell how or when I learned to read, but it was by fits and snatches, as one aunt or another in the old rumble-tumble farmhouse could give me a lift, and I am sure it increased my love and habit of reading more than the austerities of a school could have done.'[1]

And let it be remembered that emotional as well as intellectual experiences reach the child through this channel. The pleasant or unpleasant fairy tale, Doré's illustrations to the Bible, Dante and Milton, the atmosphere of the 'comic', rarely leave the sensitive child untouched, whether for good or ill. Often the effect is transitory, but sometimes the impressions received from Doré or Grimm may last through life. There is a danger in over-simplifying the complex influences of early childhood, but the significance of the intellectual environment is evident, and the attempt to trace its effect is always interesting and often fruitful.

Books are peculiarly the food of the mind. Sheila Kaye-Smith notes this fact clearly in speaking of her own development: 'I am mentally as much the books I have read, as I am chemically the food I have eaten; their sequence, too, is very much the sequence of my life.... In writing about them, I am not merely taking the reader into a library, but along the road which I myself have travelled through the years, and telling what, though it cannot strictly be called an autobiography, is nevertheless my own story.'[2]

Reading is a major experience of life, and we are indeed the books we have experienced. Contrariwise, the life of a book, or of a library, is realised only in the lives of those who absorb it into their own being.

And what of the twentieth century? The home life that Alison Uttley remembered at her Derbyshire farmhouse would be sadly rare today. The reasons are obvious, and the ethics of the matter need not be argued here. Those whose eyes are open must surely have noted how many homes today are apparently bookless. The restricted accommodation of the modern home is a quite inadequate excuse. Every one of us has room for as many volumes as Bunyan or Blake or John Clare possessed. We have rightly learnt to

---

[1] March 3, 1826.
[2] Sheila Kaye-Smith, *All the Books of My Life*, 1956.

borrow books, but the borrowed book can never be absorbed into our lives as the book that is owned is absorbed. Moreover the word 'book' itself is commonly misused for things that are not books at all: anti-literature, popular magazines that are never regarded as permanent possessions, but are discarded as soon as the next number arrives.

These circumstances must be accepted, though not without protest, as characteristic of our day. Nevertheless there are no grounds for pessimism. There has always, since the invention of printing, been anti-literature circulating in quantity: usually in far greater quantity than true literature. The pamphlet flood of 1700, which spread the habit of reading among thousands who had never read before, was anti-literature. The similar flood of 1800 which introduced the habit to the expanding industrial population was, much of it, anti-literature. The habit being established, it could be diverted to more profitable channels by Addison and Steele, or by the Mechanics' Institutes. It is sometimes doubted whether present-day habits can so easily be diverted; and this is probably true. Some are perhaps losing the habit of reading, replacing it with the habit of listening or looking. On the other hand the production and use of books increases year by year, and good libraries of every kind are abundant today; in general far more abundant and adequate than in the days of which Flora Thompson wrote. Statistics of the public provision of libraries show this beyond doubt. No statistics of domestic libraries would have much value in themselves, but perhaps the best guide is the existence of true bookshops. One could wish these were more plentiful, for it is quite as important for a town to have a good bookshop as a good library; library and bookshop are complementary things, and both have an important part to play in the life of a town. Where there is a true bookshop, dealing in literature rather than anti-literature, and carrying a reasonably large stock, it is generally well filled with customers. It would be of interest to have a national guide to our bookshops, on the plan of the guides to recommended hotels; such a guide would be a revealing document, and one may guess that it would yield grounds for hope rather than despair.

List of Sources

The following is a list of the principal sources to which reference has been made. Classical texts are omitted.

Adamson, J. W., 'The Extent of Literacy in the Fifteenth and Sixteenth Centuries,' *The Library*, 1930, x, p. 163.
Arberry, A. J., *The Legacy of Persia*, 1953.
Arnold, Sir T. and A. Guillaume, *The Legacy of Islam*, 1931.
Barraclough, G., *Social Life in Early England*, Hist. Assoc., 1960.
Baskerville, G., *English Monks and the Suppression of the Monasteries*, 1937.
Baynes, N. H. and H. St. L. B. Moss, ed. *Byzantium*, 1948.
Beckwith, F., 'Eighteenth Century Proprietary Libraries', *J. of Documentation*, 1947, III, p. 85.
Beljame, A., *Men of Letters and the English Public in the Eighteenth Century*, 1948.
Bennett, H. S., *Chaucer and the Fifteenth Century*, 1947.
  English Books and Readers, 1475–1557, 1952; *1558–1603*, 1965.
  The Pastons and their England, 1932.
  'The Production and Dissemination of Vernacular MSS. in the Fifteenth Century', *The Library*, 1946, I, p. 175.
Bevan, E. R. and C. Singer, *The Legacy of Israel*, 1927.
Birley, R., 'The History of Eton College Library', *The Library*, 1956, p. 231.
Blake, Dorothy, *The Minerva Press, 1790–1820*, Bibl. Soc., 1939.
Bolgar, R. R., The Classical Heritage, 1954.
Brunskill, Elizabeth, 'Eighteenth Century Reading', York Georgian Soc. Occ. Paper, No. 6, 1950.
Bullough, G., *Narrative and Dramatic Sources of Shakespeare*, vols. 1–5, 1958–65.
Byron, R., *Byzantine Achievement*, 1929.
Central Council for the Care of Churches, *The Parochial Libraries of the Church of England*, 1959.

LIST OF SOURCES

Černý, J., *Paper and Books in Ancient Egypt*, 1952.
Chadwick, Mrs. N. K., *Poetry and Letters in Early Christian Gaul*, 1955.
— ed. *Studies in Early British History*, 1954.
— and others. *Studies in the Early British church*, 1958.
Chambers, R. W., *The Lost Literature of Medieval England*, 1925.
— *Thomas More*, 1935.
Charlesworth, M. P., *The Lost Province*, 1949.
Chaytor, H. J., *From Script to Print*, 1945.
Clark, J. W., *The Care of Books*, 1901.
Clarke, A. L., 'Leibniz as a Librarian', *The Library*, 1914, p. 140.
Collingwood, R. G. and J. N. L. Myres, *Roman Britain and the English Settlements*, 1936.
Craster, Sir Edmund, *History of the Bodleian Library, 1845–1945*, 1952.
Crump, C. G. and Jacob, E. F., *The Legacy of the Middle Ages*, 1926.
Dalziel, Margaret, *Popular Fiction 100 Years Ago*, 1957.
Dawson, R., *The Legacy of China*, 1964.
Defoe, Daniel, *A Tour through the Whole Island of Great Britain*, 3 v., 1724–26.
Dobson, Austin, *Eighteenth Century Vignettes*, 3 series, 1892–6.
Douglas, D. C., *English Scholars, 1660–1730*, rev. ed. 1951.
Ducket, E., *The Wandering Saints*, 1959.
Edwards, Edward, *Memoirs of Libraries*, 2 v., 1859.
Fletcher, W. Y., *English Book Collectors*, 1902.
Fox, L., ed., *English Historical Scholarship in the Sixteenth and Seventeenth Centuries*, 1956.
Frere, S. S., Verulamium, three Roman cities, *Antiquity* 38, 1964, p. 103.
Galbraith, V. H., *Historical Research in Medieval England*, 1951.
Gardner, Alice, *Theodore of Studium*, 1905.
Gasquet, F. A., *Henry VIII and the English Monasteries*, 7th ed. 1920.
Ghirshman, R., *Iran*, 1954.
Gibbon, Edward, *Decline and Fall of the Roman Empire*, 1776–88.
Gibson, Strickland, *Some Oxford Libraries*, 1914.
Glanville, S. R. K., *The Legacy of Egypt*, 1942.
Greenaway, G. W., *Saint Boniface*, 1955.
Guillaume, A., *Islam*, 1954.
Gunther, R. T., *Early British Botanists and their Gardens*, 1922.

LIST OF SOURCES

Hamlyn, H. M., 'Eighteenth Century Circulating Libraries', *The Library*, 1947, p. 197.
Hansen, E. V., *The Attalids of Pergamum*, 1947.
Harrison, J. and P. Lasslett. *The Library of John Locke*, 1965.
Haverfield, F., *The Roman Occupation of Britain*, 1924.
   The Romanisation of Roman Britain, 1923.
Hecht, J. Jean, *The Domestic Servant Class in the Eighteenth Century in England*, 1956.
Hessel, A., 'A History of Libraries'. Translated with supplementary material by Reuben Peiss, 1955.
Highet, Gilbert, *Poets in a Landscape*, 1957.
Hiscock, W. G., *John Evelyn and his Family Circle*, 1955.
Holme, Thea, *The Carlyles at Home*, 1965.
Hudson, J. W., *History of Adult Education*, 1851.
Hughes, Philip, *The Reformation in England*, vol. I, 1952.
Hussey, J. M., *Church and Learning in the Byzantine Empire, 867-1185*, 1937.
   The Byzantine World, 1957.
Jackson, Kenneth, 'On the Vulgar Latin of Roman Britain', in U. T. Holmes and A. J. Denomy, ed. *Medieval Studies in Honor of J. D. M. Ford*, 1948.
Jayne, Sears, *Library Catalogues of the English Renaissance*, 1956.
Jones, M. G., *Hannah More*, 1953.
Jones, Stephen Kay, *Dr. Williams and his Library*, 1948.
Kaufman, Paul, 'Borrowings from the Bristol Library, 1773-1784,' *Bibl. Soc. of Virginia*, 1960.
   'The Eighteenth Century Forerunner of the London Library', *Bibl. Soc. of America*, LIV, 1960.
   'English Book Clubs and their Role in Social History', *Libri*, 1964, pp. 1-31.
   The rise of Community Libraries in Scotland. *Bibl. Soc. of America*, LIX, 1965.
Kendrick, T. D., *British Antiquity*, 1950.
Kenney, J. F., *The Sources for the Early History of Ireland*, 1929.
Kenyon, Sir F., *Books and Readers in Ancient Greece and Rome*, 2nd ed., 1951.
Ker, Neil, *Medieval Libraries of Great Britain*, 2nd ed., 1964.
Keynes, Sir Geoffrey, *Bibliography of William Blake*, 1921.
   Blake Studies, 1949.

LIST OF SOURCES

'Books from Donne's Library', *Trans. Cambridge Bibl. Soc.*, I, 1953, p. 64.
'The Library of Edward Gibbon'; a catalogue of his books, 1940.
'The Library of William Cowper', *Trans. Cambridge Bibl. Soc.*, III, 1959, p. 47.
Knowles, David, *The Monastic Constitutions of Lanfranc*, 1951.
The Monastic Order in England, 1940.
The Religious Orders in England, 3 v., 1948–59.
Leach, A. F., *The Schools of Medieval England*, 1916.
Lewis, C. S., *English Literature in the Sixteenth Century*, 1954.
Lewis, R. and Maude, Angus, *The English Middle Classes*, 1949.
Lewis, Wilmarth S., *Horace Walpole's Library*, 1958. (Sandars lectures, 1957).
Loomis, R. S., *Arthurian Literature in the Middle Ages*, 1959.
Meecham, H. G., *Letter of Aristeas*, 1935.
Moorman, J. R. H., *Church Life in England in the Thirteenth Century*, 1948.
Moritz, C. P., *Travels Chiefly on Foot through Several Parts of England*, Berlin 1753: Eng. ed. 1795.
Munby, A. N. L., *The Libraries of English Men of Letters*. The Library Association, 1964.
Phillipps Studies, 5 v., 1951–60.
Mynors, R. A. B., 'The Latin Classics known to Boston of Bury', *In Fritz Saxl 1890–1948*, ed. D. J. Gordon. 1957.
Oldman, C. B., Munford, W. A. and Nowell-Smith, Simon, *English Libraries, 1800–50*, 1957.
Owst, G. R., *Literature and the Pulpit in Medieval England*, 1933.
Preaching in Medieval England, 1926.
Petersson, R. T., *Sir Kenelm Digby*, 1956.
Plant, Marjorie, *The English Book Trade*, 1939; 2nd ed. 1965.
Poole, A. L., ed. *Medieval England*, 2 v., 1958.
Pollard, A. W., *Fifteenth Century Prose and Verse*, 1903.
Pollard, Graham, 'Changes in the Style of Bookbinding, 1550–1830', *The Library*, 1956, p. 71.
Powell, J. U. and Barber, E. A., *New Chapters in Greek Literature*, 1st series, 1921. 2nd series, 1929.
Power, Eileen, *Medieval English Nunneries*, 1922.
Powys, A. R., *The English Parish Church*, 1930.

LIST OF SOURCES

Reid, J. C., *The Mind and Art of Coventry Patmore*, 1957.
Roberts, C. H., *Buried Books in Antiquity*, The Library Association, 1962.
'The Codex'. *Proc. Br. Acad.*, 1954, pp. 169–204.
Robinson, J. Armitage, *The Times of S. Dunstan*, 1923.
Rostovtzeff, M., *Social and Economic History of the Hellenistic World*, 1941.
Runciman, Steven, *Byzantine Civilisation*, 1933.
The Fall of Constantinople, 1965.
Sadleir, Michael, *The Northanger Novels: a footnote to Jane Austen*, 1927. (Eng. Assoc. Pamphlet No. 68).
Sandys, Sir J. E., *History of Classical Scholarship*, 3 v., 1900–8.
Savage, E. A., 'Notes on the Early Monastic Libraries of Scotland', *Edinburgh Bibl. Soc.*, 1928, XIV.
Old English Libraries, 1911.
Schmidt, Friedrich, *Die Pinakes des Kallimachos*, Berlin, 1922.
Skeat, T. C., 'The Use of Dictation in Ancient Book Production', *Proc. Br. Acad.*, 42, 1956.
Southern, R. W., *The Making of the Middle Ages*, 1953
Steinberg, S. H., *Five Hundred Years of Printing*, 1955.
Stenton, Sir Frank, *The Bayeux Tapestry*, 1957.
Stenton, Lady, *English Society in the Early Middle Ages, 1066–1307.* 1951.
Sutherland, James R., *The English Critic*, 1952.
Swete, H. B., *Introduction to the Old Testament in Greek*, 1900.
Symonds, Thomas, *Regularis Concordia*, 1953.
Tallon, Maura, *Church of Ireland Diocesan Libraries*, Dublin, 1959.
Thompson, J. W., *Medieval Libraries*, 1939. Repr. with supplement, 1957.
Thomson, M. A., *Some Developments in English Historiography during the Eighteenth Century.* 1957.
Tillott, P. M., *A History of Yorkshire: the city of York*, 1961. (Victoria County History).
Tompkins, J. M. S., *The Popular Novel in England, 1770–1800*, 1932.
Turville-Petre, G., *Origins of Icelandic Literature*, 1953.
Vincent, W. A. L., *The State and School Education, 1640–60*, 1950.
Waddell, Helen, *The Wandering Scholars*, 1927. Rev. ed. 1934.
Wallas, Graham, *The Life of Francis Place*, 4th ed. 1925.
Webb, R. K., *The British Working Class Reader, 1790–1848*, 1955.

Weekley, M., *Thomas Bewick*, 1953.
Weiss, R., *Humanism in England during the Fifteenth Century*, 2nd ed. 1957.
Wheeler, R. E. M. and T. V., *Verulamium*, 1936.
White, J. W., *The Scholia on the Aves of Aristophanes*, 1914.
Wiles, R. M., *Serial Publications in England before 1750*, 1957.
Wilkinson, L. P., *Ovid Recalled*, 1955.
Winchester, Barbara, *Tudor Family Portrait*, 1955.
Wormald, Francis and Wright, C. E., *The English Library before 1700*, 1958.
Wright, F. A., *History of Later Greek Literature*, 1932.
Wright, L. B., *Middle-class Culture in Elizabethan England*, 1935.

Index

Abingdon, printing press, 137 n.
accentuation, Greek, 31
Act against Superstitious Books and Images (1550), 124
Acton, Lord, his library, 263
Addison, Joseph, 232; on *Baker's Chronicle*, 222; on Tom Folio, 216–17
Adelard of Bath, translator, 60
adult education, *see* Mechanics' Institutes
advertisements tax, 277
Ælfric Grammaticus, 107–8
Æthelstan, king of English, 140
Æthelwold, S., 105, 106, 107
Æthelwulf, king of Wessex, 99
Agathias, historian and poet, 49
Agricola, governor of Britain, 85, 86
Al-Azhar mosque, Cairo, 52
Alcuin, 101–2
Aldfrith, king of Northumbria, 101
Aldhelm, 99–100
Alexander the Great, his Homer, 198; tomb plundered, 25
Alexandrian Library and Museum, 24–41; archive collections, 40; architecture, 114; bibliog. and ed. work, 31–5, 37, 146–7; book stock, storage, 30–7; cataloguing, 32–4; copying, 30, 32, 38; decline, 38–40, 51; fire, 36–7, 72–3; librarians, 26–7; readers, 38–40; *see also* Callimachus
Alfred the Englishman, 60
Alfred the Great, 99, 102–4
Al-Ma'mun, caliph, 50
Ambrosian Library, printing press, 218
Ames, Joseph, antiquarian, 217
Ammianus Marcellinus, on Alexandrian Lib., 36; on Roman libs., 78–9
Ammonius Saccas, 38, 50
Ananias of Shirak, 62
Andronicus of Rhodes, 65
Anglo-Saxon chronicle, 103

Anglo-Saxon studies, 17 c., 212
Anna Comnena, *Alexiad*, 58
Annual register, founded, 254
anti-literature, 293
Antioch, public lib., 81; university, 45
antiquarian research, motives for, 210; *see also* Society of Antiquaries
Antony, (?) takes books from Pergamum, 36, 37
Apollonius of Alexandria, 40
Apollonius Rhodius, 27, 28–9
Appian, historian, 38
Arab civilization, medieval, 50–3
arabic numerals, introduction, 134
Arabic translations of Greek texts, 51–2
Aratus, poet, 27
archive collections in antiquity, 33, 40
Arethas, bp., his books, 53–4
Aristarchus of Samothrace, 35, 37
Aristeas, letter of, 30
Aristophanes, ed. at Alexandria, 31
Aristophanes of Byzantium, at Alexandrian Lib., 27, 31, 33, 34–5, 147
Aristotle, at Athens, 24; MS in Patmos, 46; works, in M. Acominatus' lib., 60; Jewish commentaries, 39; tr. Arabic, Hebrew, 51–2
arithmetic, at Canterbury, 98; at Constantinople, 55
Arthur, king of Britain, 95
astronomy, at Canterbury, 98; at Constantinople, 55
Athelney abbey, 104
Athelstan, *see* Æthelstan
Athenaeus, bibliog. and writer, 32, 34, 38
Athenian Gazette (*Mercury*), 232; on learned women, 243–4
Athens, decline of learning, 38–9, 45, 49–50, 59–60, 62; libraries, Greek, 24, 80; Trajan's, 113, 117; Lyceum colonnade, 113

INDEX

Atticus, his copyists, 121 n.
Augustan poets, 65-8 *passim*
Augustine, S., at Canterbury, 98
Augustine, S., bp. of Hippo, writes on vellum, 147
Aulus Gellius, on Alexandrian Lib., 36
Ausonius, at Bordeaux, 89; on book collecting, 75; works known to S. Columban, 94
Austen, Jane, writing conditions, 253
Avicenna, 52, 53
Azo of Bologna, 49

Babylon, archives, 33-4
Bach, copying MSS, 157
Bacon, *New Atlantis*, academy, 210; *Of Building*, omits library, 207
Bagdad, cultural centre, 50, 51
Bagford, John, title-page collector, 217
Baker's Chronicle, 221-2
Bale, John, bp., 140, 141 n.; *Scriptores Britanniae*, 135
Banks, Sir Joseph, his library, 258-9
Baronius, Vatican annals, 214
Barrie, J. M., *Window in Thrums*, 67 n.
Bartholomaeus Anglicus, *De proprietatibus rerum*, 181
Bateman, Christopher, bookshop, 217
Bates, Wm., library bought by Dr Williams, 236
Bath abbey, reformed, 106
Baudri, abt. of Bourgueil, 149
Bayeux tapestry, 111
Bayly, L., *Practice of piety*, 219
Beckford, Wm., his library, 260
Bede, 101; on Theodore and Hadrian, 98; works tr. Alfred, 103
Behn, Mrs Aphra, 240, 243
Belvedere House School, Bath, 247
Benedict, S., of Aniane, 105-6
Benedict Biscop, founds monasteries and library, 100-1, 118-19
Benedictine rule, 105-7, 109; tr. and printed, 137
Bentley, Richard, keeper, Royal Lib., 168, 213
Berytus, law school, 45, 47, 49
Beverley, parish library, 74
Bewick, on country reading, 256-7

Bible, early printing, 138; MSS, Constantinople, 47, 49; earliest codices, 147; medieval, 121; saved at Dispersal, 125; tr. Septuagint, 30
bibliographies, ancient Greek texts, 31-5; earliest current, 231
Bibliothèque Nationale, Sir K. Digby's books, 204
binding styles, 16 c., 161
Birkbeck, George, 280
Birmingham Library, 235
Blake, Wm., his books, 219-20
Bloomfield, Robert, his books, 221
Boccaccio, *Decameron*, 239
Bodleian Library, collections, 195, 196, 201, 204, 216; heating system, 154; Plato MS, 53; size, 167
Bodley, Thomas, at Oxford, 127
Boethius, on his library, 78; works tr. Alfred, 103
Bollandists, scholarship, 24
Bologna Univ., law school, 49
Bolton, Edmund, plan for nat. academy, 210
bombycine, 46
Boniface, S., 100
book clubs, 234-5, 281-2
book collecting for show, 68-71, 74-8
book titles, classical texts, 32
book trade, Roman empire, 69, 75-6, 87, 118; 18 c., 228-9, 231-3; 19 c., 262; 20 c., 293
books, burning, 72-4, 126; inflammability, 74; influence on life, 291-3; storage, 32-3, 204-7, 215. *For other relationships see the specific topic*
'books', div. of Greek texts, 31, 34
books as living things, 173-4
books in wills, 184-5, 240
booksellers, *see* book trade
Bordeaux, Gallo-Roman university, 89
Boston, John, of Bury, 134-5
botany, 16 c. and 17 c., collection, 226
Bracton, *De legibus . . . Angliae*, 49
Bradshaw, Henry, bibliothecal memory, 33
Bridgettines, Syon, 138, 181
Bristol Library Society, 235, 263-4
Britain, Roman, 81-96, 98; inscriptions,

301

INDEX

Britain, Roman,—*continued*
85, 86; libraries 83–4, 93–4; towns, 82–8; villas, 87, 88, 90, 117
British Museum, collections, 209–10, 258–60, 262
Britton, Thomas, musical coal-man, 217
broadsides, 232
Brontë, Charlotte, 241, 284
Brougham, Lord, on popular education, 280–2, 284
Brown, Robert, Banks' librarian, 259
Browne, Sir Thomas, his library, 203; on Pineda's citations, 195; on too many books, 72
Brucheium, 29
Bunyan, John, his books, 219
Burie, Wm., founder, Guildhall lib., 125
Burney, Charles, his library, 258
burning books, 72–4, 126
Burton, Robert, 161, 195, 270–1
Bury St Edmunds, library, 160
Byrhtferth, of Ramsey, 107
Byzantine age, 42–63; *see also* Constantinople

Caerleon, Roman town, 83
Caerwent, Roman town, 83, 84
Caesar, damage to Alex. library, 36–7
Cairo, Al-Azhar mosque, 52
Callimachus, 25–34
Cambridge, colleges founded, 129
Cambridge Univ. lib., collections, 167–8, 214, 260–2, 265; losses (1550), 124
candles, lighting, 153–6
Canterbury, cathedral and monastery, 98–9, 115, 160
Canute (Cnut), in Rome, 99
Carlyle, Thomas and Jane, 275
Carnegie, Andrew, buys Acton's library, 263
Caroline minuscule, 107
Carpenter, John, *Liber albus*, 184
carrels, monastic, 122
Carter, Elizabeth, studying, 155
Carthusians, copyists, 181
Casanova, Giacomo, 169–70
Castiglione, *Il Cortegiano*, 198
Catachetical School, Alexandria, 38, 40
cataloguing, 166–7, 215–16

cathedral libraries, 18 c., 235–6; *see also* Durham, Winchester
Catullus, his use of books, 66
Cave, Edward, *Gentleman's magazine*, 232
Cavendish, Margaret, d. of Newcastle, 68, 240, 241
Caxton, Wm., 136, 137
Ceolfrith, 101
Cervantes, *Don Quixote*, quoted, 288
Chapone, Hester, 246, 248
charters, 99, 104, 105
Chaucer, *Canterbury tales*, MSS extant, 182; his books, 176–7
cheap publications, 278, 281; *see also* pamphlets, serial publications
Chester, rows, 118
childhood reading, 287–92
China, civil service, 45; historiography, 58
Chirche, Robert, and his apprentice, 180
Christian church, preserves Latin culture, 43, 90–6; *see also* monasteries
Christian use of Alexandrian lib., 38, 39
Christine de Pisan, 240 n.
Christodoulos, 46
Chronicles, medieval, 133
churches, architecture and fittings, 180
Cicero, his books, 36, 65, 69; his copyists, 121 n.; on Roman education, 64–5
circulating libraries, 231 n., 234–7, 246, 248–51; dangers of, 282–3; needed by nonconformists and scientists, 263–4
Cirencester, Roman town, 83
civil service, Byzantine, 55; Chinese, 45
Clare, John, his books, 220–1
Clark, Edward Daniel, 53
classification, Naudé, 165–6
classical texts, in Eng. trans., 181; transmitted through monasteries, 94, 111
Claudius Ptolemaeus, uses Alex. lib., 38; works tr. Arabic, Hebrew, 51
Clavell, Robert, *Catalogue of Books*, 231
Clement of Alexandria, 38, 39
cloister, library architecture, 113, 115–23
Cluny, 106, 107, 109, 118

INDEX

Cnut (Canute), in Rome, 99
codex form of book, 145-7, 151
Codex Sinaiticus, 47, 121 n.
Codex Vaticanus, 47, 121 n.
coffee houses, 231, 234
coins, hist. source material, 82
Colchester, Roman town, 82, 83
Coleridge, book borrower, 264, 268-71; his reading, 235; on novels, 250
colonnade, library architecture, 113-15, 116, 119-23
commonplace books, 15 c., 181
composite volumes, Alexandrian lib., 31
Constantine Porphyrogenitus, 54
Constantine the Great, has Bible copied, 47, 121 n.
Constantinople, art and arch., 48, 49, 55; civil service, 45-6; education, gen., 44-5; intellectual life, 51, 57-63; siege (1204), 58, 60, 61; universities, 45, 49, 54-5, 73
Copyright Act (1709), 228
Cordova, cultural centre, 50, 51
Cornwall Library and Literary Society, 235
Cory, William, on Pepys' library, 202; his *discipulae*, 252
cost of books, Byzantine, 54; medieval, 148; *see also* cheap publications
Cotton, Sir Robert, his library, 161, 193; plans for nat. academy, 210
Council of Chalcedon, forbids education of laymen, 46
Counter-Reformation, scholarship, 213-14
courtesy books, 181; *see also* deportment books
courtyards, architecture, 116-18; *see also* cloisters, colonnades
Coventry, Sir Wm., his study, 203
Cowley, Abraham, on bookish retirement, 66
Cowper, Wm., his books, 222-3
Cox, J. C., on parish registers, 73
Crabbe, George, on cottage bookshelf, 257; on serials, 233
Crates of Mallos, 35, 64
Crome, Walter, books in will, 185
Cromwell, Thomas, his books, 198
Curzon, Robert, book collector, 262

Damascius, wanderings of, 38-9
Davies, Sarah Emily, 242
Dee, John, his library, 161, 194
Demetrius of Phalerum, plans lib. for Alexandria, 24, 114; proposes tr. Pentateuch, 30
Demetrius of Tarsus, in Britain, 86
democracy, Britain, 19 c., 276-7
Demosthenes, death, 24
deportment books, 239-40; *see also* courtesy books
De Quincey, his library, 217 n., 265-6
Descartes, death, 154-5
devotional books, 14 c. and 15 c., 181-2
Diamond Sutra scroll, 51
Dick, Robert, geologist, 286-7
dictation, in MS copying, 121 n.
Didymus, editorial work, 37
Digby, Sir Kenelm, 204
digests, *see* epitomes
Dio Cassius, on Alexandrian lib., 36
Diodorus Siculus, on use of parchment, 34
dispersal of monastic libs., 124-42
dissolution of the monasteries, 124-42
Dobson, Austin, *Eighteenth century vignettes*, quoted, 119, 223-5
Doctor Williams' Library, 236
Doddridge, Philip, on bookclub, 234
Dodsley, Robert, publisher, 254
Domesday Book, 111-12
domestic architecture, 15 c., 183
domestic libraries, 173-293
Don Quixote's library, 288
Donne, John, his books, 161, 195
Drummond, David, founds library, 197, 198
Dublin, Marsh's library, 162
Du Cange, 214
Duck, Stephen, 255-6
Dugdale, *Baronage* and *Monasticon*, 210-11
Duke Humphrey's lib. destroyed, 124, 125
dummy books for sale, 71
Dundee, public library, 197-8
Duns Scotus, texts misused, 140
Dunstan, S., abp. of Canterbury, 105, 106
Dunton, John, bookseller, 232

INDEX

Durham Cathedral, library, 109, 115, 122
Durie, John, keeper, Royal Library, 168, 201

Edessa, Nestorian school, 45
education, *see* Mechanics' Institutes; schools
Edward, Thomas, naturalist, 286, 287
Egbert, abp. of York, 101
Egypt, ancient, civil service, 45; medieval learning, 52
Elia, *see* Lamb, Charles
English language, development, 179-82
English prose, early use of, 103, 108
Epaphroditus of Chaeronea, 76
Ephesus, libraries, 81
Epicurus, school, library, founded, 24
episcopal libraries, 175-6
epitomes, Byzantine, 54, 55; monastic, 134
Erasmus, 127
Eratosthenes, pupil of Callimachus, 27
Esdaile, Arundell, poem on Callimachus, 28
Ethel-, *see* Æthel-
etiquette manuals, 181; *see also* deportment books
Eton College library, 125
Euclid, in monastic collections, 60
Euripides, ed. Aristophanes of Byzantium, 31
Eusebius, medieval use of, 94, 95, 102
Eustathius, abp. of Thessalonica, 59, 61
Evelyn, John, 163, 203-4
eyesight of writers, 155, 156-7

Fatimites, royal library and mosque, 52
fiction, *see* novel reading; circulating libraries
Fielding, H., literate heroines 245
Fisher, Douglas, boyhood reading, 290
Fisher, John, his library, 160-1, 191
Fleury abbey, 105, 160, 107
France, monasteries, suppression, 141
Franks, barbarian invasions, 60, 61
friars, 131-2
Froissart, 133
Fuller, Thomas, on books, 67

Galen, works, middle ages, 50, 60
Gandisapora, university, 45
gas-lamps, 156
Gaul, relationship with Britain, 81, 86, 88, 95-6; Roman civilization, 86, 88-90
Gaza, university, 45
Geneva, circulating library, 236-7
Gentleman's Journal, 232-3
Gentleman's Magazine, 232
Geoffrey de Lawarth, his library, 176
geometry, at Constantinople, 55
George of Cappadocia, his books, 47-8
Germanus, S., bp. of Auxerre, 92-3, 95
Germany, monasteries, suppression, 141
Gibbon, Edward, daylight studies, 156-7; his *Horace*, 198-9; his library, 225
Giddy (Gilbert), Davies, against popular education, 277-8
Gilbert (Giddy), Davies, *see* Giddy
Gilbert, Sir Humphrey, plans for nat. academy, 210
Gildas, 93
girls' schools, 18 c., 247-8
Glastonbury abbey, 104, 105
glazing, cloisters, 119, 122
Gloucester, cloister carrels, 122
Glubb, Sir John, on history, 14 n.
Goldsmith, Oliver, his library, 232; on patronage, 229
Goodyer, John, botanist, 226
Gower, John, MSS extant, 182; tomb, 194; writings, 179
grammar, at Constantinople, 55
grammar schools, 229-30
Gray, Gilbert, bookbinder, 280
Gray, Thomas, his books, 223, 231 n.
Greek language, ecc. use, 11 c., 109; taught at Canterbury, 7 c., 98, 99
Greek learning, *see* Greek language; Greek texts
Greek minuscule, 54, 57
Greek Orthodox Church, 62
Greek texts, bibliographies, 31-3; conservation, Alexandria, 24-41, 256; Byzantium, 42-63, 256; dissemination through Europe, 61-4; division into 'books', 146-7; losses, 61; trans-

mission through Arabic, etc., tr., 50, 51, 60
Greek uncial, 57
Gregory Nazianzen, S., 44, 45
Gregory the Great, works known to S. Columban, 94; tr. Alfred, 103
Grenville, Thomas, his library, 259
Grey friars, Oxford, 131
Grey of Fallodon, on burning books, 72
Grolier, Jean, his library, 161, 199
Grosseteste and Franciscans, 131, 132, 175
Grosvenor, Lord, on popular education, 283–4
Grotius, Hugo, escape from prison, 205
Guildhall library, books removed by Somerset, 124–5

Hadrian, abbot of SS. Peter and Paul, 98, 99
Hadrian, emp., visits Alexandrian Mus., 38
Hain, *Repertorium bibliographicum*, 142
hall-window, place for books, 221–2
Hamilton, Sir Wm., on learned women, 241–2
Handel, his blindness, 157
Hannah (O.T.), praying, 119
Hardwick Hall, Derbyshire, 152 n.
Harley, Robert, book collector, 162, 217
Harvard College, books from Sir K. Digby, 205
Hazlitt, on girls' education, 247–8; on literary footmen, 254; on reading, 213; takes Hunt's books, 272
Hearne, Thomas, 211, 213, 217
Heber, Richard, his library, 260
Hebrew translations, Greek texts, 51–2
Hemans, Felicia, 252
Hermann the German, 60
Henry VIII, plans for schools, 130
Henshaw, Thomas, 153
Herodotus, on use of parchment, 34
Hexham, monastic library, 101
Hickes, George, 212
Higden, *Polychronicon*, 134, 180
Hilton, W., *Scala perfectionis*, 182
historical study, its value, 13–23

historiography, Byzantine, 58; 16 c., and 17 c., 212–14; 18 c., 233
History of the works of the learned, etc., bibliog., 231
Hobbes, Thomas, on reading, 213
Hoccleve, Thomas, scribe, 120, 156
Holdenby House, Northants, 152
Home, Michael, on using M.I. library, 285–6
Homer, ed. Zenodotus, 31; in M. Acominatus' lib., 60; school text, Constantinople, 44; tr. Latin, 72
Hooker, Richard, 195
Horace, his library, 66; known to S. Columban, 94; on verse writing, 68
humanist studies, monastic, 136, 139; 16 c., 126–7, 186–94; 17 c., 210
Hunayn Ibn Ishaq, translator, 50
Hunt, Leigh, on Cicero, 65 n.; on his and others' libraries, 255, 272–4
Huth, Henry, his library, 259
Hyginus, Palatine librarian, 78
Hypatia, 38

Iceland, literary creativity, economic influences, 150
Iconoclast period, 50–4
illiteracy, *see* literacy
Ina, king of Wessex, 99
incipit, as title, 32–3
indexes, alphabetic, introduction, 134
India, and Near East, 29 n.; libraries, 53
Innerpeffray Library, 197
Ireland, monasteries, 94, 96, 141
Irish saints, 94, 96, 151–2
Irish wandering scholars, 91
Irving, Washington, novel-reading heroine, 251–2
Isidore, bp. of Seville, his library, 78, 121; on writing in winter, 122; used by Nennius, 102
Italy, monasteries, suppression, 141, 142

Jackson, Holbrook, *Anatomy of bibliomania*, 199, 219, 271
Jarrow, monastery, 100, 101, 109
Jerome, S., works known to S. Columban, 94
Jesuits, high regard for books, 214 n.
John de Trevisa, translator, 180–1

INDEX

John Italus, 55
John Mauropous, 55
John Tzetzes, 58–9; on Alex. lib., 27, 30–1
Johnson, Maurice, 235
Johnson, S., *Dictionary*, serial reprint, 233; his lib., 223–5; on *Anat. of melancholy*, 270; on literacy, 245
Johnson, Thomas, apothecary, 226
Johnson family, of Glapthorn, library, 192
Jonson, Ben, his books, 196–7
Josephus, MS in Patmos lib., 46
Julian the Apostate, his books, 47–8
Justinian, 45, 49
Juvenal, known to S. Columban, 94; on Latin in N. Europe, 86

Kaye-Smith, S., on her reading, 292
Keats, needs library, 264
Kederminster Library, 208
Kenney, James, steals Lamb's book, 269
Kibworth Book Society, 234
Kiev, monastery, 57
Kinglake, on childhood love of Homer, 291; on Lady H. Stanhope, 213
Kingsley, Charles, on clever women, 242
Kirkman, Francis, bookseller, 237
knowledge, exceeds capacity of personal libraries, 263–5
Knox, John, plans for education, 130
Koran (Qurán), transcribing, 121

Lackington, James, on reading, 256
ladies' maids, education, 254–5
Lamb, Charles (Elia), 155; his books, 67, 266–72; on novels, 249–50
Lambeth Library, at Cambridge, 201
Lane, Wm., Minerva Press, 249, 250
Lanfranc, abp. of Canterbury, 109–11
Langland, *Piers Plowman*, MSS extant, 182
Langley Marish parish library, 208
Languish, Lydia, her reading, 246
Laslett, Peter, on Locke's library, 216
Latimer, bp., on religious houses, 130
Latin language, Byzantium, 47, 48; Roman Britain, 85–7, 94; med. Eng., 98, 103

Latin texts, tr. Eng., 103, 180–3; transmission, 78–9; *see also* monastic libraries
La Tribu, Mme, circulating library, 236–7
Lawrence, T. E., his books, 199
Layton, Richard, dean of York, 140
Leaper, Mary, 256
learned societies, 17 c., 231
lecterns, library furniture, 205, 206
Lee sisters, of Bath, 247
Legh, Sir Thomas, Visitor, 140, 141 n.
Leibniz, as librarian, 154, 169
Leicester, Roman town, 83
Leland, John, antiquary, 140, 141 n.
lending libraries, *see* book clubs, circulating libraries
Lennox, Charlotte, *Female Quixote*, 251
Leo III (Isaurian), 50, 73
Leo the Wise, pupil of Photius, 54
Leobgatha, abbess, 238
Letter of Aristeas, 30
Libanius, teacher at Antioch, 45
librarian's duties (Naudé), 166–7
librarianship as vocation and study, 19–21, 26
libraries, architecture, 164, 207; decoration, 77–8; furniture, 166, 191–2, 195, 200–8; heating, lighting, 154–5, 164; history, 22–3; size, 160–3, 175; *see also specific topics*
library, first English, 99
library economy, 18–19, 162–9
libraries, comparative sizes, 160–3
licensing of publications, 228
lighting, buildings, 152–7; churches, 180; libraries, 154–5, 164
Linnaeus, his library, 259
Linnean Society founded, 259
Lintot, B. B., catalogues, 231
Lipsius, *De bibliothecis syntagma*, 23, 214
literacy, aided by nonconformism, 264; female, 238–55; medieval, 44, 103, 108, 175–83; 16 c., 178; 18 c., 229–31, 264; 19 c., 276, 278
literary creativity, economic factors, 146, 149–51
literary criticism, 230–1
literary heroines, their reading, 245–7
literary research, value of, 71

306

INDEX

literary societies, 234-5
Liverpool Lyceum, 235
Locke, John, his library, 215-16
London, John, Visitor, 140, 141 n.
London, Roman town, 82, 83
London Library, 18 c., 263; 19 c., 263, 275
Longinus, uses Alexandrian lib., 38
Lucas, R., *Plain man's guide to heaven*, 219
Love, Nicholas, *Mirror of the blessed life of Jesus*, 182
Lucian, on book collecting, 74
Lucullus, book collector, 65
Luddenden Library, 235
Luddington, parish registers, 74
Lumley, John, Lord, his library, 161, 193
Lyceum, books, 30
Lydgate, 134

Mabillon, Jean, 214
Machiavelli, *Il principe*, 198
Madden, Sir Frederic, on Phillipps, 262
Madox, Thomas, historian, 213
Mahomet II, 61, 62
Maistre, Joseph de, on education, 279
Maittaire, typographer, 217
Malmesbury abbey, reformed, 106
Mamoun (Al-Ma'mun), caliph, 50
Manorial libraries, 18 c., 221-2
MSS, collections, 209, 258-62
Map, Walter, 132
Marcus Aurelius, on getting lib. books, 113
Marie de France, 238
Marsh, Narcissus, his library, 162
Marsiglio of Padua, *Defensor pacis*, 198
Martial, his books, 67; on codex, 151; works read in Britain, 87
Martineau, Harriet, 252
Matthew, Tobie, abp. of York, 264
Mazarine Library, 162-3
Mecca, Great Mosque, 116
Mechanics' Institutes, 280-7
medicine, medieval study, 51, 55
Mellon, Paul, gift to Bodleian, 216
Ménagier de Paris, *Traité*, 239-40
Menander, plays first produced, 24
Michael Acominatus, bp. of Athens, 59-60, 61
Michael Psellus, 44, 55

Milton, his blindness, 157; his books, 197; on woman's duty, 243 n.; *Paradise lost*, Digby's copy, 204
Minerva Press, 249, 250
minuscule, Greek, 54, 57
Mohammed (Mahomet) II, 61, 62
monasteries, Byzantine, 46, 56-7, 59; Continental, 105-9 passim; degeneracy, 128-32; dissolution, 124-42; English, 104-11; Irish, 94, 96, 141; Lanfranc, 109-11; teaching, 46, 130-2; visitations, 140-1
Monastic constitutions (Lanfranc), 109-11
Monastic libraries, arch., fittings, 115-23; Byzantine, 56, 59; catalogues, 109, 135; contents, 101-3; dispersal, 124-42, 192; librarian, 110-1; loans, 110; scriptoria, 56-7, 105, 107, 132-4, 137
monastic muniments, 125
Montagu, Lady Mary Wortley, 244, 248
Montaigne, his library, 199-200
Montrose, 5th earl of, his books, 198
Moore, bp., education, 230; library, 162, 213
More, Hannah, educationist, 247, 248, 255, 278
More, Sir Thomas, 188-91; daughters' Latin, 240; on contemporary literacy, 178
More, Wm., prior of Worcester, 138-9
More, Sir Wm., his library, 191-2
Moritz, Charles P., on reading in England, 228-9, 238
Morley, Lord, gives library to Cambridge, 263
Moslem learning, middle ages, 50-3, 61
Motteux, P. A., *Gentleman's Journal*, 232
Mount Athos monastery, 46, 57
Moxon, Joseph, *Mechanick exercises*, 233
Musaeus, poet, 49
museum collections in libraries, 166
music, at Constantinople, 55; MSS destroyed at dispersal, 125
mysticism, Byzantine, 55-6

Napoleon, maltreats, his books, 198
Naudé, Gabriel, *Avis pour dresser une bibliothèque*, 162-7
Nennius, *Historia Brittonum*, 102

INDEX

Neo-Platonism, 38, 50
Newton, Sir Isaac, education, 230; library, 214-15, 216
Nicetas Acominatus, 58, 60
Nicolson, Wm., bp. of Carlisle, 212, 213
Ninian, S., missionary, 90-1
Nisibis, university, 45
Nollekens, Joseph, saves candles, 154
nonconformists and libraries, 236, 263-4
North, Marianne, flower painter, 252
Norwood, Gilbert, on Alex. Lib., 72
novel reading, 246-51; *see also* circulating libraries
nunneries, med. England, 129, 130, 133, 138

Odilo, abbot of Cluny, 118
Odo, abbot of Cluny, 106
Oecumenical College, Constantinople, 50
Olympus, Mt, monastery, 46
Ommiades, library, 52
oriental books and MSS, in Selden's lib., 201
Origen, neo-Platonist, 38, 40, 50
Origins of the English library, 13
Orosius, on Alexandrian lib., 36; works tr. Alfred, 103
Osborne, Dorothy, 240, 241
Oswald, S., 104, 105, 106
Oughtred, Wm., mathematician, 153-4
Ovid, destroys *Metamorphoses*, 73; his use of books, 65-6; known to S. Columban, 94
Oxford, colleges, founded, 129; libs., 124, 127, 133, 140; religious orders, 131, 175
Oxyrhynchus papyri, hist. source mat., 27, 40

Palaeography, study of, 212, 214
Palladas of Alexandria, teacher, 40
pamphlet publications, 232, 233, 293
paper, duty on, 277, 281; writing mat., 148
papyrus, rolls, storage, 77; writing mat., 144-8
parchment, MSS at Patmos, 46; rolls, Persian archives, 34; writing mat., 145-8

Paris, Matthew, historian, 133, 239; on Verulam lib., 84
parish libraries, 142, 228
parish registers, 73-4
Parker, abp., prints Ælfric's *Paschal homily*, 108
Paston family, 185-6
Patmore, Coventry, his reading, 274-5; against clever women, 241
Patmos, monastery, 46, 57
Patriarchal School, Constantinople, 46; Library, 47
Patrick, S., 91-2, 94
patronage, literary, 229
Paul the Silentiary, poet, 49
Pelagius, a. of earliest extant British writings, 91
Penn, Margaret, girlhood reading, 290
Pepys, Samuel, his library, 161, 164, 201-2; borrows *Hudibras*, 237
Pergamum, arch. remains, 32, 37; library, 36, 37, 114
periodicals, *see* serial publications
Peripatetics, Athens, 27; books in Rome, 65; name, 113
Persius, his library, 67
Peterborough abbey, reformed, 106
Petrarch, his pocket Augustine, 198
Petronius, *Satyricon*, quoted, 68
Petrus Godefridus, on women's writing, 239
Phillipps, Sir Thomas, his library, 154, 260-2, 272; printing pr., 218
philosophy, at Constantinople, 55
Photius, patriarch, 53, 61
Pindar, ed. Aristophanes of Byzantium, 31
Pius II, pope, on Constantinople, 58
Place, Francis, 279 n., 283-4
Plato, Academy, 24; ed. Aristophanes of Byz., 31; MS from Patmos, 53; on history, 14
Plato, abbot, 56-7
Pliny, the elder, his reading, 67, 68; on books, 225
Pliny, the younger, his library, 67, 77; works sold Lyons, 69
Plotinus, 38, 50
Plutarch, on Alexandrian lib., 36, 37; on Britain, 86

308

INDEX

pocket editions, 158-9
Poggio, on English scholarship, 127
Pole, card., on religious orders, 130
politics as reading matter, 227-33 *passim*
Polybius, Greek historian, 64
Polybius, sec. to Emp. Claudius, 71-2
Pope, Alexander, on book collectors, 218; on female literacy, 245; spurious quotation, 223
population, 19 c., 276
Portugal, monasteries, suppression, 141
Pratt, Anne, botanist, 252
prayers for royal family introduced, 106
prejudice, male, against learning in women, 238-53 *passim*
Priestley, Joseph, promotes circulating libraries, 263
printing, earliest, 51; effect, on lit. production, 149-50; on monasteries, 136-9; on scholarship, 190; licensing, 228
Prise, Sir John, Visitor, 140, 141 n.
Proclus, neo-Platonist, 38, 50
Procopius, historian, 48
proprietary libraries, 235; *see also* circulating libraries
pseudonyms, women writers, 241
Psellus, Michael, 44, 55
Ptolemy I, Soter, 25
Ptolemy II, Philadelphus, 25; founds Brucheium, 29; his librarian, 33
Ptolemy III, founds Serapeum, 29
Ptolemy IX, robs Alexander's tomb, 25
Ptolemy (Claudius Ptolemaeus), 38, 51
Public Libraries Bill (1850), 279
publishing, licensing, 228; *see also* book trade
punctuation, Greek, 31, 145, 147; medieval, 120 n.
Pynson, R., printer, 137

Qurân, transcribing, 121

Rabelais, *Gargantua*, libs. in, 207
Ralegh, Sir Walter, favourite book, 198
Ramsay, Allan, circulating library, 236
Ramsey abbey, 106, 107
Rawlinson, Thomas, 'Tom Folio', 216-17
reading, aloud, 119, 285, 287-91; environmental factors, 150-9; in monasteries, 55, 105, 107, 110-11; 18 c., 227-37, 253-7; *see also* literacy
Reformation, effect on monasteries, 139
regional surveys of library history, 22
Registrum librorum Angliae, 135
Regularis concordia, 106, 107, 109
religious books, early printing, 137-8
religious orders, educational work, 130-2; *see also* monasteries
Reynolds, Richard, 138
rhetoric, at Constantinople, 55
Rich, Sir Richard, arch-ruffian, 139-40; examines Sir T. More, 191
Richard de Bury, 175
Richard de Swinfield, bp., 176
Richardson, Samuel, his reading, 213; *Pamela*, 253
Robinson, Mary, 247
roll form of book, 145-8 *passim*
Rolle, Richard, extant MSS, 182
Roman Britain, *see* Britain, Roman
Roman empire, book trade, 69, 75-6, 87; public libs., 78-81, 113-17; universities, 49, 88-9; villa libs., 64-9, 78, 84, 89
Roman Empire of the East, and West, contrasted, 42-4
Roman law, codification, 49
Rossano Gospel, 49
Rotherham, abp., founds school, 179
Rousseau, borrows books, 236-7
Royal Library, books destroyed, 1550, 124; 17 c., 168-9, 201
Royal Society, 209, 210, 231
rural areas, lack libraries, 286
Rusticus, bp. of Lyons, his library, 78
Ryckes, John, *Image of love*, 138
Rymer, Thomas, ed. *Foedera*, 213

St Albans, chronicles, 133; monastic library, 115, 133-4; printing press, 136, 137 n.; *see also* Verulam
Salonika, *see* Thessalonica
sand, writing material, 143
Santa Sophia, 48
Sault, Richard, mathematician, 232
Saxon period, 97-112
Scandinavia, monasteries, suppression, 141

309

INDEX

scholastisccism, 126–7, 139, 140
schools, endowed at dissolution, 129–30; for girls, 247–8; monastic, 46, 130–2; 15 c., 179–80; 17 c., 229–30; 19 c., 277–80
science, Moslem study, 57; needs libs., 263; 17 c. meaning, 210
Scipio Africanus Minor, as scholar, 64
Scot, Michael, mathematician, 60
Scotland, domestic libs., 16 c., 197–8; monasteries, 135 n., 141; oldest pub. lib., 197
Scott, Sir W., boyhood reading, 291–2; education, 220; on book collecting, 219
scribes, medieval, 119–22, 132–3
scriptoria, 56–7, 105, 107, 132–4, 137
Scrope of Masham, books in will, 185
Selden, John, his library, 157, 161, 201
Seneca, 64–9; on Alexandrian lib., 36; on book collecting, research, 70–2; on history, 14
Septuagint, tr. at Alexandria, 30
Serapeum, 29, 39, 114
Serenus Sammonicus, the younger, 76
serial publications, 231–3; 281
servants, literacy, 253–7
service books, destroyed, 16 c., 124, 125; early codices, 147; printed, 137–8
Sevenoaks, Wm., founds school, 179–80
Shaftesbury abbey, 104
Shakespeare, his sources, 196; 2nd folio, sale, 204
Sheridan, on women's reading, 246
Shirley, John, scribe, tr., 182–3, 194
Shirley family pedigree, 148
Sicily, centre, Arabic-Latin tr., 60
Sidonius Apollinaris, his books, statue in Ulpian lib., 79, 92, 115; on cl. texts for Britain, 95; on villa libs., 78, 89
Silchester, Roman town, 83–7 *passim*
slates, writing materials, 144
Sloane, Sir Hans, 162, 209
Smith, Sir James Edward, botanist, 259
Smith, S. Kaye-, on her reading, 292
Smith, Sir Thomas, his library, 194
Smollett, *History of England*, publication, 233; literate heroine, 245
Smyrna, library, 81

Society of Antiquaries (f. c.1586), 192
Society of Antiquaries (f .1717), 209, 210, 231, 235
Socrates, on book collecting, 75
Southey, Robert, his reading, 235, 264
Sowerby, *English botany*, 259
Spain, monasteries, suppression, 141; Moslem civilization, 52; *see also* Cordova; Toledo
Spalding Gentlemen's Society, 235
spectacles (optical), 156–7
Spectator, 232
Spelman, *Glossary*, 211
Spence, Thomas, radical, 277
Spenser, his reading, 196
Sponheim, abbot of, *De laude scriptorum*, 137
stalls, libraries, 206
stamp duty, 277
Stanhope, Lady Hester, no reader, 213
Steele, Richard, 232; on women, 244
Sterne, on fate of *Tristram Shandy*, 222
Stevenson, R. L., boyhood reading, 289, on lamps, 156
stichometry, 32, 34
stone, writing material, 144
Stow, John, 194
Strabo, on Alexandrian lib., 36; on ibis, 29; on Smyrna, 22–3
studies (study rooms), 204; *see also* domestic libraries
Studios, monastery, 55, 56–7
subscription libraries, *see* book clubs, circulating libraries
Suidas lexicon, 54; on Alexandrian lib., 27; on Callimachus, 27, 32
Sulla, book collector, 65
summaries, *see* epitomes
Swift, Jonathan, buys spectacles for Stella, 157; his 'little language', 119; on female literacy, 244–5
Swinfield, Richard de, bp., 176
Symeon the Young, 55–6
Synesius, bp., his library, 40–1; on contemporary learning, 38, 39, 44
Syon monastery, library, 138, 160
Syon nunnery, 138, 181
Syriac MSS, B.M., 262; tr. Greek texts, 50

INDEX

Tacitus, *History* copied, 145; on Roman education, 68
Talbot, Robert, 141
Tanner, Thomas, 212-13
Tate, Nahum, on books, 66
Tatler, 232
Tavistock, printing press, 137
technology as revolutionary force, 17-18
Templars, suppressed, 129
Tennyson, *Princess Ida*, 242
Theodore of Studios, 46, 56-7
Theodore of Tarsus, abp. of Canterbury, 45, 98, 99
Theodore Prodromus, on scholars' penury, 59
Theodosius II, reorganizes Imperial university, 48
Theon, uses Alexandrian lib., 38
Theophilus, patriarch of Alex., 39
Thessalonica, 59
Thomas à Kempis, *Imitation of Christ*, 182
Thompson, Flora, on using M.I. lib., 285
Thorney abbey, reformed, 106
Thornton, Marianne, on education, 279
Thorpe, Wm., on literacy, 178-9
Thou, J. de, his library, 161, 199, 206
Thucydides, in Acominatus' lib., 60
Tibullus, Greek models, 67
Timgad, 81, 83, 84
Toledo, centre of learning, 51, 60
Tonantius Ferreolus, his villa lib., 89
translation, Alexandrian lib., 29-30; Arabic, 50-1, 60; Eng., 103, 180-3
Trebizond, Greek city, 62
Trollope, Anthony, childhood, 288-9
Turks, conquest of Constantinople, 61
Tychicus of Trebizond, 62
Tyrannion, Sulla's librarian, 65
Tzetzes, *see* John Tzetzse

uncial, Greek, 57
union catalogues, monastic libs., 135
Uttley, Alison, on farmhouse reading, 256, 287-8

Valens, emp., adds copyists to Lib., 48
Varro, works requested 5 c. Gaul, 95

Vatican, Codex Vaticanus, 47, 121 n.; Joshua Roll, 49
vernacular, development, 103, 108, 179-82
Verulam, Roman town, 82, 83, 88, 92; villa library, 84
vicarage libraries, 18 c., 221-2
Vienna Genesis, 49
villa libraries, 64-9, 78, 84, 89
Virgil, in middle ages, 72, 94, 101
visitations, to monasteries, 140-1
Vitruvius, on Aristophanes of Byz., 33; on aspect of libs., 68

wall-shelving, 208; *see also* libraries, furniture
Walsingham, Thomas, 133
Walpole, Horace, his library, 218; midnight scholar, 155; on patronage, 229
Walton, Izaac, his library, 195 n.
wandering scholars, 61-3, 91
Wanley, Humfrey, palaeographer, 212
Watts, Thomas, bibliothecal memory, 33 n.
wax tablets, 144, 149
Wearmouth, 100, 101, 109, 119
Weller, Sam, writing, 119
Wesley, John, encourages reading, 264
Wesley, Samuel, *Athenian Gazette*, 232
Wharton, Henry, scholar, 212
Whethamstede, ab. of St Albans, 133-4
Whitaker, T. D., on circulating libraries, 282-3
Whitby abbey, restored, 109
Whitelands Training College, 279
Whittington, R., founds Guildhall lib., 225
Wilford, bookseller, catalogues, 231
William de S. Carilef, 109
William of Malmesbury, 133
Williams, Daniel, est. library, 236
Williams, Gilly, on H. Walpole, 218
wills, books in, 184-5, 240
Winchelsea, Lady, 240, 241
Winchester Cathedral, 104-7 *passim*, 112
windows, 152-3
Wise, Thomas, his library, 260
Wolfenbüttel, library, 154, 168, 169
Wollstonecraft, Mary, 252
women, readers and writers, 238-55

INDEX

Woodforde, James, *Diary of a country parson*, 221
Woolf, Virginia, on intellectual freedom for women, 241, 243, 252
Worcester Cathedral, 10 c., 104, 106
Wotton, Thomas, his library, 193
Wren, Sir Christopher, wall shelving, 208
Wright, James, on library hospitality, 211
Wright, Joseph, philologist, 264-5
writing aloud, 119-20, 121
writing, creative, economic factors, 146, 149-51
writing materials, 143-52
Wroxeter, Roman town, 83-4, 85
Wyclif, translations, 181
Wynkin de Worde, 138

Xiphilinus, 55

Yearsley, Ann, 255
York, Minster lib., 235; S. Mary abbey, 109; school f. Egbert, 101-2

Zenodotus, ed. Homer, 31; head, Alexandrian lib., 27
Zenon, Egyptian business records, 40

For Product Safety Concerns and Information please contact our EU representative GPSR@taylorandfrancis.com
Taylor & Francis Verlag GmbH, Kaufingerstraße 24, 80331 München, Germany

www.ingramcontent.com/pod-product-compliance
Lightning Source LLC
Chambersburg PA
CBHW070750020526
44115CB00032B/1610